# NEW FUTURES:
## The Challenge of Managing Corporate Transitions

# NEW FUTURES:
# The Challenge of Managing Corporate Transitions

John R. Kimberly _____
The Wharton School
The University of Pennsylvania

Robert E. Quinn _____
The Nelson A. Rockefeller College of
Public Affairs and Policy
State University of New York

DOW JONES-IRWIN
Homewood, Illinois 60430

A classroom edition of this book under the title *Managing
Organizational Transitions* is available through Richard D. Irwin, Inc.

This publication is designed to provide accurate and
authoritative information in regard to the subject matter
covered. It is sold with the understanding that the
publisher is not engaged in rendering legal, accounting, or
other professional service. If legal advice or other expert
assistance is required, the services of a competent
professional person should be sought.

*From a Declaration of Principles jointly adopted by a Committee
of the American Bar Association and a Committee of Publishers.*

ISBN 0-87094-470-3

Library of Congress Catalog Card No. 83–73364

*Printed in the United States of America*

1 2 3 4 5 6 7 8 9 0 ML 1 0 9 8 7 6 5 4

# Preface

The restructuring of AT&T is perhaps the single largest corporate transition in history. There is virtually no precedent for it. Large numbers of AT&T executives have struggled with how to shape the new future that lies ahead, spawning at least a temporary boom in the practices of hundreds of external consultants. There are few ground rules. There is enormous uncertainty. The stakes are extraordinarily high.

The case of AT&T is only the most visible instance of a phenomenon that is becoming more and more common—major change in the structures, the process, and/or the strategies of corporate entities in this country. Whether driven by changing markets, new technologies, or governmental mandate, the challenge confronted by executives is the same: how to move an organization from one configuration to another.

Our interest in corporate transitions has its origins in earlier theoretical work on organizational life cycles and in a variety of consulting assignments. On the theoretical side, we both had been working for a number of years on longitudinal studies of organizational creation and development and had found the life-cycle metaphor useful for capturing many of the dynamics in the earliest years of a firm. Yet we both found the metaphor less useful in getting a handle on the later years. Once a firm became relatively well established and had moved from the entrepreneurial to the managerial stage, events, issues, and problems became less predictable in both their substance and their timing. Crises of leadership and performance, changes in strategy, and corporate reorganizations often occurred, but in no particular sequence and at no particular time.

On the practical side, we both were involved in consulting assignments quite independent of one another, which involved major organizational changes. We were thus confronting many of the nitty gritty operational issues associated with large system change.

The idea for this book came during a discussion we had at a conference in Albany in the spring of 1982. We were certain that lots of others were involved in guiding organizational transitions, and felt that it would be worthwhile to identify some people who had had hands-on experience in managing the transition process and encourage them to write about their experiences. The accounts, we felt, would be valuable in and of themselves. But, in addition, we believed that comparative analysis of the cases might lead to some useful generalizations about the process.

The process we used to identify cases and authors was nonsystematic. We relied on word of mouth and an announcement in the *Administrative Science Quarterly*. Of the more than 20 proposals we considered, we chose 7 based upon our desire to ensure a diversity of organizational settings and of type of transitions. Each author was asked to describe the situation, the setting, and the flow of events and outcomes and to articulate the managerial principles or guidelines that might be gleaned from the example. In addition to the 7 cases, we decided to include four contributions of a more conceptual nature, contributions which we felt helped either to clarify or to raise useful questions about the transition process.

Before and after these 11 chapters are our introductory and concluding chapters. The introductory chapter outlines our approach to the analysis of transitions and the concluding chapter proposes a set of guidelines for the manager confronted by the prospect of a major change in structure, process, or strategy in his or her own organization.

The process of putting this book together has been both fun and educational for us. A subset of the chapters was formally presented to a most receptive audience at the Academy of Management meetings in August of 1983 in Dallas. The authors of various chapters have been by and large receptive to our editorial exhortations and to the stringent deadlines imposed by the publisher. Now that the book has been written, we are anxious to hear from you about how well its contents map onto and illuminate the world of experience.

**John R. Kimberly**
**Robert E. Quinn**

# Contents

# 1

## The challenge of transition management

John R. Kimberly
*The Wharton School*
*The University of Pennsylvania*

Robert E. Quinn
*The Nelson A. Rockefeller College of*
*Public Affairs and Policy*
*State University of New York at Albany*

Acquiring a new company? Making a significant change in executive leadership? Developing a new strategic thrust? Contemplating a major internal reorganization? Each of these actions will affect your organization significantly. Yet, often needless fallout is created in the process of making the transition that each of these actions requires.

A transition is a major change in organizational strategy, structure, or process. Transitions may be precipitated by a variety of factors, such as declines in performance, perceptions of new opportunities, changes in legislation, or the development of new technologies. They may take a variety of forms, such as increasing formalization of structure, redefining principal operating units, broadening or narrowing market definitions, or engineering a shift in culture. Despite these differences, they have a number of things in common. The stakes are usually high. The number of people involved is large. The emotional context is intense. The timing is unpredictable. The potential for unproductive conflict and negative outcomes—both personal and organizational—is great.

We have written this book for two reasons. First, transitions are an increasingly frequent fact of organizational life. Managing them effectively is a real and significant challenge for the executive. Second, transitions are

1

generally undermanaged. As a result, they often produce more negative upset than is necessary in both the short term and the longer term.

Our objective in this book is to set out the very best current managerial thinking on how most effectively to manage the transition process. We have gone to experts for answers. Each chapter is written by someone who is either a practicing manager or an active consultant to management. The book distills from their broad experience a set of guidelines for the manager who is either confronted by the prospect of a transition in his or her own organization or is trying to learn from previous experience.

## WHY NOW?

Transitions are an increasingly frequent fact of organizational life. Why should this be the case? What accounts for the need for managers to be more skilled now than ever before in the techniques of effective transition management? Five factors help answer these questions.

1. *Downturns and upswings in the economy are forcing businesses of all types to think more in strategic terms.* The recent recession forced many businesses to rethink their strategies. As a result, some began to divest, others began to reorient their product and market objectives, and still others undertook internal reorganizations to enhance efficiency and/or to realign structure with strategy. Each of these actions represents a major transition, and each requires careful planning and astute execution. As the economy recovers, we can anticipate a renewed wave of transitional activity oriented toward repositioning to take advantage of the upturn.

2. *Many new high-tech companies are being built around emerging technologies.* One of the most common transitions in the business world is that from an entrepreneurial to a professionally managed organization. The pain and problems that go along with this shift are well documented and examples are plentiful. The 1980s are witnessing a virtual explosion of new companies being built around emerging technologies, primarily in the information and biotechnology fields. As these companies grow, each will face the prospect of a major transition. Some will make the transition successfully. Most will not. Reflection on how others have managed the process can improve the odds.

3. *Mergers and acquisitions continue to be a principal strategic option for many businesses.* We can anticipate that the rate of mergers and acquisitions will continue unabated. They will be particularly common in three industries: financial services, information services (computer hardware and software production, marketing, and servicing), and health care. As banking becomes increasingly deregulated, as interstate banking becomes more common, and as financial services becomes increasingly the strategic orientation of the major players, a variety of organizational combinations, each representing a significant transition for the affected parties, will be inevitable.

Many experts are predicting a major shakeout in the computer industry, but at the same time there is continued growth stimulated by new technological developments. An explicit strategy of many of the larger firms is to acquire the new technology through merger rather than through in-house research and development (R&D). So we can anticipate a great deal of organizational mating in the next few years.

In the health care industry, mergers and acquisitions will continue to be driven by growth strategies pursued by the investor-owned segment of the industry and by the problem that the autonomous hospitals have in gaining access to capital.

Changing legal ownership, that is, the fact of merger or acquisition, does not guarantee a successful transition. Effective management of the process by which a Connecticut General and an Insurance Company of North America, a Bendix and an Allied, or an American Express and a Shearson become integrated distinguishes the more- from the less-successful ventures. Yet there is plenty of evidence from stories in the popular press alone that some of the more glamourous weddings have not been followed by strong marriages. How do you improve the odds?

4. *Current concern for increasing productivity has led many businesses to experiment with new management systems.* Relatively lean times force careful examination of operating principles, assumptions, and systems. Widespread concern with productivity is in part a function of response to constrained resources and in part recognition of the widespread perception that the United States as a country is losing ground in the international marketplace. The popularity of Ouchi's *Theory Z* and Peters and Waterman's *In Search of Excellence* is evidence of management's search for solutions to the productivity problem.

Many companies are currently experimenting with new ways to manage, experiments which often require substantial revision of existing operating principles, assumptions, and systems. The more sophisticated among them realize that more than engineering is involved; entire organizational cultures have to be transformed. This represents yet another form of transition, likely to become more common yet needing to be carefully managed to be successful. How do you go about transforming an organization's culture?

5. *Rapid development of new information-related technologies is forcing user businesses to rethink and redesign their internal operations.* We are on the very front edge of a wave that will transform the way most organizations do their business. Application of information technology is in its infancy. Whether the particular example is robotics, electronic banking, telecommunications, or the "office of the future," fundamental change is the touchstone. Some businesses will manage the technological transition from today to tomorrow much better than others. Inadequate management will prove to be enormously costly. Effective management of these transitions will separate the long-term winners from the losers.

## MANAGING TRANSITIONS

Transitions are generally undermanaged. What tends to be undermanaged is the behavioral rather than the technical side of the process. There are two principal reasons for this. First, technical issues generally have a "right- and wrong-way" mentality associated with them. Errors may be identified and remedies found. Performance capacities in the technical sense can be determined and verified. Investment of time, energy, and thought in issues which are believed to be finite and bounded is attractive. There is an underlying logic which engages managerial action. Second, behavioral issues are both less concrete and easier to dismiss ante facto. The technology for dealing with the behavioral side of the transition process *appears* both underdeveloped and easier for the line manager to master. The manager is likely to believe that intuition and common sense will be sufficient, if indeed he or she thinks at all systematically about the behavioral side.

Seduced by the "right- and wrong-way" mentality which accompanies and reinforces thinking about the technical side, managers let their attention become dominated by problems which have the illusion of concrete solutions. This tendency produces two results. First, fascination with the technical hampers hard evaluation, and managers sometimes find themselves trapped in a situation from which escape is difficult. Chosen courses of action set boundaries on subsequent choices and bad decisions escalate. Some of the most visible examples of this sort of problem involve computer hardware and software decisions, where previous investments limit how managers think about future options. A second, and more pervasive, result is that the behavioral side of the transition process is undermanaged and is permitted to evolve more by default than by design.

The principal theme of this book is that the behavioral side can be managed more effectively. We are not arguing that managers ought to focus on the behavioral *at the expense of* the technical aspects. Our position instead is that the most elegant of technical solutions depends ultimately on people for its success. No organizational transition—in strategy, in structure, or in process—will be successful unless its impact on preexisting patterns of interests, incentives, and interdependencies among the people responsible for and affected by it are understood and effectively redesigned. This simple idea is certainly not new. But, unfortunately, there is no guarantee that simple ideas will be used. In a sense, then, this book is a reminder.

The book is much more than a reminder, however. It is also a repository of current versions of the simple idea. How are contemporary managers using the idea? To what effect? What guidelines or principles can be taken from their experiences and applied elsewhere? In our view, the book will be successful to the extent that you may be forced to think more systematically about the behavioral side of the transition process and/or to the extent that you find some of the practices others have used helpful in your own organization.

## THE PLAN

The book is organized according to our perspective on the major types of transitions that most organizations face: restructuring, repositioning, and revitalizing. Restructuring refers to major changes in how an organization defines its basic components and their interrelationships. An example of restructuring would be a change from a functional to a product or matrix form of organization. Restructuring generally involves changes in reporting relationships, changes in the distribution of authority, and, hence, changes in the roles that key individuals play. Repositioning refers to major changes in how an organization defines its relationship to the various markets it serves. Repositioning may involve adding new product lines, eliminating old ones, and/or changing the level of support for existing ones. Radical repositioning may even involve getting completely out of one or more businesses altogether or getting into new ones. And revitalizing refers to major changes in how an organization defines its style of operations. Here, we are generally concerned with changes in process. Revitalizing may involve moving from a less- to a more-centralized decision structure, from a less- to a more-participatory managerial structure, or from a more- to a less-formal style of operations. Whatever the specific changes, the net result of revitalizing is a change in organizational culture.

As the case studies richly illustrate, these three types of transitions rarely occur in isolation. More typically, they occur in various combinations, and occasionally in concert. The most common type is restructuring, and changes in structure can and do take place in the absence of major changes in strategy or process. To prepare the way for his successor, for example, a CEO may realign the next echelon of management in such a way that each of the three most obvious candidates has a similar title and areas of responsibility which will allow them to demonstrate their strengths and perhaps uncover weaknesses. This is done without making any changes in overall strategy or in style of operations. Neither repositioning nor revitalizing, however, occurs alone. Each requires some restructuring, and often a major change in strategy will be impossible to achieve without changes in both structure and process. Figure 1-1 on the following page illustrates the four basic types of transitions commonly encountered.

Type I transitions are the most common. Restructuring is the transitional cornerstone. Every transition involves some changes in patterns of authority and in the relationships among people and positions in the hierarchy. Many transitions, however, involve more than restructuring. If they involve changes in strategy as well, they are Type II. If they involve changes in process as well as changes in structure, they are Type III. And if they involve all three, they are Type IV. The managerial challenge is most complex in this latter case and least complex—although still formidable—when restructuring is undertaken independent of a change in strategy or in process.

Generally, the principal motivator of the transitions will be clearly one

**FIGURE 1-1**     Types of transitions

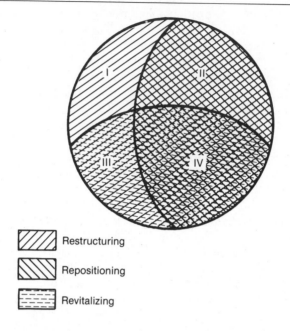

[/////] Restructuring

[\\\\\] Repositioning

[-----] Revitalizing

of the three. A decision to add a new product will require changes in structure. Or an effort to transform the basic operating style will result in rethinking strategy. The very nature of transitions, however, is that their effects on the organization are widespread and that, while they may be undertaken for one reason, they may have consequences that go far beyond those that relate directly to the original rationale.

Dividing the book as we do into sections titled "Restructuring," "Repositioning," and "Revitalizing" obviously implies greater simplicity than there is in fact. Case studies found in each section illustrate instances where the *principal* motivation was structural, strategic, or processual. As you will see, the reality of effective transition management requires an appreciation of how the three are linked.

The case studies themselves were deliberately chosen to encompass a variety of settings. Thus, you will find such diverse sites as an airline, a university, a multinational conglomerate, and a high-tech manufacturing firm. Our objective in seeking diversity was to increase the generalizability of the results. To the extent that there are common themes, you can be relatively sure they will apply to your own situation.

## THE MENU

The book is divided into four principal parts. Each of the first three parts, "Restructuring," "Repositioning," and "Revitalizing," contains one essay and two or three case studies reflecting the type of transition denoted by the title. The fourth part, "Reviewing," contains two essays, one intended to raise questions about how we think about transitions, and the other identifying common themes in the case studies and suggesting a set of general guidelines for the manager confronting the prospect of a transition in his or her own organization.

The general problem of *restructuring* refers to how an organization defines its basic components and the relationships among them. Restructuring may occur in a variety of settings: big or small, young or old, fat or lean. It may be systemwide or targeted to a particular unit or subunit. In this volume, we focus on one particular instance of restructuring, the transition from the entrepreneurial to the professionally managed stage in the evolution or an organization. This transition involves a number of specific problems, perhaps the most fundamental of which is how to balance the need for flexibility with the need for control in the face of what is often very rapid growth. Too much flexibility can result in chaos and dissipation of resources; too much control can stifle creativity and dampen individual initiative.

The case studies in this section focus on two young organizations confronting the agony and ecstasy of rapid growth. Quinn and Anderson describe a small high-tech firm in the Midwest. They explore the failure that emerges from past success and the difficulty that organizations have in dealing with such a paradox, and present a method for facilitating the transition toward formalization. Hackman describes the case of a new, rapidly growing, highly successful airline committed to a distinctive, nontraditional set of values about how its employees should relate to the parent organization. The case is particularly interesting because the restructuring one would expect, given the experience of most organizations, has not yet occurred. Hackman uses the case to raise a number of questions about the future of this airline and about alternative approaches to management. The final essay by Craig Lundberg places restructuring in the broader context of organizational change. Lundberg abstracts a general approach, focusing primarily on what he calls the "transformational case."

Few organizations hold still for long. New markets open up. Old markets disappear. New products are developed. Old products become obsolete. New legislation is passed. Old legislation is repealed. Myriad forces lead to repositioning. *Repositioning* is a strategic response to problems or opportunities intended to enhance performance. It generally requires restructuring. And it always involves rethinking one's relationship to the marketplace and thus may result in narrowing one's focus to increase control or in expanding one's focus to broaden the opportunity set. Cutback and divestiture are examples of the former and horizontal and vertical integration are examples of the latter.

The three case studies illustrate different forms of repositioning and their implications. David Warren's retrospective on Antioch University chronicles the consolidation of a system that had grown too rapidly and distills the managerial principles that were used to bring that organization through a financially and emotionally difficult period in its history. Amy Sales and Phil Mirvis describe how a small corporation, which had been acquired by a much larger one, struggled to retain its identity and they highlight the importance of managing what they call acculturation. Steve Shortell and Tom Wickizer review the results of a series of experiments in vertical integration in the world of health care, where the fundamental challenge is managing change in the context of a highly professional value system where the professionals are both dominant and highly autonomous. Stuart Albert's essay on delete designs completes this section. Albert argues that effective repositioning requires discontinuity. Managers need to develop skills in deleting old activities and their associated rituals and symbols before new activities can be effectively installed.

Occasionally, an organization will fall into the equivalent of a deep sleep. When this happens, and when it is recognized, the problem is revitalizing. Both case studies in this section describe how mature organizations have attempted to reawaken themselves. Rosabeth Kanter focuses on Honeywell and Lee Barrett and Cortlandt Cammann examine the National Steel Corporation. The principal lesson derived from these cases is that revitalization requires cultural change and that such change does not emanate from decrees from on high but rather from a process which requires patience and careful management. In the final essay of this section, Noel Tichy and Dave Ulrich argue that leadership is the single most important ingredient in helping revitalize a mature organization. Citing several contemporary examples, they identify a number of prerequisites for successful revitalization efforts, and discuss the attributes of effective transformational leaders.

The final section of the book, "Reviewing," contains two chapters. Ken Smith challenges the way we think about transitions by contrasting older cybernetic theories with newer ones. His point is that the way we think affects the way we act and that we ought therefore to explore alternative ways of framing problems before acting on them. This chapter is the most difficult but conceptually the most provocative contribution to the volume. Our final chapter scans the others and distills the results. The purpose of this chapter is really to try to answer the question we posed at the outset: What is the best current thinking on how to manage organizational transitions effectively? A number of themes that run through the other chapters are identified and used to build a general model of the transition process. Eight guidelines are then derived for managing transitions. Based as they are on the leading edge of current practice, these guidelines provide a set of useful action-oriented insights for the manager who is facing the prospect of a transition in his or her own organization.

# PART I

# Restructuring

# 2

## Formalization as crisis: Transition planning for a young organization

Robert E. Quinn
David F. Andersen
*The Nelson A. Rockefeller College of*
  *Public Affairs and Policy*
*State University of New York at Albany*

Just as individuals move through distinct life stages, organizations also move through marked phases or life cycles; and just as the movement into a new life stage is often a time of crisis for an individual, so it is for an organization. At the individual level, increasing strain is experienced as people attempt to reduce uncertainty and wrestle with complex questions having significant implications for key relationships and self-identity. In such situations, there often appears to be no "right" answer. As perspective is lost, desperation and a sense of panic grow, and often lead the individual to engage in a series of self-defeating behaviors that exaggerate rather than solve the overall problem. At the organizational level, managers experience a very similar phenomenon. The uncertainty and strain become intense as they wrestle with key issues about strategic directions and organizational arrangements. Here also there often appears to be no right answer, and the selection of a remedy often intensifies the illness.

In this paper a single organizational transition—that from a young and flexible organization to a more mature and formal one—is examined in some detail. We argue that this formalization transition is predictable as a general phenomenon, yet most-often traumatic and seemingly chaotic for the managers who must live through such a transition. A three-stage planning process is proposed for managing these formalization transitions. This planning process is illustrated with a case example.

Organizational transition is a process of adaptation. The organization has been in some type of steady state or equilibrium when some stimulus affects the environment, organizational design, or strategic orientation in such a way as to cause an incongruous relationship among these three factors. Once the incongruity is introduced, a variety of forces eventually move to counteract the disequilibrium. With this view in mind, Miller and Friesen (1980) define a transition as "a package of changes that occur between the onset of the imbalance or stress and the time when some equilibrium or tranquil interval is reached." In a study of the phenomenon, they were able to empirically identify nine "archetypes" or organizational transitions. Among some of the more readily recognizable are the movements toward consolidation, stagnation, maturation, fragmentation, formalization-stability, and entrepreneurial revitalization.

For the manager, transitions are particularly difficult because resources are fully strained and the system is highly vulnerable. An inappropriate decision can initiate a period of decline which may even result in dissolution. The problem is compounded by the fact that points of reference are embedded in the past. These points of reference sometimes act as incentives to return to and preserve the previous steady state, rather than move to some new and uncertain condition. Also, there is a tendency to use restricted problem-solving or search strategies. Cyert and March (1963, p. 121) point out that the search for solutions is often founded on the two assumptions that "A cause will be found 'near' its effect and a new solution will be found 'near' an old one." These tendencies contribute to the probability of selecting an "obvious" solution that, in fact, initiates a poorly understood cycle of events that result in a still worse overall condition. Perhaps the best illustration of this point is Roger Hall's (1976) study of the death of the old *Saturday Evening Post*.

Hall's study focuses on variables such as circulation revenue, advertising revenue, production expense, relative growth of readers and revenue, subscription rate, advertising rate, and total readers. Using a system dynamics approach, he constructed a complex simulation model of the interrelations among variables and how they shift over time. Through this model, Hall shows that certain commonsense management decisions actually contributed to the death of the magazine.

The *Post* moved into one of its final transitions when *Look* magazine became increasingly competitive and a circulation war erupted. In pursuit of growth, the company dropped the subscription rate and increased promotional spending. The only way to cover the promotional expenditure was to raise the advertising rate. However, the rate of increase in readers did not match the rise in advertising rate and thus the real price of advertising increased, leading advertisers to purchase fewer pages. Because of a policy linking editorial pages to advertising pages, the magazine grew thinner and the subscription yield from trial subscriptions fell off. This caused a drop in profit margin which pushed the company to the brink of bankruptcy and set up the conditions for the demise of the organization.

Unaware of the underlying dynamics of the system, management was unable to break out of the cyclical trap. According to Hall, there was a solution:

> As mentioned earlier, the root cause of the sagging profit margin lies in the positive feedback loop relating the number of pages in the magazine, and hence its cost, to the number of readers: (1) as the readership increases, (2) the price of advertising decreases stimulating advertising sales, (3) the increased number of advertising pages leads to the addition of more pages of editorial content, (4) the increased volume of pages attracts more trial subscribers to convert to regular readership, which leads to accelerated readership growth and a feeding back of the outcome to further reducing the price of advertising, and so on, until (5) a feedback effect results in which costs rise more rapidly than the revenues and the profit margin is reduced.
>
> If the management were aware of this process, then one might expect it to prevent the production costs from running away by controlling the number of pages in the magazine. Obviously some relationship between advertising and editorial content must be maintained, otherwise the magazine will become all advertising as the readership grows and the price of advertising declines. An obvious way out of this dilemma is to fix the amount of advertising by controlling the price of advertising. Keeping the advertising "rate" per thousand readers constant will achieve this.

In the above case, management could not handle the transition because it could not understand the shifts that were taking place in the underlying dynamics of the system. Most transitions, in fact, take place because such shifts are occurring. In most cases, because the numerous complex interconnections between variables are not understood, management is unaware of these subtle shifts, and is unprepared to engage in the counterintuitive thinking that is required in order to break out of the problem cycle.

## FORMALIZATION: THE FIRST MAJOR TRANSITION

In this paper we focus on what is often the first major transition for a growing, innovative organization—the movement toward formalization. This transition is particularly troublesome and is seldom expected, understood, or well managed.

In a recent paper, Quinn and Cameron (1983) integrated the literature on the life cycles of new organizations with the competing values framework of effectiveness criteria (Quinn and Rohrbaugh, 1983). From this integration, they formulated a four-stage model of early development in new organizations. As shown in Figure 2–1, the four stages are entrepreneurial, collectivity, formalization and control, and elaboration of structure. During each of these four stages, organizations tend to emphasize differentially each of eight possible classes of organizational values. By plotting each of these organizational value orientations on an eight-point star, Figure 2–1

**FIGURE 2-1**    Effectiveness values during the early stages of development

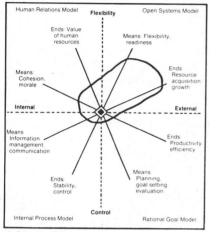

1. Entrepreneurial stage

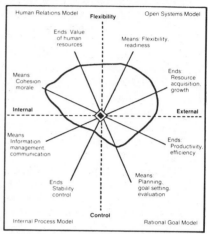

2. Collectivity stage

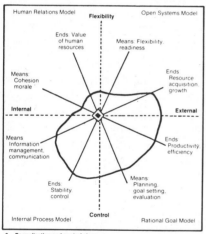

3. Formalization and control stage

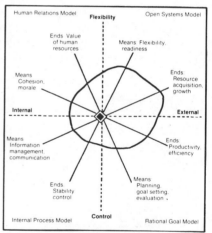

4. Elaboration of structure stage

Source: Reprinted by permission of Quinn and Cameron, "Organizational Life Cycles and Shifting Criteria of Effectiveness: Some Preliminary Evidence." *Management Science*, Vol. 29, no. 1, January 1983, p. 43. © The Institute of Management Sciences (Providence, R.I., 1983).

portrays in graphic form the organizational orientation in each of the four life-cycle stages. In the first stage, because it is necessary to reach some threshold of survival, the managerial preoccupation is with growth, resource acquisition, flexibility, and readiness (the "circled" area). In the second stage (collectivity), this circle or profile widens. While the concerns of the first are still operative, there is now a heavy focus on cohesion, morale, and human resource development. This is a very exciting period, when people enter a new and growing system and have the freedom to maximize their individual creativity and growth. Usually, there is a powerful father figure and an ideology that supports the innovative climate. The "core" group or management "team" is both cohesive and aggressive. People tend to work long hours and exert enormous energy.

In the next stage (formalization), the emphasis moves dramatically from the criteria in the open system and human relations quadrants (top half of figure) to the criteria in the internal process and rational goal quadrants (bottom section). Information management, communication, stability, control, planning, and goal setting all take on higher importance. Thus, this transition represents the most dramatic change in the early evolution of organizations.

Miller and Friesen (1980, p. 285) call this transition maturation and indicate that it:

> . . . represents a maturation of sorts. It heralds the transition to a more professional management approach, often from an entrepreneurial one. As firms grow older, larger, and more complex, there is a greater need to delegate some of the decision-making tasks to functional and lower-level managers, to professionalize and institutionalize the intelligence-gathering and information-processing functions, and to integrate the efforts of decision makers by formal means (e.g., committees and planning sessions) rather than by charisma alone.
>
> The first change that normally occurs is the boosting of the intelligence system. Whereas managers may have gathered information quite informally on their own, systems and departments are set up to gather certain types of information routinely and to disseminate this information to the appropriate decision makers. Also, formal inventory controls, profit centers, cost-accounting systems, and quality controls are implemented.

Based on a review of four cases, Miles (1980) proposes three explanations for the formalization process. First, there is often external pressure. The central office of a large corporation may press for conformity to companywide policies or synchronization to the normal rhythms and performance demands. The control agencies in a government may demand compliance with normal budgeting, accounting, and regulatory procedures. Second, the growth process creates pressures toward formalization. Growth tends to generate a reduction in the frequency and comprehensiveness of personal contacts among key members of the original core group and between the original and new people in the system. This condition tends to result from the physical distance and organizational subdivisions which usually accompany increases in size. Finally, there is the problem of maturation among individual members of the system. One of the negative functions of the challenge, creativity, and intense effort during the collectivity stage is that individuals tend to burn out. Also, the prospect of more routine tasks and formal relations serves as an incentive for the more creative people to leave. This allows for replacement by people who are more willing to usher in the formalization process.

Scholars have varied in their evaluative reactions to this phenomenon. Some see the process as necessary to the continued functioning of the system. Miller and Friesen (1980) seem to take a neutral stance as they present the transition and, in nonevaluative terms, point out a series of costs: leadership becomes more risk-aversive; there is less probability of proactive strategies in which competitors are beaten in the race to enter new markets; there is the emergence of bureaucratic traditions and accompanying resistance to change; there is an element of conservativeness in managerial decisions as groups of policy makers must be ready to defend their conclusions. Lodahl and Mitchell (1980) take a very different position as they argue that mechanisms must be built into innovative organizations so as to prevent formalization, or what they call drift. They suggest a "cycle of vigilance" in which there is an evaluation of the match between the innovative ideology and existing conditions. When there is an incongruence between these two, they argue that appropriate corrective action should then be taken.

While we would certainly allow for the position of Lodahl and Mitchell, our own feeling is that in the majority of cases the transition is probably inevitable. Further, the initial question is not necessarily how to prevent or facilitate formalization, but how to grasp and understand what it is that is taking place. Once there is comprehension, then there can be choice about prevention or facilitation. For most young and growing organizations, this first crisis is a forbidding, mysterious drama. Unfortunately, the members of the organization are not dispassionate observers in the audience, but inexperienced, on-stage actors striving to perform without a script, in a rapidly unfolding spectacle.

The problem of transition is costly in both financial and human terms. There is often a fall-off in performance and prolonged conflict. People fail to understand that a predictable macro process is occurring, but tend instead to see their painful experience as idiosyncratic. They interpret it through a micro lens and look for individuals and groups to blame. Each coalition chooses a different scrapegoat: the external interests with their "evil intentions" to destroy a system they do not understand or appreciate, the top administrator's "inability to manage," the core group's "naiveté" around the maintenance of the original ideology, the bureaucratically oriented new members and their lack of "appreciation" for the "real purpose" of the organization.

The inability to see the overall phenomenon as an unfolding macro process is closely paralleled by the inability to see the underlying patterns of interconnected, dynamic, cyclical actions which initiate and control the problem. By this we mean the kind of system dynamic relationships illustrated in the study of the *Saturday Evening Post*. The formalization process is a classic problem for system dynamics, and at least two students of the field have turned some initial attention to the issue (Andersen, 1981; Richmond, 1981). In the remainder of this paper we describe a process for formalization planning. It is designed to aid organizations in developing a comprehensive analysis of where they are in the transition process, and then to develop an understanding of underlying dynamics that drive their problem.

## FORMALIZATION PLANNING

Formalization planning consists of a three-stage process in which strategic choice, organizational capacity, and longitudinal impact are each considered. The proposed three-stage process provides managers or organizational interventionists with a series of specific techniques to diagnose the situation, to detail specific steps that might be used to control or manage the formalization process, and finally to assess the impacts over time of specific managerial initiatives. In order to illustrate the process, we will describe a recent case experience.

### The focal system

The organization in this case was a corporation of approximately 150 people located in a large Midwestern city. Over the first 8 years of existence, the organization maintained a relatively steady size of approximately 40 people. A decision by a new executive director to diversify services and move into three new areas of activity met with considerable success, and in a 2-year period the organization grew from 40 to 150. At the time of the present intervention, the organization had nearly all the characteristics of a stage 2 (collectivity stage) organization as described in the Quinn-Cameron (1983) life cycles model (see Figure 2–1). The organization was highly flexible and responsive, and relied heavily on informal communication and intuitive decision making. The executive director worked closely with a cohesive management team. This group was skilled at confronting complex problems and generating creative solutions. Innovation and aggressiveness were highly valued, and the executive group took great pride in the growth of the organization and in "the group's" ability to manage. People in this group faced enormous time pressures and worked extraordinarily long hours, seldom taking personal leave.

While members of the executive team were proud of the accomplishments of the organization, there was a growing concern about a lack of planning. Members of the executive group were sensing increasing conflict over strategic alternatives, and some were concerned by an increasing number of internal problems. As these difficulties increased in frequency, a decision was made to hold an executive retreat. At that retreat the organization's management team, working with external consultation, initiated a multistage planning process designed to deal with increasingly frequent problems centering on the organization's planning, staff-development, and information-management capabilities. That is, the management team began to explicitly chart a course through the organization's formalization transition. A three-stage planning model that emerged from the management retreat and follow-on meetings is discussed below.

### Strategic choice

The first stage in the formalization planning process is concerned with strategic choice. There is an examination of the general strategic orientation and an evaluation of alternative strategic directions. In the present case, approximately nine hours were spent in this part of the process. An administration of the strategic orientation instrument developed by Snow and Hrebiniak (1980) based on the Miles and Snow (1978) typology showed a heavy emphasis on the prospector and reactive orientations. These two orientations are very different. The first suggests a heavy emphasis on opportunity seeking, an emphasis on being the first into new product and market areas, and an emphasis on competition. The second suggests a lack of a consistent product-market orientation, a lack of aggressiveness and risk taking, and a tendency to go where forced by environmental pressures. The contrast in these two perspectives led to an extended discussion, resulting in the clarification of a major difference in perspective between two subgroups within the executive team. While one group felt that the organization was reactive and greatly needed to increase its aggressiveness, the other felt that the organization was lacking in continuity and stability and was in great need of consolidation and definition of goals. This conflict would continue throughout the two-day retreat.

After a discussion of these two orientations, a list of all the major present and potential strategic activities was generated and then prioritized. As might be imagined, this process was characterized by considerable disagreement and much of it concerned the organization's capacity to support alternative strategic activities. The discussion particularly focused on whether or not the organization should continue to expand.

### Analysis of performance

In the second phase of the retreat, the group was assisted in a seven-hour diagnosis of the performance characteristics of the organization. The first task in this diagnosis was an administration of the Competing Values Effectiveness Questionnaire. The Competing Values Effectiveness Questionnaire is an instrument designed to elicit a manager's perception of the degree to which an organization is oriented toward each of the eight value dimensions within the competing values model. When results from the questionnaires are plotted on an eight-point star (one point for each of the eight dimensions of effectiveness), a graphic profile of the organization's orientations is derived. In this case, scores from the management team were averaged to create the group profile of the base organization's orientation as shown in Figure 2–2. Notice that this profile closely resembles the typical stage 2 (collectivity) organization as depicted in Figure 2–2.

The second task in the performance analysis planning stage involved using the profile of organizational orientation presented in Figure 2–2 to generate a list of possible steps for future managerial action. After a discussion of the profile in Figure 2–2, the nominal group technique was employed to generate lists of action statements for each area of the competing values model.

The generation and discussion of the action statements did much to clarify the meaning of the profile in Figure 2–2 and to aid in the assessment of the capacity of the organization. A summary of this discussion, organized by each of the four quadrants of the competing values model as shown in Figure 2–2, is presented below:

**FIGURE 2-2**   A performance profile of the organization

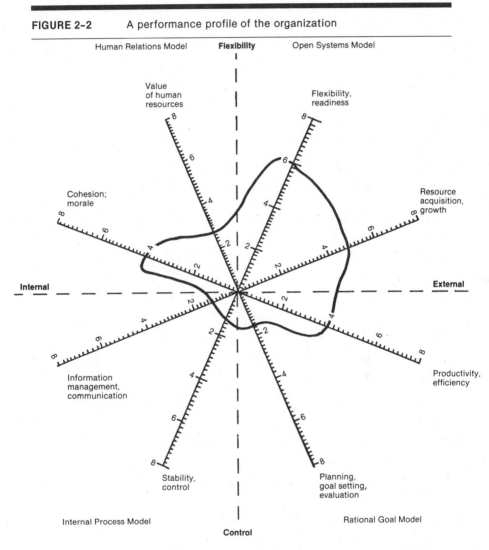

**Open systems model.** In terms of flexibility, it was felt that the organization was very good at adjusting to changes and to sudden crises, but there was some concern over the ability to move into new areas of activity in a timely, systematic fashion. Several statements suggested the need for a decision system and an organization structure that would support and preserve flexibility. There was also an expression of the need to be careful about "buying flexibility at the cost of internal integrity." In considering growth, the executive team expressed a great deal of concern about getting the expansion process under control. There were a number of statements about planned growth; linking growth patterns to the goals of the organization; developing a capacity for program development, research, and analysis; and generally taking a more comprehensive, thoughtful, and "whole organization" approach to expansion.

**Rational goal model.** The criteria in the lower right quadrant of Figure 2–2 are productivity and efficiency, planning, goal-setting and evaluation. In considering productivity—efficiency, the group first pointed out the need for stronger second-level management. For a number of reasons, they felt that it was very difficult to delegate key tasks to subordinates, and this problem left the executive team overloaded. They also indicated a need for the development of standards in the areas of quality control and production. In considering planning, it became clear that this area was in need of planning and evaluation activity. This was true in a macro-micro sense, and in a long-range, short-range sense. The group pointed out the need to set aside a regular time for formalized, timely planning with wide involvement and a commitment to stick with specified objectives. They also pointed out the need for the establishment of clearer time lines and benchmarks for major activities and for a more effective link between the budget-making and planning processes.

**Internal process model.** Of all the quadrants in Figure 2–2, the one in the lower left appears to be the most neglected. In the discussion of stability control, it became clear that internal coordination was an area of growing concern. The group called for clearer specification of role expectations and job descriptions, procedures for resolving conflict over internal resources such as copying and word processing, and the need for consolidation and standardization in certain units. In the area of information management and communication, it was agreed that there was a need for a number of changes. These included the formal recording of certain policies and procedures, the establishment of a corporate file system, the development of data banks, and a cutback on unnecessary paper flow. In this area it was also agreed that there was a need for increased sharing of verbal information and a number of mechanisms were suggested.

**Human relations model.** The upper left quadrant includes cohesion, morale, and the value of human resources. For some time the organization had prided itself on the fact that there was high cohesion and morale. It was therefore very unsettling when some people argued convincingly that morale was falling off, particularly at the levels below the executive team. The three most concrete suggestions for addressing the problem were to hold more staff meetings, to hold unit retreats, and to shift evaluation and budgeting functions to the unit heads. The most extensive list generated had to do with the development of human resources. These included: increased hiring, better training and development, better salary and reward system, development of career ladders, better matching of skills and jobs, increased delegation, development of a personnel manual, and more systematic affirmative action efforts.

## Longitudinal impact analysis

By the end of the second phase of the formalization planning process, the management team had analyzed the organization's performance along each of eight key dimensions and had suggested action steps that could be used to improve organizational performance and ease the formalization transition. Two key questions remained to be answered. First, would these action steps actually achieve desired ends over time? More to the point, what implicit assumptions was management making in assuming that these steps would work? Second, do predictable "reverse pressures" exist within the organization that would work against management's attempts to take these actions?

The final step in the formalization planning process was designed to examine the proposed action steps in some detail in order to determine why management believed they would work and what types of pressures embedded in the standard operating procedures and operating norms of the organization might prevent these actions from being effective over time. For example, implicit in the notion of developing information and management communication functions more fully (an action step associated with the internal process model) was the belief that such systems could help to routinize agency operations, thereby encouraging the emergence of the management team's immediate subordinates into a truly effective middle-management team. However, such a long-range growth strategy would have to be balanced against a possible short-run slump in overall task performance as the management team pulled out of direct involvement with production decisions and spent more time developing new functions (such as information management and planning).

In a word, investing the management team's time in developing new functions implied a promise of greater future growth, but also a near-term danger as the management team underwent a sharp transition in roles—moving from direct production activities to more indirect planning, control, and goal-setting activities.

System dynamics diagramming was proposed as a tool for making management's implicit growth assumptions explicit and open for discussion and for analyzing future possible barriers to implementation (Forrester, 1961; Roberts, 1978). Although system dynamics analyses often culminate in formal computer simulation models (as in the *Saturday Evening Post* case cited previously), in this case a simple diagrammatic analysis of the causal feedback loops controlling agency growth was employed. Follow-up to the present effort may involve formal simulation modeling.

The longitudinal impact analysis proceeded in several steps. First, the major feedback loops believed to be controlling present agency growth were uncovered and discussed. Next, the feedback loops that would be touched off if the management team were to invest in greater planning, information, or training activities were tentatively identified. The implications of these causal influences were then discussed and their implications over time more fully explored. Since these proposed management interventions have not yet taken place, the "data base" for the causal feedback diagrams is the subjective beliefs and implicit assumptions of the management team. Hence the purpose of the system dynamics-based intervention is less to validate "true" causal structure (since the proposed effects are future-possible, not already existing) and more to make explicit management's assumptions concerning what will be the consequences of various strategic choices.

In the discussion below, two action steps proposed by the management team are examined in some detail—the management team's decision to invest time in staff training and development and the decision to invest more managerial time in planning and goal-setting activities.[1]

**Staff training and development.** Figure 2–3 illustrates one of several causal loops that drive successful growth within the young and aggressive corporation. A highly cohesive management involved with organizational production decisions is highly productive. High team productivity leads to a high task-completion rate. Success at past tasks encourages the team to take on new and more challenging tasks. These new tasks increase the overall production load on the central team, leading to pressure to expand the central team size. Increased task accomplishment and sustained team cohesion are possible through the marginal expansion in the size of the management team.

However, this simple diagram, capable of partially explaining the aggressive behavior on the part of the management team, also contains the first hint that such an aggressive management strategy cannot continue to work indefinitely. Continued growth would assume that the central management team could continue to expand indefinitely. As informal communication needs become greater and interpersonal relationships more complex, the central management team will cease to function cohesively at some point determined by a "maximum team size."

This "maximum" effective size for an informal management team may be 7, 11, or even 27 members. The point remains that, given such a maximum, this limit will ultimately constrain the continuing growth of the organization. As the team size approaches this maximum, pressure will mount to formalize operations, to create a more efficient middle-manage-

---

[1]Because of time limitations, this occurred several days after the retreat. In future applications of this process, we intend to build this step into the initial design.

**FIGURE 2-3**      Simplified analysis of forces causing rapid growth and eventual leveling of organizational activities

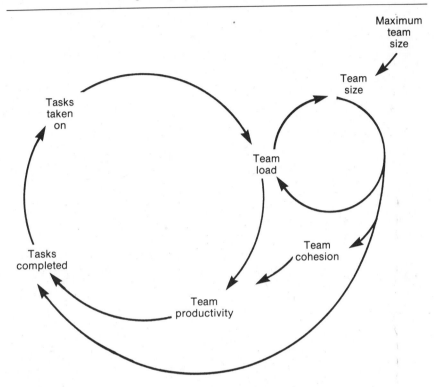

ment layer, and, in general, to shift production decisions from the top management team.

In sum, Figure 2–3 suggests that, over time, an aggressive and cohesive management team is the central force responsible for the system's rapid growth during its youth. However, implicit in this very management strategy are the seeds of future stagnation as the management team becomes overwhelmingly involved in production decisions and loses its cohesive nature as the team grows in size and complexity. A strategy to formalize system operations and to divest the central team of some portion of these responsibilities is needed.

Diagrams such as Figure 2–4 can be used both to document why training activities can enhance long-run performance and to diagnose short-run pressures that may prevent the training proposal from being truly effective. As shown in Figure 2–4, team time invested in the training and development of subordinates will lead to an able core of middle-level managers. As the ability of this new layer of management increases, the central team will delegate a greater and greater portion of production decisions to middle management. Subordinate productivity will then augment the productiv-

**FIGURE 2–4**     Causal analysis of training as a mechanism to sustain organizational growth

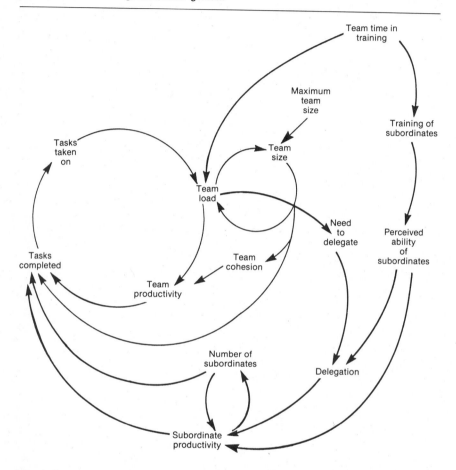

ity of the central management team, enhancing overall task completion. The number of subordinates will also be able to grow without the need to maintain team cohesion (given the more formal structure of middle management) and, hence, the system will be able to transcend the earlier growth limit imposed by maximum team size. That is, the management team will come to believe that staff training and development could, in the long run, bring about a more-formalized organizational structure through the development of a new layer of middle management.

However, this strategy is not without its own problems. Notice that Figure 2–4 predicts that increased team effort in training will also have the near-term and undesirable effect of increasing the central management team's overall load. Especially in times of high task pressure, it would appear that the central team would not have the time and energy to devote to developing a middle-management team. Hence a paradox arises. At exactly those points in time when the central management is most pressed, the development of subordinates will be the least likely to occur. However, it is at exactly this point in the system's growth that an investment in middle-management capabilities is most necessary. If the management team continues to pursue the same strategy that has yielded success in the past (that is, heavy reliance on the team's own cohesive structure to accomplish tasks), future success in the long term will not be possible. At this critical point in the young organization's life history, patterns of behavior that have produced success in the past will paradoxically lead to stagnation in the future.

**Planning and goal setting.** Figure 2–5 demonstrates how this rather simple causal analysis may be extended to incorporate other aspects of management's implicit growth strategy, as identified in earlier phases of the formalization planning process. At the management retreat concern was

**FIGURE 2-5** Causal analysis of planning as a mechanism to sustain organizational growth

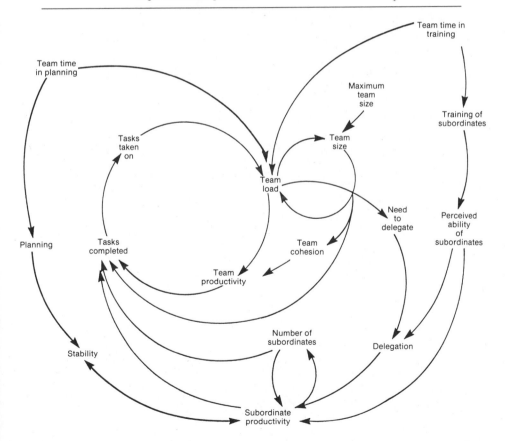

expressed over developing greater long-range planning capabilities within the organization. As shown in Figure 2–5, such a strategy could have the ultimate effect of enhancing agency stability and, hence, the ability of the newly emerging middle-management layer to function more productively. However, this strategy evokes the same type of paradox as that shown in Figure 2–4. In the short run, effort devoted in planning is taken away from direct production activities. Again, at the very times when such an investment in planning would be most warranted, it would also be least likely, given the pressures on the management team, coupled with their established patterns of behavior.

As a final point, notice that even at the rather simplistic level of analysis as that shown in Figure 2–5, it becomes quite difficult to unravel the consequences of implicit assumptions concerning a proposed strategy for growth. For example, Figure 2–5 presents the management team with three choices for the investment of their efforts: continue to be involved in production, spend time developing and training the middle-management team, or spend time developing agency planning functions. Given a limited amount of time and effort, unaided intuition gives few hints concerning how these three competing functions should be handled, especially given that the long-term versus short-term effects of various growth strategies may be dramatically different. For this reason, system dynamics analyses often proceed to the state of formal computer simulation, so that management can precisely specify implicit assumptions concerning the strength of various influences and have the computer unfold the consequences of such assumptions accurately and quickly.

The three rather simple diagrams just discussed all point to the need for more-formal analysis of a given growth strategy. If an explicit "model" (be it causal influence diagrams or a more-formal computer model) of the transition strategy cannot be thought through and made to work "on paper," it would appear highly unlikely that such a fuzzy strategy would work in reality. On the other hand, an explicit model of the growth strategy through the transition, while reassuring, is still not a guarantee that such a strategy will work. Furthermore, the causal loop diagrams also help to identify pressures within the organization that will "work against" the proposed innovations. Paradoxically, these reverse pressures are embedded in the same standard operating procedures and organizational norms that have caused the organization to grow and flourish during its stage 2 (collectivity) life-cycle phase.

## SUMMARY AND DISCUSSION

The literature on organizational growth suggests that many organizations will move through predictable life stages, and that the transition from one life stage to the next will be accompanied by a crisis of transition. Using one organization as a case study, we have examined a series of techniques for helping an organization to grow through and prosper during such a transitional crisis—specifically focusing on the formalization crisis within young organizations.

We have proposed a three-stage "formalization planning" process. The strategic choice process identifies key aspects of management's orientation and lays out which areas may be most in need of more attention by management. The performance-analysis process identifies specific operational areas of organizational performance that may need managerial attention. By focusing on broadly defined functional areas, management brainstorms specific strategies to manage the formalization crisis. Finally, the longitudinal impact analysis forces management to be explicit about the organization's normally implicit growth assumptions. By committing to paper a formal and explicit causal model (in the form of causal loop diagrams) of agency growth, the overall soundness of management's strategic growth plan can be scrutinized and discussed. Further, possible impediments to implementing growth strategies (often embedded in the organization's own standard operating procedures and norms) can be identified through the longitudinal impact analysis. Throughout, the emphasis of all three techniques is on getting management to formally and explicitly articulate a formal strategic plan for dealing with the formalization crisis in a young organization.

## REFERENCES

Andersen, D. F. "A System Dynamic View of the Competing Values Approach to Organizational Life Cycles," pp. 160–87. *Public Productivity Review* 5, 1981.

Cyert, R. M., and J. G. March. *A Behavioral Theory of the Firm.* Englewood Cliffs, N.J.: Prentice-Hall, 1963.

Forrester, J. W. *Industrial Dynamics.* Cambridge, Mass.: MIT Press, 1961.

Hall, R. I. "A System Pathology of an Organization: The Rise and Fall of the Old *Saturday Evening Post,*" pp. 185–211. *Administrative Science Quarterly* 21, 1976.

Lodahl, T. M., and S. M. Mitchell. "Drift in the Development of Innovative Organization." In *The Organizational Life Cycle,* ed. J. R. Kimberly, R. H. Miles, and Associates. San Francisco: Jossey Bass, 1980.

Miles, R. E., and C. C. Snow. *Organizational Strategy, Structure, and Process.* New York: McGraw-Hill, 1978.

Miller, D., and P. Friesen. "Archetypes of Organizational Transition," pp. 268–99. *Administrative Science Quarterly* 25, 1980.

Quinn, R. E., and K. Cameron. "Organizational Life Cycles and the Criteria of Effectiveness," pp. 33–51. *Management Science* 29, 1983.

Quinn, R. E., and J. Rohrbaugh. "A Spatial Model of Effectiveness Criteria: Towards a Competing Values Approach to Organizational Analysis," pp. 363–77. *Management Science* 29, 1983.

Richmond, B. M. "Endogenous Generation of Structural Change in System Dynamics Models: An Illustration from Corporate Context." Paper presented at the 1981 System Dynamics Research Conference, Institute on Man and Science, Rensselaerville, New York, October 14–17, 1981.

Roberts, E. B. *Managerial Applications of System Dynamics.* Cambridge, Mass.: MIT Press, 1978.

Snow, C. C., and L. G. Hrebiniak. "Strategy, Distinctive Competence, and Organizational Performance," pp. 317–36. *Administrative Science Quarterly 25,* 1980.

# 3

# The transition that hasn't happened[*]

J. Richard Hackman
*Yale School of Management*
*Yale University*

It is commonly assumed that a new organization, as it grows and matures, proceeds through a series of developmental transitions—that is, changes in the direction of the organization, in how it is structured, or how it functions. Objectives and ways of operating that may serve a firm well during start-up, for example, often must be modified later when the challenges of getting underway are replaced by those having to do with the maintenance and growth of the organization in a changing environment.

This is an account of a young, fast-growing organization that seems *not* to be exhibiting the kinds of developmental transitions one would expect to observe. The account is necessarily unfinished: As this is written, the firm has been operating for only two and a half years. It would be premature, therefore, to try to draw conclusions about the dynamics and consequences of its unusual pattern of growth and development. Yet the way this organization has developed is sufficiently unique and counter to traditional wis-

*This paper was prepared as part of a research project on team effectiveness supported by the Office of Naval Research (Organizational Effectiveness Research Program, Contract No. 00014-80-C-0555 to Yale University). The assistance of Fred DeLeeuw of People Express Airlines in providing financial and operating statistics is gratefully acknowledged. The measures of organizational climate reported here were compiled by Dan Denison and Richard Saavedra at the University of Michigan, and are used with their permission. My understanding of People Express has been greatly enriched by conversations with Susan Cohen, Aubrey Cramer, Dan Denison, and Robert Helmreich in the course of our collaborative work with the firm.

dom that it may be instructive to describe what has transpired, to assess the apparent consequences for the firm to date, and to see if there are lessons about transitional processes that can be learned from its experience.

## The firm

The organization we will examine is People Express Airlines, Inc., which describes itself as follows:

> The Company is a certificated air carrier which commenced operations on April 30, 1981, with three aircraft serving four cities. The Company currently provides . . . service to 16 airports in the eastern United States. It utilizes 21 Boeing 737 aircraft and operates from a hub at Newark International Airport. . . .
>
> The Company has adopted a simple pricing policy for each of its routes under which two prices (peak and off-peak) are offered. The Company's price levels are substantially lower than the standard coach fares of other airlines that were in effect prior to the announcement of the Company's service on such routes, although the Company's competitors have matched its prices on many of [its] routes. . . . The Company's price strategy is designed to stimulate demand by inducing passengers who would otherwise travel by automobile, bus or rail, or who might not travel at all, to take advantage of the speed and convenience of air travel, thereby increasing the total market for the Company's services.
>
> People Express has made substantial efforts to minimize its costs in order to be able to offer its low prices. The Company has achieved significant increases in aircraft productivity by flying its aircraft a high number of hours per day and by redesigning the interior configuration of its aircraft to allow additional seating capacity. In addition, through simplified reservations, ticketing and passenger processing procedures, the Company is able to provide passenger convenience, while utilizing fewer personnel and facilities than are required for similar operations by other airlines. The Company has developed an organizational structure that promotes the involvement of all its people in the management of the Company. All full-time employees of People Express are stockholders of the Company, and each performs more than one function in the Company's operations.[1]

The major aspirations of the firm are summarized by 6 precepts, formulated early in the life of the organization by the 16 top managers, and now used throughout the firm as the primary guides for decision making about organizational policies, structures, and practices. The precepts are:

1. Service, commitment to the growth of people.
2. Best provider of air transportation.
3. Highest quality of management.
4. Role model.

---

[1]Prospectus for a 1,000,000 share offering of common stock, April 26, 1983, page 3.

5. Simplicity.
6. Maximization of profits.

The organization that has emerged relies heavily on member self-management for guiding work activities (the management hierarchy has, in practice, only three levels), with relative equality of "perks" within the firm. There is a pervasive emphasis on teams as the unit for accomplishing work and making decisions, with all employees serving more than one function. Everyone, including middle and senior management, performs regular line work, and there is no full-time support staff. Staff work is covered on a rotational basis by flight managers (who are pilots), customer service managers (who provide cabin service on the aircraft), and maintenance managers. Compensation relies heavily on profit sharing and stock ownership. All employees are required to purchase stock as a condition of employment, and are periodically given the opportunity to purchase additional shares at favorable rates.

### The role of the researcher

The data used in this paper are drawn from documents and reports generated by People Express in the course of its business, from research my colleagues and I have conducted in collaboration with the organization, and from my own observations of the organization and conversations with its members.

In interpreting what I have to say about the development of the organization, the reader should understand the character of my involvement with it. I began work with the People Express as an occasional consultant in December 1980—eight months after the firm was incorporated and four months before it began operations. My involvement increased both in extent and breadth thereafter, and has included research, consultation, and management training activities.

I have spent a great deal of time observing the line operations of the firm and the meetings of various management groups and task forces—sometimes as a part of formal research or consultative work, other times simply to better understand what was going on.[2] In addition, I have spent many hours in informal conversations with individual managers at People Express, both listening to their views of the organization and trying to formulate and articulate my own.

With high access to the organization has come a considerable personal investment in it. Beyond my interest as a scholar in understanding the organizational experiment that is People Express, I have come to care about the

---

[2]My access to the organization and its members appears to have been limited only by constraints on my own time. I have been allowed to attend all meetings and events I wanted to attend, and have no evidence of something being deliberately scheduled so as to preclude my being there.

firm and the people in it. The aspirations of the firm are consistent with my own values, and I want the organization to succeed. Even though my primary professional commitment is to learning, and my main contribution to People Express has been to help members learn things about organizations and about their behaviors that will help them in their work, I am not a disinterested outside observer.

### The notion of an organizational transition

Transitions pervade organizational life, and the other chapters in this book illustrate diversity both in the kinds of transitions that occur in organizations, and in the ways organizations deal with them. Here I use the term very simply, to refer to significant changes in (a) the primary tasks or goals of an organization, and/or (b) the strategy an organization employs to achieve those aspirations. Transitions, then, are major alterations in *what* an organization is trying to do or *how* it is doing it, alterations that have nontrivial implications for how the human and material resources of the organization are deployed and managed.

Transitions often occur in response to external demands or opportunities (for example, changes in the economy, in competitor behavior, in capital or labor markets, in government regulations), but also are responses to changes in the internal state of a firm. As an organization moves from start-up to steady state, or as it enters a period of growth or retrenchment, significant alterations may be required in the aspirations of the firm or in its internal structures and systems.

Of special interest for People Express are the kinds of transitions that may occur as a firm surmounts the start-up hurdle and enters a period of sustained growth. One way of viewing that process, that identifies a number of specific crises an organization faces as it grows, has been proposed by Larry Greiner in an article titled "Evolution and Revolution as Organizations Grow."[3] Greiner suggests that the development of an organization can be characterized as a series of evolutionary periods of growth, punctuated by times of revolutionary change. During revolutionary periods management structures and practices that previously were satisfactory are found to be inadequate for present needs, and there is a time of upheaval and turbulence as managers search for new practices that will guide the firm through the next evolutionary period. The alternating cycles of evolution and revolution proposed by Greiner are illustrated in Figure 3–1.

Of special interest for our purposes are the early phases of growth: the time of initial growth through creativity, the crisis of leadership, followed by growth through direction and the crisis of autonomy. According to Greiner, creative evolution involves intense entrepreneurial activity by the founders, long hours of work motivated by the hoped-for benefits of ownership, frequent and informal communication, and control through immedi-

---

[3]*Harvard Business Review*, July–August 1972, pp. 37–46.

**FIGURE 3-1**     The five phases of growth

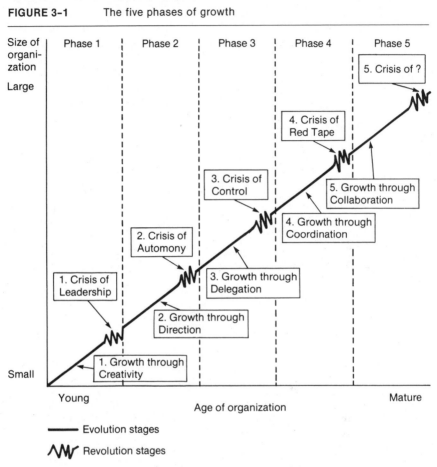

Source: Reprinted by permission of the *Harvard Business Review.* An exhibit from "Evolution and Revolution as Organizations Grow" by Larry E. Greiner, July–August 1972, p. 41. Copyright © 1972 by President and Fellows of Harvard College; all rights reserved.

ate feedback from the marketplace. But as the company grows, it encounters the crisis of leadership, a time when individualistic and creative activities must give way to getting things organized, when structures and systems must be introduced to coordinate and control the enterprise. The need, Greiner suggests, is to locate and install a strong business manager, someone more tempermentally suited to the new managerial tasks than the founders—but who must, nonetheless, be acceptable to them. The founders may not recognize this need, or they may be unwilling to take the necessary step to the side, and as a result some organizations fail to survive this crisis.

Next, according to Greiner, comes growth through direction, a period of sustained growth guided by competent, directive management. The firm is likely to be reorganized along functional lines, job assignments become more specialized, control systems (for example, budgets, work standards, incentive programs, accounting procedures) are installed, communication becomes more formal, and a management hierarchy is created. Direction is provided by the top manager and his or her staff, leaving little room for autonomous decision making by lower-level managers and supervisors. This evolutionary period begets the crisis of autonomy, in which lower-level managers demand greater decision-making latitude, something the directive top managers may not be disposed to provide—and something the lower-level managers may not be ready to handle given their lack of experience as decision makers.

For organizations that survive this crisis, Greiner suggests, there are more to come: The alternating cycles of evolutionary growth and revolutionary crisis continue indefinitely. While it is not possible to predict the number of months or years that will elapse between times of revolutionary transition, Greiner argues that the *slope* of the line in Figure 3–1 depends on whether the firm is in a high- or low-growth industry. When the organization is in a high-growth situation with rapidly expanding markets, evolutionary periods will be relatively short, and revolutionary crises will come more quickly.

## GROWTH AND TRANSITION AT PEOPLE EXPRESS

Did People Express exhibit the period of informal, creative growth Greiner suggests is characteristic of young, entrepreneurial organizations? Has it subsequently experienced the leadership crisis, gone through a time of growth through direction, and encountered the crisis of autonomy? Or has the firm followed a different pattern of growth, with different kinds of transitions?

In starting to address these questions, we will look first at the rate of growth of People Express from April 1981, when it began operations, through June 1983. This should give us an idea about the degree of potential *need* for transitional changes in the organization's early years. Then we will examine selected data from the life history of the firm, to determine whether and how the organization *has* reoriented or restructured itself in response to the external shocks and internal challenges it has experienced. After reviewing this evidence, we will assess the performance of the firm, draw some inferences about the relationship between its developmental patterns and its effectiveness, and close with some speculations about the implications of the People Express experience for the future development of the firm.

### The growth of the firm

People Express Airlines, Inc., was incorporated in April 1980. In May of that year it obtained its first external financing ($200,000 from the venture capital subsidiary of Citicorp), in October obtained certification from the

Civil Aeronautics Board to operate as passenger carrier, and in November successfully offered 3,000,000 shares of stock at 8-1/2 per share. The Federal Aviation Administration granted the airline an operating certificate on April 25, 1981, and flight operations began on April 30, one year after incorporation. The company initially operated 3 airplanes (the first deliveries of 17 used Boeing 737s ordered from Lufthansa) and served 4 cities: Newark (headquarters and the hub of operations), Buffalo, Norfolk, and Columbus, Ohio.

The company has grown rapidly and steadily since then. Figure 3–2 shows the number of aircraft operated, and the number of passengers flown, at the end of each fiscal quarter. The number of aircraft increased from the initial 3 to 22 in June 1983—including 10 Boeing 727s (with many more on order) and 1 leased Boeing 747 used for transatlantic service. The number of passengers carried also has grown steeply in the company's 26 months of operation, reaching a high of 1,236,000 passengers in the second quarter of 1983 when data collection for this paper ended. The number of cities served has grown from the initial 4 to 19. The revenues and assets of the airline, shown in Figure 3–3, have increased in parallel with the number of passengers and aircraft flown. Operating revenues reached a high of $64,304,000 and assets were $187,014,000 in the second quarter of 1983.

**FIGURE 3–2**     Growth in number of aircraft and number of passengers

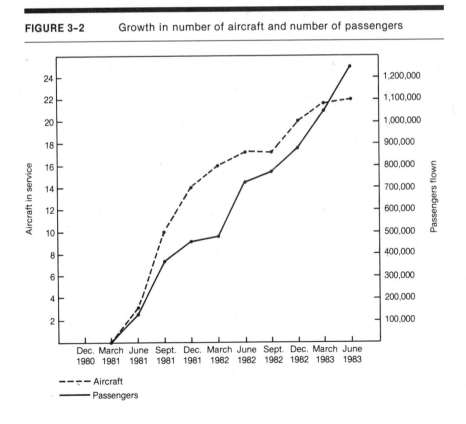

**FIGURE 3-3**     Growth in operating revenues and total assets

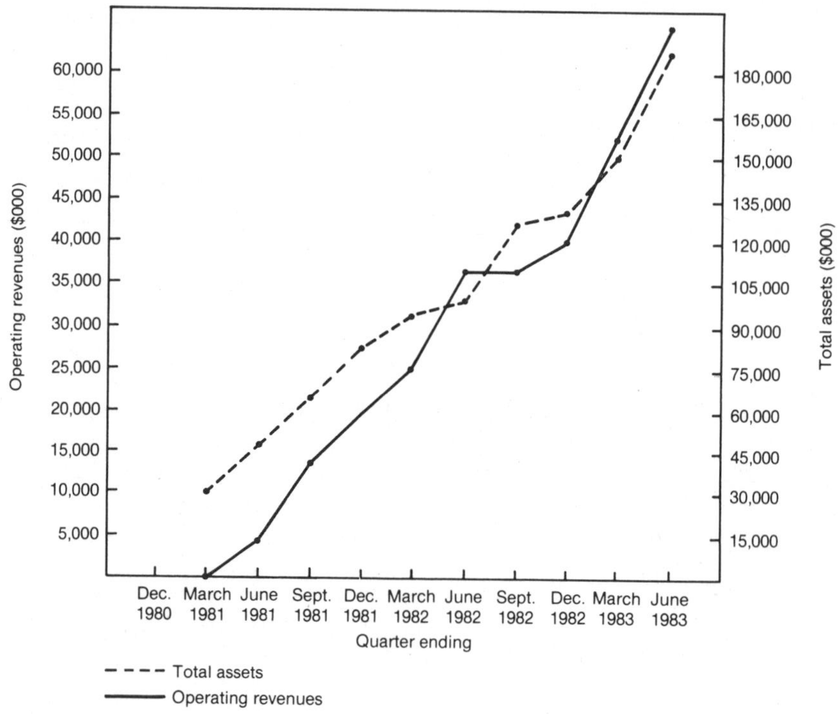

Growth in personnel is shown in Figure 3-4. At the end of March 1981, there were 37 persons on the payroll, including the chairman, the president, 6 other managing officers, and 8 general managers who together comprised the top-management group of the company. An additional 66 persons were in training at that time, preparing to join the organization before operations started one month later. In June 1983, there were 1690 full-time organization members, plus 1479 part-time employees (predominantly college students working as sales agents in reservations) on the payroll.

The bottom part of Figure 3-4 shows the growth in management personnel. There were 16 senior managers when the organization began operations, there are 16 senior managers now, and (except for 1 resignation and 1 promotion, to be discussed later) they are the same individuals. In August and September of 1982, a new middle-management role (called "team manager") was created and 44 individuals were promoted to that position. (No appointments to middle- or senior-management positions have been made from outside the organization since the initial top-management group was formed.) By the end of June 1983, a total of 94 middle and senior managers, each of whom was expected to spend time in line operations as

**FIGURE 3-4**  Growth in personnel

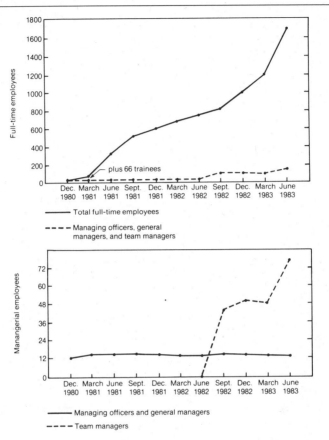

well as in management work, was available to lead a workforce of more than 3,000 people.

Although the airline industry as a whole has been in a period of some disarray in recent years, People Express exploited the oportunity provided by deregulation in a way that resulted in very fast growth. If Greiner is right that organizations in growth environments move quickly through cycles of evolution and revolution, we should observe transitions appearing at People Express at a rapid clip.

### Searching for signs of transitions

We turn now to evidence from the history of People Express to see if signs of significant transitions can be found. What is presented here is in no way a comprehensive history of the firm. It is, instead, a focused and selective summary of those events and activities that may help us understand how the organization has grown and changed in the first two and one half years of its life. Since our interest is organizational transitions, we will give special attention to (a) external shocks and internal crises (because they may serve to stimulate transitions), (b) activities that tended to affirm or change the company's primary aspirations, and (c) activities that tended to promote or inhibit change in the firm's strategy for accomplishing its tasks and achieving its aspirations.

**Before start-up.** The idea for the airline was hatched in Houston by Don Burr, who had been president of Texas International Airlines and who became chairman of People Express. He convinced Gerald Gitner and Melrose Dawsey (who also were formerly with Texas International) to join him as the founding group of managing officers, with Gitner as president of the fledgling airline. Other managing officers and general managers were recruited, and the emerging management team spent countless hours together hearing the chairman's vision for the new enterprise, laying plans for the policies and structure of the firm, securing capital, and negotiating for aircraft and facilities.

By the time the team moved (in January 1981) from Houston to its new general offices in the old North Terminal at Newark International Airport, the basic strategy and structure of the airline had been determined. There would be four teams of top managers: (a) finance and administration, (b) marketing, (c) people (human resources), and (d) flight operations and in-flight service (actually, two overlapping teams). Each managing officer and general manager would be a member of more than one team, just as each flight manager (FM), customer service manager (CSM), and maintenance manager (MM) would work in more than one area.

It was an exciting, creative time: The challenges were great, but successes were frequent. And each new person recruited brought new ideas and enthusiasm to the group. The work was a mix of planning ("How do we get this airline organized?") and production ("How can we get enough people recruited and trained to start up on schedule? How can we get the facilities ready and obtain the FAA certification we need in time?"). Production activities seemed always a bit behind schedule, there were not quite enough people to do what was required, and sleep became a scarce commodity for many members of the start-up team. Yet people were genuinely engaged by the chairman's vision for the airline and the plans and aspirations that emerged were grand.

I, too, was caught up in the enthusiasm. Asked to do some thinking about the design of the organization, I came up with a long laundry list of ideas and issues. We had fascinating discussions about them, and if anybody noticed that implementing the ideas was far beyond the practical reach of an understaffed group of managers who had to start an airline in a couple of months, nobody said anything. But what absolutely *had* to get done got done.

**April 30, 1981: Start-up day.**　Some random images from my notebook:

The bus driver, the cab driver, the hotel clerk, the parking lot attendant, spying an identification badge: "How are you all doing?" "Good luck now." An officer unable to resist, hopping on one of the first flights at the last minute, to applause from the crew. It's infectious.

Everybody pitching in with everything. A banker from California, a key figure in arranging financing for the airline, sitting in the reservations office alongside a captain just back from his day's flying, booking flights and trying to keep up with the flood of incoming calls. A general manager, his voice filled with emotion: "For the first time in my career, I'm in an organization where you can help someone out and be thanked for it rather than resented."

Smoke filling the conference room while the senior management team reviews the first day's operation. The chairman emerges, asks a consultant standing in the hall to call the fire department, re-enters the room, closes the door, and the meeting continues.

A team of three CSMs, back from their first trip, sorting through a pile of money on the conference room table (the same conference room, the *only* conference room), trying to balance the dollars they have with the number of passengers they flew. And then discovering that they are not sure what they are supposed to *do* with all that money.

Euphoria: passengers enthusiastic, congratulatory calls, flowers from parents and from vendors, hugs in the hall. "We pulled it off." We really *are* a different kind of airline." "There's no stopping us now." And then stillness at the end of the day. The chairman in his office, alone with a pile of bonus checks, one for each member of the start-up team. Quiet, brief, personal conversations with each person as checks change hands. It has begun, but now it begins. Just what has been set in motion today?

**Summer 1981: Reality strikes.**　Start-up was just what a start-up is supposed to be: a time of enthusiasm, creativity, informality, collaboration, improvisation, and amazing entrepreneurial drive. It couldn't last forever, and it didn't. The external shocks were severe. After service was announced for Cleveland (but before it was begun) two competitors slashed their Cleveland prices, wiping out People's anticipated price advantage. Traffic throughout the industry went soft, and passenger loads were lower than hoped for. Problems that disrupted operations developed with vendors supplying ground services. And then, on August 3, the Professional Air Traffic Controllers Organization (PATCO) went on strike. Landing slots at key airports were severely restricted in number, passengers stayed away from airlines in droves, and it looked as if a life-threatening situation was developing.

Internal problems were surfacing as well. Those employees who thought that the pace would slacken after start-up were discovering that they were wrong: The staffing shortfall got worse, and the workload got higher.

Missed birthdays and anniversary dinners, forgiven by friends and families before start-up, now added to the stress on already-stretched managers at all levels of the organization. And things were not getting organized. Meetings ran over into the scheduled start of subsequent meetings, the management teams were not functioning well, advisory councils (which were designed to provide input into policy decision making by CSMs, FMs, and MMs) were not getting off the ground, and people throughout the organization, especially pilots, were getting frustrated and restive.

Yet, again, what absolutely had to be done got done—the chairman made sure of it. A decision to terminate plans for Cleveland service and to go to Boston instead was made in an afternoon meeting, and by evening all relevant parties had been informed and redirected. Pressures to put standard airline structures and systems into place (for example, a dispatch function staffed by full-time dispatchers) were resisted despite their clear short-term advantages, because such changes would "tear the fabric" of the airline.

At the end of August, I videotaped a talk on People Express for a group of human resource professionals, and used the occasion to reflect on what seemed to be working well, and what had turned out to be especially difficult for the airline. I commented favorably about the commitment of the organization to self-management, about the use of teams as performing units, about the learning that was happening throughout the firm because of staff cross-utilization, and about the inventiveness of the organization in creating structures consistent with its vision while simultaneously growing fast in a crisis-ridden environment. I noted the extraordinary quality of the people in the organization, pointed to data showing that the overall climate of the organization (as measured by our survey) was as high as I had ever seen, and attributed much of the success of the organization to the chairman, who had held fast to his ideals despite much pressure to compromise them in small ways. Difficulties I discussed included problems in getting things communicated throughout the firm, in helping people learn the skills they needed to be good self-managers, and slowness in turning the corner from starting up the airline to operating it. The process of developing structures and systems for the routine management of the organization, I said, was not coming along fast enough; too much remained squarely on the shoulders of the chairman, and I doubted that that could remain the case for much longer.

**Late fall 1981: The pressure builds.** I was wrong. In the fall of 1981, the chairman began to take on even more responsibility, particularly for the operation. The partnership that was supposed to have developed between the chairman and the president (with the former guiding the overall development of the firm, and the latter having primary operational responsibility) was not working out as well as had been hoped, and both parties were unhappy about that.

The economy and air traffic control situation were still serious problems—although the company seemed to be coping with them at least as well as anybody else (the addition of Florida routes, for example, diminished the air traffic control problem and generated substantial revenue). Responsibility for many operational matters remained diffuse, and the organization continued to be understaffed and understructured. There was, now, a daily operations briefing which helped to coordinate activities. And some members of the start-up team had been asked to serve as "coordinators" (albeit with the same formal job title and salary) to provide additional assistance in managing the operation. The coordinators were supposed to rotate back into regular line work after six months, and be replaced by other CSMs, FMs, and MMs. But the organization was finding itself dependent on them—and the coordinators were feeling overworked, frustrated with the ambiguity of their role, and underappreciated. While it seemed clear that something would have to be done soon about "the coordinator problem," nobody was sure what that should be.

As the pressure built, the chairman continued to hold fast to the initial vision of the company, and teach it whenever and to whomever he could. Then, around the first of December, he asked each of his 15 top managers to write down his or her views of the key precepts of People Express, and a special meeting was held to discuss, prioritize, and codify those views. Out of that meeting came the six precepts listed earlier in this chapter, and a renewed commitment to structure and manage the organization in accord with them. It was a major step in the evolution of the firm, in that those six brief phrases came to serve as a firm handhold for people throughout the organization—something to rely on when faced with conflict or uncertainty in deciding how to handle a difficult situation.

**Early 1982: Movement toward restructuring.**    By February 1982, it was clear to the top-management group that something had to be done to get things organized. The small changes that had been made (for example, restructuring the responsibilities of senior managers to give greater priority to operations) had not put much of a dent in the general looseness and informality of the overall organization. Because the structure was not working, too many small problems to be solved and decisions to be made found their way to senior managers—who became so occupied with them they could not make the investment of time required to get the structures working as intended, and thereby relieve some of the burden on them. A number of senior managers were having difficulty coping with their workloads, and were not at all sure what to do to make things better.

Moreover, morale in the flight-manager group, always a concern, now appeared to be quite low—and sinking. Communication problems seemed to be getting worse, and the advisory councils still had not started to function as intended. And most salient of all was the resignation of the president (the first—and still the only—departure of a senior manager from the firm). As the chairman added the duties of the president to those he already had, some senior managers began to act in ways that suggested they had their eyes on the open presidency. In all, the time seemed ripe for a significant organizational transition.

Soon after the president's departure, the chairman appointed a "restructuring task force," with an initial charge of looking into the coordinator problem—but an implied mandate to look at the structure of the company more broadly. The task force, composed of six managing officers and general managers, began by seeking ideas, company-wide, on what to do about the role of the coordinator. Ideas and suggestions literally poured in; many were creative, and almost all were highly constructive in tone. Encouraged, the restructuring task force began to develop the criteria they would use in evaluating alternative designs for work roles at People Express, suggestions were sought from the People Advisory Council and from the coordinators themselves, and the mood of the organization seemed to lighten perceptibly. It was almost as if a barrier had been removed from a roadway, releasing vehicles to accelerate toward a most attractive destination.

**April–May 1982: Work and celebration.** Two events occurred in this period that expressed the renewed optimism of the organization. First was a party to celebrate the anniversary of the start of operations. Everyone was invited, and it seemed that almost everyone came: The hall was packed with celebrants who reminisced about the year, cheered a slide show that somehow captured the spirit of the organization through candid photographs, and shared the kind of feeling that only those who have been through some trying times together can share. Those CSM coordinators who had been with the organization since before start-up had especially wide smiles—a happy and welcome change for what had been a rather disaffected group. They had presented their own ideas about restructuring to the structure team earlier that day in a report titled "Proposal to Enhance and Define the Present Organizational Structure of People Express Airlines . . . prepared and submitted by The Founding C.S.M.'s." The proposal had received rave notices, and it was hard to tell whether the coordinators or the senior managers to whom it had been submitted were more pleased. In all, it was an uplifting evening, a time that symbolized much that was special about People Express and that offered hope for even better things to come.

The other event was the first major retreat of senior management, held at a secluded hotel in Florida in mid-May. The structure group used much of the time there to develop a rough first cut at its proposals and then, with some trepidation, made an oral presentation to the chairman (who had studiously avoided involving himself in the on-going work of the team to that point). The chairman was most supportive of what the team had to say. He encouraged the team to get its ideas down on paper, and to begin thinking about an implementation plan. The structure group returned to Newark with a full head of steam, fleshed out its proposals, and outlined a detailed report that would be used to communicate and explain the proposed changes throughout the organization. Things appeared to be very much on track for getting in place the kinds of roles and structures the firm would need for the next phase of its growth.

**Summer 1982: Derailment.** As the structure team got nearer and nearer to finishing its work, it became harder and harder to go the rest of the way. Finally, after several postponements, a comprehensive 24-page report was produced and distributed. The document (a) reviewed the history of the firm and explained why changes were needed, (b) described the process the structure team had used to gather information and develop ideas, (c) set forth the criteria employed to evaluate and refine alternative designs, (d) described in detail the new managerial roles and organizational structures to be introduced (including the new "team manager" role), (e) gave examples to illustrate how the structure would work in practice, and (f) laid out a plan for implementing the new structure. The report was carefully read and well received throughout the organization. Yet the cost of producing it had been very high—both in managerial time and in the strain on the structure team itself. Indeed, the final push to produce the document so badly disrupted relations among members that they were unable to work together effectively as a team for a considerable time thereafter.

The immediate consequence of the report was the selection of about 40 CSMs, FMs, and MMs for promotion to the new team-manager role. The need for additional management had been felt for some time throughout the organization, and no one hesitated to take advantage of the opening the structure report provided. Management training activities for the new team managers were initiated at once (for some team managers, literally the morning after they were told of their promotion). The chairman was heavily involved in these training sessions, personally handling training in the precepts, the role of the team manager, and the management practices of the airline. And he faithfully attended sessions taught by others, signaling by his presence the importance he placed on the new managers' learning quickly how to manage in accord with the precepts of People Express.

The structure report also prompted a reconfiguration of senior management teams and a new management meeting schedule. But like previous changes involving the managing officers and general managers, the hoped-for changes in behavior either did not occur or did not stick. And the bulk of the recommendations were never fully implemented. (Particularly distressing to some organization members was the abandonment of a peer feedback system in mid-stream: After extensive data had been collected from the colleagues of coordinators about their strengths and weaknesses as People Express managers, feedback of those data was delayed interminably— and in many cases never occurred at all.) The structure team, still smarting a bit from the final days of preparing its report, experienced great difficulty in getting all members together for meetings, and was not able to get things back on track when meetings did occur.

It was as if the structure team, having gotten over a major hurdle in its work, was now unable to keep on running. And the organization as a whole seemed to be experiencing some of the same lethargy. The arrival of new aircraft and the opening of new cities had flattened out, and while nearly everyone I spoke with reported being busier and more pressured than ever, the organization seemed somehow heavier and slower than it had in earlier times. If the pause in the rate of growth provided an opportunity for implementing the ideas the structure team had come up with, that opportunity was not being pursued with much vigor.

**October 1982: Rededication to growth.**    Among the plans that had been slipping was the management development program. The chairman, Lori Dubose (the airline's officer with main responsibility for human resource matters) and I agreed to meet at the chairman's home in early October to assess where things stood with the program and to lay some plans for next steps. We spent the day together, and we never talked about the topic. Instead, we found ourselves reflecting on our individual and shared frustrations, disappointments, and failures. The day provided a valuable catharsis, for me if not for the others, but I left with a hollow "But now what?" feeling.

The answer came two weeks later at a meeting of the 16 managing officers and general managers, also at the chairman's home. Here is what he had to say, from my notes of the meeting, very lightly edited:

> The spark in our organization went out sometime between last March and now. I've withdrawn, have been working less, and am less happy about it. I sense the same thing in others. This came to a climax for me here two weeks ago in a meeting with Lori and Richard that was supposed to be about management development. We never even got to the issue. Instead, I spent most of the day complaining, pouring out my own anxiety. It was a good process for me. I learned a lot about me, about the company, and I've thought a lot about it since then.
>
> I think I've come up with something. This is an *entrepreneurial* company, dedicated to growth and change. That's what we do best. When that ended, a piece of what we are ended with it. Sometime after March we switched from being a new venture to being an establishment company. People started going home to sleep. We lost the momentum. And we're not particularly good at maintenance. I know I'm not good at it; it doesn't engage me.
>
> Do you share this view? If so, think about re-gunning the engines and doing more of what we set out to do three years ago. What we ought to do, given our present lethargy and the economic times, is set out on a new growth path, and get some aggressive plans in place.
>
> We know how to do some things. We know how to do Part 121 [FAA certification]. We know how to market. We know how to buy airplanes. We know how to maintain them. But why muddle along doing what we know how to do? It's not reaching our potential. By next spring, we ought to be ready to

make the next big push. What's to stop us? What are the constraints? Equipment? No. Money? No. Facilities? No. The FAA? No. The constraint is the people. But really that's not a constraint either. There are a thousand young people just like you already in the company, ready to go. And we can hire more. So our only *real* constraint is people who are knowledgeable and experienced enough to operate well in our kind of organization.

Communications. Supporting people. That's why our discussion today [the official agenda was to discuss implementation of the structure package] is so important. The people process is our only real secret, the lynch pin to our ability to move forward. It's the most important thing we have to do.

So we should set a new horizon, a bigger vision. If we are not excited, our people won't be either. We've got to do better than four to eight new planes a year. We've got to rededicate ourselves to our people-oriented direction. We've lost track of it, and we have to get back with it because that is where our future is.

A couple of minutes later, the meeting was interrupted for an urgent telephone call for the chairman. The call turned out to be from the firm's Washington lawyer. There had been a new development in negotiations about Newark-London service, and People Express would now have a good shot at getting the route if it could make a commitment immediately.

"Can we be ready to fly to London next July?" Laughter. Excitement. Of *course* we can!

**Spring 1983: The plate is full.**     I have few data about the winter of 1982–83, because I was not around much. I had some doubts about the ability of the airline to achieve its new aspirations without first addressing certain organizational issues that had not yet received much attention— such as improving the way teams and task forces were designed and managed, strengthening the advisory council system to provide improved two-way communication between the top-management group and the rest of the organization on policy-related issues, and getting the structure team (which was still having difficulty with the implementation of its report) moving forward with its work (particularly its plans to assist managers in the functional areas improve how work was structured and managed in those areas). But my initiatives on these and other issues were not picked up, I was not as assertive as I could have been about my view of their importance, and I drifted away from the organization for a time.

Things were busy while I was away. Airline traffic had softened in the last quarter of 1982, competitors in the Florida market were drawing away business with very low fares, and the company posted a loss for the quarter, breaking a string of three consecutive profitable quarters. Much attention was given to making sure that the first quarter of 1983 would once again be profitable.

Entrepreneurial activity was also at a high pitch. Negotiations were underway for the purchase of a large number of Boeing 727 aircraft and the lease of a 747 for London service, and task forces were busy throughout the organization: preparing to open service to new cities, obtaining FAA certification for two new aircraft types, and getting cockpit, cabin, ground, and maintenance personnel trained to operate the new aircraft and fly them to their new destinations. While all this was going on, the volume of reservations calls continued to grow—exceeding the capacity of both reservations equipment and personnel (part-time and temporary employees) to handle them—and significant managerial time was spent working on that problem. And, finally, an external consultant was engaged to gather data about people's understanding of the company precepts and to draft some language about them. These materials, after review and revision by the top-management group, were to be used in training and communication sessions to further strengthen organization members' understanding of the precepts and their ability to use them in their work.

In early spring, my associate Susan Cohen and I restarted work with the structure group, based on our continuing hope that the team could become a powerful tool for addressing some of the problems of organizational design and management that continued to frustrate members of the firm. The work did not go well, and eventually the chairman decided that he personally would have to assume the leadership of the structure team for a time. Action agendas were developed for dealing with a number of pressing "people issues," special top-management task forces were formed to improve the quality of in-flight service and ground operations, and the pace of management training activities picked up. There was a sense that progress was being made—but people were feeling stretched very thin, and signs of stress and tension were visible throughout the organization.

**Summer 1983: A new start-up.** The arrival of the 747 aircraft in May was an occasion for much celebration, and the pace of activity picked up even further as traffic improved and as preparations were made to introduce new equipment and new cities. At the end of June, the chairman decided that he needed to let people know that he recognized the considerable sacrifice that they had made during what was probably the most demanding month of the airline's life. Here are excerpts from the memorandum he sent to everyone at People Express:

> I am personally and painfully aware that in a place known for its primary aspiration—an intense, unyielding and demanding commitment to people, ourselves, and our customers—precepts 1 and 2, June has proven to be an extraordinarily difficult month for these same people.
>
> There have been tears of joy and sorrow as our heroes and champions have struggled to cope with the truly extraordinary demands of an historic month. Historic, both in terms of our intent to be the best airline and also the public demand for our product.
>
> First, in terms of the public clamor to use what we produce, we carried nearly a half million customers in June. That is an annual rate in excess of 5 million people and has made us one of the largest airlines in the world in a little over two years from start-up. Before we begin each new day the public has

already reserved every available seat and well beyond in virtually every market. . . . Our unique problem, if you could call it that, is because we are so inordinately productive, the demand for our product is outstripping our ability to produce it. In short, while we routinely talk about operating at virtual capacity we are in a real sense operating beyond our practical capacity. This is not new to us, but in June the pressure and tension of this demand was greatly intensified by the following multiple and cumulative factors:

Introduction of 4 new cities.

Introduction of international service to London.

Introduction of 4 additional aircraft.

Introduction of 727, including the certification ordeal.

Introduction of 747, including the certification ordeal.

Introduction of training—747, 727, recurrent, and Flight Pass (for example, one third of Flight Managers in 727 training).

Introduction of true hub and spoke (105 departures from Newark . . . ).

Introduction of 2,000 new connectors per day . . . .

Introduction of West Arcade [new gates in the North Terminal].

Introduction of Flight Pass and new Paxtrax program [ticketing and boarding pass systems].

Introduction of new reservations system, people and facility.

Introduction of 150 new full time and 1,500 part-time people.

[There follows a detailed discussion of some of the problems encountered during the month, and some of the successes experienced in dealing with them.]

While all of this was an incredible feat, it is not something we will have to do again. It is not the norm. It is not our future.

It will, in time, however, prove to have been our awesome demonstration of the power of the individual. It will similarly come to be seen as one of those periods in our development when we put a huge building block in place and immeasurably enhanced our defensive and offensive capabilities. . . . The intent of our effort, which we in fact accomplished, was to enhance our competitive survivability. This greatly ensures that we can build a place strong enough to allow us to aspire to enjoy the promise of our precepts. . . .

Now . . . we urgently need to and will be focusing renewed energy on how information is best communicated in our organization. . . . We are currently working hard on some exciting ideas to improve our organizational design, particularly relating to a more extensive development of the team manager/team leader structure. This effort is being designed to provide each individual with a direct verbal communication link to what's going on and what should be going on. As this is being accomplished, we will also develop additional devices and techniques to supplement our central verbal chain of communications.

In this regard and also to further understand our recent experience, we have set aside all day Wednesday, July 6, for scheduled open door sessions. Managing officers and general managers will be available for your questions and comments. A sign-up sheet will be posted with times in 15-minute increments. This will be followed at 6 p.m. by a question and answer session at the Holiday Inn. . . .

Finally, let me take this opportunity to say that *I do* recognize the extraordinary effort that everyone contributed in June and I am personally grateful for this dedication, care, and concern. Put in context over the years and not forgetting the difficulties, we should be extremely proud of what we accomplished in June and it will serve us extremely well in the future. I look forward to hearing from as many of you as possible on Wednesday as a symbol of our rededication to each other and our efforts to enhance communication about everything that concerns us.

## Did transitions occur at People Express?

Recall that an organizational transition, as we are using the term in this chapter, involves significant change in the aspirations of the organization (that is, in its primary tasks or goals), or in the strategies used to pursue those aspirations. Is there evidence for such transitions at People Express?

**Changes in primary tasks or goals.** In reviewing company documents and my own notes from observations and interviews, the material on which the historical account of the organization was based, I could not find a single datum suggesting that alterations in the major tasks and goals of the firm were ever even considered. On the contrary, the evidence is that the basic vision of organization has been constantly reinforced, disseminated, and strengthened throughout the life of the firm thus far.

Initially a set of ideas in the mind of the chairman, the vision was shared first with the founding officers, then with the full group of 16 managing officers and general managers, and eventually with everyone in the organization—and even with recruits considering applying for a position with the firm. And, while fairly general at first, the vision was gradually sharpened through constant discussion and debate early in the life of the firm, and then was articulated in a set of six brief phrases, now known by nearly everyone in the company as "the precepts."

There were a number of external shocks to the company early in its life (for example, the PATCO strike, a sharp reduction in demand for air transportation, aggressive pricing by competitors) that could have prompted a major change in corporate strategy or philosophy—shocks that did, apparently, contribute to changes in direction by at least two competitors who also began operations as low-cost, low-fare airlines, New York Air and Midway Airlines. At People Express, however, external (and internal) difficulties seemed only to prompt greater tenacity in holding to the precepts of the enterprise.

The precepts now are well understood and widely used throughout the airline, are rigorously taught to each new class of recruits and each new group of team managers, and seem to be stamped permanently into the fabric of the firm. The basic direction of People Express, as summarized by the precepts, has not changed—and, for the foreseeable future, seems unlikely to.

**Changes in strategy for pursuing corporate aspirations.** Although various structural changes have occurred at People Express (for example, devices for dealing with specific communication and coordination problems), and while managers have made resolve after resolve to get more organized and more disciplined in their work, the basic strategy the firm has used in organizing and executing its work has not changed. Nor is there evidence that the alternating cycles of evolution and revolution described at the beginning of this chapter have occurred at People Express. Indeed, at almost exactly the time one would have expected the "crisis of leadership" (that is, when a strong business manager would take precedence over the entrepreneur at the helm of the organization), the president (whose major responsibility *was* the operation of the airline) resigned—and his duties were assumed by the chairman. The period of "growth through direction" under the business manager's leadership never occurred, and the "crisis of autonomy" was never reached.

There were ample opportunities for transition to a more "businesslike" organization. There have been problems in coordinating the operation, in hiring enough people to run the airline and getting their work organized well, in dealing both with customers (who have had trouble even getting through to make a reservation) and vendors (some of whom have had a bit of difficulty comprehending the absence of secretaries, receptionists, and support staff), and so on. And there have been times of clear failure in managers' attempts to get the organization to work the way they wanted it to work, and to perform at the level they wanted it to perform. My notes are full of quotations documenting the struggle and the pain: "We just cannot keep operating like this." "We *have* to get better organized." "I'm in meetings so much of the time I can't get any work done." "We can't seem to get anything implemented and followed through." "I can't take any more of this pressure and stress."

But whenever times have been especially tough (for example, in the fall of 1981 when the environment was particularly pernicious, or in the late fall of 1982 when the "crisis of lethargy" was encountered), the response has been the same: a rededication to the *growth* of the airline, greater efforts to sharpen and teach the *precepts*, and an increased commitment to the *people* of the airline. Those emphases have been present at People Express since it began, and there is no reason to expect they are about to change. Indeed, when data collection for this chapter ended in mid-summer of 1983, People Express looked in many ways like a start-up organization—one with thousands more people than the group that started the airline in the spring of 1981, but with many of the same dynamics.

## CONCLUSIONS

We seem to have here an organization that has not, at least not yet, experienced the kind of transitions we have come to expect from the research literature on organization development and life cycles. How are we to make sense of what has happened at People Express, and what are the implications of the organization's experience for its future development?

We will look first at the organization's performance, to see if there is any evidence to suggest that the absence of major transitions has impaired the effectiveness of the firm. And then we will briefly explore some alternative ways of understanding the history of People Express to date.

### Organizational performance

Although we cannot undertake here a full anlaysis of the data on how People Express has performed, we will sample evidence from four domains: (a) measures of cost and load, (b) profitability, (c) stock-market performance, and (d) employee attitudes and motivation.

**Cost and load.**    A standard measure of productivity in the airline industry is cost per available seat mile (ASM)—that is, how many cents it costs to fly an airplane seat one mile. As it began operations, People's cost per ASM was about eight and one half cents, less than industry averages but not substantially so (perhaps because the firm expensed most of its set-up costs, rather than capitalizing and amortizing them). Costs dropped to a low of 5.2 cents in the second quarter of 1982, and have exhibited an increase since then of two tenths of a cent per quarter (see Figure 3–5).

**FIGURE 3-5**    Passenger loads and operating costs

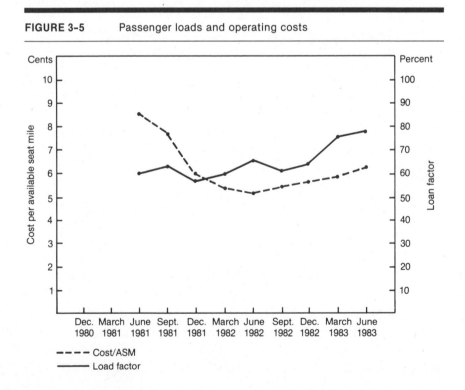

Another widely used measure, this one having more to do with marketing and service quality than with cost efficiency, is load factor: the percentage of available seats filled with revenue passengers. Load factors are highly sensitive to passenger demand, which in turn varies with the health of the economy, so they must be interpreted with caution. In the first seven quarters of operations, People's load factors hovered around 60 percent, a respectable number given the economic times, and somewhat higher than a number of the airline's competitors. In the first two quarters of 1983, loads increased substantially, reaching a high of 78.6 percent (a *very* high load factor) in the second quarter.

**Profitability.**    Two measures of gain or loss are shown in Figure 3–6: gain or loss from operations, which assesses the degree to which operational revenues exceed the cost of operating the airline, and net gain or loss, which is the profitability of the airline considering all sources of income and all expenses.

People Express showed a gain from operations before the end of its first year of operations, and has not posted an operational loss since then. The

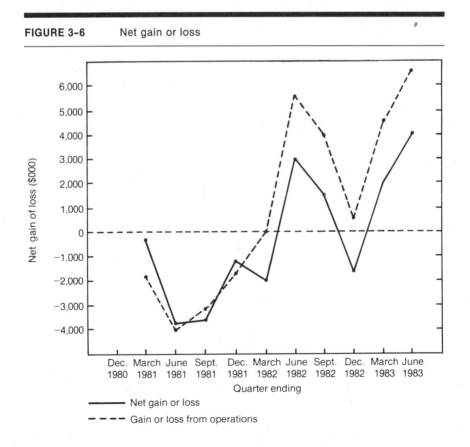

**FIGURE 3-6**     Net gain or loss

firm became profitable in the second quarter of 1982, showed a loss in the fourth quarter of that year (when coincident economic, competitive, and internal problems appeared), and increased its profitability substantially in the first two quarters of 1983. It was one of a handful of profitable airlines in the 1982–83 period.

**Stock-market performance.** The quarterly highs and lows for People Express stock are shown in Figure 3–7. Except for a dip late in 1981 (during the PATCO strike), the price of the company's stock has increased steadily—and, in 1982–83, steeply. The stock has traded at 40 times earnings or better, suggesting that the financial community has had considerable confidence in the growth potential of the firm.

**Employee attitudes and motivation.** The "climate" of the organization has been assessed at regular intervals using an attitude survey developed in collaboration with members of the organization. Average scores for selected items are shown in Table 3–1 from surveys administered in July 1981 (just two months after start-up), December 1981, September 1982, and August 1983. (See page 54.)

The items with which people most strongly agreed (averaged across the four administrations of the survey) are: (a) the people with whom I work in this airline are first rate, (b) overall, I am quite happy with my job at People Express, (c) owning stock in People Express makes people try especially hard to help the airline succeed, (d) the overall quality of the upper-management team at People Express is excellent, and (e) the work I do is challenging and involving. Respondents expressed the greatest *disagree-ment* with these two items: (a) there is a lot of conflict and tension between Customer Service Managers and Flight Managers, and (b) the "team concept" at People Express is a joke. Overall, the attitudes of organization members, as captured by the survey, are quite positive.

How have those attitudes changed over time? There is a definite pattern for many of the items: Scores from the first administration of the survey are most positive, they drop a bit in December 1981, drop a bit more in September 1982, and then rebound in the most recent administration to around the December 1981 level.

Some items do not fit this pattern of decline and recovery. The items in the "colleagility" category, for example, are consistently positive across the four administrations. The perception that People Express might be growing too fast was highest in December 1981 (after the first growth spurt), and higher then than in August 1983 (during a time of more substantial growth). Scores on the item reflecting how well-informed people feel about the performance and future plans of the airline are only middling, as are scores on the item asking about the clarity of what self-management means at People Express, despite a considerable expressed commitment by top management to these matters.

**FIGURE 3-7**     Stock price

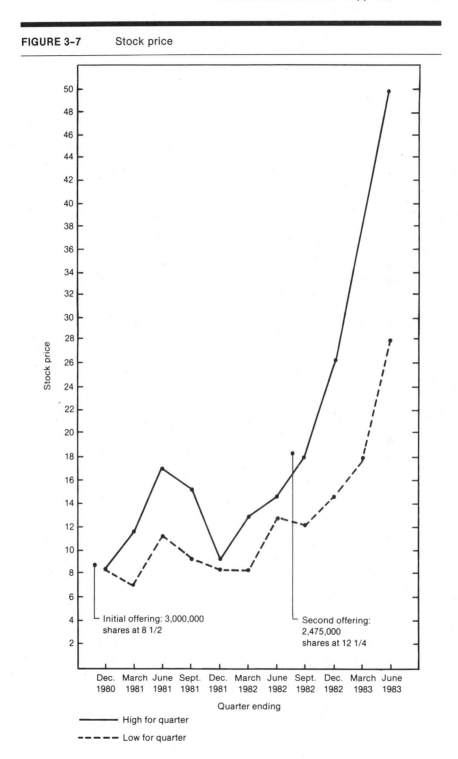

**TABLE 3-1**   Overall responses to selected climate survey items

| | Survey date | | | |
|---|---|---|---|---|
| | July 1981 | December 1981 | September 1982 | August 1983 |
| *Motivation and satisfaction:* | | | | |
| Overall, I am quite happy with my job at People Express. | 6.4 | 5.7 | 5.5 | 5.7 |
| I feel frustrated a lot of the time in this organization. | 3.7 | 3.9 | 4.4 | 4.3 |
| The work I do is challenging and involving. | 6.2 | 5.6 | 5.2 | 5.7 |
| I have many opportunities to exercise self-management in my day-to-day work. | 5.7 | 5.1 | 4.9 | 5.4 |
| I have many opportunities for personal growth and career development in this airline. | 5.6 | 5.3 | 4.8 | 5.2 |
| *Colleagility:* | | | | |
| The people with whom I work in this airline are first rate. | 6.0 | 5.8 | 5.9 | 5.9 |
| There is a lot of conflict and tension between Customer Service Managers and Flight Managers. | 2.1 | 2.3 | 2.4 | 2.3 |
| The "team concept" at People Express is a joke. | 2.6 | 2.6 | 2.9 | 2.8 |
| *Management:* | | | | |
| The overall quality of the upper management team at People Express is excellent. | 6.2 | 5.8 | 5.2 | 5.6 |
| If you raise questions about how this airline is managed, you are likely to get in big trouble. | 2.6 | 3.9 | 4.4 | 3.6 |
| I am kept well informed about the performance and future plans of the airline. | 4.4 | 4.7 | 4.0 | 4.4 |
| Management does not provide me or my team with the kind of support and guidance we need to do our work well. | 2.8 | 3.0 | 3.7 | 3.4 |
| *Governance, policy, and ownership:* | | | | |
| It is clear what "self-management" means at People Express. | 4.4 | 3.9 | 4.0 | 4.5 |
| Owning stock in People Express makes people try especially hard to help the airline succeed. | 6.0 | 5.6 | 5.5 | 5.8 |
| The advice and ideas of the "advisory councils" are taken very seriously by the top management of the organization. | 4.4 | 4.4 | 3.8 | 4.0 |
| People Express is growing and expanding too fast. | 3.5 | 4.4 | 3.8 | 4.0 |

*Note: 1 = strongly disagree; 7 = strongly agree.

**Summary.**    Overall, data on operational performance (cost and load), profitability, stock-market performance, and employee attitudes suggest that the airline has been performing well—particularly when the performance of People Express is compared to that of other airlines during what has been a time of considerable turmoil for the industry. There was a drop in performance on most of the indices in the last quarter of 1982, but results since then suggest that the company has recovered well and that it remains on a high-growth, high-performance track.

### Understanding the People Express experience

People Express has not experienced the kinds of organizational transitions that usually are observed in the early years of an organization's life—and has enjoyed considerable success nonetheless. How are we to understand this?

One possibility is that the organization has had no real *need* to alter its aspirations or its strategy for pursuing them. It may be, for example, that transitions usually result from an organization's inability to deal satisfactorily with the external and internal challenges that confront it (such as being unable to compete successfully in the marketplace or to sustain adequate levels of member work motivation). If this proposition has validity, then there are two circumstances under which one would *not* expect to observe organizational transitions. One is when a firm is in an environment so munificent that success is virtually assured. If, for example, there are only a few organizations that can provide a product or service for which there is great demand, then even firms that are poorly organized and managed can do well—at least for a time. Second, success in some kinds of business has little to do with a firm's internal structure or with how it organizes and manages its human resources. This might be the case, for example, for a business whose profitability depends mostly on the skill of a buyer in obtaining key materials at a low price, on the creative output of a small team of scientists, or on the market acceptance of the work of creative artists.

Can a case be made that such circumstances existed at People Express? The data reported in this paper suggest not. For one thing, the environment was far from munificent. As noted earlier, the organization faced several life-threatening external challenges; indeed, the environment was so unforgiving that many low-fare airlines that began operations after deregulation have been unable to survive. Moreover, organizational and human resource considerations are critical to airline profitability. Airlines are labor intensive as well as capital intensive; airline operations require high flexibility of employee behavior and complex coordination of resources in real time; and airline employees have both substantial responsibility for their firm's assets and high leverage on its costs and revenues. It would be difficult to argue either that People Express in its early years enjoyed an environment so munificent that success was virtually guaranteed, or that its internal structures and management practices were objectively irrelevant to its operational and financial performance.

So it does not appear that People Express was free of the kinds of challenges and performance demands that often prompt significant organizational transitions in other organizations. Perhaps, then, the management of the firm simply did not *realize* that it might be a good idea to reconsider the direction or structure of the firm in response to those challenges and demands. The data do not support this explanation either. The pressures to evolve from start-up mode to a more structured organizational form were intense, and they came from many sources. Bankers, regulators, consultants, and organization members all proposed, at various times and in various ways, that the organization needed to become more structured and better organized. Specific ideas that were suggested ranged from developing detailed procedures for handling certain operational matters to hiring full-time staff to support overworked line managers to incorporating design features previously adopted by established and successful competitors. Such advice was always fended off.

How, then, *has* People Express responded to the challenges it has faced thus far? The answer to this question is perhaps best captured in a comment the chairman often makes when asked why the company is organized and managed as it is: "What are we doing here? What we are doing is learning how to *unleash the power of the individual* in ways that have not been done before and in ways that even we do not yet fully comprehend."

In this context, it becomes easier to understand why, when times have been particularly difficult, the response invariably has been to better articulate the vision of People Express, to reaffirm the firm's commitment to the development of its people, and to set forth on a new growth path. These devices have one thing in common: Each of them serves to engage, direct, and motivate organization members. The vision of the firm is something most members find attractive and worthy of their commitment. The wide-open design of work and the absence of complex organizational structures spur members' motivation to produce and minimize bureaucratic barriers to their productivity. And the incessant growth of the firm (there is always a new city to open, a new aircraft to certify, or new training to be done) keeps people learning and stretching, just to stay abreast of a very fast-moving enterprise. It is as if extraordinary motivation and commitment, coupled with a clear sense of the direction of the entity, can somehow compensate for the absence of the kinds of structures, roles, and management practices that many organizations introduce soon after the rush of start-up has subsided.[4]

As the data in the previous section suggest, the strategy of the firm seems to have worked reasonably well so far. Can the organization operate indefinitely in this way, or is a day of reckoning about to come? There are at least

---

[4]I am indebted to Connie Gersick for pointing this out.

three responses to this question. And as will be seen below, they differ sharply in what they imply about likely future developments at People Express.

1. *People Express has merely put off the inevitable.* A significant transition in how the firm does its business *must* occur, and when it does, the organization will probably pay a considerable price for having deferred so long doing what long-term viability requires.

Every time it looked as if a major transition was about to occur at People Express, a crisis appeared or a spurt of growth was initiated, and attention turned to those pressing matters. One could argue that this pattern cannot continue indefinitely, and that one of these days the consequences will catch up with the organization. Even though it may be painful to visit the dentist, it will eventually hurt more if you keep putting it off.

There is some evidence in support of this interpretation. While there has always been plenty of stress and pressure at People Express, some individuals have recently reported that their personal pain is now more than they can continue to handle. And there is more tension in the relationship between the chairman and his top-management group than has been present before. It looks as if *something* needs to happen to lower the heat a bit, and that something may be the long-deferred transition.

On the other hand, if a significant transition were going to happen at People Express, it really should have happened by now. I have made statements similar to those above a number of times in the life of the organization, and several times thought I saw a transition starting to happen. In each case I was wrong. At some point, one must start to entertain the possibility that what looks like the early stages of a transition is, in fact, simply business as usual for the organization.

2. *People Express has avoided the need to make a significant organizational transition.* With no small measure of struggle, the firm has managed to get through the critical period in its life when the pressures for a transition to more traditional aspirations and structures were greatest. Those pressures will now attenuate, and the organization can continue to grow and develop in its own unique fashion.

While the organization did encounter enormous pressures to become better organized and to adopt more conventional airline structures and systems (especially just after the first few months of operation, early in 1982 just before the president resigned, and again late in 1982), the time of vulnerability may now have passed. And having survived thus far with the precepts and management practices of the firm intact, the firm may now be relatively free to proceed from here on its own terms.

There is evidence in support of this interpretation as well. People in the organization, particularly top managers, are somewhat less intense than they used to be about the need to structure the organization in ways that make things more stable and predictable. And there is a more relaxed attitude now about certain symbols (such as the possibility of having wings and stripes on pilot uniforms, something that previously would have been viewed as wholly inconsistent with the precepts). Senior managers at People Express appear to have developed greater trust in the sturdiness and integrity of the core values of the firm than they had before, as well as an enriched personal understanding of those values and a greater facility in using them in their work. This, in turn, may have made it easier for these managers to tolerate ambiguity in organizational structures, and to give others more latitude in determining how other parts of the organization develop.

Indeed, lots of things *are* getting designed and structured throughout the organization, largely from the bottom up, and in ways that are consistent with the precepts. Customer service managers, flight managers, maintenance managers, and team managers are taking significant initiatives in figuring out how to design and manage the work in their own areas, and there is a sense throughout the organization that the firm is gradually getting both more organized and better managed. Apparently the entrepreneurial spirit of People Express has started to spread, and people are going ahead with their own initiatives to put in place what needs to be put in place to get the work of the organization done the way it is supposed to be done.

There is, on the other hand, still a great deal of looseness in the firm, and a great deal of frustration, duplication of effort, and slippage in getting things implemented. A number of organizational structures and programs, viewed as critical even before start-up, remain relatively undeveloped (for example, the advisory councils, the management development program, the communication program). And, finally, some people in the organization continue to use its underbounded character to rationalize their own less-than-excellent performance, or to forgive poor performance by others. So even if it is true that the track has now been laid for the future growth and development of People Express, there is still a good distance to travel before the firm will be able to realize the full promise of its precepts.

3. *People Express has somehow transcended the conventional dynamics of organizational life cycles.* The organization is about to provide a model of a truly different way to function as a profit-making business in this society. It is not a matter of having deferred or avoided the kinds of transitions that most organizations experience; it is, instead, that this organization is in the process of creating a new and qualitatively different organizational form, one for which traditional thinking about the processes of organizational growth and development is simply not appropriate.

There is also some evidence to support this interpretation. Many trends one commonly observes as an organization grows are simply not present at People Express. There has been, for example, zero growth in the number of senior managers in the firm, despite the fact that the organization as a whole has grown to more than 3,000 full- and part-time members as of June 1983. And, although the presidency has been potentially available for more than a year, there is no overt evidence of jockeying for position among the 15 senior managers (and, in recent months, a lessening of covert maneuvering as well). Indeed, the boundaries defining the special "turf" of middle and senior managers have been getting harder to discern, not easier, in the last year: Collaboration is the rule among people who in most organizations would view themselves as competitors, and sharing of personal motives among senior managers has been on the upswing in the last year. These things are simply not supposed to happen in a hard-driving, entrepreneurial organization as it matures and as senior managers start to stake their future claims.

On the other hand, the firm is still extremely chairman-dependent. He watches the performance of the enterprise more closely and in greater detail than anyone else, sets the priorities, informally chairs most meetings he attends, and is the main teacher of the precepts. And when things start to cool down a bit, it is he who quickly turns up the heat. The empowerment of the other senior managers at People Express, both individually and collectively, has been increasing only gradually—and may have to accelerate if the firm is, in fact, to become a qualitatively different kind of organizational entity.

So what do we have here? An organization that has merely put off its inevitable transition for a time—and will pay the price for it later? Or one that managed to get through its period of vulnerability to transitional processes relatively unscathed by them? Or one that is transcending the conventional dynamics of organizational growth and development? Or is there yet another way of understanding the absence of significant transitions at People Express, one that has eluded this observer?

There is no clear answer to these questions at this point in the organization's development. What does seem clear, however, is that the next chapters in the life of People Express, whatever they may reveal, will also be lively, interesting, and as informative to students of organizations as what has transpired thus far.

---

# 4

# Strategies for organizational transitioning*

Craig C. Lundberg
*Graduate School of Business*
*University of Southern California*

Organizational transitions signal a break from the familiar, that is, they imply a major shift in the organization's character, nature, and functioning. Transitions thus signal a change in historicity and control; in flux are the values and ideals, the structures and ways of operating that have characterized the organization for some period of time. Accustomed patterns which have served as templates for interpreting experience and taking action become tenuous and new processes come into existence. A different future is anticipated and the transition period unfolds more or less intentionally. That organizational transitions occur has long been recognized. How to manage transitions, however, remains as yet relatively obscure.

To be sure, organizational changes of all kinds are becoming more frequent. In part, this represents a contemporary world of several paralleling revolutions, for example, technological, informational, and logistical, of major changes in social values, of increasing environmental turbulence and uncertainty, of demographic and generational imbalance, of new ideas and methods about appropriate management, and of resource constraints and

---

*The author wishes to acknowledge the provocative encouragement of A. P. Raia in nurturing the ideas of this essay, and the helpful comments of W. Bennis and I. Mitroff.

inventions (e.g., Drucker, 1969; Roeber, 1973). The frequency of organizational change thus is partly a response to conditions both internal and external. In addition is the simple fact that we now, as never before, have models and competencies about change, and these induce a sensitivity about and a proclivity toward change. We now possess a sizable literature on organizational change (for example, Peters, 1982), a body of knowledge based on observations and experience with actual change attempts, failures, and successes. Our knowledge and practice, however, focus on the internal fine-tuning of purposive organizations and their improved alignment to their relevant external environments. To raise questions about the management of those organizational changes we have termed transitions immediately pinpoints two notable omissions in the change literature—missing are change models concerning the dynamics and structures of major system shifts, that is, organizational transitions, and change strategies, that is, those macro models which guide major change endeavors.[1]

In the essay, we shall explore the heretofore unexamined area at the interface of change strategy and organizational transitions. Any endeavor that focuses upon the juncture of two previously underconceptualized areas will, of necessity, be somewhat speculative and this essay is admittedly so. Our interest is more to sketch some of the possibilities and opportunities of this arena than to offer either doctrine or prematurely sophisticated theory or empirical substantiation. Thus, what follows is a conceptual essay which outlines strategies for organizational transitioning.[2]

The significance of this purposed endeavor is both obvious and subtle, potentially of practical as well as theoretical importance. It has been noted (Mohr, 1982; Pfeffer, 1982) that progress in the organizational sciences continues to be constrained by a lack of adequate conceptual frameworks. It is timely to move from myth toward theory and the major means are conceptual frameworks that permit us to notice the anomalies that lead to inquiry, which subsequently enhances our frameworks until our increasing sophistication can engender the systematic research that results in theory (Lundberg, 1982b). Therefore, even speculative reasoning which is carefully done and which probes the pragmatic dimensions of a major, increasingly crucial phenomenon, has utility, for it begins to inform and guide practice

---

[1]Although strategies for intervention exist (for example, Beer, 1980) and it is popular to speak of planned change, action research, educative, revolutionary, social diffusion, and other such approaches on "strategies" (for example, Burke, Hornstein, 1972; Huse, 1975), strategy as a pattern of resource developments and environmental interactions that indicate how an organization will achieve change objectives is notably absent. Beer and Driscoll (1977) come closest in their discussions of the dilemmas that constitute strategic considerations for creating and managing change. The explicit use of organizational transitions in and for change is likewise scarce. For an exception, see Beckhard and Harris (1977).

[2]Note the shift here from the noun transition to the verb transitioning, denoting our emphasis on process. To paraphrase the philosopher Max Otto (1949): "Much trouble might be saved if the noun transition never comes into use and everyone uses instead a verb like transitioning or transitioned. We are so much in the habit of believing that a thing must somehow exist corresponding to every noun in the language."

and to stimulate inquiry. Recently (for example, Beyer and Trice, 1982), the relevance and effective utilization of knowledge have become the new slogans in the organization sciences. These terms indicate the several efforts now underway to heal the rift between "rigorous" and "applied" organizational scholars. On the one hand, theoretical elegance and empirical rigor have ruled organizational studies for nearly two decades, resulting in a historical focus on statics over dynamics, on abstraction over praxis.[3] Change and action have been relegated to the related fields of management and organization development—which, in turn, have engendered a somewhat narrowly constrained view of change phenomena, processes, and their models as realignment and increased congruency of organizational elements (Lundberg, 1982a). Attention to the strategy of organizational transitioning may encourage efforts on two fronts. First, it may widen managerial and organizational development perspectives and lead to more developmental approaches and, second, organizational scholars may be encouraged to attend to and appreciate more the study of organizations as developmental systems.

The essay is composed of five parts, each of which is a nearly independent unit which builds sequentially on those preceding it. In the first part, we map the conceptual territory. Strategic organizational transitions and their facilitation are differentiated from other change perspectives and the relevant organization strategy and change literature are briefly reviewed. The second part clarifies organizational transitions. Initial frameworks for understanding transition types, transition stages, and the conditions associated with transitioning are also offered. The third part argues the need for transitional strategy. In addition, dimensions of strategies are suggested and, with them, a classification of transition strategies put forth. The facilitation of strategic transitioning is taken up in the fourth part, with some discussion given to facilitation activities. The fifth and final part of the essay recapitulates the argument and concludes with suggestions for some next steps in the conceptual development of strategic transitioning.

## TOWARD THE CLARIFICATION OF STRATEGIC ORGANIZATIONAL TRANSITIONING

At the outset of this essay, organizational transitions were characterized as the period when an organization shifted from one configuration of relatively stable cultural patterning to another. A transition is from one stage of relatively smooth and continuous operation to another. Organizational transitions encompass major transformations which distinguish one period of organizational history from another (Starbuck, 1965, 1968). The general meaning of organizational transitions, therefore, refers to fundamental changes of an organization's basic nature—a transition from one more or less congruent configuration of character, even culture, to another.

---

[3]Leading, even advanced, texts on organization structure and design often ignore organization change altogether. See for example, Khandwalla (1977) and Mintzberg (1979).

Organizational transitions appear to be bounded in terms of both time and form (Freeman, 1982). While major organizational changes have been subject to the metaphors of biology for some time (Kimberly, 1980), from cell division (for example, Haire, 1959; Ijiri and Simon, 1971) to population ecology (for example, Aldrich, 1979), the dominant analog has become the life cycle. The organization life-cycle perspective clearly offers a counterpoint to the often arid, ahistorical, and overly static orientation to organization research which predominates in the field. Organizations are created, grow and mature, decline, and sometimes end. It appears that organizations do experience common patterns of growth and change (for example, Dale, 1960; Filley, 1962; Starbuck, 1971; Feldbaumer, 1973; Kimberly, 1976; Kimberly and Miles, 1980). Birth, life, and death thus comprise the most general life-cycle framework. Many models of the stages of the organizational life cycle now exist, as does a debate pro and con on whether there is a deterministic sequence. Nevertheless, the life-cycle perspective postulates "stages" which are fundamentally different from one another and thus points to transitions between stages.

The field of organizational change and development (OD) offers a quite different perspective on organizational transitions. Although numerous definitions of the field exist and none appears to be more central than others, many do state that OD improves or changes organizational culture (for example, Burke and Hornstein, 1972; French and Bell, 1973; The Conference Board, 1973). Much of what goes on in OD is predicated on moving an organization from what it is to what it would prefer to be (Lundberg, 1974; Margulies and Raia, 1978). Sometimes this is mostly a matter of getting some part of an organization into a better fit with other parts or with the whole. Typical foci of interventions are role clarifications, better teamwork, socio-technical systems work, enhanced intergroup relations, and the like. Whatever the interventional mode, they are negative feedback-dominated and are best categorized as organizational change (Lundberg, 1980). The other main line of work in the field is concerned with achieving a better fit between the organization and its domains and environment. Typical interventions here are open systems planning, structural redesign, and better management of the system interfaces. These adaptive adjustments are the highly intentional counterpart to the process of when an innovative organization becomes an institution, what Lodahl and Mitchell (1980) have termed *organizational drift*. The most recent conceptualization of this focus on system-environment adjustment is transorganizational development (Cummings, 1983). In all of these "external" fits a combination of both positive and negative feedback mechanisms is involved and they all are best categorized as developmental (Lundberg, 1980).[4] Both organizational change and development explicitly conceive of the stage be-

---

[4]Most organization change and development is value-laden. Espoused values are power equalization, humanism, and collaboration. Many recent movements capture one or more of these normative themes in their labeling, for example, quality of work life, workplace democratization, Quality Circles.

tween the present state and the future desired state as one of transition. Beckhard and Harris (1977, p. 5), for example, conclude, "It should be thought of as a state of affairs in itself, requiring a governance or a management structure and specific work plans and controls unique to that state."

Recently, a new conception of organizations has appeared that provides for still another perspective on organizational transitions. Borrowing analogically from Kuhn (1970), Brown (1978) introduced the conceptualization of organizations in terms of paradigms. Paradigms are a way of looking at things, a way of doing things, embodying procedures for enquiring about the world and beliefs about cause and effect, as well as of appropriate standards of practice. The earlier view that the task of organizational leadership is to give meaning and purpose to activities by the provision of myths and beliefs (for example, Selznick, 1957) has been reinterpreted by Pfeffer (1981) as the articulation of the organization paradigm. Whereas major change in a science is through paradigmatic revolution (Kuhn, 1970), fundamental organization changes have been characterized with a parallel imagery (Sheldon, 1980). Rounds (1981) has reported on the role of information and, hence, meaning as paramount for this order of change. The concept of organizations as paradigms thus postulates cycles of change and stability where basic changes are equivalent to paradigmatic revolutions. The movement from one organizational paradigm to another therefore encompasses a transition of major scope. The transition is from one relatively closed system of meaning to quite a different one.

The life-cycle, organizational change and development, and organizational-paradigm perspectives have in common a view of organizational transition from one stage or state to another quite different stage or state. They vary somewhat, however, in their views about the scope and pacing of transitions and the degree to which transitions are a natural phenomenon or one which is intentionally guided. In the remainder of this essay, we shall focus on the management of major transitions, that is, on those transformational changes in an organization's character and culture which are, in part, intentionally influenced. Whereas major transitions embrace what previously were termed organization changes and organization development, we here acknowledge that transition scale and nature are more encompassing, more strategic.

*Organizational strategy* is the phrase given to the ways by which an organization matches its competencies and resources with the opportunities and risks created by environmental change in ways that are both effective and efficient over time (Hofer and Schendel, 1978). As a separate field of study, strategy is quite recent. At the outset, corporate strategy, for example, Ansoff's (1965) classic, ignored change completely. Even the recent interest in corporate planning (for example, Naylor, 1979) treats organizational changes in terms of strategy implementation, that is, as a change tactic. Even the most eclectic and contemporary of strategic management texts (Rowe, Mason, and Dickel, 1982) retains implementation as the change concern. The literature on strategy and planning seemingly is obscured by a rational action perspective that, to date, has overshadowed attention to strategic organizational transitioning.[5] The literature on change strategy likewise has little to add. *Strategy* here tends to refer to the sequencing of interventions when it is used at all. An organization's business strategy is typically viewed as a constraint on its change endeavors (Lundberg, 1982a). Although strategic transitions were implied by the early spokespersons in the OD field, its practice and models no longer reflect its original renewal and revitalizing functions. In fact, Burke (1982) suggests that it is becoming a cooling-out process for changes that managers wanted anyway and more easily facilitates problem solving and fixing things rather than engendering different ways of problem solving and encouraging basic changes.

From time to time, there is a major, fundamental change of organizational character and culture.[6] This shift can occur with revolutionary swiftness or more slowly by drifting, but usually signals movement in the organizational life cycle. Such fundamental changes are typically induced by environmental changes and require organizational change to reestablish internal congruencies as well as organizational development to realign the organization with its environmental domains. Yet, major organizational transitions are more than changeful and developmental, they are also paradigmatic and strategic.

## TOWARD A MODEL OF ORGANIZATIONAL TRANSITIONS

The development of organizations' literature seems collectively to point to several stages in the life cycle of emergence and decline of organizations. The earliest models of organizational life stages primarily examined the consequences of growing scale and diversification. Other early models emphasized stages brought on by cycles of crisis. The models which followed examined the influence of cultural, economic, and technical factors. Of late, stages-of-development models have been related to differences in other contextual factors as well as strategy, structure, and decision-making styles. The parade of such models continues to grow (for example, Chandler, 1962; Lippitt and Schmidt, 1967; Downs, 1967; Scott, 1970; Greiner, 1972; Channon, 1973; Weinshall, 1973; Torbert, 1974; Lyden, 1975; Lavoie and Culbert, 1978; Adizes, 1979; Miller and Friesen, 1980). These models differ from one another in two ways: the number and, therefore, type of stages, and the degree to which organizations follow the stages sequentially. Some closure was recently given to these issues by Miller and

---

[5]The rational action perspective is well described by Pfeffer (1982). Planned change and planning theories tend to be highly rationalized activities, some would go so far as to say rationalizations (Pfeffer, 1978).

[6]Organizational culture is here understood to be those assumptions, that is, taken-for-granted beliefs, concerning nature, truth, relationships, etc.; values, that is, generalizable ideals, standards and goals; and perspectives, that is, situation-specific rules of conduct and norms that provide a common meaning for system members.

Friesen (1982) who, on the basis of a literature review and a large empirical study, have discovered a rough sequence through five common organization life stages: birth, growth, maturity, revival, and decline. Other scholars are still tentative, specifying a creation, transformation, and decline sequence (for example, Kimberly and Miles, 1980). Even here, there are a variety of transformations possible.

The state of knowledge about organizational life cycles and, hence, major transitions, is such that a rigorous specification of the number and type of stages is probably unwarranted. Given that transitions are major periods of strategic, even paradigmatic development, we are left with postulating organizational life cycles composed of a series of quasi-stable states with transitions interposed. Even this, however, enables the conception of simple and more-complex cases. The simple case has an organizational emergence, formation, or creation stage, a transition to a quasi-stable state, followed by another transition to a decline and ending stage. More-complex cases would contain two or more quasi-stable states with transitions to, between, and after. The creation state and transition states powerfully shape the character of organizational development through the choices made about ideology, organizing, planning, learning, external relations with constituents, stakeholder influence, and membership definition—in short, about the development of organizational culture.

Regardless of the number of stages in an organization's life cycle, we may note that there are essentially just three types of transitions. One may be termed *emergence transition*. It defines the transition from when an organization is simply a possibility to its identifiable creation. A second type of transition may be labeled *transformational*. These transitions are those that punctuate the stages in the "mid-life" of organizations, the quasi-stable states variously concerned with growth, renewal, revival, and so on. The third transition type signals the beginning of decline, and may be termed the *termination transition*.

Each type of transition takes place in three analytically separable but actually overlapping phases. In the change literature, these phases are popularly called unfreezing, change or movement, and refreezing, after the usage of their discoverer, K. Lewin (1951) and early advocates (for example, Lippit, Watson, Westley, 1958; Bennis, Schein, Steele, and Berlew, 1968). Here we shall relabel them inducement, management, and stabilization to keep their reference to organizational transitions clearer. The *inducement phase* involves stimulation, withdrawal from former equilibrium conditions and overcoming natural resistance forces, and recognition that the transition may be necessary and/or even desirable. The *management phase* involves information manipulations, recruitment and utilization of powerful agents, the diffusion of constructs, and the redefinition of the situation, the organization's mission, and so on. The *stabilization phase* is the time when the transitioning is institutionalized, that is, obtains persistence of performance and existence as a social fact (Goodman, Bazerman, and Conlon, 1980). After stabilization, the transformed social processes and actualities take on a rulelike status in social thought and action (Meyer and Rowan, 1977). Reinforcement, reward allocation, procedure formalization, and similar processes are devices commonly used for stabilization.

The designation of three transitioning phases maps into the three types of transitions as shown in Figure 4–1. In the remainder of the essay, however, we shall limit our attention to transformational transitions. There are two reasons for this: (1) They are presumed to be the more common and (2) so little is really known about emergence and termination.

Organizational transitions not only occur between quasi-stable states, but they also seem to be associated with certain conditions. Although development of organizations over time can be considered as a natural mode of organizational behavior, there is as yet no theoretical consensus as to which forces generate development or hold it back (Child and Kieser, 1981). In the model of organizational transitions being elaborated here, we specify three kinds of conditions associated with transitions. Two kinds refer to those internal and external conditions that permit and enable, respectively, transformational transitions. These are thought to be those conditions more or less necessary for effective transitioning to occur. The third kind of conditions, precipitating conditions, are those which bring pressures to bear on an organization for transition. These categories are intended to correspond to the debate in the literature over the significance of environmental forces as opposed to managerial action, over organizational dependence as opposed to autonomy.

**FIGURE 4–1**    An initial classification of transition types and transitioning phases

| | Phases of transitioning | | |
|---|---|---|---|
| Types of transition | Inducement | Management | Stabilization |
| Emergence | | | |
| Transformational | | | |
| Termination | | | |

*Permitting conditions* are defined as those aspects of the internal organizational situation that seemingly allow for transitions to occur. Four such permitting conditions are hypothesized. The first is that there is available some surplus of change resources. Transformational transitioning will require resources in addition to those necessary to carry on the main business of the organization. Thus, additional resources are needed. Whether they constitute managerial time and energy, financial resources, or whatever, this organizational "slack" permits the system to invest some of its resources in change. A second permitting condition is system readiness. This rather ill-defined construct refers, at the organizational level, to that which at the level of individuals we would call an open state of mind. It is the collective sense on the part of organization members that they, or some influential coalitions, can endure change. The endurance of changing more accurately refers to the members' willingness and ability to live with the anxiety that comes with anticipated uncertainty. The third condition is that a minimal degree of system coupling exists. Organizations with very autonomous components cannot easily undertake major transitioning simply because of the additional integrative and coordinative tasks that would be needed. It seems, therefore, that some minimal but as yet unspecifiable intraorganization informational linkages need to exist. The fourth permitting condition has to do with agent power and leadership. There has to be some stability in managerial membership and some degree of strategic awareness and competence in the power coalitions. Although the agents of transitioning may include staff personnel and/or consultants, many are eventually and inevitably managers. Whoever, an ability to envision alternative organizational futures seems useful, as is skill in communicating them. Whether transitioning agents elect power or collaborative tactics, or a centralized or decentralized approach, or whether individuals or system structure are the initial targets of changes (Beer and Driscoll, 1977), these choices will reflect many circumstances of course, for example, the degree of membership homogeneity, the extent of the hierarchical structure, and so on. There are, as noted, several competencies and conditions prior to and permitting of transitioning.

*Enabling conditions* are those external to the organization which increase the likelihood of transition occurrence. Here we specify just two general enabling conditions, both of which indicate the ease or difficulty an organization will experience in transitioning. The first we term the *degree of domain forgiveness*. In the relevant immediate environment of an organization, there are conditions of scarcity or abundance, stability or instability, and resource concentration or dispersion (Aldrich and Miller, 1982) which, in combination, determine the degree of threat to an organization posed by its competition and the economic cycling of the industry (Khandwalla, 1973; Miller and Friesen, 1978). The second enabling condition specifies the *degree of organization—domain congruence*. It is hypothesized that a too great or a too little incongruence between the system and its domains will make transformational transitions seem overly threatening, overly risky, or totally unnecessary. With only modest congruence, the challenge can, and may, be perceived as opportunistic. In essence, these two conditions indicate whether or not the environmental domain will be supportive of an organization's transformational transitioning.

From time to time, organizations also face conditions which *precipitate* transitioning. The literature has stressed the links between organizational structure and environment (for example, Burns and Stalker, 1961; Thompson, 1967; Lawrence and Lorsch, 1967; Perrow, 1970; Khandwalla, 1973; Meyer and Associates, 1978), typically showing how environmental challenges must be dealt with through structural adaptations. Here we speculate that, beyond the challenges which come from the environment—actually incorporated above in our enabling conditions—there are additional pressuring factors, both internal and external to the organization, which set the stage for transition. One kind of pressure has to do with organizational growth or decrement. Boulding (1953) notes three classes of growth: simple, which is organization size; populational, where the composition of one or more organizational components increases in heterogeneity; and structural, where increases in the aggregation of organizational parts means the number of relationships increases. Each creates transformational pressures. The pressure from decrements, that is, the opposite of the three classes of growth, comes from feelings of pain or dissatisfaction and the need to generate or maintain energy for continued functioning. A second precipitating condition stems from the organization's stakeholders. Stakeholders, all of the claimants inside and outside the organization who have a vested interest in it, provide sources of organizational purpose and strategy. A third kind of precipitating condition is in the real and perceived crises an organization experiences. Some crises stem from the environmental uncertainty associated with rates of industry innovation and unpredictability of competitor and consumer actions. Other crises arise from the buildup of resource deprivations and excesses, such as skills, ideas, materials, morale, and so on. It is the accretion of indicators that key members attend to that creates this precipitating condition. The final kind of condition exists in atypical performance demands on the organization. An unexpected greater or lesser level of organizational performance tends to be pressureful. Here, performance demands placed on the system from the marketplace and the public and interpreted by the organization's intelligence system, which the organization is unprepared for, serve to build up pressures for transformation.

With the existence of a threshold amount of enabling and permitting conditions and the pressures experienced from an as-yet-unspecifiable degree of precipitating conditions, organization transformational transitions may be triggered.[7] The image is of tensions which build up and can no long-

---

[7]In this discussion, triggers and triggering events are conceived as more specific than in other treatments. Tichy (1980), for example, lists environmental and technological changes, shifting agreement among organizational members about goals, production focus and structures, and changes in membership composition as triggering events—what in this essay are either precipitating or enabling conditions.

er be ignored, which are released through the stimulus of a particular event or activity. Here we can only indicate the classes of triggers and a few examples. Events in the environment which abruptly create a calamity are one class. Examples are sharp recessions, unexpected innovations by competitors, or natural disasters. A related class of triggers, also environmental, are composed of opportunities, such as the discovery of unexpected market niches, the sudden availability of new venture capital, and technological breakthroughs. A third class are major unresolvable managerial conflicts, or some crisis caused by a major management shake-up or blunder. The fourth and fifth classes of trigger events are revolutions. The installation of a new management team or a "young Turk" coup would be examples of a revolution from within. Revolutions from without might be triggered by such events as political interference or a corporate takeover.

In this part of the essay, we have sketched our conception of strategic organizational transitions. Although emergence and termination transitions were identified, we chose to focus upon transformational ones, transitions between the quasi-stable states or stages of ongoing organizations. Three types of conditions under which transformational transitions occurred were specified, namely, internal permitting conditions, external enabling conditions, and precipitating conditions. The first two types of conditions set an organization up for a transition, whereas the latter type of condition provides the pressures for transition. Given these conditions, when trigger events occur, they initiate the unfolding of the transition in three phases— inducement, management, and stabilization. Taken together, these conditions and phases constitute a first model of organizational transforming transitions. Figure 4–2 summarizes this model diagrammatically.

## ON TRANSITION STRATEGIES

Prior parts of this essay have argued the existence of organizational transitions, attempted to clarify and characterize them, and sketched an initial model of one presumably common type—transformational transitions. We now need to look more closely into this type of transitioning. Although we have postulated a three-phase unfolding of transitions as well as their preconditions, as yet we have not dealt with the states bridged by transitions nor have we examined strategic orientations or the types of strategies available for transitioning. It is these matters to which we now turn.

If transitions are the periods when an organization changes its basic characteristics and culture, then, put simply, transition strategy is the plan for transforming one organizational culture to another. We presume that transition strategy will in part reflect both the former organizational culture and that which is anticipated. The study of organizational cultures is relatively underdeveloped and recent. Since no particularist classification of organizational cultures currently exists, we can indicate only in a general

---

FIGURE 4-2     A model of transformational transitioning

Under circumstances of

*Internal permitting conditions*   in conjunction with   *External enabling conditions*

A surplus of change resources
System readiness
Some system coupling
Agent power and leadership

Domain forgiveness
Organization-domain
   congruence

and

*Precipitating conditions*

Organizational growth and
decrement
Stakeholders
Real and perceived crisis
Performance demands

an organization which experiences certain

*Trigger events*

Environmental calamaties
Environmental opportunities
Managerial crisis
External revolutions
Internal revolutions

may lead to *transformational transitioning*
which unfolds in phases of:

Inducement
Management
Stabilization

---

way the array of cultural possibilities.[8] Culture is anchored in the epistemological structures which are dominant among a culture's members. Here we content ourselves with indicating in only a rough way the variety of these structures. Our constructs of reality seem to vary in two major dimensions, as follows. One dimension concerns the way we conceive of the wholeness or fragmentation of "reality." At one extreme, there is homogeneity, that is, organizations are viewed as a single entity and the ways we choose to fragment it are understood to be arbitrary. Members of homogenetic organizational cultures accept this reality as basic, natural, and desirable. At the other extreme, there is heterogeneity, in which organizations are viewed as having a multiplicity of components which have a reality independent of our observations. Again, this is seen as basic, indispensable,

---

[8]Maruyama (1980) has examined the diversity of cultural and epistemological forms through his "mindscapes" construct. McWhinney (1982) attacks the same issues from a different perspective, the value-influenced view of reality.

and desirable. The second dimension of "reality" contrasts underlying beliefs that organizations are either homeostatic or morphogenetic. The former is stability-oriented, whereas the latter is change-oriented. In one sense, these orientations reflect a difference in our concepts about our freedom of choice in changing the way things happen. On the one extreme, it is taken as dogma that all things are foreordained or predetermined; and, on the other extreme, that anything can be changed if enough intentionality, focus, and energy are brought to bear. With these two dimensions of reality, we can construct a two by two matrix of the extreme alternative positions as shown in Figure 4–3.

Recall that this figure merely sketches the space wherein types of organizational cultures are positioned. While there may be a preponderance of organizational cultures in one quadrant for some combination of industry, nation, and historical period, we assume that the distribution may sometimes be quite wide-spread. An organization entering a transition will anticipate just two choices—the transition will be to another quasi-stable state within one of these quadrants, or to a different one. The latter choice implies a greater change of organizational culture and no doubt quite a different strategy of transitioning. The probability of transitioning intentionally and the scope of the endeavor would seem to vary from very low in the heterogenistic-homeostatic quadrant (i.e., stability of parts), to very high in the homogenistic-morphogenic quadrant (i.e., a changeful whole).

Transformational transitions can be characterized in terms parallel to the typology of organizational culture. This is useful to do because the features of the transition will reflect the quasi-stable cultural stages the transition bridges. Transformational transitions will reflect two dimensions attributed to all organizational strategies. One is the organization's basic time orientation, that is, organizations will vary along a continuum from being primarily reactive to the past to being largely anticipatory of the future. The other dimension of transitions concerns the organization's mission concern, that is, whether the organization is prepared simply to reformulate its present mission, or anticipates creating a distinctively new one. With these two dimensions, we can again construct a two by two matrix which identi-

---

**FIGURE 4-3**    Organization culture types

|  | Homeostatic | Morphogenetic |
|---|---|---|
| Homogenistic | Ho/Ho | Ho/Mo |
| Heterogenistic | He/Ho | He/Mo |

fies the possibilities of fundamental transition orientations. The four quadrants thus specified are shown in Figure 4–4. These quadrants indicate four rather different strategic orientations for transitioning. As such, they inform both practice and meaning. To be "responsive" (that is, to essentially be concerned with a strategy through which the organization responds to its past situation by bringing its mission into conformance), is quite different from being "proactive" (that is, where the strategy is based upon creating a distinctively new mission which anticipates some future circumstances for the organization). Likewise, to be "adaptive" (that is, a strategy where the prior mission is modified to anticipate the probable future) is quite different from "designed" (that is, where the strategy is not only brought up to date but explicitly reflects the system's emerging themes and values). We may further indicate these fundamental orientations to transitioning with reference to several social technologies. Most of what are the conventional interventions of organizational change would seem to fall into the responsive quadrant. The systemwide planning process known as opensystems planning (Krone, 1974), with its emphasis on preplanning for anticipated social and technical environments, appears to illustrate the orientation of the adaptive quadrant. The orientation of the quadrant designated as designed is illustrated by Mason and Mitroff's (1981) strategic assumption surfacing and testing (SAST) technique which was invented to uncover the critical assumptions on which organizational strategy rests. The final quadrant, proactive, may be illustrated by the technique of Nanus (1982) called QUEST (quick environmental scanning technique), which provides a broad and comprehensive first approximation to the environmental trends critical to strategic decisions.

Having examined the fundamental orientations of transitions, we now enquire into the dimensions of transitional strategies. Here we continue our discussion on transformational transitions. The model of transitioning outlined a sequence of three phases that a transition goes through; we now need to go further and enquire into the questions which enable us to differentiate alternative transition strategies. The first question concerns the

---

**FIGURE 4-4**     Fundamental transition orientations

| | Time orientation | |
| --- | --- | --- |
| *Mission concern* | *Reactive* | *Anticipatory* |
| Reformulative | "Responsive" | "Adaptive" |
| Creative | "Designed" | "Proactive" |

*pace* with which the transition process begins. Here we are asking whether the inducement phase is swift or slow. The second question asks about the comprehensiveness of the transition, that is, what is the *scope* of the transition. The scope of the transition may vary from narrow to wide. A narrow scope is confined to the organization itself, whereas a wide scope includes the organization and at least portions of its domain (that is, it is transorganizational). The third question asks about the *time span* of the whole transition process from inducement through stabilization. This may be conceived as either relatively short or relatively long. Combining the three dimensions of pace, scope, and time horizon, and assigning just the two states to each used above, a transition strategy space can be constructed. Figure 4–5 portrays the cube that results.

Obviously, the strategic alternatives presented in Figure 4–5 are extremes and no strategy need adhere to them, for middle courses are not only possible but may be desirable. But the agents of transitioning probably should be clear about how the transition program measures up with respect to each dimension. In considering ways to facilitate transitioning, agents may use these dimensions and the eight alternative strategies outlined as guides. Here we must acknowledge that transitioning is not completely under the control of any agent. Nevertheless, the agents who control organizational resources and possess strategic facilitation competencies can probably enhance their influence if a transitional strategy is explicitly followed. The eight general transitional strategies are listed in Table 4–1.

Table 4–1 shows us that the eight generic transaction strategies are to be understood as being utilized in organizations with one of four fundamental orientations toward transitions. Although space does not permit exampling

---

**FIGURE 4-5**     A classification of transition strategies

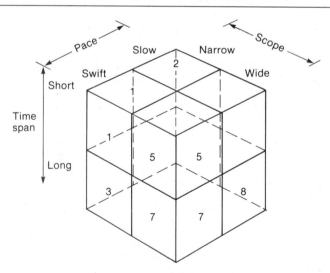

**TABLE 4-1**     Generic transition strategies

| Strategic dimensions | | | Generic transition strategies |
|---|---|---|---|
| Pace | Scope | Time span | |
| Swift | Narrow | Short | 1. Precipitous |
| Slow | Narrow | Short | 2. Perturbation |
| Swift | Narrow | Long | 3. Segregational |
| Slow | Narrow | Long | 4. Inculcation |
| Swift | Wide | Short | 5. Metamorphosis |
| Slow | Wide | Short | 6. Pervasive |
| Swift | Wide | Long | 7. Saturational |
| Slow | Wide | Long | 8. Permeating |

of the resultant 32 possibilities, some sense of this array of possibilities can be gained with some representative exampling. Divestiture, as when a business sells one of its divisions, is a precipitous strategy for a system under the responsive transaction orientation. A metamorphosis strategy, under the adoptive orientation, would be exampled by so-called turnaround business strategy. When a new plant is designed from the ground up, according to socio-technical principles, we witness a segregational transitional strategy for an organization with a proactive transaction orientation. Joint ventures example the saturational strategy under an adaptive orientation. The perturbation type of strategy under the designed transactional orientation may be exampled by organizational centralization or decentralization. The pervasive transition strategy, for a responsive orientation, might be exampled by an organization which promotes a company union. The intervention which Zand (1974) calls a collateral organization (that is, creating a structure which parallels the existing one which eventually will be the only one), is an example of the inculcation transaction strategy for organizations with a proactive orientation. A permeating transition strategy, for organizations with an adoptive orientation, is exampled by what Brown, Aram, and Bachner (1974) have identified as a consortium, the intentional interdependent linking up with other systems.

## THE FACILITATION OF TRANSFORMATIONAL TRANSITIONING

Transformational transitioning occurs when an ongoing organization with one of four fundamental orientations to transition enters into the three phases of transitioning in accordance with a generic transition strategy. In this part of the essay, we will confine our attention to the intentional activities of transformational transitioning. By intentional, we merely mean that some members of the organization are both aware of and more or less in control of the activities undertaken to transform the organization. The intentional activities of each phase of a transformation (that is, induction, management, and stabilization) occur in what here is termed *cycle of planned change processes*. This cycle of planned change processes begins with a diagnosis, which informs planning, which, in turn, guides action. This sequence of diagnosis, planning, and action processes constitutes a cycle for each phase of the transition. Figure 4–6 portrays the nine kinds of activities that occur in intentional transformational transitioning.

This sequence of intentional activities outlines a "process" plan (Beckhard and Harris, 1977) which serves as a road map for transformation transitioning. It is implied that attention to each activity in sequence will contribute to greater transitioning effectiveness. The three cycles will of course contribute to vigilance in transitioning because the action taken in each cycle is input to diagnosis. This is important since organizational transitioning is not directed toward specific end states to the degree that most familiar kinds of organization change are. Of course, these cycles will appear quite differently, depending on which transaction strategy is operative. A swift pace, for example, will mean that the induction stage will appear truncated, whereas a slow pace will allow the cycle of change processes to receive, relatively, a lot of attention.

The phases of transition will be subject to several strategic considerations.[9] These strategic considerations essentially indicate the range of alternative practices available to the facilitators of transitioning. Four strategic considerations have been identified as significant. Although we will discuss them as if the facilitating agent must choose between extremes, obviously middle courses are available and sometimes desirable. The first strategic consideration applies to the induction phases of transitioning. Here the choice is between an induction phase which is centrally controlled by one or a few agents (that is, by decree), or decentrally shared by most organization members (that is, through data discussion). Clearly, those generic strategies with a swift pace and/or a short time span will prompt more centrality of induction. A decentralized induction will hinge on the facilitator's ability for setting expectations for other members (King, 1974). A second strategic consideration asks the facilitating agents to choose between activities which either build a power base or where widespread trust and mutual influence are engendered (that is, more collaborative). A third strategic consideration concerns whether the content of the transformation or the processes of transformation will receive the bulk of attention. These second and third considerations are especially pertinent for the management phase of transitioning. The choices made will depend in part on the intrinsic power of the facilitating agent and on the time span of the generic strategy undertaken. Without much time for transitioning and little power, facilitators will tend to develop a power base and concentrate on content.

---

[9]This terminology is used by Beer and Driscoll (1977) although the strategic considerations in this essay are only partially influenced by theirs.

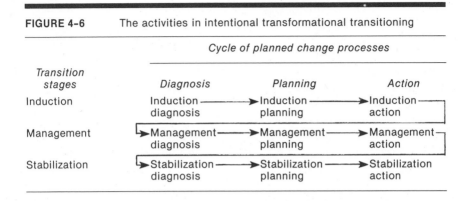

FIGURE 4-6    The activities in intentional transformational transitioning

| Transition stages | *Cycle of planned change processes* | | |
| --- | --- | --- | --- |
| | *Diagnosis* | *Planning* | *Action* |
| Induction | Induction diagnosis ──────▶ | Induction planning ──────▶ | Induction action ──┐ |
| Management | ┗▶Management diagnosis ──────▶ | Management planning ──────▶ | Management action ──┐ |
| Stabilization | ┗▶Stabilization diagnosis ──────▶ | Stabilization planning ──────▶ | Stabilization action |

Given a long time span and more power, the facilitators would, and more likely would be able, to be collaborative and to be more process concerned. The ways in which these strategic considerations influence the management phase will be conditioned by the stress levels and resource strains anticipated, the agent's capability of providing appropriate myths and beliefs, and the number of incentives available. A fourth strategic consideration has to do with whether energy will be devoted to changing structures or individuals. The choice of changing individuals involves training and educational experiences to modify attitudes, knowledge, and abilities. Individuals are also changed by structure indirectly by changing the social structures that shape behavior. This consideration will impact the stabilization phase of transitioning. Again, the time span for transitioning is important—the structural choice being swifter. The persistence of stabilization, once enacted, will be a function of factors, such as the nature of reward systems; group forces, for example, cohesion; and transmission mechanisms, for example, socialization (Goodman et al., 1980).

## SUMMARY AND PROSPECTS

This essay has advocated a developmental perspective on organizations. Our primary concern has been to conceptualize the management of strategic organizational transitions. Organizational transitions were defined as those periods in an organization's life cycle when there is a major change in the character and culture of the organization, that is, of a paradigmatic quality. Strategic organizational transitioning was differentiated from organization change and organizational development, which it embraces, and conceived as an intentional endeavor. Three types of organizational transitions were specified (that is, emergent, transformational, and termination). The essay then narrowed its focus to deal solely with transformational transitions. These occur when an organization is in a quasi-stable state, nominally under one of four types of organizational culture.

Transformational transitions are possible when certain external enabling and internal permitting conditions exist. When additional, precipitating conditions exist and one or more trigger events happen, transformational transitioning may begin. Transitions occur in three phases, labeled inducement, management, and stabilization. Organizations are posited as holding a fundamental transitional orientation that reflects the prior type of organizational culture, that is, an orientation that is either responsive, adaptive, designed, or proactive, depending on the organization's mission concern and time orientation. We then outlined eight generic transitional strategies based upon the pace of the inducement phase, the time span of the transitioning, and the scope of the transition. The transformational organizational transition unfolds within a transition strategy of three successive cycles of planned change processes, each cycle having a sequence of diagnosis, planning, and action activities.

This essay, as was earlier noted, has been essentially speculative. Although the dynamic perspective adopted is relatively recent among organizational scholars, the increasing turbulence of the modern world strongly suggests new conceptualizations and new kinds of research. With environmental turbulence comes pressure for the sort of major organizational transitions explored here. Managers and scholars alike need to understand such transitions as never before. The delineation of organizational transitions and, especially, the patterning of transformational transactions into distinguishable strategies, establishes a new frontier of conceptualization. While the models and frameworks of this essay are admittedly tentative, they do enable us to begin. With models such as are put forward here, the work of understanding transitioning can begin in earnest. As a first step, these models can serve to order the many richly descriptive, existing accounts of organizations over time. There is no doubt that our conceptualizations will soon give way to more refined and valid ones as longitudinal inquiry proceeds. What that evolution of thought and experience portends is indeed stimulating to think about.

## REFERENCES

Adizes, I. "Organizational Passages: Diagnosing and Treating Life-Cycle Problems in Organizations," pp. 3–24. *Organizational Dynamics* 8, no. 1, 1979.

Aldrich, H. E. *Organizations and Environments*. Englewood Cliffs, N.J.: Prentice-Hall, 1979.

Aldrich, Howard, and S. Miller. "The Evolution of Organizational Forms: Technology, Coordination, and Control." In *Research in Organizational Behavior*, Vol. 4, ed. B. Staw and L. L. Cummings. Greenwich, Conn.: JAI Press, 1982.

Ansoff, H. Igor. *Corporate Strategy*. New York: McGraw-Hill, 1965.

Beckhard, Richard, and R. T. Harris. *Organizational Transitions: Managing Complex Change*. Reading, Mass.: Addison-Wesley, 1977.

Beer, Michael, and J. W. Driscoll. "Strategies for Change." In *Improving Life at Work*, ed. Richard Hackman and J. Lloyd Suttle. Santa Monica: Goodyear, 1977.

Beer, Michael. *Organizational Change and Development: A Systems View*. Santa Monica: Goodyear, 1980.

Bennis, Warren G., E. Schein, F. I. Steel, and D. E. Berlew. *Interpersonal Dynamics* (rev. ed.). Homewood, Ill.: Dorsey Press, 1968.

Beyer, Janice M., and H. M. Trice. "The Utilization Process: A Conceptual Framework and Synthesis of Empirical Findings," pp. 591–622. *Administrative Science Quarterly* 27, no. 4, 1982.

Boulding, Kenneth E. "Toward a General Theory of Growth," pp. 326–40. *Canadian Journal of Economics and Political Science* 19, no. 3, 1953.

Brown, L. Dave, J. Aram, and D. Bachner. "Interorganizational Information Sharing: A Successful Intervention that Failed," pp. 533–54. *Journal of Applied Behavioral Science* 10, no. 4, 1974.

Brown, Richard H. "Bureaucracy as Praxis: Toward a Political Phenomenology of Formal Organizations," pp. 365–82. *Administrative Science Quarterly* 23, no. 3, 1978.

Burke, W. Warner, and H. A. Hornstein, *The Social Technology of Organization Development*. Washington, D.C.: N. T. L. Institute, 1972.

Burke, W. Warner. *Practices and Principals of Organization Development*. New York: Little, Brown, 1982.

Burns, Tom, and G. Stalker. *The Management of Innovation*. London: Tavistock, 1961.

Chandler, Alfred D. *Strategy and Structure*. Cambridge, Mass.: MIT Press, 1962.

Channon, Derek F. *The Strategy and Structure of British Enterprise*. London: Macmillan, 1973.

Child, John, and A. Kieser. "Development of Organizations over Time." in *Handbook of Organizational Design*, ed. P. C. Nystrom and W. H. Starbuck. New York: Oxford University Press, 1981.

The Conference Board. *Organization Development: A Reconnaissance*. New York: American Management Association, 1973.

Cummings, Thomas G. "Transorganizational Development." in *Research in Organizational Behavior*, ed. B. Staw and L. L. Cummings. Greenwich, Conn.: Jai Press, 1983.

Dale, Ernest. *The Great Organizers*. New York: McGraw-Hill, 1960.

Downs, A. *Inside Bureaucracy*. San Francisco: Little, Brown, 1967.

Drucker, Peter F. *The Age of Discontinuity: Guidelines to Our Changing Society*. New York: Harper and Row, 1969.

Feldbaumer, W. C. "The Management of an Entrepreneurial Crisis." Ph.D. Dissertation, College Park: The Pennsylvania State University, 1973.

Filley, Alan C. "A Theory of Small Business and Divisional Growth." Ph.D. Dissertation, Columbus: The Ohio State University, 1962.

Freeman, John. "Organizational Life Cycles and Natural Selection Processes." in *Research in Organizational Behavior*. Vol. 4, ed. B. M. Staw and L. L. Cummings. Greenwich, Conn.: Jai Press, 1982.

French, Wendell, and C. Bell. *Organization Development*. New York: Prentice-Hall, 1973.

Goodman, Paul S., M. Bazerman, and E. Conlon. "Institutionalization of Planned Organizational Change," in *Research in Organizational Behavior.* Vol. 2, ed. B. Staw and L. L. Cummings. Greenwich, Conn.: Jai Press, 1980.

Greiner, Larry E. "Evolution and Revolution as Organizations Grow," pp. 37–46. *Harvard Business Review* 50, no. 4, 1972.

Haire, Mason. "Biological Models and Empirical Histories of the Growth of Organizations." in *Modern Organization Theory*, ed. M. Haire. New York: John Wiley and Sons, 1959.

Hofer, Charles W., and D. Schendel. *Strategy Formulation: Analytical Concepts.* St. Paul: West Publishing, 1978.

Huse, Edgar F. *Organization Development and Change.* St. Paul: West Publishing, 1975.

Ijiri, Y., and H. A. Simon. "Effects of Merger and Acquisition on Business Firm Concentration," pp. 83–97. *Journal of Political Economy* 79, 1971.

Khandwalla, Pradip N. "Viable and Effective Organizational Designs of Firms," pp. 481–95. *Academy of Management Journal* 16, no. 3, 1973.

Khandwalla, Pradip N. *The Design of Organizations.* New York: Harcourt Brace Jovanovich, 1977.

Kimberly, John R. "Contingencies in the Creation of Organizations." Copenhagen: Joint Eiasm/Dansk Management Center, 1976.

Kimberly, John R. "The Life Cycle Analogy and the Study of Organizations: Introduction." in *The Organizational Life Cycle*, ed. J. R. Kimberly, R. H. Miles and Associates. San Francisco: Jossey-Bass, 1980.

King, Albert S. "Expectation Effects in Organizational Change," pp. 221–30. *Administrative Science Quarterly.* 19, no. 2, 1974.

Krone, Charles. "Open Systems Redesign." in *Theory and Method in Organization Development: An Evolutionary Process*, ed. J. D. Adams. Arlington, Va.: NTL Institute for Applied Behavioral Science, 1974.

Kuhn, Thomas S. *The Structure of Scientific Revolutions.* 2d ed. Chicago: University of Chicago Press, 1970.

Lavoie, D., and S. A. Culbert. "Stages in Organization and Development," pp. 417–38. *Human Relations* 31, no. 4, 1978.

Lawrence, Paul, and J. Lorsch. *Organization and Environment.* Boston: Harvard Business School, 1967.

Lewin, Kurt. *Field Theory in Social Science.* New York: Harper and Row, 1951.

Lippitt, Gordon L., and W. H. Schmidt. "Crises in a Developing Organization," pp. 102–12. *Harvard Business Review*, March 1967.

Lippitt, R., J. Watson, and B. Westley. *The Dynamics of Planned Change.* New York: Harcourt Brace Jovanovich, 1958.

Lodahl, Thomas M., and S. M. Mitchell. "Drift in Developing Innovative Organizations," in *The Organization Life Cycle*, eds. J. R. Kimberly and R. H. Miles. San Francisco: Jossey-Bass, 1980.

Lundberg, Craig C. "Organization Development: Current Perspectives and Future Issues," a paper presented to the Southwest Chapter of the American Institute for Decision Sciences, 1974.

Lundberg, Craig C. "On Organizational Development Interventions: A General Systems–Cybernetic Perspective." in *Systems Theory for Organization Development*, ed. T. Cummings. New York: John Wiley and Sons, 1980.

Lundberg, Craig C. "What's Wrong With OD?" pp. 17–23. In *Organization Development: Managing Transitions*, E. J. Pavlock ed. Washington, D.C.: American Society for Training and Development, 1982a.

Lundberg, Craig C. "Planning Theory: Myth, Anomaly, Inquiry." Working Paper, School of Urban and Regional Planning, University of Southern California, 1982b.

Lyden, F. J. "Using Parson's Functional Analysis in the Study of Public Organizations," pp. 59–70. *Administrative Science Quarterly* 20, no. 1, 1975.

Margulies, N., and A. P. Raia. *Conceptual Foundations of Organizational Development*. New York: McGraw-Hill, 1978.

Maruyama, Magoroh. "Mindscapes and Science Theories," pp. 589–608. *Current Anthropology* 21, no. 4, 1980.

Mason, Richard O., and I. I. Mitroff. *Challenging Strategic Planning Assumptions*. New York: John Wiley and Sons, 1981.

McWhinney, Will. "Resolving Complex Issues," Working Paper, Enthusion, Inc., 1982.

Meyer, John W., and B. Rowan. "Institutional Organizations: Formal Structure as Myth and Ceremony," pp. 340–363. *American Journal of Sociology*, 83, no. 3, 1977.

Meyer, Marshall W., and Associates. *Environments and Organizations*. San Francisco: Jossey-Bass, 1978.

Miller, Danny, and P. H. Friesen. "Archtypes of Strategy Formulation," pp. 921–933. *Management Science*, 24, no. 4, 1978.

Miller, Danny, and P. H. Friesen. "Archtypes of Organizational Transition," pp. 268–299. *Administrative Science Quarterly*, 25, no. 2, 1980.

Mintzberg, Henry. *The Structuring of Organizations: A Synthesis of Research*. Englewood Cliffs: Prentice-Hall, 1979.

Mohr, Lawrence B. *Explaining Organizational Behavior*. San Francisco: Jossey-Bass, 1982.

Nanus, Burt, "QUEST: Quick Environmental Scanning Technique," pp. 39–45. *Long Range Planning* 15, no. 2, 1982.

Naylor, Thomas H. *Corporate Planning Models*. Reading, Mass.: Addison-Wesley Publishing, 1979.

Otto, Max. *Science and the Moral Life*. New York: A Mentor Book, 1949.

Perrow, Charles. *Organizational Analysis: A Sociological View*. Belmont, Calif.: Brooks Cole Publishing, 1970.

Peters, David R. *Organization Change and Development and Related Fields: A Readers Guide to Selected Resources*. Malibu, Calif.: School of Business and Management, Pepperdine University, 1982.

Pfeffer, Jeffrey. *Organizational Design*. Arlington Heights, Ill.: HHM Publishing, 1978.

Pfeffer, Jeffrey. *Power in Organizations*. Marshfield, Mass.: Pitman, 1981.

Pfeffer, Jeffrey. *Organizations and Organization Theory*. Boston: Pitman, 1982.

Roeber, R. J. C. *The Organization in a Changing Environment.* Reading, Mass.: Addison-Wesley, 1973.

Rounds, J. "Information and Ambiguity in Organizational Change." Paper presented at the Carnegie-Mellon Symposium on Information Processing in Organizations, Pittsburgh, Pa, 1981.

Rowe, Alan J.; R. O. Mason; and K. Dickel. *Strategic Management and Business Policy.* Reading, Mass.: Addison-Wesley, 1982.

Scott, Bruce R. "Stages of Corporate Development: Parts I and II." Boston: Harvard Graduate School of Business Administration, Intercollegiate Case Clearing House, 1970.

Selznick, Philip. *Leadership in Administration.* Evanston, Ill.: Row, Peterson, 1957.

Sheldon, Alan. "Organizational Paradigms: A Theory of Organizational Change," pp. 61–80. *Organizational Dynamics* 8, no. 4, 1980.

Starbuck, William. "Organizational Growth and Development." in *Handbook of Organizations*, ed. J. G. March. Chicago: Rand McNally, 1965.

Starbuck, William. "Organizational Metamorphosis," in *Promising Research Directions*, ed. R. W. Millman and M. Hottenstein. Academy of Management, 1968.

Starbuck, William H. *Organizational Growth and Development.* New York: Penguin Books, 1971.

Thompson, James D. *Organizations in Action.* New York: McGraw-Hill, 1967.

Tichy, Noel M. "Problem Cycles in Organizations and the Management of Change." in *The Organizational Life Cycle.* ed. R. Kimberly and R. H. Miles. San Francisco: Jossey-Bass, 1980.

Torbert, William R. "Pre-bureaucratic and Post-bureaucratic Stages of Organization Development," pp. 1–25. *Interpersonal Development* 5, no. 1, 1974.

Weinshall, Theodore D. "Study of Organization Size and Structure," in *Management Research*, ed. D. Graves. Amsterdam: Elsevier, 1973.

Zand, Dale. "Collateral Organizations: A New Change Strategy," pp. 63–89. *Journal of Applied Behavioral Science* 10, no. 1, 1974.

# PART II

**Repositioning**

# 5

---

# Managing in crisis: Nine principles for successful transition

David L. Warren, Ph.D.
*President*
*Ohio Wesleyan University*

---

## THE MANAGEMENT OF TRANSITION

The twin forces of persistent inflation and declining enrollments have left a majority of the nation's 3,000 colleges and universities struggling to define *how* they will survive and *who* they will serve. The innate conservatism of the higher education community has made institutional change, or even the consideration of such change, a central issue of debate among faculty, trustees, and alumni. Those presidents who have failed to manage effectively the transition from the prosperity of the early 1970s to the frugality and scarcity of the 1980s have become the victims of this transition. A premium has been placed on the management of institutional adaptation by those who must endure it. It is for this reason that the Antioch transition and crisis deserve special review.

Antioch College is a name synonymous with change in higher education. Its history is charted by transitions from one major curriculum organizing theme to another. During its 130-year history it has dramatically restructured itself by introducing such pioneering ideas as alternating work and study, democratic governance by faculty and students, and international study.

Antioch's restructuring from college to national university in the midst of difficult economic times and internal crisis is the subject of this study in management transition.

## INTRODUCTION

Antioch has been undergoing a fundamental organizational transformation since a decision by its board of trustees in 1959 to create a network of learning centers beyond the residential college in Yellow Springs, Ohio. As a consequence of this decision, 32 network learning centers had been created in this country and abroad by 1976. This rapid growth was not without problems, however, and in that same year Dr. William Birenbaum was hired as president to consolidate these far-flung learning centers into a coherent, unitary system. It was Birenbaum's strategic plan to streamline and unify these disparate learning centers into a "national" university, with stabilized financial and academic policies implemented through new system-wide standards for tenure, tuition, financial aid, staffing patterns, development, and faculty-student intercampus transfer. Birenbaum intended to strengthen markedly the governance powers of the president and trustees to implement these changes, as well as to phase out those centers judged to be fiscally or academically unsound.

However, in May 1979, these plans were seriously threatened by the failure of Antioch to meet its payroll. Antioch thus faced the specter of bankruptcy. Surveying the situation, Birenbaum seized upon this crisis as an opportunity to speed the transition from college to national university. For a period of seven and one half months the fate of the institution hung in the balance, while Birenbaum worked skillfully to accomplish major organizational changes. When the district court in Washington, D.C. ruled on January 11, 1980, that the Antioch School of Law could not secede from the financially troubled university, the period of crisis ended.

During the crisis triggered by the missed payroll, Birenbaum steered the institution toward his strategic goal of a reconstructed national university. I was a participant in many of the decisions implemented in the midst of this accelerated transition period, and in reflecting on the events of this period, I have abstracted nine "principles of practice," subdivided into structural, symbolic, and process—by which Birenbaum governed. This chapter will explore these principles, and their utility in moving an institution through a given crisis toward a new organizational form and function.

## ORIGINS OF CRISIS

On May 29, 1979, Antioch University failed to meet a payroll for its 869 employees. As a result of this missed payroll, the institution was thrown into a period of crisis which threatened its life. At a time when over 150 liberal arts colleges had gone out of business in a period of 10 years, the prospects of Antioch's survival seemed dim indeed. However, as this chapter will indicate, Antioch endured this crisis and turned it to its own advantage, as it had numerous other crises during its distinguished 130-year history.

Antioch was born into crisis 130 years ago. Its founding president, the celebrated public school educator Horace Mann, suffered through a series of confrontations with faculty and students during the first nine years of the university's history. In 1865 the college went into bankruptcy and was purchased by one of the trustees for the sum of $20,000.00. In 1881, and again in 1919, Antioch's fiscal fragility pushed it into bankruptcy, but each time devoted alumni and concerned residents of Yellow Springs, Ohio bailed it out.

Antioch's reputation as a progressive, alternative institution has been a significant contributor to its financial problems. The college repeatedly challenged the norms of the mid-19th century by establishing the nation's first full curriculum for Blacks and later for women. In 1921, the noted flood control engineer Arthur Morgan became president and introduced what became the trade mark of Antioch: the cooperative education program. Co-op education proposed that students alternate between classroom studies and work in gainful employment outside the college. Morgan maintained that students needed to mix the theoretical and the practical to achieve a proper balance of learning. His view is still held not only by those at Antioch College, but by some 1,200 other institutions of higher education which have adopted the co-op plan. In the 1930s Antioch pioneered international education and in the 1940s established the college as a laboratory for democracy, where students and faculty joined with the administration in making critical decisions regarding curriculum and hiring. Each of these Antioch innovations—education for minorities and women, co-op education, and campus democracy and international education—were both well ahead of their time and costly to implement. With only a tiny endowment, the college consistently lived on the edge of insolvency.

In 1959, the physician James Dixon became president of Antioch College and launched the institution on one of the most ambitious experiments in higher education. He proposed that Antioch College, the small liberal arts institution located in the village of Yellow Springs in southeastern Ohio, expand itself both nationally and internationally. He proposed that Antioch create a network of learning centers which would allow "bypassed populations" to enjoy the benefits of an Antioch education. These bypassed populations were those Americans who were disenfranchised and dispossessed, and primarily minority in race and female in gender. Under Dixon's 16-year presidency, Antioch College mushroomed from one liberal arts campus in southern Ohio to a network of 32 learning sites, scattered across the United States and 4 continents. Antioch expanded its frontiers to include Alaska, Appalachia, Austin, England, Switzerland, and India. In being scattered geographically, Antioch's modest resources were also scattered. Key faculty members left the campus at Yellow Springs to set up these far-flung centers, or to provide administrative oversight to such centers started by other independent organizations with which Antioch was affiliated. Funds to start up and underwrite these new centers were siphoned off from the college budget, and the institution's focus became divided between the "mother" campus and its offspring.

Two forces were at work in this expansion of the college. The first force grew out of missionary zeal, a belief among trustees, faculty, administrators, and students that an Antioch education was the most dynamic in America, and that bypassed Americans ought to have the opportunity to share it. Thus, Antiochians established programs in Cambridge, San Francisco, and Columbia, Maryland, and the flag of the college was raised. The second force for expansion arose from Antioch's association with ideological entrepreneurs. These were individuals who approached Antioch with the proposal that a particular institute, organization, or group was congruent with the Antioch ethic, and should thus be allowed to employ the Antioch name. The exchange seemed very straightforward; the organization received the Antioch name and its accreditation, and Antioch came to utilize that institution's base of operation, and to join in common ideological cause with its members. Thus, the "network" developed both wholly owned Antioch centers and "affiliate" relationships with institutions which maintained separate incorporation.

The pressures of the late 1960s and early 1970s—spiraling inflation and energy costs and declining enrollments and federal support—began to take their toll on the undergraduate college in Ohio. More importantly, in the fall of 1972 minority students at the college protested an attempted cutback in their financial aid package. They claimed that the administration had committed itself to an agreement that no such reduction would occur during their matriculation. The administration denied this claim, and the students launched a strike action which lasted through the fall and winter of 1972–73. That strike was joined by the local maintenance union.

The college's finances, management, and enrollment emerged from the strike in shambles. One million dollars in endowment was liquidated to cover expenses; enrollment dropped by a full 50 percent, and as a consequence 25 percent of the faculty were laid off. The credibility of President Dixon's academic and administrative policy was dealt a fatal blow. Though Dixon survived until 1975, he no longer commanded the mandate necessary to govern effectively. The reputation of Antioch as a creative academic institution became overshadowed by media focus on mismanagement and internal strife.

Following the strikes and concurrent start-up of the Antioch School of Law in Washington, a counterreformation was instigated at the college. A cross section of faculty, students, and alumni began to lobby vigorously for a rollback of the network concept. Debates within the Antioch faculty raged over whether the college should continue to support the network, or whether all of its resources—fiscal, managerial, and academic—should be returned to the struggling college in Yellow Springs. This debate continues even today, but in 1975 it was the final cause of President James Dixon's demise. He was unable to maintain a consensus regarding the viability of the network within the faculty and alumni at Antioch, and he was fired in the spring of 1975.

## TRANSITION

William M. Birenbaum, an educator with a distinguished history of progressive ideas, was hired in the spring of 1976 to become president of Antioch in September of that same year. Birenbaum's past had prepared him well for Antioch. He had been a special assistant to the president of the University of Chicago, Robert Hutchins, in the early 1950s, and had been the dean of the New School of Social Research in New York. In the late 1950s and early 1960s he served as vice president of Long Island University's Brooklyn campus, and later directed Robert Kennedy's Bedford-Stuyvesant experiment in urban education. Immediately preceding Antioch, he served as president of Staten Island Community College. His numerous books and papers reveal a strong identification with the progressive ideology of Antioch College, and he was selected after a vigorous and highly charged search process.

Birenbaum began his presidency with three assumptions: that the institution needed to centralize its authority, to stabilize its fiscal and academic practices, and to revitalize its mission. The presidency Birenbaum inherited had been gutted by the controversies surrounding the relationship of the college to the network learning centers. Governance authority resided neither within the president's office nor within a 38-member board of trustees, which itself reflected the divisions among faculty and student, alumni and administration, and among the college and the learning centers. Each center controlled its own finances and academic policy, and each had the ability to create liability for all others. Birenbaum was clear that the power of the presidency needed to be reinstated and that the trustees needed to reclaim their proper fiduciary and supervisory roles.

Birenbaum's own informal survey of the learning centers, based on conversations with colleagues around the country and on the available materials, persuaded him that a dramatic reduction in sites would be probable. Not only was the institution undercapitalized, but no budgetary policies were in place to control the repeated cash shortfalls caused by faulty enrollment and overhead projections. Additionally, the quality of teaching and learning at several of these centers left grave doubts as to whether the name "Antioch" should be attached to the enterprise.

Birenbaum saw as his third major challenge the necessity to restate the mission of the institution. It was clear to him that a consensus would have to be shaped anew as to the role and the form of delivery of an Antioch education. Was the institution to incorporate both a traditional and residential, rural college setting for 18- to 22-year-olds, with settings which were part-time, nonresidential, and urban and designed for older, fully employed, and married students? If so, then certain ideological themes would have to be identified and interpreted which would give meaning to each part and to the whole. Out of the tension and diversity of the institution, Birenbaum was intent on identifying a basis for compromise and unity.

Shortly after his appointment, Birenbaum convened three task forces to address these fundamental concerns. He tapped for the first David Apter, an Antioch College graduate and professor of political science at Yale University. Apter was asked to chair a commission which would recommend a governance structure for the institution. The single most important finding of the Apter Commission was that Antioch College should amend its articles of incorporation to become Antioch University.

In January 1978, the college did become a university by the laws of the State of Ohio. In doing so, the relationship of the college at Yellow Springs to the then 32 learning centers was made legal and binding.

Birenbaum moved swiftly on the question of stabilizing the fiscal and educational quality of the institution. He persuaded Theodore Mitau, a highly distinguished professor from the University of Minnesota and former chancellor of the Minneosta State College system to conduct visits to selected Antioch learning centers. Mitau established evaluation teams which addressed the ability of a center to implement its educational mission based on its tuition, local development activities, and faculty strength. His teams included not only faculty members of the local sites, but members from the network, the college, and individuals outside Antioch. Though these reviews were still in progress when the "payless May" arrived, Mitau had already concluded that the number of centers must be reduced. In his preliminary survey, he was convinced that Antioch's modest resources were dangerously over extended, and that its most valuable asset—its educational reputation—was at risk. The Mitau Commission findings later served as the basis for terminating centers in Texas, West Virginia, Maryland, and California.

On the issue of revitalizing the institution's mission, Birenbaum himself assumed the leadership role. In the spring of 1978, he began publication of a series of presidential papers. In these he discussed the priorities and purposes of the national university, and described the manner in which Antioch's management would be improved in order that its resources could be more effectively deployed. In these papers he used such terms as "consolidation," "quality control," "centralization," "multiunit programs," and "national base." By using these concepts, Birenbaum shifted the debate from the question of *whether* there was going to be a national university to *what* would be the nature of this national university which had now been established in law.

Even as Birenbaum was reframing the debate, however, he was discovering that Antioch's legacy of rapid expansion had left him with enormous fiscal and managerial problems. There was simply not sufficient cash to meet the ever-increasing payroll, nor was there adequate managerial talent to implement the organizational changes which he proposed.

I was hired in November of 1978 to implement the findings of the Mitau Commission on quality, the Apter Commission on the design of the national university, and the president's own interpretation of Antioch's special mission in the 1980s. In the winter of 1978 I found Antioch to be an institution scattered geographically and administratively, and divided in its purpose. Antioch had centers located in 14 states and on 4 continents. The president and I, the chief academic officer, had our offices in New York City; the finance vice president was located in Yellow Springs, and our director of academic affairs was based in Washington, D.C. The face of every Antioch center bore a separate identity, although each asserted that it carried the Antioch tradition. My office, located at Antioch "Central" in New York City, was on the third floor of a building in the Battery section of lower Manhattan. I distinctly recall my first visit to the building several weeks before I was hired. I recall commenting to the president that Antioch's national office could well pass as a CIA front. There was nothing which distinguished this particular office from a dozen others occupying the third floor of 17 Battery Place, except for the hand-stenciled word "Antioch" on the doorway.

Antioch Central was located in New York for several reasons: because it was New York City and a major location for Antioch alumni; because it was a center for communication and banking in America; and because many corporations had their headquarters in New York City. The office was intended to be the symbol of the national university. While located in a major metropolitan city, it was modest in its trappings. This particular office contained three smaller offices and a secretarial stenographic area. In and out of this office flowed the business of running the 32 centers scattered around the country and the globe.

Four days after I assumed my position as university dean for academic affairs, I went on the road for Antioch. My first stop was in Baltimore, Maryland, where one of Antioch's major centers of 300 students was located. The building which Antioch Maryland had under lease was located on Charles Street across from the Monumental Life Insurance Company. This building was located in a space easily available to the very substantial number of older, married, and fully employed persons who were students at Antioch Maryland. The vast majority of those enrolled at this center were black. Some 35 minutes away, another Antioch flag had been planted in the "new town" of Columbia, Maryland. In the late 1960s the urban planner James Rouse had created the planned town of Columbia out of the rolling hills of Maryland. He had invited Antioch to establish a learning center there, out of his belief that Antioch shared with him a vision of the future: that new communities should be planned where education would be responsive to its environment, and that the old urban neighborhoods should not be destroyed but converted to new uses. The center I visited at Columbia enrolled primarily the white upper-middle class, and was devoted to the ceramic arts. The program at Antioch Columbia centered in a small building in a shopping mall. The business transacted there was primarily sculpturing and other hand crafts.

I later discovered that Antioch Columbia was viewed by many to be the prototype of the "network," that early elaboration of the university beyond Yellow Springs. What distinguished Columbia as part of the early network was its jealous control of its own curriculum, its own careful definition of what it meant to be Antioch, and its annual habit of passing on deficits to the national office. From Columbia we were only an hour's drive away from the Antioch School of Law, located in Washington, D.C., on 16th Street.

The School of Law is perhaps the university's most experimental effort in extending the concept of work and study to new disciplines. The law school was a cooperative effort between Jean and Edgar Cahn, visionary educators in urban law, and the faculty and administration at the college. The School of Law was launched in 1972 with $800,000 of college funds and the good name of the institution. I found the law school to be filled with the intellectual tension and ideological fervor which I had come to associate with Antioch. While my visit was brief, I left Washington, D.C., with a distinct impression that the School of Law would play a major part in the success or failure of this emerging university.

On the flight to Dayton, Ohio, I gave long thought to what I would find at Antioch College. I knew of its reputation through following its recent legal struggles in the press, when it had sought to depose its then-president Jim Dixon. Prior to William Birenbaum's appointment, Antioch, of course, was renowned for its numerous innovations in higher education, and in particular its work and study model and its concept of community government. After a half hour drive from Dayton, I arrived at the village of Yellow Springs, and to this day I will not forget the effect it had on me.

The college is located in this tiny village of 5,000 people, nestled in southwest Ohio. The college *is* in many ways the town, dominating it by its rich history, its tradition, and by the employment which it provides local citizens. What I was unprepared for was the disarray which I found in the physical plant and in the morale of faculty. The struggles of the previous decade had left deep and visible marks on all who had participated. In every conversation, I detected fear and cynicism regarding the future of the college as it was related to a national university.

It was on that trip that my own ideas came clearly into focus regarding what the national university could mean, but had not yet become. To establish the substance of the national university, it would be necessary to accomplish the following: (1) to link together these dispersed campuses through a common fee structure, admissions policy, and faculty standards; (2) to develop a series of courses offered among several campuses, such that students could pursue a joint curriculum in a variety of settings—urban, rural, and international—over the course of two to four years; (3) to introduce through these network campuses an opportunity for students to learn through the Antioch style of work and study, community government, and self-directed learning; and (4) to bring to each of these centers distinguished teachers who could be attracted only to an institution with Antioch's name and tradition, and who would wish to teach for brief but intensive periods at several of its centers.

The Antioch learning style is rooted in the general belief that study in the classroom must be directly related to practical work in the marketplace. In addition, how one learns is critically influenced by the learning community in which one lives and participates. Finally, Antioch believes it important that the learning environment include the most contrasting and clashing ideas, so that individuals can choose among them.

Almost six months passed before I was able to visit the greatest number of Antioch learning centers. I never did avail myself of the opportunity, I regret, to visit Antioch Hawaii or Antioch London. However, I did, on a half dozen to 10 occasions, commute from my home in New Haven, Connecticut to each one of the following major centers of Antioch: Philadelphia; Keene, New Hampshire; San Francisco; Los Angeles; Seattle; Denver; and of course, to the major program at the law school in Washington, D.C. and to the college in Ohio. The geographic diversity of Antioch created enormous administrative problems. It was simply not possible to convene an afternoon meeting to discuss a given problem in the curriculum, or to plan a development brochure or to discuss some issue regarding admissions. The vast majority of work was conducted over the phone and by mail, and was thus accomplished in a vacuum from one's peers.

The consequences of this geographic dispersion are and have been far-reaching. Every organization needs a minimum level of trust, common communication, and convenience; all three of these were absent to any necessary degree at Antioch. Consequently, most every transaction was shrouded in suspicion, and all important decisions became highly charged, with local interests being pitted one against the other, and all against the central administration. All of this of course was exacerbated by the mounting financial stress under which the university operated. Deans, in their role as executive managers of the local centers, jealously guarded information regarding enrollment, collection of tuitions, and fund raising. While in most universities it is time-consuming to collect such information, rarely does the process reduce itself to hand-to-hand combat. Local managers, fearful that their revenues would be expropriated for purposes contrary to their own views, would set up private checking accounts and hide money in shoe boxes. The university, which was in a perpetual state of cash difficulty, found its dilemma compounded by the lack of credible information regarding accounts payable or receivable at any one center.

Central management found it most difficult to assess enrollment projections made by local centers. As central administrative control began to increase, local managers would make more and more optimistic projections on enrollment for their fall and spring semesters. They would do so in order to maintain and enlarge their own staffs, based on enrollment. When enrollment shortfalls occurred, they would not be known about for at least three to four months, during which time local employees would entrench themselves either as teachers or administrators.

The Antioch to which I came in 1978 was an institution burdened more than served by its geography, its tradition of local autonomy, and its willingness to experiment with the most limited of resources. William Birenbaum estimated that during the period from 1973–77 enrollment at the college at Yellow Springs dropped from 2,400 to 1,200; that $1.2 million of unencumbered endowment money had been converted into operational funds expense, and that some $3 million in bank loans had been made at the approximate cost of $.25 million in annual interest. Looking at the period from 1970–77, the university had created a $6 million operating deficit for itself and was laboring under an accounts payable portfolio of over $2.5 million dollars. Antioch was technically insolvent in 1978.

A clear division of opinion existed regarding the future of the national university. On one side stood those stalwarts who believed in the college and its future free of the learning centers. Many alumni and the majority of those at Yellow Springs were of the firm belief that the "network" centers had bled the college of its treasure and of its good name, and were about to plunge it into bankruptcy.

Conversely, those from the network who were neither graduates nor faculty members at Yellow Springs believed that the college was afloat today because of their bailing and rowing. The data are somewhat uneven. During that period of 1970 through 1977, only three Antioch learning centers accumulated surpluses: Antioch West a little short of $200,000, Philadelphia approximately $175,000, and Antioch New England approximately $50,000. However, the law school had generated a $1.25 million deficit, or about 24 percent of the entire deficit generated during that period of time. The college at Yellow Springs had generated a deficit of over $2 million. The political reality in this matter depended on what one most needed to believe. However, what was clear beyond any doubt was that, unless some plan was devised to deal with the prospect of empty pay envelopes in May 1979, no centers would remain beyond the grasp of bankruptcy proceedings.

Antioch entered the last week of three of my first six months, unable to meet its payroll. Through a series of inventive cash flow manipulations, the administration was able to avoid the calamity which a payless month would surely create. However, during the first week of May 1979, all available data indicated that unless some $2 million was raised in a period of 21 days, the university would not only miss its payroll to 869 employees, but would also forfeit interest payment on its $3 million loan. It was during this period that I came to understand in a painfully detailed way the fiscal, legal, and accrediting status of Antioch.

Birenbaum saw in the specific cash flow problem of May 1979 both an immediate crisis with which he had to contend, and an opportunity to shape the future of the university. The tactical steps which he took to cope with the cash flow problem were similar to those which a surgeon in an emergency room might take: First he had to save the patient before he could return that person to certain healing and life-altering behaviors.

In the crisis of the payless May, he saw an opportunity to increase and magnify his own transition objectives:

1. To centralize governance authority in the president and to strengthen the trustees.
2. To stabilize fiscal and academic practices.
3. To revitalize the Antioch mission.

Birenbaum consistently acted with these objectives in mind, even as he struggled to prevent Antioch from slipping over the precipice of bankruptcy.

## MANAGING THE TRANSITION

President Birenbaum, assessing his emerging crisis, took five tactical steps to cope with the potential consequences. First he convened the trustee's executive committee and a select group of administrators from each of the centers. At that meeting the problem of the $2 million cash flow shortfall was outlined, and suggestions were solicited as to how to meet this problem. The director for development proposed a "cash" fund raising campaign with key alumni and friends of the school. At the same time the vice president for finance outlined his plan to slow payments to major creditors, in hopes that sufficient cash could be reserved to meet the payroll. Those present at the meeting were each assigned designated donors, and were dispatched to try and raise substantial sums of money.

Second, several days after this meeting, the "cabinet," composed of the deans from the major learning centers, was flown to New York City. I was assigned the responsibility of convening them over the course of almost seven working days. The purpose of the cabinet work group was to design a reconstruction or reorganization of the university, such that each of the centers would have some greater sense of security, ownership, and freedom in managing its own affairs. At the heart of these discussions was the crucial and recurring debate at Antioch: Should the university devolve into a series of separate corporations joined together only by the name Antioch, and protected from one another's fiscal deficiencies; should the college at Yellow Springs be set free from the 32 centers, and allowed exclusive rights to the name "Antioch"; or should the strongest learning centers be retained as wholly owned parts of the national university and the weakest centers closed?

Third, the president set into motion the exploration of Chapter 11 proceedings. He dispatched me to meet with the law firm of Fried, Frank, Harris and Shriver to determine which steps might need to be taken for the university to avoid bankruptcy proceedings.

Fourth, the president maintained careful contact with key members of the board of trustees, even as he held himself aloof from any meetings with the deans.

Fifth, an emergency meeting of the board of trustees was set for May 30, June 1, and June 2 in Washington, D.C., at which the direction of the university would be determined.

The May 1979 payday came and went at Antioch and the pay envelopes were empty. On the same weekend that this payless day transpired, the board of trustees met in Washington, D.C. to determine the fate of the institution. At that meeting several major decisions were made which controlled events of successive months. First, it was determined that the university would not go into Chapter 11, but would rather use Chapter 11 guidelines to deal with institutional creditors. On the recommendation of legal counsel, the university approached all of the creditors to whom it owed $1,000 or more. The majority of them agreed to accept payments equivalent to 15 cents on the dollar, in exchange for which the university would maintain a cash and carry relationship for the future. All creditors under $1,000, numbering almost 1,200, were paid in order to eliminate nuisance lawsuits.

Second, the principal new creditor group in the university, the now unpaid employees, were advised that they would be reimbursed through five installments spread out over 15 months with 6 percent interest.

Third, it was determined that the university would not reorganize itself into separate corporations and would not separate the network from the college. Rather, it was agreed that the university would centralize and administer all cash management, all academic program review, all tenure decisions, all enrollment projections, and all personnel policies. These new policies represented a dramatic reversal of a 20-year pattern of decentralized decision making which had created substantial local autonomy, but had left the central administration and the trustees with insufficient administrative and fiduciary control.

All of these ideas were summarized in a 15-point plan presented by the president to the trustees. This was a plan conceived almost entirely by the president with only a handful of individuals privy to its content. The plan included proposals for strengthening academic programs at the college at Yellow Springs, and a pledge to make the coming fiscal year "The Year of the College." It was also agreed that the budget for the fiscal year 1979–80 would be delayed until such time as the full impact of the creditors' strategy was in place.

The payless May and the events of the trustees' meeting triggered a new chain reaction of decisions by those both within and out of the university. The vice president for finance, and his wife, the director of development, both submitted their resignations effective within 15 to 30 days, respectively. The dean of Antioch International was relieved of responsibility due to illness and absence from post. The dean of Antioch Maryland was relieved of responsibility for failure to perform. Several trustees resigned. The university's principal creditor, Winters Bank of Ohio, foreclosed on the university's defaulted loan payment, thus liquidating $3.1 million of the university's modest $5 million endowment. And a review of the university's accreditation status was launched by the North Central Association, with a focus on Antioch's fiscal and management capacities. These events all transpired within a period of 30 days after the missed payroll.

In spite of these chain-reaction events, the university endured, and as of this writing remains intact. President Birenbaum's tactical activities during the month of May prepared him for the worst-case outcome of the missed payroll. He identified the financial variable as the key problem, and thus instituted an attempt to raise sufficient monies to meet the payroll. That work group convened the first week of May, and raised $100,000 in three weeks, with a private promise of a $750,000 loan from a trustee who, over the next three years, would loan or donate over $8 million.

Second, he looked to the question of organizational stability; by convening the deans and provosts and asking me to coordinate their work on the reorganizational plan, he kept his finger on the pulse of their thinking. He was aware through a variety of sources of any new strategic moves which they might contemplate for separation, for bankruptcy, or for affiliation with some other institution.

Third, the president looked hard at the university's legal flank by dispatching me to work with legal counsel on the contingency of bankruptcy proceedings. Early on it became evident to me that the president at no time intended to declare bankruptcy; however, he was determined to know every contingency related to Chapter 11 proceedings, so that he might repel any efforts by creditors or trustees to declare the institution bankrupt.

Fourth, the president was at all times conscious that his ability to govern was derivative of trustee authority, and that in particular he must maintain the confidence of the chairman of the board of trustees and the chairman of the executive committee of the board. The president worked with these two individuals, as well as the trustee who was the key donor to the institution, and thereby was prepared to present to the trustees a survival plan in which he knew they had confidence. The president therefore carefully, consciously, and in a calculated manner managed the financial, organizational, legal, and governance issues. Had any one of these factors not been handled well, the institution might well have capsized during this period of peril.

The trustee meeting following the payless May of 1979 became the arena in which the president played out his own larger strategy. He came equipped with a master plan to respond to these key factors, and he did so with full knowledge that no other constituent group had a coherent plan in hand. He chose not to reveal the content of his plan to other than a handful of trusted advisors, and to reserve the presentation of it until all others had spoken their minds. His timing was superb and the impact was as he intended. He received a unanimous vote of confidence and was urged to move forward in the implementation of the 15 points contained in his plan.

Even as Birenbaum was coping with the known aspects of the crisis, an additional unknown factor was in the making. The co-deans of the Antioch School of Law had concluded that the university would go bankrupt, and they wished to have the law school secede before the university's demise.

They resolved, therefore, to hold $1.5 million in tuition in escrow, rather than forward it to the central administration to meet university obligations. This decision brought into dramatic focus a long-standing dispute between Antioch School of Law and the other Antioch parts.

The Antioch School of Law, located in Washington, D.C., was established by act of the trustees in December 1971. The doctor of jurisprudence program is organized around a clinical curriculum of work and study, where the faculty are both practicing attorneys and classroom instructors. The central purpose of the school is the use of law as an instrument of justice and social change.

Many of the faculty, students, and administrators had been attracted to Antioch School of Law by the presence of the co-founders Jean and Edgar Cahn. The Cahns had established themselves as progressive and innovative in the field of legal education, with a special emphasis on public-interest and poverty law.

During the period preceding the payless May, the Cahns attempted to exercise academic and fiscal autonomy from the directives of the central administration. The law school deans and faculty had initiated new degree programs without the approval of the president and trustees, and had generated accumulated deficits of nearly $3 million.

When the university failed to meet its May 1979 payroll, the Cahns set in motion a plan to "liberate" the School of Law from the university. Acting in defiance of directives from myself, the president, and the trustees, the Cahns decided to retain, for the sole purposes of Antioch School of Law, $1.5 million in tuition which was being collected for the summer and fall terms.

A period of protracted negotiations followed, during which the Cahns were repeatedly directed to comply with university guidelines. When, on November 5, 1979, the Cahns ignored a final order from the president and trustees to comply, the university informed all banks in Washington, D.C. holding "Antioch" funds to freeze those accounts. The banks complied. The Cahns then sought a temporary restraining order against the university's instructions to the banks.

The district court agreed to hear the dispute and I was assigned to work with legal counsel. The Cahns quickly translated their motion for a temporary restraining order into a motion to allow the law school to secede from the university.

The fundamental issues confronting the judge were twofold: who owned and who governed the School of Law? While these were issues quite specific to the dispute at hand, they were issues now being asked by every learning center and the college at Yellow Springs. Was it possible for any of these centers to declare its independence, unload its liabilities on the remaining centers, and yet retain the name of Antioch?

The court heard testimony and reviewed documents for eight weeks. Finally, on January 11, 1980, Judge Revercomb ruled that the university trustees were the proper fiduciaries and final governors of the affairs of the law school. The deans were instructed to forward all tuition funds and to comply with university directives. Immediately upon receiving Judge Revercomb's ruling I phoned the Cahns and, on President Birenbaum's instruction, requested their resignations. The president had sought to remove the Cahns as financial agents at the same time that the bank accounts were frozen. However, Judge Revercomb had interceded and prohibited any action by the president and trustees which would alter the "status quo" as it stood on November 5.

The Cahns refused resignation and at 5:00 p.m. that same day they were fired in any and all capacities at the Antioch School of Law. A period of turmoil then followed, when the Cahns attempted to override Birenbaum's decision through student and faculty protest, and appeals to funding sources and accrediting agencies. Each of these strategies failed, and with it the Cahn's future with the school which they had created.

The decision handed down by the District of Columbia district court marked the end of the crisis period. By Judge Revercomb's opinion, the legal status of the university was reaffirmed, as was the authority of the president and trustees as "owners and governors" of all parts of the university. Dissidents in various centers of the university and at the college, who had hoped for a decision "liberating" the law school (and by implication themselves) from any central control, were gravely disappointed.

Any prospect for other battles of liberation which would return fiscal and academic power to the centers was dashed. And with Revercomb's decision the constitutional and fiscal period of crisis ended.

Birenbaum skillfully used the district court opinion and the payless crisis to accelerate the transition for Antioch from college to national university. He was able to focus the trustees, faculty, student body, and alumni on the fundamental question of the university's future. His own 15-point plan made it clear that he intended to preserve the residential college in Ohio, to retain the School of Law in Washington, and to continue with strong centers in San Francisco, Seattle, and Los Angeles, and the Antioch New England center located in Keene, New Hampshire. The crucial variable associated with each of these centers was an academic program which met the Antioch standard of quality, as defined by the president, the Mitau Commission, the Apter Commission, and the majority of the alumni. Birenbaum demonstrated that this plan held the best hope for moving Antioch through this period of potential calamity to a time of greater safety and institutional well-being.

The 15-point plan served as Birenbaum's blueprint for pursuing his transition objectives. It outlined revised governance policies which would centralize authority in the president and trustees; it spelled out new fiscal and academic policies, including the creditors' plan which would introduce necessary stability; and it provided a "bully pulpit" from which to restate the institution's mission.

The legal challenge by the deans of Antioch School of Law created an additional forum within which the issues of governance, finance, and institutional identity were further clarified. Together, the payless May day and the law school confrontations created a seven-month period wherein Birenbaum aggressively and skillfully pursued his transition objectives. The principles of practice described in the next section were successfully employed by Birenbaum during this seven-month period of crisis to accelerate the transition of Antioch from 32 to 11 learning centers.

## PRINCIPLES OF PRACTICE

The phenomenon surrounding the Antioch missed payroll suggested to me certain principles of practice regarding organizational crisis, and how these principles can assist strategic transitions within an institution. Let me summarize several of them which seem to me the key to success of an institution's survival.

The principles subdivide into three categories of three each: structural, symbolic, and process.

The *structural* principles represent actions which will result in material, substantive changes in the way the institution functions:

Principle 1: Capitalize on the crisis.
Principle 2: Be bold and aggressive in announcing and implementing a plan.
Principle 3: Make the hard decisions as quickly as possible in order to cut one's losses.

In cases where structural principles were invoked, administrative positions were established or eliminated, individuals hired or fired, policies created or revoked, and major legal or fiscal decisions implemented.

*Process* principles reflect the necessity to cope with matters of governance, day-to-day operational procedures, and the relationship of the institutional parts, to the whole:

Principle 4: Recognize that executive power derives ultimately from the appointing authority.
Principle 5: Understand the limits of your resources.
Principle 6: Develop a multifaceted strategy to preserve and protect the institution during its immediate crisis.

Process principles recognize that careful attention must be given to the fiduciaries and stewards of the institution; that one must maintain a realistic, prudent view of the institution's fiscal and legal resources, and the assessment given it by the public; and that bearing all of this in mind, a plan of action must be created, amended, and carried out.

*Symbolic* principles concern themselves with institutional esprit, with the organization's sense of history and future, and with the fashion whereby individuals identify with it, support it, and will act to see it survive:

Principle 7: Seize upon the crisis as an opportunity to analyze the institution both in historical and contemporary terms.

Principle 8:   Interpret the circumstances of the crisis for the media.
Principle 9:   Employ the crisis as an opportunity to restate the mission of the institution.

Where symbolic principles of practice are asserted, several actions will likely follow: Mission will be examined and debated; the media will provoke internal debate about historical decisions, and prospective actions; and the image of the organization can be modified, altered dramatically, or sustained.

## THE STRUCTURAL PRINCIPLES

The first principle can be stated simply: *capitalize on the crisis*. The president saw in the midst of the confusion of May 1979 an opportunity to implement major changes, both in the personnel structure and administration of the institution. At a time when others were looking merely to meet the payroll and to pay creditors, the president was giving careful consideration to new directions for the university. In particular he focused his attention on the college at Yellow Springs. Since his appointment in 1976, the president had been moving steadily to reorganize the curriculum and the administrative structure of the college by reducing 21 departments to 12 divisions. Even at this time it was clear to him that the provost of Antioch College was not the right person for the job and needed to be removed. Initial steps were set in motion to achieve this objective. Beyond this, however, the president declared that 1979–80 would be the Year of the College, and that both intellectual and material resources would be focused on Yellow Springs and its relationship to the national university.

The acute organizational problems of Antioch Maryland and Antioch International provided the president with an opportunity to vacate and then fill critical executive positions. In addition, with the departure of the university registrar, vice president for finance, director of development, and business manager at Antioch College, the president moved quickly to appoint to those positions individuals in whom he had confidence. In response to the refusal of the law school deans to forward tuition revenues, Birenbaum secured a court order requiring them to do so. He then fired them and brought the school under tighter fiscal and academic control. Most significantly, through a calculated process of spin-off, consolidation, and termination, the president engineered the reduction of learning centers from 32 to 11 between May 1979 and March 1982.

Two: Be bold and aggressive in announcing and implementing a plan of action. The 15-point plan which Birenbaum unveiled at the trustees' meeting in June 1979 became the blueprint which he was to implement. He distributed the plan to all members of the university community, but also made it available to friends and colleagues in higher education, in business, and in the media.

Because the plan was both comprehensive in its strategy and bold in its language, it had a simultaneous effect on two groups: Birenbaum's sharp critics were held at bay and his strongest supporters were armed with a manifesto.

Three: Make the hard decisions as quickly as possible in order to cut one's losses. Birenbaum saw that he had to deal quickly with his creditors, the one group which more than any other could cast the institution into bankruptcy. The strategy proposed by outside counsel was the plan he adopted, and through it he was able to either mollify, pay off, or delay creditors in sufficient numbers to keep the institution afloat. Over $1 million was forgiven by the university's creditors through this plan. Organizationally he needed the full cooperation of his deans in order to keep the institution working. There was considerable fear that faculty would stop teaching and that clerks, secretaries, and administrators would simply refuse to come to their desks until such time as they were paid. He proposed to pay all employees of the university who had missed payroll over a period of 15 months with 6 percent interest. Birenbaum gambled that these payments, plus the loyalty of the employees and the fact that they had no other immediate place to go, would keep them in place. He was correct.

Birenbaum knew that he was now managing an institution with absolute bare-bones administrative staff. He decided to bring in several consultants with fiscal backgrounds to advise him on a plan to implement the creditors' strategy and to begin to reduce costs at the centers. Subsequently, Birenbaum hired as consultants two former vice presidents for finance, one from Skidmore and one from Columbia University. He weighed their advice and counsel as to how to proceed regarding financial strategy during the months of June, July, and August. Because these individuals were not in the long-term employment of the university, and because they came from institutions of considerable repute, their advice was seen as credible. Those administrators who had to act upon it and those trustees who were ultimately responsible for their institution received their recommendations in good faith. By his decisions to relieve certain administrators, deans, and provosts of their posts, he found a quick solution to several long-standing problems of inadequate management skills. The programs in both International and Maryland were losing money at a disproportionate rate, and the president saw in the crisis a chance to alter that management team.

## THE PROCESS PRINCIPLES

Four: Recognize that executive power derives ultimately from the appointing authority. Birenbaum understood that the power of his presidency rested with the trustees. He never confused popular sentiment with the specific governing authority reserved in the hands of the trustees. Therefore, he maintained a steady flow of paper from his office to all members of the board of trustees. He was in telephonic communication on a regular basis with members of the executive committee, particularly the chairman of the board and chairman of the executive committee. Birenbaum was mindful that his predecessor James Dixon had been unseated unceremoniously by the board of trustees for failing to maintain their confidence. This was a mistake he was determined not to make.

Five: Understand the limits of your resources. Birenbaum designed a master plan that looked for short-term remedies for survival within the institution, but recognized that the long-term solutions would have to come from outside. With respect to short-term solutions, he instituted dramatic reductions in staff, cutbacks in purchase of supplies and materials and in the reduction of expenditures for transportation, telephones, etc. Birenbaum recognized, however, that the long-term solution to Antioch's problems resided in the resources of new students not now enrolled at Antioch, in new monies not now available to the institution, and in the reduction of learning centers. He therefore began to promote his concept of a unique national university scattered across the United States and four continents, which would represent a progressive alternative in learning for students from ages 18 to 80 in America. At the same time he began to steadily phase out, consolidate, or make free-standing some 20 learning centers.

At Antioch he wished potential students and donors to see an institution focused on the future, prepared to cope with the influence of technology, and with factors such as changing family patterns, new models of organization and management, and new patterns of living and transportation. The persistent paradox of Birenbaum's strategy is that he had to put the vast majority of his time and resources into short-term solutions to guarantee that the ship would not sink; and yet he was aware that the solution to Antioch's crisis was to chart a course toward new markets, imaginative programs, and cultivation of the liberal-progressive sources of money in the country.

At a time when the liberal-progressive wing of American political thinking was in disarray, Birenbaum sought to gain their attention and support. Time and money were both of the essence, and Antioch was short of both.

Six: Develop a multifaceted strategy to preserve and protect the institution during its immediate crisis. The steps which Birenbaum took throughout the late spring and summer of 1979 constituted such a strategy. He used the crisis as an opportunity to intervene in the organization of life at Antioch, to tell the story of the institution in his own terms, and to make those decisions which needed to be made. He captured the initiative with the press, and was on the offensive in characterizing the events surrounding the difficulties of Antioch. At all times he kept in mind the interests of those groups, any one of which might bring about the demise of the institution. He provided a plan which would speak to the questions in the minds of these constituent groups, and then surrounded himself with a handful of trusted personnel who implemented the plan as designed.

## THE SYMBOLIC PRINCIPLES

Seven: Seize upon the crisis as an opportunity to analyze the institution both in historical and contemporary terms. In a series of reports to alumni, faculty, students, and friends, the president pointed out that the critical origins of the immediate crisis were rooted in the 1959 decision to expand into a "network," and in the strikes of 1972–73 when the college's enrollment was cut in half and 25 percent of its faculty was laid off. In addition, he pointed out that, on three other occasions in Antioch's history, the institution had gone into bankruptcy and still survived.

Beyond this and more importantly, however, the president spoke of the changing face of higher education. He suggested that the future of the institution rested importantly in urban centers with older, married, full-time employed students. This declaration by the president represented a radical shift from the orientation of the majority of Yellow Springs alumni and faculty at the college. They had come to believe with almost religious fervor in the concept of the residential college and in the effect it might have on the lives and minds of its students. It was their desire to replicate the conditions of the residential college in all of the sites, or to eliminate those sites altogether.

In addition, the president suggested that Antioch reflected the crisis confronting all small, liberal arts, rural colleges in the country. He pointed to spiraling tuitions and inflation, and diminishing purchasing power of the modest endowments held by such colleges. Moreover, Birenbaum suggested that the liberal arts curriculum was perhaps the issue at greatest risk for these colleges. The new computer technology rising up in industry had yet to have a full and sharp effect on higher education, and Birenbaum was now proposing that the computer play a major instructional and administrative role in higher education. Birenbaum was thus setting up a test in which the survival of Antioch became synonymous in the minds of many in higher education with the survival of liberal arts education.

Eight: Interpret the circumstances of the crisis to the media. Birenbaum sought out *The New York Times, Newsweek, Time,* and the local daily newspaper. He spoke forthrightly of the institution's fiscal difficulties, and emphasized steps to be taken to meet the problem. He called upon creditors to cooperate in this plan, and spoke of the prospect of Antioch turning a new fiscal corner. The gamble which he took here was substantial. Publicity regarding Antioch had been uniformly negative over the period of eight years, and he was now seeking in the midst of this crisis to turn that publicity to his advantage. He succeeded in attracting positive coverage from two important national publications—*The New York Times* and *The Chronicle of Higher Education.*

Nine: Employ the crisis as an opportunity to restate the mission of the institution. Birenbaum selected ancient and honorable themes which would be recognized immediately by alumni and faculty at Yellow Springs and which would resonate with those individuals and centers beyond the college. While speaking of the college as the centerpiece of the university, Birenbaum also spoke of ensuring the quality of an Antioch education wherever it might be provided. He honored the connection between work and liberal education. He recognized that new designs in community learning must be developed so that the students could learn in the most conducive fashion.

Finally, Birenbaum restated the fact that Antioch existed to provide an education to those who had been bypassed, disenfranchised, or left behind in America. In restating these Antioch themes, Birenbaum was able to rally a substantial majority of faculty, students, alumni, and staff to the flag which he was now carrying. Birenbaum now recognized clearly that he needed to maintain a consensus among those key constituent groups in order that his national plan for the university might have a chance to succeed. He therefore appealed to the practical necessity of institutional survival on one hand, and the ideological and inspirational elements of institutional mission on the other.

## SUMMARY

Where taken together, the structural, process, and symbolic principles of practice provide the embattled executive with a framework for coping with crisis. This paper has demonstrated how one president of one beleaguered institution used them with exceptional skill.

On several occasions during this crisis period, legal, fiscal, or governing questions arose to threaten William Birenbaum's continued presidency. In every instance he maintained a cool resolve and outflanked either the opposition or the issue at hand. Many in the organization predicted its imminent demise, and waited expectantly for the collapse of the institution. During these months, as I worked closely with the president in the capacity of the number two administrator, I often wondered myself whether the institution could endure the constant assaults on its well being. A number of individuals predicted the death of the institution and made reference to it in writing and at frequent public meetings.

I took it upon myself to reread a well-known book, *On Death and Dying* by Elizabeth Kübler-Ross, and determine whether her principles of behavior for dying patients were principles applicable to Antioch. She has observed that individuals confronted with death go through a series of stages which include shock, denial, anger, an attempt to make an accommodation with the forces at work on the individual, depression, and then finally a quiet acceptance of the reality that death will come. Birenbaum's performance in the midst of this crisis contradicted all the key elements in Kübler-Ross's construct. While others were in shock, he was in control. While many were denying the facts of institutional difficulty, he was asserting them. While many were angry with the distress and prospects for change, he was enthusiastic about the promise they held. Some proposed accommodations which would have essentially stripped the institution of its integrity, and he resisted those aggressively. As a countermeasure, he restated the principles and purpose of the institution as he understood them, and rallied a clear majority. While an increasing number slipped into depression, he exhibited exceptional energy and purpose. And finally, while many resigned themselves to the collapse of the institution and looked elsewhere for new jobs, he asserted a new optimism about the future of Antioch and about those who would remain with it. Throughout, his performance was remarkable.

New academic and fiscal policies are now in place which empower the president and trustees to establish tuition, fees, and enrollment targets, approve and phase out programs and learning centers, grant tenure, adopt systemwide personnel policy, and review appointments of deans.

Only 11 of the original 32 centers have been retained, and the statement of current fund balances shows a June 30, 1983 surplus of $28,862, as compared to a June 30, 1977 deficit of $2,374,354. And, of necessity with the decline in centers, has also come a decline from 1977 figures of 869 employees and 4770 full-time students to the 1983 figures of 515 employees and 3238 full-time students.

## CONCLUSION

The transition process from college to university begun by William Birenbaum in 1976 is still underway at Antioch. However, that transition was dramatically influenced by the failure of the institution to meet its May 1979 payroll. Birenbaum seized upon that crisis and bent it to the purpose of institutional restructuring. In doing so he stabilized fiscal and academic practices, centralized governance authority, and established a national university. In 1984, the face and form of the institution reflect his efforts.

William Birenbaum accepted the unhappy task of scaling back Antioch's commitments to a level commensurate with its resources. In doing so, he accepted the unrelenting truth that the reach of Antioch's dreams had exceeded the grasp of its means.

Over the course of the last 20 years, whole learning communities were created and dissolved, and careers lost and derailed at Antioch.

Along the way, significant human and capital resources were committed to restructure Antioch College into the university as it came to exist.

As one surveys the field of American higher education, Antioch's experiment of transforming itself "in medias res" from college to university remains unparalleled, singular, and monumental in its scope and intent. This small liberal arts college at Yellow Springs, Ohio sought to become a unique, inventive, and progressive national university. In its effort, it developed an enormously diverse student body, a far-flung geography, and alternative curricula. Antioch also drove itself to the edge of bankruptcy before it was rescued.

William Birenbaum exercised enormous courage, keen insight, and shrewd political judgment in leading Antioch through its payless May day and subsequent reorganization. The principles of practice—structural, process, and symbolic—employed by William Birenbaum saved that university. Their application in other managerial settings can provide the imperiled institutional executive with a guideline for action.

# 6

# When cultures collide: Issues in acquisition

Amy L. Sales
Philip H. Mirvis
*Boston University Graduate School of Management*

*The key role for me is keeping the culture well*

(President of DC, 1981,
three years after being acquired)

DC was an independent firm; GrandCo was a multibillion dollar U.S. conglomerate. DC's president was "very committed to participative management," while GrandCo had "an organizational culture dominated by the power of the aristocrats." Early in 1978 DC was acquired by GrandCo, and the two cultures came into contact. DC found that participative management was Greek to GrandCo. "They never heard of that . . . it's like going to another planet." Integration into GrandCo became problematic for DC. DC executives questioned how they could implement "effective integration"; at the same time they warned that "the benevolent . . . authoritarian value system of GrandCo will find its way into DC unless we work very hard to prevent it."

These words, from DC people, denote aspects of their culture, of contact between cultures, and of culture change. Their firm, and their lives, were in the midst of transition following the acquisition and they viewed this partly from a cultural vantage. This cultural viewpoint not only colored perceptions of the acquirer but also shaped cross-cultural relations and acculturation.

## BACKGROUND ON THE DC ORGANIZATION

DC is a manufacturing firm with over 1,000 employees. In addition to its main plant, which is in a large, industrial, Midwestern city, it has several domestic divisions and international affiliates. It has been a leader in its product market.

DC had been a family company until it became a public corporation in 1970. Also in that year, the son of DC's founder assumed the presidency of the company. An organization psychologist was called in at that time to consult with the new president and DC's top-management group (TMG). Based on his diagnosis, a 10-year organization development plan was established. As part of this work, the TMG developed a management philosophy expressive of a value system based on "the authority of knowledge . . . the sharing of power and decision-making authority . . . informed choice . . . (and) the commitment that results from effective participation." Over the next five years, the TMG and the new president worked to bring this philosophy to life in DC—they established, in philosophy and practice, an advanced form of participative management.

## THE ACQUISITION

Between 1970 and 1978, DC created three new divisions and experienced growth in its sales and income. In 1975 and 1976, DC management, needing capital to fund further planned expansion, considered the possibility of being acquired. One of the firms they contacted was GrandCo.

GrandCo, headquartered in an East Coast urban center, was a multibillion dollar U.S. corporation comprised of some 30 subsidiaries. It was a highly successful organization which had actively acquired companies; yet, it had never made an unfriendly takeover bid. The management style of GrandCo was traditional and conservative: decision making was top-down and the hierarchy was well respected. Beyond a few meetings between the presidents of GrandCo and DC, close ties were not established.

By 1977, DC was able to meet its financial needs on its own, and decided to remain independent. However, the sale in that year of an unprofitable division in the company suddenly made DC a prime target for a takeover attempt.

Early in 1978, an unfriendly takeover bid was made by a company with a record of taking full control of subsidiaries and "milking" their profits. DC turned to GrandCo, who at once made a counteroffer of over double the DC trading price and, in a "White Knight" acquisition, rescued DC from the undesirable bidder.

Some weeks later, GrandCo owned 90 percent of DC's stock and, instead of a 7-person board and 2,500 stockholders, DC's president now reported to a group vice president of a conglomerate.

### The research

Our studies of DC began in the mid-1970s and, after the acquisition in 1978, focused on reactions to that event and consequent changes in the organization. In 1979, Mirvis and a colleague, Mitchell Marks, administered a survey to all DCers and interviewed a sample of over 20 employees, including top and middle managers, staff personnel, and the consulting psychologist. In 1981, the present authors studied the relations between the cultures of DC and GrandCo and their effect on DC's way of life. Throughout this period, tapes of meetings in DC, memoranda, and correspondence were also reviewed.

The reader is cautioned to be sensitive to limitations in the data. Our evidence is limited to only one side of the story. By agreement with DC, we interviewed only DC personnel and made no contact with GrandCo people. In addition, the data are subjective and by no means an accurate reflection of GrandCo's culture or even of the culture of DC. It is precisely this subjectivity, however, that provided the perceptual and emotional base for DC's management of the post-acquisition transition.

## TRANSITION: CROSS-CULTURAL RELATIONS

The many models of the development of cultures all include a final stage of differentiation wherein a culture is unified, made distinct from others, and seen by its members as preferable to life in another culture. Our focus here is on what happens when such a differentiation is challenged—when cultures collide in an acquisition. There are many other exemplars of such collision, for example, the contact between two societies that results from the migration of peoples, a military invasion, and the annexation of territory. For all such contacts, we propose, there is a developmental transition with identifiable phases. Each phase, moreover, poses unique problems for the culture involved in the transition and the ways these problems are resolved ultimately affect cultural integrity. Let us turn to three generic phases.

**Phase 1: Threat to culture.** An invasion poses an obvious threat to a culture but the prospect of meeting new peoples, encountering new ways, and starting life again, as in migration, also inevitably threatens the continuity of the past. In many ways, the unfriendly bid for DC seemed like an invasion. The initial reaction of DC management was shock and dismay. Following discussions with lawyers, financial analysts, and among themselves, the feelings of the group shifted to injustice and anger underlain with anxiety.

The sale to GrandCo was a reprieve, but still implied transition and change. The reservoir of uncertainty, unresolved concerns over loss, and the sense of crisis in DC spilled over into reactions toward the sale. At a TMG meeting called to "grieve" the past and prepare for the future, the somber tone gave way to a militant stance: DCers had so far played their cards well and what was needed now was a good first show of strength. Following the meeting, rhetoric gave way to strategy as the TMG vowed to avoid GrandCo's steering and to preserve their company's values.

**Phase II: Cross-cultural contact.** Contact across cultures can affirm or challenge the integrity of a culture. In cases of military invasion or territorial annexation, the threat to a culture resides outside of it. In migrations, as well, there is a dominant group and a subdominant group, or minority. In the present case, GrandCo bought DC and thus assumed a dominant position. This position was evident in the several meetings between the top managers of the two firms in the first year following the sale. In the first meeting, it was learned that DC's management would be reporting to a group vice president, as GrandCo expected, rather than to the president, as DC had hoped. At a later one, it was determined that DC would have to adopt GrandCo's planning, accounting, and reporting systems. And, in the final one, DC learned that to survive in the alien culture of GrandCo, it had to change the way its leaders represented the company's financial and business plans.

Cross-cultural contacts create change not only at the cultural interface but also within the respective cultures involved. For example, the bad feelings and mistrust DC's president held toward his new boss set the tone in DC: Many DC managers felt uneasy about the GrandCo vice president yet were equally concerned their own boss would "screw up" the new relationship. In addition, some personnel in DC were affected directly by the acquisition. Managers had to adjust to the working styles of their GrandCo counterparts, and accountants had to accommodate new procedures. There were also indirect effects: People in DC had heard of conflicts over reporting relations and policies and found their bosses obsessed with the acquisition.

Such internal changes—in a culture's leadership and membership and in its philosophy and public pronouncements—shape and are shaped by cross-cultural contact. In DC, the strong preference to remain independent and preserve the culture, when coupled with a militant strategy and "we-they" orientation toward GrandCo, all served to polarize cross-cultural relations and promote conflict. As a result, DC was keeping score and the losses in the first year reverberated through the organization.

**Phase III: Acculturation.** There are many forms of acculturation following acquisitions, including the integration of the companies, the assimilation of one within the other, or the withdrawal of one from the other. Our model of cross-cultural contact is developmental: The final form of acculturation depends very much on how each stage is managed.

To effectively manage these stages, they—and the problems each entails—must first be understood. The case described herein illustrates a set of these problems and the data are presented in depth to promote understanding. An underlying question concerns the dynamics that shape and drive this development of cross-cultural relations. There are many at the personal, interpersonal, intergroup, and interorganizational level that are no doubt operational (Mirvis, Marks, and Sales, 1982). Our concern here is with culture, and the fit between two cultures. It centers on the way that culture and cultural differences shape perception, arbitrate experience, and regulate action during these phases of the cross-cultural relationship. And it focuses on the factors that influence acculturation following an acquisition and how they account for cultural transitions and change. Let us begin, then, with a working definition of organizational culture.

## Understanding culture

Organizational culture is a term borrowed from anthropological conceptions of society that explain how peoples live and organize themselves. The analogy between societal and social organizations is made because both exist within an environment—geographic, political, and economic; both have relations with other interests, other societies and firms with whom they have varying degrees of exchange, interdependence, and competition; and both must adapt to survive.

In the world of biological and ecological survival, the focus is on species and populations. But in the world of social survival, human action and human meaning are key reference points. Human action represents the surface realm: language, knowledge transmission, and behavior in culture-specific domains, including traditions, customs, and rituals. Such action is organized through norms, roles, and role relationships. Underlying this realm is the one of values and meaning, wherein assumptions about the natural world, human nature, society, and the self give significance to communication, purpose to socialization, design to behavior, and legitimacy to organization. Connecting these realms is philosophy, the societal paradigm that provides a map for action and a means for interpreting and evaluating its consequences (Condon and Yousef, 1975; Padilla, 1980). To understand DC's culture, and their perceptions of GrandCo's, we consider these three realms of culture: philosophy, values, and action (represented by interpersonal and business-related behaviors). Although we speak of three realms, we emphasize that cultures are unified and internally consistent: Philosophy expresses values; values are manifest in normative behaviors; and behaviors give meaning to the underlying philosophy. A unified culture thus becomes "the social glue that holds the organization together" (Baker, 1980).

## 1979: DC CULTURE ONE YEAR AFTER THE ACQUISITION

*Our managerial philosophy is the important thing to retain; the rest will follow.*

(Officer of DC, 1979, a few months before
taking early retirement due to the acquisition)

GrandCo and DC were distinct societies which had developed unique cultures, given their particular histories and business environments. At the time of the acquisition, there were differences in geographic location, size, capital and labor markets, structures, and business outlooks. Such differences, not uncommon in conglomerate acquisitions, naturally influence cross-company relations. Added to these were cultural differences—in philosophy, values, and behavior—made manifest in various arenas of organizational life, including reporting practices, planning systems, decision-making processes, budgetary responsibilities, and interpersonal interactions. Such differences become symbols of divergent visions of what it means to be a business. It was these that first posed a threat to DC as the question was raised: Does DC have to adopt GrandCo's policies and practices? It was these that soon colored cross-cultural contact. Differences in various practices, for example, were seen by DCers as representing differences in basic values and attitudes. And it was these that ultimately influenced the cultural integrity of DC.

A key element of a culture is its integrity. At DC, the *philosophy* of decentralized participative management is seen in the *behavior* of DC people ("At DC you can go to the real source of information, you don't have to go through the hierarchy or the party lines at all times") and in their *beliefs* and *values* ("Who can make a better judgment than the guy who's on the scene anyway?"). In cross-cultural relations with GrandCo, then, it was DC's values and attitudes, as much as specific policies, that were being challenged. And when policy changes were mandated, DCers wondered whether they could accept them and remain "authentic" and true to their managerial philosophy.

The following is a shorthand account of the cultural differences between DC and GrandCo, as noted by DCers one year after the acquisition.

| Philosophy | |
|---|---|
| *GrandCo* | *DC* |
| Political | Familial |
| Benevolent, authoritarian | Participative management |

We begin with each organization's philosophy of management, for it provides the public rationale linking behaviors and values within each organization.

Interviewees said that DC, with its strong people orientation, promoted the family feeling which stemmed from its size, location, and founding family. In contrast, GrandCo, as a profit-oriented system, was described as political, and keen political acumen was seen as necessary for success. The differences in the management styles of the two firms were often described in textbook terms. GrandCo was said to have a benevolent-authoritarian culture which presumed that right answers exist and are to be handed down. By contrast, DC's participative management style was seen as assuming a more open, questioning stance. These ideological differences were variously characterized as "free choice versus authoritarian management," "theory Y versus theory X," "model II versus model I," or "people-oriented versus technocrats."

*Values*

| GrandCo | DC |
|---|---|
| Financial, numbers people | Operations people |
| Power of the aristocrats | Authority of knowledge |
| Indirect communication lines | Direct communication lines |
| Low level of responsibility | High level of responsibility |
| High "protect-your-ass" | Low "pya" orientation |

Values, manifest in the behaviors of organization members, are consistent with the organization's philosophy. GrandCo was described as an organization with a financial orientation, supported by an enormous financial and accounting staff. DC, in turn, was viewed as populated with more operating people and fewer financial or legal "types." The implication was that GrandCo, unlike DC, valued above all financial information and careful attention to accounting detail.

GrandCo was also seen by people at DC as dominated by the power of the aristocrats at the top. The ruling group made the decisions that were communicated down the hierarchy, and everybody else knuckled under. By contrast, DC was seen as reflecting the authority of knowledge and decentralized decision making, which necessarily encouraged communication across all levels. The differing degrees of centralization of power were seen, for example, in the level of budgetary responsibility in the two organizations: At DC, managers of divisions could authorize any capital expenditure up to $50,000; at GrandCo anything over $10,000 had to have top-management approval.

Finally, DC people found a heavy "protect-your-ass" orientation in GrandCo. This was evident in the constraints on budgetary responsibility, in the expectation that DC managers be aware of details, in a norm that there be no surprises, in an emphasis on fault finding, and in other attitudes and behaviors that DC people characterized as "flank protection," and contrary to their own organization's norms.

*Interpersonal behavior*

| GrandCo | DC |
|---|---|
| Product-oriented | Process-oriented |
| Command | Request |
| Problem solving fast when routine, slow when complex | Problem solving slow but implementation fast |
| No confrontation | Confrontation |
| Limited disclosure | Open disclosure |

Behaviors in an organization can reflect aspects of the organization's philosophy and value system. DC people described GrandCo as very "business-like, crisp, decisive, dynamic . . . chop-chop." By contrast, DC spent more time in the process of decision making, looking at alternatives. At GrandCo, when the head of a division made a decision, "everybody hopped to." At DC, many matters were discussed with a group—even when the decision was a particular person's responsibility. As a result of these differences, GrandCo was seen as being effective in addressing cut and dried problems, but slow in responding to novel ones. At DC, in contrast, the decision-making process was seen as invariably slow, but the "implementation is concurrent with the decision, and that's where the speed is."

DC people found GrandCo to be dominated by command power, and its consequent "Yes, sir" attitude. When GrandCo personnel planned a visit, they would call and say, "I'm just calling to let you know I'll be there next Wednesday at 9 A.M." At DC, such visits would have clear objectives, be discussed beforehand, and arranged at a mutually convenient time.

DC placed an emphasis on one-to-one meetings and open confrontations. It was regarded as "inappropriate and ineffective to discuss relationship problems without directly involving the people concerned." At GrandCo, however, "you never meet alone" with anyone and open confrontations were avoided. GrandCo people were described as not used to any kind of confrontation, because "no one confronts them . . . literally." Instead, third-party comments were used at GrandCo to convey concerns about relationships and performance problems.

A final example of differences in normative interpersonal behaviors concerns the handling of information in the two organizations. In direct contrast to DC, GrandCo was seen as guarded about disclosing business information, particularly operating results; DC management believed in full disclosure of business results, good and bad, to all employees.

| Business-related behaviors | |
| --- | --- |
| *GrandCo* | *DC* |
| Monthly reports | Quarterly reports |
| Two planning meetings per year | One planning meeting per year |
| Realistic targets | "Stretch" targets |
| "Broadway" theatre | Theatre-in-the-round |

The last cultural component concerns differences between DC and GrandCo in their business-related behaviors and expectations. For example, GrandCo required monthly reports on business results, whereas DC had been used to presenting quarterly progress reports to its board. In addition, GrandCo placed a premium on thoroughness, extensive documentation, and elaborate financial analyses, whereas DC's board had been less concerned with details. There were differences, as well, in the ways results were reviewed and received. DC's board had been filled with good listeners who were free with both compliments and criticism. "Even challenges were given in a sort of reinforcing, caring fashion." By contrast, GrandCo officials were not characterized as good listeners and they seemed to DC people to concentrate on the negatives. "If they find a flaw," noted one manager, "they never let us forget it."

DC had been accustomed to one planning meeting per year; GrandCo required two. In their planning, GrandCo emphasized the establishment of conservative, realistic goals, and viewed unfavorably efforts that fell short of objectives. By contrast, DC was accustomed to encouraging risk taking in budgets and to setting stretchy targets. The norm was to "go for the big one . . . stretch as far as you can." Managers felt that it was better to be short of an ambitious target than to meet a lesser one.

Differences were seen as well in the way in which planning meetings were conducted. GrandCo meetings were described as having a "Broadway" quality with a heavy emphasis on rehearsed speeches and elaborate audio-visuals. Meetings at DC often involved all management levels in "theatre-in-the-round" discussions marked by vigorous participation. The implication to many was that GrandCo managers were spectators to a performance, while at DC everybody was a participant.

## IMPLICATIONS OF THE FIRST-YEAR DATA

This listing of cultural differences between GrandCo and DC demonstrates clearly three major cognitive processes of DC personnel during the year following the acquisition—polarization, evaluation, and ethnocentrism. These processes, in fact, are commonly found in instances where cultures come into contact with each other and the concept of an in-group and out-group forms.

### Polarization

The most striking feature of this listing is its polarization. Interviewees did not describe the two cultures by emphasizing the unique characteristics of each, but rather used the same dimensions in describing both of them in order to highlight contrasts. As interviewees would place the two organizations along a continuum, they tended to push them to extreme opposite poles (that is, DC is *highly* participative; GrandCo is *extremely* autocratic).

Another aspect of polarization is that each cultural group is seen as monolithic: DC was described as if *all* DC managers practiced participative management with unflagging consistency; GrandCo was described as if *no* one there had ever heard of participation. Individual differences, shades of commitment, or vacillation in behaviors were not noticed.

### Evaluation

A second feature of the cultural listing is its evaluative flavor: For each dimension described, DC people placed a positive value on their pole and a negative value on GrandCo's. The outcome of the contrasts is that DC was seen as good and GrandCo as bad.

There were, of course, real differences between DC and GrandCo. But it is possible for persons, groups, or cultures to be different from one another without necessarily being better. For example, objectively, GrandCo's size might warrant a more-centralized structure; but, subjectively, it was seen by DC people as different from their decentralized model and thus a "techno-structure."

### Ethnocentrism

Finally, the expression of cultural contrasts, with its polarized and evaluative flavor, showed strains of ethnocentrism, as it demonstrated that DC was unable, unwilling, or perhaps not yet ready, to see behaviors and events from the point of view of the other.

Ironically, many people at DC felt that DC was more relativistic than GrandCo. Although proud of their philosophy of management, DC people said they recognized that their management style was not right for everybody. On the other hand, GrandCo was initially regarded as having an absolutist view of the world. Many stated that GrandCo viewed its way as the right way and that it was not interested in learning more about management processes and practices. Moreover, according to one interviewee, any challenge to the assumption that GrandCo's way is best, "gets them upset, very uptight, and tends to generate a perception of ingratitude." Yet DC's stance was probably every bit as absolutist as GrandCo's.

\*  \*  \*

Why did DCers develop a polarized, evaluative, and ethnocentric view of GrandCo? One explanation concerns *culture learning*, which takes place when one culture comes into contact with another. A lesson from cross-cultural training is that people's culture is so much a part of them and their lives that they are unaware of it, unable even to define or describe it, until it comes in conflict with or is placed in contrast to another culture (Hall, 1959). In some respects, then, DC people were learning about their own culture during this time. For example, reporting business results on a quarterly basis may never have seemed unique to DC or representative of one aspect of culture (for example, decentralization and high levels of individual responsibility). Rather, it was "just the way things are done," an unquestioned behavior—until the demand was made on them by GrandCo that they report monthly.

Such culture learning took place in DC around business-related behaviors, like financial reporting and business planning, and also around interpersonal behaviors and values, like commands versus requests. Just by coming into close contact with GrandCo's culture, DC arrived at a clearer understanding of its own. This culture learning served to highlight differences between the two and to polish the cultural lens through which DC would focus and interpret its perceptions of GrandCo.

Beyond this, we believe that the threat to the DC culture posed by the acquisition heightened polarization and evaluation. When DCers described themselves positively and denigrated GrandCo, it was often in reference to valued aspects of the DC culture that could be challenged by the acquisition. Polarization and evaluation created a strong cultural identity within DC and a definite preference for DC over GrandCo. One DC executive crystallized this view: "We are proud of this style we have used. We are convinced it contributed to our years of continuing record earning and our tremendous growth record. Therefore, we are going to do everything we can to protect it, to improve it, and to let GrandCo see how good it is."

The ethnocentric perception of GrandCo by DC also influenced the threat involved in the acquisition by leading DCers to stereotype GrandCo people; that is, to form generalizations about them as a group. Through stereotyping, all GrandCo people could be seen as benevolent autocrats, for example. Stereotypes are formed because they are functional: They reduce complexity; they help people organize their social world, retain information about others, and anticipate what a particular member of a stereotyped group is like and how he or she will behave (Hamilton, 1980). After the acquisition, DC was facing great uncertainty: Suddenly it had to deal with a large and complex parent company run by a host of unfamiliar executives and staff personnel. The new parent company had a language, symbols, norms, and values unknown to DC. Stereotyping was a way for DC to cope with complexity by simplifying it.

It should be noted that the processes of polarization and evaluation undoubtedly operated on both sides. GrandCo had its own perceptions of the DC culture and its own. Their pride in their culture, their perception of themselves as a "White Knight," and their generosity in paying such a handsome price for DC made DCers seem ungrateful. These, in turn, could have led them also to see polarized differences between the two organizations and to devalue DC's policies, norms, and values. For instance, GrandCo could have viewed realistic goals, extensive measurements, and elaborated plans as essential to hard hitting management. DC, then, would have been seen as soft and undisciplined with respect to finance.

The result of these polarized, evaluative views was, in the course of the first year of cross-cultural contact, miscommunication, misunderstanding, and conflict. Even where there was some shared understanding, each side's ethnocentrism kept them from total agreement. Members of the two cultures would observe the same objective behavior but, given their cultural biases, place a different value on it. Thus the two companies seemed to agree that GrandCo was "crisp and decisive" at meetings, whereas DC "wallowed in the process, looking at endless alternatives." Yet DC people denigrated GrandCo's decisiveness and prided themselves on their process skills. GrandCo, we were told, held the opposite opinion.

As much as these cognitive processes produced cross-cultural conflict, they also served a function within DC, maintaining a bond among top managers and enforcing a strategy aimed at the survival of the DC culture. Polarization, evaluation, and ethnocentrism serve to create a positive social identity for the "in-group" (Jaspars and Hewstone, 1982)—a requisite for the maintenance of that group's culture. DC developed a stereotyped view of GrandCo based upon limited contact and data gathering. The polarized descriptions of GrandCo and of DC were probably learned within DC—passed on from one member to another—and maintained because of DC's strategy that first year of protecting its own boundaries by keeping GrandCo at arm's length. This meant that DC's perceptions of GrandCo would be self-sealing and that its strategy, based upon an anticipation of conflict, would become a self-fulfilling prophesy.

## BETWEEN 1979 AND 1981

Between our rounds of data collection in 1979 and 1981, life went on at DC, relations among the top managers of DC and GrandCo matured, and DC began its acculturation. Two broad factors contributed to this movement. First, DC's top managers, at a meeting in 1980, abandoned their strategy of repelling the enemy and devised ways of proactively managing the relationship in search of preserving their culture. Second, time passed: From 1979 to 1981, DCers had more experience with GrandCo people and could "reality-test" past stereotyped perceptions. Moreover, DC came to be less threatened by the acquisition at this point and could approach GrandCo with more realism and less saber rattling.

Several important decisions were undertaken in DC during these years, two of which are included here: the DC decision to shift to a market-oriented structure and the selection of a new executive vice president. We have chosen these particular events because interviewees saw them as landmark decisions in the organization, and because they offer insight into the subtle nature of organizational acculturation.

### Shift to a market-oriented structure

In 1980 a top-management task group was formed to consider whether DC should adopt a market-oriented organizational structure which would join divisions with common markets. The arguments in favor of the new structure emphasized financial gains; those opposed stressed the loss of family feeling and opportunities for participation in smaller divisions. At issue, in a sense, was DC's philosophy of satisfying both human and financial needs. The decision was finally made in mid-1981: DC shifted to a market-oriented structure, and two of its major divisions merged.

### Executive vice president selection

In 1980, as had been planned prior to the acquisition, the president and chairman of DC, while retaining his position as chairman, turned the presidency over to the then executive vice president. Thereafter, succession planning for a new executive vice president began. The GrandCo group vice president was invited to participate in the selection process—the first time he had taken part in the participative decision-making process at DC.

The selection process had symbolic meaning for DC. With the inclusion of the GrandCo group vice president, the process represented a move toward further integration of the two companies. It was also a test of the autonomy of DC and its power to determine its own future. Moreover, the selection process was a living example of the DC values—authority of knowledge, integrating organizational and individual needs, informed decision making, and so forth. It was thus a strong validation of the health of the DC culture.

The selection narrowed to two final candidates. While both were well-qualified for the job, each offered DC different strengths. One, with a background in human resources, had a deep understanding of and commitment to participative management; the other, with a background as a line manager, had operating experience and a strong drive for DC's growth. There was divergent speculation in DC as to how the final decision was made, but regardless, early in 1981 the former line manager was named executive vice president of DC.

## 1981: DC CULTURE THREE YEARS AFTER THE ACQUISITION

*The benevolent, well-intentioned, authoritarian value system of GrandCo, as the power group, will find its way in unless we work hard to prevent it.*

(DC manager, 1981)

Three years after the acquisition, some aspects of organizational life and culture at DC remained unchanged by the acquisition. Many of these were related to basic differences between GrandCo and DC which will always exist because of the location of the two firms, the different industries they are in, and consequently their differing personnel and material needs. Such differences, even three years after the acquisition, continued to influence each organization's culture and the process of accommodation. At the same time, other aspects of DC life and culture had conformed to GrandCo's ways or indicated a compromise between the two.

We turn now to a selective description of the fit between the organizations' cultures and changes in the DC culture, looking again at philosophy, values, and interpersonal and business-related behaviors.

### Philosophy

In 1981, DC people described their own company as still committed to following the values of participative management, which remained a way of life at DC. GrandCo too, was seen as unchanged in its philosophy of management. Said one DCer, "They think they are ethical but they aren't . . . their values are still 'authority of power' and 'benevolence'. . . . They are still old-fashioned in their managerial approach. So really nothing is new."

At the same time, the GrandCo group vice president, who in many ways represented GrandCo to people at DC, showed both an increased appreciation of the DC style and organizational climate and continuing skepticism of its value. On the one hand, he was seen as "more willing to play our type of game than he was originally" and "intrigued" by DC's style. The selection process had been his first experience with participative group process. He saw that it was "not quite as flaky and kooky as he thought it was initially," and he was "overwhelmed with the quantity of work that these people do, and the quality of it." On the other hand, he continued to "needle the hell out of us about the time it takes to make decisions," and, said one, DC's philosophy of management was "still all Greek" to him.

In terms of general atmosphere, GrandCo was seen as unchanged, and GrandCo people were still described as political animals. But we questioned whether DC, too, would remain unchanged and keep its family feeling. DC had always been organized into small operating units in order to keep the family feeling and involve all levels of employees in participative decisions. The decision to join existing units into a larger division to create a market-oriented structure brought the issue of size and employee relations into question. DC had come to believe that it would be possible to maintain a "sense of smallness" with its associated advantages in a large division. The decision to shift to the new structure was made participatively and implemented in ways commensurate with DC's philosophy (for example, with team-building efforts between merging divisions and the use of DC's participative selection process for choosing the manager of the newly created division). Still, it is notable that GrandCo had favored the creation of the new division from the start and regarded it as a sensible business move.

## Values

There remained sharp differences in values between DC and GrandCo culture in 1981, but there was also an increased acceptance of the other's values. For example, while GrandCo managers were still perceived as numbers people, there was more appreciation of their financial acumen. "I think financially they are tough and they're competent," said one interviewee. "They keep us on our toes, and that's relatively healthy."

There was some indication as well that GrandCo, at least in the person of the group vice president, was coming to better understand DC's value on authority of knowledge. His participation in the executive vice presidential selection process could be interpreted as an openness to valid data, a willingness for the decision to be guided by the authority of knowledge and not the authority of the vice president's power.

In 1981, GrandCo was still seen by DC people as having more of a protect-your-ass orientation. Most GrandCo people were still called fault finders; yet it was noted that two GrandCo executives had gone out of their way to be complimentary. At the same time, DC began to criticize its own fault finding: Several DC managers acknowledged that it was easy for them to criticize GrandCo and that they had to make a special effort to stop doing so. Moreover, DC often rejected direct confrontation and openness with GrandCo people as not the best strategy. DCers were advised to "vary your approach" when dealing with GrandCo. In this way, DC's attitude toward GrandCo could be seen as akin to flank protection—another GrandCo characteristic.

### Interpersonal behaviors

Differences in what was deemed appropriate behavior in each culture still irritated people at DC although the differences in 1981 were more predictable and, therefore, less likely to lead to misunderstandings. The most annoying behavior was GrandCo's continued use of third parties rather than the DC mode of direct confrontation. For example, one executive noted, "Third-party comments are the only way to know what your relationship with (the group VP) is."

Avoidance of direct confrontation was especially evident in performance appraisals. In essence DC's president had to do his own performance review because GrandCo's "idea of a performance appraisal is to go out for dinner some night, have a couple drinks, and talk about how things are going." At DC, in contrast, performance appraisal had always been a part of managing individual and organizational growth; for DC, attention to performance appraisals was a symbol of managing people, not products.

Another irksome difference in behaviors was GrandCo's handling of data. On the one hand, GrandCo was still seen as limiting disclosure of information, particularly operating results, and the head of GrandCo was described as "holding his cards close to his chest." On the other hand, when GrandCo had confidential information from DC, they were "promiscuous" with the data, passing it around with no regard for confidentiality. Indeed, during the selection process for the executive vice president, the GrandCo group vice president had circulated psychological assessments of the candidates throughout GrandCo's top management. DC members, in contrast, said they treated public information as truly public, and they treated with great discretion material labeled private.

### Business-related behaviors

By 1981, DC had adopted the business-related practices required or expected by GrandCo. DC was preparing monthly reports on business results and two planning documents per year. They had done a good job of assimilating the GrandCo accounting system and they had finally learned to live with the auditors and accountants from GrandCo. Moreover, DC had adopted the "Broadway style" of presenting business plans, consistent with GrandCo's expectations and practices. Presenters studied the script and rehearsed the lines to perfection before their performances at GrandCo. DC would dazzle GrandCo at these planning meetings and it was reported that, over time, DC budgets were not as frequently or aggressively challenged.

Yet, there was still considerable frustration with the amount of paperwork and details GrandCo required in budget preparation—"We almost spend too much time in doing planning work as opposed to running an operation." Thus, although DC complied with GrandCo's norm for frequent and thorough financial information, they did so somewhat begrudgingly: They had adopted the surface behavior without the underlying value.

Finally, we noted in 1979 that GrandCo emphasized the establishment of conservative, realistic goals, while DC was accustomed to setting stretch targets. In 1981 we found that DC had maintained its goal-setting practices, contrary to GrandCo's norms. DC top management still went "for the big one" and budgeted "aggressively." This adherence to challenging goal setting is particularly remarkable, given that, under the GrandCo system, DC executives could jeopardize their bonuses by such budgeting.

## INTERPRETATION OF THE THIRD-YEAR DATA

In order to understand the nature of the transition, we compared 1981 and 1979 in terms of changes in DC's perceptions and attitudes and changes in their organizational culture.

### Changes in perception and attitude

First, let us return to the processes of polarization, evaluation, and ethnocentrism which were clearly in evidence in 1979.

Overall, we continued to find polarization in descriptions of the two organizations, but it was somewhat less pronounced in 1981. Specifically, there was less tendency to view GrandCo and DC as monolithic units. Rather, DCers mentioned some increase in the GrandCo group vice president's understanding of their culture and some appreciation of their culture on the part of certain other GrandCo executives. On their own side, interviewees remarked on colleagues at DC, such as their newly promoted financial officer and the recently appointed executive vice president, who were more comfortable than other DCers with GrandCo's style and more understanding of GrandCo's values.

Likewise, ethnocentrism and the evaluative stance it fostered continued to exist in 1981, although to a somewhat lesser degree than previously. There was evidence that each side still perceived its way as being best. At DC, for example, there was still occasional bad mouthing of GrandCo people, which one manager believed was merely DC "trying to pat ourselves on the back."

At the same time, there was also more openness and flexibility in DC's perception of GrandCo and of itself. For example, one manager noted that

GrandCo does not practice participative management to the same extent DC does, but he accepted the fact that few companies do. Another urged DC to understand what the business world must look like to GrandCo with their 30 or 40 subsidiaries: "We have to kind of pay attention to their needs and their situation. We are not the only business they run or have."

Some decrease in polarization and ethnocentrism would result from the decrease in actual behavioral and structural differences between the two firms: For instance, DC had assimilated the GrandCo accounting system; DC was moving toward a market-oriented structure with larger divisions; DC had perfected its "Broadway" style presentations, and so on. However, much of the decrease correlated with changes in DC's attitude toward GrandCo and with improvements in the GrandCo-DC relationship.

The relationship had improved as GrandCo became more comfortable with DC and its managers and as DC came to feel less "intimidated, overwhelmed, and paranoid." With time, GrandCo came to view and treat DC executives and other personnel more as people of equal status, as competent managers GrandCo could respect. Relations at the top, between DC's president and the GrandCo group vice president, improved considerably between 1979 and 1981, thus demonstrating for others, perhaps, that positive contact between members of the two organizations was sanctioned by their leaders. Moreover, GrandCo's involvement in DC, brought about by the initial exigencies of the acquisition, had peaked during the first two years and now very much depended on the particular issue at hand; and DC no longer viewed every contact as interference. "In 1979, 1980 . . . no matter what they did, it was interference. It was bad and so forth. I think we are on the other side of that," explained one DC manager. With these shifts, polarization could be replaced with a more tempered view of GrandCo; the defensive function of polarization and ethnocentrism was no longer needed as extensively as before.

## A MODEL OF ACCULTURATION

*I have thought of integration up to this point as like an amoeba that integrates any foreign object in its midst. That's only one concept of integration. I haven't really explored other models of integration that might be equally possible.*

(DC executive, 1980)

By 1981, DC had moved into the stage of acculturation in its relationship with GrandCo. The overt threat to the culture had subsided and DC and GrandCo managers had developed working relationships. There were some changes in DC's policies and practices, and in managers' behaviors and attitudes. Yet other policies and practices were unchanged, contrary to GrandCo's wishes, and there remained strong differences in the two cultures' norms and values.

To understand acculturation in DC, then, we need to conceptualize it in terms of its various forms (Berry, 1980). Following are eight possible types of acculturation that result from cross-cultural contact:

integration—multiculturalism or pluralism

assimilation—melting pot or pressure cooker

rejection—withdrawal or segregation

deculturation—marginality or ethnocide

*Integration* is based on the desire for basic unity, along with the toleration of cultural diversity. With integration, the acquired firm has pride in its distinctiveness and lives in peaceful co-existence with the new owners. When more than one cultural group is present in a society or corporation, it is a *plural* society; but when, in addition, the diversity of the cultural groups is valued, it is a *multicultural* society.

Thus, one option for DC was that it could maintain its own culture, either despite GrandCo's pressure or desires that DC change or with GrandCo's sanction that DC maintain and further its own culture. This latter pattern of acculturation, in fact, became the desired model for DC. "The relationship," said one DC executive, "should be a step above acceptance, something along the lines of encouragement."

*Assimilation* assumes the desirability of maintaining the institutions and cultural patterns of the dominant group as standard. The *melting pot* occurs when the acquired firm moves freely toward the culture of the new owner; the *pressure cooker* occurs when it is coerced. Both the melting pot and the pressure cooker lead away from a plural or multicultural society toward a unicultural one. These patterns of acculturation are the amoeba model which threatened DC, as DC's leadership believed that eventually it would end up adopting GrandCo's patterns, either through force or gradual, perhaps even unwitting, absorption of cultural elements.

*Rejection* has two forms: withdrawal and segregation. *Withdrawal* is self-segregation or flight, a basic form of adaptation to intergroup conflict; *segregation* means that group distinctiveness and separation are enforced by the dominant society. In other words, aside from the formal, financial relationship of the two organizations, DC could remain a completely separate organization: While there would be nominal union, everyday life and activities would go on as before. Such separation could be initiated by either DC (for example, choosing not to send memos of DC meetings to the GrandCo vice president) and/or GrandCo (for example, ignoring DC).

In fact, in our experience, the latter scenario is improbable: Acquiring firms invariably want to incorporate their new property (Thompson, 1982); it is the acquired firm which would use withdrawal as a protective strategy.

*Deculturation* means giving up the native culture, not taking on the culture of the dominant group, and remaining outcasts to both. Given the forces operative after an acquisition (ethnocentrism, the acquired firm's desires for self-protection, the acquirer's desire for control or influence), deculturation is most unlikely. It may, however, be an individual option, wherein some people at DC might remain outside of the culture of both GrandCo and DC either by choice (*marginality*) or by force (*ethnocide*).

### Levels of acculturation at DC

In 1981, we find that no one model of acculturation predicts all the changes in DC or describes all aspects of the GrandCo-DC relationship. Rather we find elements of integration, assimilation, and rejection.

**Elements of integration.** Three years after the acquisition, the conditions for integration had been met to some extent. As noted above, cultural integration is based on the desire for unity. By 1981 there was evidence that DC had come to accept its status as a GrandCo subsidiary. While this level of acceptance may not equal a desire for unity, it would enhance the likelihood of achieving a multicultural corporation.

Integration requires as well a toleration for diversity. In DC's eyes, GrandCo would tolerate their management style as long as results were good; DC, too, was coming to accept the fact that GrandCo had a style different from theirs and one which probably could not be influenced.

Integration also means that the subdominant group has pride in its distinctiveness: DC's self-pride is seen in the continued polarized descriptions of GrandCo and DC, which effectively emphasized DC's distinctiveness. DCers spoke of the self-confidence of their managers, and of the fact that DC still did not "fall in line" like GrandCo's other subsidiaries.

In 1981, interviewees reported that the integration of DC and GrandCo had been proceeding well during the past two years and that the relationship between the two organizations had improved. One DC executive who had rated the GrandCo-DC relationship 3 to 4 out of 10 in 1979 gave the relationship a 6 to 7 in 1981. The improvement was attributed to DC delivering promised increases in profits and sales. In his view, as DC met its commitments, GrandCo's confidence in DC and respect for its management style increased. Others noted that many conflicts had been resolved at crossover points, where unreconciled differences were acceptable to both GrandCo and DC.

Basic differences between DC's and GrandCo's philosophy, values, and norms for interpersonal behaviors remained, along with some moderation in attitudes towards these differences. DCers continued to cite the family feeling in their organization and the basic honesty of DC managers as cultural exemplars. Commitment to open disclosure of data, to the authority of knowledge in decision making, to collaborative problem solving, to direct communications and high levels of responsibility, and to the organization development program—as reflected in the selection process and performance appraisal system—were expressed in action and word.

We find, then, a situation based in part on the model of integration. GrandCo tolerated DC's management style and many elements of DC's culture. Yet, while DC's style had been accepted by GrandCo, it had not been encouraged. GrandCo-DC integration was leading to pluralism, not multiculturalism where diversity would also be appreciated and valued.

**Elements of assimilation.** At the same time, in some aspects of organization life, DC was assimilating into GrandCo and giving up pieces of its cultural identity. We noted above that in key areas having to do with business practices (accounting, reporting requirements, authorization limits, and so on), GrandCo exerted its influence and DC adopted its systems. And we noted that some DC managers adopted GrandCo's style in their personal behavior (for example, dress habits, "flank protection").

More telling, perhaps, were organizational events which suggested that assimilation was occurring unwittingly. The two key events during this time were the shift to a market-oriented structure and the selection of the new executive vice president.

The decision to reorganize into a market-oriented structure had long been favored by GrandCo and by DC's soon-to-be executive vice president, but not by DC's president. The decision, we have noted, was made and implemented in keeping with DC's philosophy. However, the outcome of the decision could be seen as a move away from smaller divisions, which allow for the DC family feeling and high levels of participation, and a move toward larger profit centers. The executive vice president selection process resulted in the selection of the candidate with operating experience over the candidate with expertise in participative management. Indeed, one interviewee questioned whether the new executive vice president really understood DC's management philosophy. Thus, while a participative selection process had been used, the outcome could be interpreted as favoring operational knowledge and bottom-line accomplishments over a people-oriented and humanistic culture. Both the decision on the new organization structure and the executive vice president selection might represent a cultural value shift away from placing primary importance on people toward placing it on business and profit concerns.

To the extent that assimilation has occurred at DC, it was of the pressure cooker, and not the melting pot, variety. On the organizational and group level, DC has not moved freely and willingly to adopt GrandCo's cultural forms. Rather, assimilation has occurred as a result of GrandCo's expectations, influence, and demands, all backed by the greater power and control GrandCo holds in relationship to DC.

**Elements of rejection.** As noted above, a subsidiary may react with withdrawal; but it is unlikely that the acquirer will impose segregation. In the present case, GrandCo was inevitably involved in DC. GrandCo insisted on gaining control over many of DC's business operations, at least partially to counteract the concerns of GrandCo's accountants that GrandCo had paid too much for DC. Moreover, GrandCo necessarily exerted enormous power over DC through control over its resources and the promotion of DC's top people. It was suspected by some that GrandCo used their influence politically to promote "safe" candidates who were more like others in GrandCo. In contrast to this imposition by GrandCo, DC's initial strategy was "Repel all boarders" and "Keep the bastards at arm's length."

Thus, during the first two years after the acquisition, GrandCo was operating along the lines of the pressure-cooker model of acculturation, while DC was using the model of withdrawal. In 1980, for instance, the GrandCo group vice president requested copies of the minutes of DC meetings. Even at that stage, DC was loathe to include him in this information; they reluctantly decided to send him some information on an experimental basis.

DC eventually became more open and proactive in its relationship with GrandCo, and DC managers and other employees came to enjoy good one-to-one relations with their GrandCo counterparts. Yet, by 1981 there still remained elements of withdrawal. GrandCo continued to be a "phantom over the shoulder" of DC people and there was the perception of a constant threat that GrandCo would swoop down on DC in the event of a business downturn. Moreover, DC's president had assumed a policy of act and advise with regard to organizational changes. He would take action before consulting with GrandCo to avoid the possibility that GrandCo would flex its muscle power and block movement at DC.

Withdrawal is a defensive posture: It expressed DC's negative orientation toward its new owner and protected it from being lost to the amoeba. Thus, withdrawal was more prevalent during the early post-acquisition period of high conflict and perceived needs for self-preservation and persisted only to the extent that GrandCo continued to be seen as a threat.

## MANAGING ACCULTURATION

Managing acculturation in any group or society in contact with another culture means managing a cultural transition. An acquired organization is a special case, however, for acculturation following an acquisition is often marked by conflict for at least three reasons. First, it involves a large power differential between groups. This raises a broad question: Is the subsidiary allowed to choose how it will accommodate and relate to the acquirer? Second, it often involves a unidirectional flow of cultural elements from the dominant group. The broader question is: Does the acquired group have a positive relationship with its new owner? Finally, it often involves resistance on the part of the subdominant group. Culture is central to a group's identity and view of reality; most groups, therefore, do not give up their culture lightly. The broader question is: Does the acquired group retain its own identity?

Answering these questions helps in identifying the factors that shape the form of acculturation that develops in a firm following its acquisition.

These factors have been used to predict the outcomes of cross-cultural relationships in broad terms (Berry, 1980) and may help to explain the mixed form of acculturation that developed in DC. They are summarized in Table 6–1.

## Q1. Power and choice in the form of acculturation

The takeover attempt of DC, which preceded its "White Knight" acquisition by GrandCo, left DC managers feeling powerless and lacking ways

**TABLE 6-1**     Diagnostic questions for acculturation

| Q1 | Q2 | Q3 | | Varieties of acculturation |
|---|---|---|---|---|
| Is the new subsidiary (DC) allowed to choose how it will accommodate and relate to the acquirer (Grand-Co)? | Does the acquired group (DC) have a positive relationship with its new owner (GrandCo)? | Does the acquired group (DC) retain its own cultural identity? | | |
| (To what extent . . . . . . does the acquirer have power over the subsidiary in various domains? . . . is the subsidiary allowed to choose in various domains?) | (To what extent . . . . . . are relations positive in various domains? . . . do members of the organization have positive relations with the acquirer? . . . do the two organizations agree on means and goals? . . . is the relationship instrumental for each?) | (To what extent . . . . . . is identity maintained in various domains? . . . do members of the organization retain the native culture? . . . does change affect both surface behavior and underlying values?) | | |
| yes | yes | yes | Integration | multiculturalism |
| no | yes | yes | | pluralism |
| yes | yes | no | Assimilation | melting pot |
| no | yes | no | | pressure cooker |
| yes | no | yes | Rejection | withdrawal |
| no | no | yes | | segregation |
| yes | no | no | Deculturation | marginality |
| no | no | no | | ethnocide |

Source: Model adapted from J. W. Berry, "Acculturation as Varieties of Adaptation" in *Acculturation,* ed. A. M. Padilla (Boulder, Colo.: Westview Press, 1980).

to prevent the sale of their company. These feelings of powerlessness, we have argued, generalized over into relations with GrandCo and were compounded by power differences inherent in the GrandCo-DC relationship. During the initial phase of contact, these feelings generated reactions toward anticipated GrandCo steering: DCers vowed to retain their culture's values and not to "kiss the enemy's ring until the results of the battle were announced."

Differences in culture and in power are prime contributors to feelings of oppression (Brown, 1982). Such feelings were commonplace during the first year following the acquisition and at its end DC crystallized its need to have freedom of choice with respect to its culture. To reach this, DC adopted a proactive strategy. First, it was agreed that achieving profit objectives was essential. Second, it was agreed that DC had to be selective in representing its interests, choosing where to be persistent and aggressive.

Turning to the model of acculturation, then, we can see that DC had limited choices in determining how it would accommodate and relate to GrandCo. In areas where GrandCo's power held sway—concerning financial reporting, DC's position in the parent company, and so forth—changes in DC were mandated. In other areas, mostly differences in policy and practice, changes were negotiated but, again, DC had limited options. In still other areas, however, DC retained its valued freedom of choice and kept its traditional ways.

We see from the model that DC had different degrees of choice in accommodating and relating to GrandCo. This would predict different forms of acculturation within DC. To focus this prediction, let us turn to relations between the two companies.

### Q2. The nature of relations between cultures

Clearly the relationship between DC and GrandCo improved over the years, but, again, there is no simple answer to whether DC and GrandCo developed a positive relationship. The relationship varied by persons and by domains. Certain interfaces between the firms did evolve into positive relations. The new executive vice president in DC, for example, developed a solid relationship with his superior in GrandCo. By contrast, other DCers continued to "bad mouth" GrandCo and see its people in polarized and negative terms. The accountants in DC adapted to changes in their system and even saw some advantages in GrandCo's reporting practices, while people in other staff areas saw GrandCo's policies as "Mickey Mouse."

A relationship across cultures is positive to the extent that the two groups agree on means and find their relationship to be instrumental for both. Here the DC and GrandCo relationship became compartmentalized. As a business relationship it proved instrumental: DC achieved its profit objectives and, in turn, received desired investment capital from GrandCo. In terms of interpersonal relations, however, there was little warmth between leaders of the two companies and each viewed the other from an ethnocentric perspective. Furthermore, there remained disagreement over the means to desired ends. DC felt its participative practices were still seen as "kooky" to the acquirer and unrelated to DC's business success.

Finally, a relationship is positive to the extent that it involves reciprocity. Reciprocity evolved in the GrandCo-DC business relationship but not in the interpersonal one. Moreover, it scarcely developed in cultural relations having to do with attitudes and values. DC at one time had fantasies of carrying the gospel of participative management to the GrandCo "heathens," but eventually had to accept that GrandCo had "little interest in being evangelized." At one time it envisioned itself as a guiding light in GrandCo. Later it recognized it was just one of many GrandCo subsidiaries.

Thus the DC and GrandCo relationship became compartmentalized, across persons and domains. Where the relationship proved instrumental and reciprocal we would predict, based on the model, movement toward integration and assimilation; where not, we predict withdrawal and, for some key persons, marginality. Let us turn now to culture retention to understand the final character of DC's acculturation.

### Q3. The retention of cultural identity

Just as DC's relationship with GrandCo varied across persons and domains, so also did the extent to which DC maintained its cultural identity. Certain people, for example, began to wear three-piece suits and ties like GrandCo personnel, while others continued to dress as always. DC changed its reporting requirements and authorization limits on budgets to fit GrandCo's policies, but it retained its performance appraisal system and practices of sharing financial information with first-line supervisors.

Aspects of cultural identity were affected in different ways. For example, although DC adopted GrandCo's accounting and reporting practices, they maintained, for a time, a second set of accounts for internal purposes and viewed frequent calls for financial details as a frustrating and foreign experience. A new behavior was in place in DC but those affected by it maintained past practices and did not assimilate the values and attitudes of GrandCo numbers people. In addition, although DC acquiesced to Grand-Co's short-term profit objectives, they assigned this objective a different meaning. At GrandCo, greater sales and margins were a means toward growth and further diversification. At DC, by contrast, they were a means for maintaining autonomy and freedom to continue its management philosophy and practices. In these ways, then, changes in surface behavior were made compatible with DC's underlying philosophy, attitudes, and values.

Despite these signs of culture retention, the model predicts that some forms of assimilation and deculturation would follow, given the relative power of the two parties and the nature of their relationship. Certainly some persons and functions moved beyond compliance with GrandCo directives to some degree of identification with and internalization of the underlying attitudes and values. In the same way, the DC culture to some extent moved into assimilation of the GrandCo way. This was most evident in DC's increased emphasis on profitability, which was seen, at least by management, as a strategic necessity to keep GrandCo's interference at bay. The effects were heavier demands on employees, reports of pressure on the shop floor, and the sense that DC managers were in a meat grinder to achieve profit objectives. The result was a cultural reperception among workers that DC was more interested in satisfying GrandCo than in meeting its own employees' needs, and that DC was now more interested in profits than people.

People expect a culture to be consistent. One story that unified the DC culture was that behavior change was a strategic necessity and that top managers' real interest in people was not sacrificed or changed. Another story, however, was that the underlying philosophy and values were changing. This story also explained the decision to shift to a market-oriented structure and to name an operations man as the new executive vice president.

Cultures live and are passed on to newcomers through stories. In the present case, both stories were live and used to explain observed changes in behavior. As a result, DC lost some of its cultural integrity. Thus, along with integration and assimilation, there were elements of deculturation by which the DC culture lost its unity—leaving some members marginal and the whole culture at risk of ethnocide.

## Final thoughts

Managing a culture in transition requires an understanding not only of the factors influencing acculturation but also the processes underlying them. This involves, in our view, managing the threat to a culture posed by an acquisition, managing conflicts involved in cross-cultural contact (both the internal and interorganizational processes), and managing the culture's integrity.

Managing the threat involves strategic and emotional preparation for the change, rehearsal of its possible implications, and the early development, where possible, of ground rules for cross-cultural contact. Managing the conflicts involves the management of internal processes of polarization, evaluation, and ethnocentrism, as well as interface conflicts resulting from differences in philosophy, values, and behavior. Managing cultural integrity involves the conscious scanning of the culture and its reexamination following change. In the end, this may require reculturation.

DC was notable in its efforts to so manage the acquisition. At the grieving meeting, managers reminded themselves not to project their anger and powerlessness into the GrandCo relationship; at meetings throughout the first year, they reminded themselves that "the enemy is us" with regard to polarization and evaluation; in contact with GrandCo people they sought forums in which conflicts could be openly and mutually addressed; and, in regard to their own culture, they strove to maintain its integrity. There were limits in each of these undertakings. Anxious, angry feelings colored the initial relationship with GrandCo; managers were unable to overcome their ethnocentrism and stereotyping in the first year; mutual problem-solving forums were never fully developed through the second. Finally, evidence of disintegration of cultural elements in DC was not fully examined following the changes from 1980 on.

All of this was hampered by a lack of mutuality, as GrandCo never saw the necessity of so self-consciously managing the process of acculturation. There are many guides to the management of acculturation but most are predicated on a mutuality of interest between the parties and the development of a common language and shared understanding by which to have a dialogue. In this case, no such language was developed and no such understanding was cultivated. DC was left on its own.

But the tasks of acculturation were accomplished. No doubt the threat to culture slowed the development of relationships, conflicts in the relationships produced varied forms of acculturation, and the integrity of the DC culture was weakened. Theoretically, culture change resulting from contact will stop when a form of acculturation is achieved that is fully acceptable to both groups and they arrive at a state of co-existence in which differences can remain without conflict. It may take years: The transition continues at DC today, but the process now is barely noticed in the organization.

> *I guess there are only a few people with a crazy fascination in keeping track of the parts of the river that have merged—which parts GrandCo, which DC . . . . It's behind us. Let's get on with whatever it is.*
>
> (Manager of DC's largest division, 1981)

## REFERENCES

Baker, E. L. "Managing Organizational Culture," pp. 51–61. *The McKinsey Quarterly*, Autumn 1980.

Berry, J. W. "Acculturation as Varieties of Adaptation." In *Acculturation*, ed. A. M. Padilla. Boulder, Colo.: Westview Press, 1980.

Brown, L. D. *Managing Conflict at Organizational Interfaces*. Reading, Mass.: Addison-Wesley Publishing, 1982.

Condon, J. C., and F. S. Yousef, *An Introduction to Intercultural Communication*. Indianapolis, Ind.: Bobbs-Merrill, 1975.

Hall, E. T. *The Silent Language*. Garden City, N. Y.: Doubleday and Co., 1959.

Hamilton, D. L. "A Cognitive-Attributional Analysis of Stereotyping," pp. 53–84. *Advances in Experimental Social Psychology* 12, 1980.

Jaspars, J. and M. Hewstone, "Cross-Cultural Interaction, Social Attribution and Inter-Group Relations. In *Cultures in Contact*, ed. S. Bochner. Oxford: Pergamon Press, 1982.

Mirvis, P., M. Marks, and A. Sales, "A Conceptual History of the Impact of a Corporate Acquisition." Unpublished manuscript, 1982.

Padilla, A. M. ed. *Acculturation.* Boulder, Colo.: Westview Press, 1980.

Thompson, D. B. "Surviving a Merger," pp. 41–44. *Industry Week*, September 6, 1982.

# 7

New program development: Issues in managing vertical integration

Stephen M. Shortell
*J.L. Kellogg Graduate School of Management*
*and Department of Sociology*
*Northwestern University*

Thomas M. Wickizer
*School of Public Health and Community Medicine*
*University of Washington*

## INTRODUCTION

The development and survival of new organizational forms is a topic of growing interest to researchers and managers alike. (Hannan and Freeman, 1977; Aldrich, 1979; Pfeffer and Salancik, 1978; Kimberly, Miles and Associates, 1980; Marrett, 1980; Carroll and Delacroix, 1982; and Pennings, 1982.) Such forms may result from the initiation of a new free-standing organization, the acquisition of one organization by another through merger or consolidation, or through "sponsorship" whereby an existing organization develops a new organization or subunit for purposes of providing a new product or service. To the extent that each of these represents new markets, products, and services different from what the organization currently provides, vertical integration is involved. As described by Williamson (1975), vertical integration exists where organizations decide to produce a product or service themselves rather than purchasing it in the marketplace. Vertical integration, particularly of the sponsorship or *coupling* form, raises a number of interesting and important questions from the perspective of both the new organization or subunit and from the perspective of the sponsoring organization itself. For example, seldom has the

**134**

effect of the new organization on the sponsoring organization been studied; rather, attention is usually limited to the survival of the newly created unit.

Among the interesting and important questions which managers must address in undertaking such activities are the following:

1. Why are we becoming involved in the new organizational form?

2. What is the relationship of the proposed activity and organizational unit to the firm's overall corporate mission and philosophy?

3. How different is the proposed organizational unit from what we are currently doing?

4. What are the likely effects on our position in the marketplace vis-a-vis our competitors?

5. Who is for and against the proposed venture? How do we maximize the amount of support and minimize the resistance?

6. How do we acquire the technical knowledge and other resources to launch the new activity?

7. What kinds of management systems do we put in place to ensure accountability and control?

8. How much autonomy do we grant the newly sponsored unit?

9. On what criteria do we evaluate its performance? For example, to what degree should we evaluate its impact on the "home base" organization in addition to performance indicators relevant to the sponsored organization itself?

These questions, while posing challenges to all managers, are particularly difficult for managers of nonprofit enterprises. This is because the environment of these organizations is frequently more complex and turbulent and because the performance criteria are often more diffuse and intangible than the financial indicators (such as earnings per share, return on investment, and discounted return to stockholder value) used by for-profit firms.

The present chapter addresses the questions posed by examining a particular form of vertical integration in the health field; namely, joint ventures between community hospitals and physicians in sponsoring primary care group practices. The analysis is based on a 7-year evaluation of 53 such ventures funded by the Robert Wood Johnson Foundation. This program was known as the Community Hospital Program (CHP) and its overall purpose was:

> To strengthen the role of community hospitals in ambulatory care by developing affiliated (not necessarily hospital-based) group practices. It is the Foundation's hope that these groups may serve as a single identifiable source

of continuing care for the whole family, with around the clock, front-line coverage and an integrated and coordinated referral system.

(National Planning Association, 1974).[1]

Subsequent sections indicate the major questions of interest, the conceptual framework and study design used and the key findings. A concluding section summarizes a number of key managerial lessons in the form of guidelines or managerial propositions for further consideration. Although the study is based on 54 nonprofit organizations in the health field, we believe the lessons learned are relevant to managing vertical linkages in other industries as well.

## MAJOR EVALUATION QUESTIONS

From a public policy and managerial perspective, four performance questions were of primary interest; two of a "social efficiency" nature and two of a "managerial efficiency" nature. The two social efficiency questions were:

1. Does the program result in a strengthened and on-going commitment of the hospital to providing organized primary care services to its community?
2. Does the program result in an improvement in the organization of access to primary care services in the community?

The two managerial efficiency questions were:

1. Does the program result in the development of primary care group practices which are financially viable?
2. Does the program contribute to the financial viability of the hospital through admissions, ancillary services use, and related means?

Thus, the major purpose of the demonstration was to determine whether grant support could assist in the *transition* of community hospitals from

---

[1]Toward this end the Foundation committed approximately $27 million in grants to 54 hospitals; each grant was for a period not to exceed 4 years and in an amount not to exceed $500,000. The funds were to be used for program planning and development, including salary support for physician and ancillary staff and funds for supplies and equipment. Physicians were to be salaried or under a contractual arrangement with the hospital. No support was provided for construction or renovation as the hospitals were required to ensure the availability of appropriate facilities. The groups were expected to break even financially by the end of the grant and to continue under hospital sponsorship.

All not-for-profit short-term municipal, county, and voluntary hospitals with fewer than 60 interns and/or residents were eligible to apply. Of the approximately 1,000 community hospitals meeting these criteria, approximately 225 submitted completed applications. From these 225, awards were made to 53 sites; one site involved co-sponsorship by two hospitals. Applicants had somewhat higher costs per adjusted admission and a somewhat higher volume of outpatient visits than nonapplicants. Those receiving awards were somewhat more likely to be religiously affiliated hospitals than those not receiving awards. There were no other differences in regard to such background characteristics as bed size, region of the country, or sociodemographic characteristics.

their dominant in-patient care orientation to a new role as providers of a wider range of primary care services to the community. Firms in other industries face similar challenges in attempting to diversify into new markets. They often involve a significant degree of institutional change and, in the present case, a rich context within which to examine a variety of issues related to organizational creation, transition, and failure along with their associated managerial challenges.

## CONCEPTUAL FRAMEWORK

As an organizational transition, the CHP primarily involved a combination of "entrepreneurial revitalization" and "initiation by fire" (Miller and Friesen, 1980). It involved entrepreneurial revitalization in that a major reason most hospitals applied for funding was to maintain or enhance their market share of patients and thereby better serve their communities. A number of hospitals were faced with growing competition for services from other hospitals and providers. At the same time, initiation by fire was also involved in that a number of hospitals did not have the managerial experience to deal with the issues raised by starting a primary care group practice.

The CHP was also extensive in the *scope* of change demanded (Zaltman, Duncan, and Holbek, 1973; Daft and Becker, 1978). It involved changes in values (for example, from an acute care orientation to primary care orientation); administrative and organizational structure (for example, reorganization or dissolution of out-patient departments and/or clinics); services (for example, emphasis on coordinated primary care services); and people (for example, recruitment of primary care physicians and managers with an understanding of primary care). It was also a relatively *complex* organizational innovation; for example, the formal definition of a hospital-sponsored primary care group practice contained 20 elements and a number of sub-elements. Finally, it was *pervasive* in that a number of hospital subsystems were involved, including the medical staff, emergency room, out-patient department, purchasing, personnel, accounting offices, and, of course, hospital administration itself. These issues of scope, complexity, and pervasiveness must be faced by all managers dealing with vertical integration.

Such changes raised a number of on-going technical, political, and cultural problems (Tichy, 1980) which had to be managed effectively if the transition was to be termed "successful." *Technical* issues involve obtaining and organizing resources to produce the product or provide the service. In the CHP, this centered on issues of physician recruitment and retention, development of management and medical information systems, patient scheduling, billing, and related issues. *Political* issues concern the allocation of power, authority, and resources within the organization and the question of who benefits and who loses. For the CHP grantees, key examples included the nature and degree of medical staff opposition to the idea, the degree of operating autonomy which existed between the group and the hospital, and the allocation of power and decision making within the group itself. *Cultural* or ideological issues involve the degree to which a new change or organizational unit is compatible with prevailing norms, values, sense of mission, and overall philosophy of the organization. For CHP grantees, examples included differences regarding what constitutes primary care, differences in physicians' motivations for joining the group, and differences in practice styles.

Experimental work suggests that technical problems tend to dominate in the early set-up phases of a group (Cameron and Whetten, 1981) with, perhaps, political issues emerging after the organization gets "off the ground" and cultural issues becoming more prominent in more-mature stages as the organization begins to reexamine its overall mission and original goals. Alternatively, Tichy (1980) suggests that these technical, political, and cultural issues may interact with each other in more complex ways over the life cycle of the organization. The CHP experience supports this notion with subsequent sections documenting the complex and subtle interplay of technical, political, and cultural factors, along with the strategies used to deal with them.

Before turning to these issues directly, it is important for managers to identify the *sources* of the technical, political, and cultural forces. One source, of course, is the nature of the organizational innovation itself. Several of the CHP characteristics have been noted above. A second source, however, is the nature of the external environment in which the innovation is embedded. A third is the nature of the management response itself in terms of the plans for implementation. Thus, from both the manager's and theorist's perspectives a relatively comprehensive framework is needed to plan and manage such an effort.

Figure 7-1 presents one framework for considering these issues. As shown, the external environment is considered in terms of a number of demand and supply factors likely to influence the development of the group practice and some additional hospital specific factors. The latter, such as existence of medical staff opposition or the presence of an idea champion for the group could be considered as either exogenous or endogenous. They are treated here as exogenous; that is, as essentially "givens" which then need to be dealt with in terms of the design and on-going management of the practice.

Managers must respond to the external environment in ways which increase the probability of success, taking into account other ventures with which the organization is engaged. These are variables directly under the manager's control and, in this case, include the design of the practice itself, staffing patterns, and information systems. Under the terms of the demonstration program, the group practices had relatively wide latitude to develop and manage these factors to influence or respond to the external environment. For example, a group serving primarily a low-income, high-percent Medicaid population would probably be better off trying to recruit

**FIGURE 7-1**     Framework for analysis of hospital-sponsored group practice implementation and outcomes*

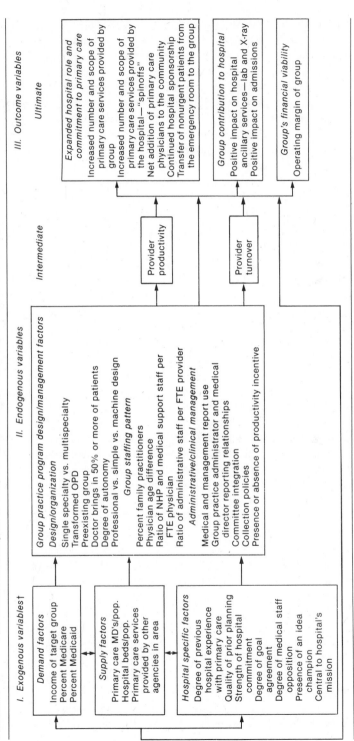

*I. Exogenous variables†*

**Demand factors**
Income of target group
Percent Medicare
Percent Medicaid

**Supply factors**
Primary care MD's/pop.
Hospital beds/pop.
Primary care services provided by other agencies in area

**Hospital specific factors**
Degree of previous hospital experience with primary care
Quality of prior planning
Strength of hospital commitment
Degree of goal agreement
Degree of medical staff opposition
Presence of an idea champion
Central to hospital's mission

*II. Endogenous variables*

**Group practice program design/management factors**

*Design/organization*
Single specialty vs. multispecialty
Transformed OPD
Preexisting group
Doctor brings in 50% or more of patients
Degree of autonomy
Professional vs. simple vs. machine design

*Group staffing pattern*
Percent family practitioners
Physician age difference
Ratio of NHP and medical support staff per FTE physician
Ratio of administrative staff per FTE provider

*Administrative/clinical management*
Medical and management report use
Group practice administrator and medical director reporting relationships
Committee integration
Collection policies
Presence or absence of productivity incentive

*III. Outcome variables*

*Intermediate*

Provider productivity

Provider turnover

*Ultimate*

**Expanded hospital role and commitment to primary care**
Increased number and scope of primary care services provided by group
Increased number and scope of primary care services provided by the hospital—"spinoffs"
Net addition of primary care physicians to the community
Continued hospital sponsorship
Transfer of nonurgent patients from the emergency room to the group

**Group contribution to hospital**
Positive impact on hospital ancillary services—lab and X-ray
Positive impact on admissions

**Group's financial viability**
Operating margin of group

*The arrows are meant to suggest that a given block of factors is expected to influence another block of factors and are not meant to suggest strict "causality." Neither is it intended that every item in each block is expected to affect every item in another block.
†We also expect that demand and supply factors will have a direct effect on provider productivity and turnover in addition to their effect through program design and program management variables.

at least one physician who could bring some paying patients into the practice in order to provide the group with greater financial stability. Such a group might also need to initiate stringent credit and collection policies, such as requiring some payment at each occasion of service.

Another example is offered by a group which faces strong market competition for its services, as might be reflected in a high ratio of primary care physicians per population and a high number of primary care services provided by other agencies in the community. Such a group might be better off by developing a multispecialty practice, permitting its physicians a high degree of autonomy, organizing along professional design models whereby the group functions essentially as a private practice, and initiating a productivity incentive payment mechanism for physicians. These kinds of design characteristics would enable the group to offer a relatively wide scope of services, recruit high-quality physicians, and in general compete more effectively in the market for primary care services.

As shown in Figure 7-1, the design and management of the practice in relationship to the environment are likely to influence two key intermediate variables; the productivity of the practice and provider turnover. These, in turn, are expected to affect the group's ability to meet the objectives of improving the organization of access to primary care, expanding the hospital's on-going role in primary care (in Figure 7-1 these two closely related objectives are grouped), having a positive financial effect on the hospital, and becoming financially viable in its own right.

From the manager's perspective, the key set of variables in Figure 7-1 are the endogenous design, staffing, and managerial system variables. It is through these "levers" that managers influence the technical, political, and cultural challenges posed by the widespread change associated with developing a new organization. However, it is important to note that while these are levers for managing such issues, they at the same time can *create further problems* of a technical, political, and cultural nature. For example, the decision to start a multispecialty rather than single-specialty group may introduce additional technical questions of having to recruit physicians from a wider variety of specialties; political problems of possible incompatibilities in practice styles; and cultural problems in terms of different perceptions of the hospital's proper role in primary care. Likewise, the decision to initiate a productivity incentive arrangement may introduce technical problems of how best to design the incentive arrangement; political problems involving whether there should be differentials by specialty; and cultural problems involving the effect of the incentive on the number of patients seen and, therefore, the amount of time which should be spent with each patient in providing high-quality, comprehensive primary care. *These examples make explicit the idea that inherent in any solution to a given problem is another set of hidden problems.*

Given the above, we generally expected that a more favorable or "benign" environment would be more conducive to the development of successful primary care group practices. Further, faced with such an environment, the organization design, staffing, and information system factors would make relatively little difference; that is, managers could make "mistakes" relative to design, staffing, and information systems without having a serious negative effect on the group because of favorable demand for its services. Specifically, favorable outcomes would be more likely the higher the income of the target community served, the lower the percentage of Medicaid patients, the less the competition as evidenced by a lower ratio of primary care physicians to population (and related measures), and the greater the extent to which the hospital was "ready" to implement the concept by virtue of its past experience. Measures of income and percent of Medicaid served reflect a construct which we call "environmental scarcity" whereas physician/population ratios and related measures reflect "environmental competition."

In addition to the influence of the environment, it is also expected that the managerial variables will be associated with performance outcomes, particularly when the environment is more hostile to group success (for example, serving a low-income, high-percent Medicaid population, having a high degree of competition, and being relatively ill prepared to develop the practice by virtue of past planning and experience). In brief, when environments are relatively favorable for launching new ventures, even poor management can look relatively good. However, when environments are less favorable, poor management becomes readily exposed and the need for truly outstanding management becomes apparent.

Among the management variables expected to be associated with more successful outcomes were the following: (1) single-specialty groups, on the theory that they are easier to manage than multispecialty groups; (2) groups that are transformed out-patient departments, are preexisting, or where at least one physician has brought in 50 percent or more of his patients, on the theory that these groups might have a head start in regard to building patient volume; (3) groups organized along professional lines characterized by limited vertical differentiation (Mintzberg, 1979; Kaluzny and Konrad, 1982) and where physicians play key roles as opposed to groups with simple structures or those organized along bureacratic or "machine" lines; (4) groups which experienced a considerable degree of functional autonomy from the sponsoring hospital in terms of personnel, purchasing, billing, and budgeting issues; (5) groups that were relatively homogeneous in regard to physician ages, on the theory that wide differences in physician ages would reflect different practice philosophies and styles leading to conflict and physician turnover; (6) higher medical and management report use which would increase the "visibility of consequences" (Becker and Gordon, 1966), providing greater opportunity to take corrective action; (7) relatively tight credit and collection policies; (8) relatively close integration of the medical director and group administrator into hospital decision-making circles, as evidenced by their participation on hospital committees; and (9) the existence of a productivity incentive payment arrangement. Before presenting the findings, the following section briefly outlines the study design and data sources.

## STUDY DESIGN AND DATA SOURCES

To examine the issues posed above, a "triangulation" approach was used involving multiple theories, concepts, measures, methods, and data sources (Denzin, 1970). Such an approach has several advantages when an evaluation is intended to deal not only with impact issues such as program outcomes but also implementation issues and, in particular, to assess the relationship between the two. Further, the approach is advantageous where true experiments are not possible. Each of the two principal components of the research, the extensive study and the intensive study, is described below. A fuller description is reported elsewhere (Shortell, Wickizer, and Wheeler, 1984).

### The extensive study

The extensive study involved analysis of all 53 funded sites using data obtained from: (1) standard quarterly financial/management reports completed by each group; (2) a specially designed annual supplemental data collection form to gather information on group management practices, services, physician turnover, reporting relationships, and other information not available through the quarterly reports; (3) information contained in each site's original application plus subsequent staff reports and correspondence; (4) information obtained from each site's Medicare cost report forms; (5) American Hospital Association data; and (6) data contained in the area resource files pertaining to characteristics of the geographic area of the funded sites.

These data were used to analyze the financial viability of each group, its impact on hospital services and financial position, the impact of the group on the hospital's commitment to primary care, and its ability to improve the organization of access to primary care in the community.[2]

### The intensive study

In order to provide detailed documentation of the development of the groups over time, in particular regarding the evolving relationships with the sponsoring hospital, a random subsample of 12 of the first 42 funded

---

[2]A companion study, also funded by the Robert Wood Johnson Foundation, was conducted by investigators at the University of Chicago to examine whether or not changes in the actual level of access to care occurred in 12 of the funded sites (L. Aday, R. Andersen et al., 1984).

sites was selected.[3] Using semistructured interview schedules, visits were made to each site on an annual basis by two members of the study team. Interviews were conducted with all relevant parties associated with the practice, resulting in descriptions of each group's mission, objectives, strategies, policies, structures, and procedures over time at a level of detail that could not be obtained from the data sources used in the extensive analysis. Between visits, groups were followed through phone call discussions with key members.

### Linking the extensive and intensive studies

The extensive and intensive approaches are viewed as mutually supportive. Data collected from all 53 sites made possible multivariate analysis of the factors associated with financial viability of the practices and their impact on the hospital, and other performance outcomes. Such associations have little meaning based on 12 cases alone. However, for those managers and physicians wishing to implement such practices, it is also necessary to know what methods and strategies can be used to maximize the probability of success. This knowledge cannot come from multivariate analysis. For this purpose the detailed case studies were necessary. For example, one might find an association between the number of outreach services provided by groups and their financial viability. This is of interest to policy makers in targeting future funding and making recommendations to future grantees. However, the managers and providers charged with actually implementing the practice would like to know what specific strategies to use in providing outreach services. What are the different approaches and what seems to work best? It is the latter information that comes from the intensive case studies. Thus, the combination of the two sets of information derived from the two parts of the study enabled the study to address the needs of both policy makers and those who implement policy, in this case, managers and physicians. In Whyte's (1982) terms it provided a better "grasp of the social principles underlying (the) effectiveness" of the social invention.

### FINDINGS

#### Overall results

The major focus of the chapter is on the managerial lessons learned, based primarily on the case study analysis. However it is useful to briefly summarize the overall findings based upon multivariate analysis of all 53 grantees (Shortell et al.) 1984)

---

[3]Six of these sites were eliminated for failure to meet initial stratification criteria. The remaining sites were selected after first stratifying on the basis of the probability of changing the community's access to care and on organizational characteristics pertaining to the likelihood that the group would be a viable entity by the end of the study period. Efforts were made to obtain a range of sites rated high, medium, and low on each of these variables. A 13th site was added at its request because of its geographical proximity to the evaluation team.

Among the variables most strongly and consistently asosciated with the hospitals' *on-going commitment to primary care* were the degree of hospital committee involvement of the group's medical director (positively related), the differences in physicians' ages in the group (negatively related), the original degree of hospital commitment (positively related), and the degree to which the group was organized along "professional" lines in terms of having control over their own personnel, purchasing, budgeting, billing, and related policies (positively related). The degree of hospital committee involvement of the group's medical director represents an important structural mechanism for integrating the activities of the group with the hospital. As will be seen, this "integration" strategy complemented the "differentiation" strategy represented by the professional organization designs characterized by a high degree of functional autonomy. Differences in physicians' ages highlights the importance of "cultural fit" in that such differences reflected different physician practice styles and orientations. In brief, groups which were more homogeneous in terms of physician ages tended to function more smoothly and thereby, to be associated with greater hospital on-going commitment to primary care. Cultural issues were particularly significant and are subsequently elaborated.

Use of a professional organizational design was also positively associated with improving the organization of access to primary care along with the use of medical residents, locating the practice in a suburban site and having a high volume of visits per full-time equivalent (FTE) physician.

Variables most strongly associated with the financial viability of the group practices themselves were the group's productivity and number of full-time equivalent physicians, and use of new health practitioners (specifically, nurse practitioners and physician assistants). These are primarily technical issues involving physician provider recruitment and retention but, as will be seen, are influenced by a number of cultural and political considerations as well. The fees charged by the group and the degree of commercial insurance coverage were also positively related to financial viability. Medical-director leadership was also found to be positively associated with financial viability, and will be subsequently elaborated.

The variable most strongly and consistently associated with financial impact on the sponsoring hospital was the number of full-time equivalent group physicians per hospital bed. This was largely a function of hospital bed size, with smaller hospitals experiencing a greater percentage impact on admissions and ancillary revenue (i.e., laboratory and radiology) than larger hospitals.

Overall, the multivariate analysis indicated that different factors were associated with different performance outcomes, suggesting the complexity of such organizational transitions. At the same time, it is important to recognize that most of the variables which were strongly and consistently associated with the different performance outcomes are "controllable" by managers through dealing with the underlying cultural, technical, and political issues which they pose. These underlying issues were the central focus of the 13 longitudinal comparative case studies; the major lessons of which are discussed below.

## Managing technical, political, and cultural issues

**The importance of culture.** In many respects, the sponsorship of primary care programs represented a paradigmatic shift for most of the hospitals involved. Such a shift is characterized by major changes in the organization's belief system and culture (Nicoll, 1979). The program involved a clash of two quite different cultures, that of high-technology, in-patient care on the one hand and primary ambulatory care on the other. Some of the more salient differences between these two kinds of care are summarized in Table 7-1. As shown, these differences primarily involve scale of operation, structure, degree of specialization, multiplicity of goals, time orientation, staff-patient orientations, and administrative-physician relationships. Lawrence and Lorsch (1967) have highlighted the fact that subunits within organizations may differ along a number of these dimensions, thereby creating the need to provide appropriate integrative mechanisms to ensure productive operation. This is a difficult task. A recent study of innovations in ambulatory primary care found that hospital-sponsored models experienced the most difficulty in implementation, with the majority eventually transferring ownership of the practice (Murrin, 1982).

There are vast differences between hospitals and primary ambulatory care group practices in their scale of operation. Procedures, systems, and

**TABLE 7-1**   Fundamental differences between hospitals and ambulatory primary care group practices

|  | Hospitals | Ambulatory primary care group practices |
|---|---|---|
| Scale of operation | Large | Small |
| Structure | Complex | Simple |
| Specialization | High | Low |
| Values | Treatment | Diagnosis and treatment, but with high emphasis on disease prevention and health promotion |
| Goals | Multiple and diverse | Singular and similar |
| Provider-patient contact | Usually one week | Minutes to hours |
| Staff-patient orientation | Patients "captive"; staff comes and goes | Staff "captive"; patients come and go |
| Administrative-physician relationship | More impersonal; structured through committees | More immediate and personal; direct day-to-day contact |

decision making required for hospitals tend to be overwhelming when considered in the context of ambulatory care. In similar fashion, the complex organizational structure of the hospital based on the relatively "loose coupling" (Weick, 1976) of the administration, nursing staff, and voluntary medical staff is markedly different from the simpler, more-integrated organization of a small primary care group practice. In such a practice the physicians, nurses, and administrative support staff are more immediately tied into the success of the practice, and the relatively small size allows for closer interaction.

The degree of specialization is significantly greater in hospitals than in primary ambulatory care. One of the main consequences is that hospital employees who transfer to ambulatory care settings have difficulty because administrative and ancillary support staff in ambulatory care are required to do many things. The jobs are less specialized and more general. For example, a clerk might be required to do some reception work and patient scheduling in addition to patient billing. —

The values of hospitals tend to be different from those of primary ambulatory care group practices. The central value of the hospital is in treatment of acutely ill patients. In primary care, more attention is given to prevention, education, and health-maintenance activities. In some of the more family practice-oriented sites, more attention is given to considering the family and the patient's larger socio-cultural environment than is typically the case in the hospital.

The goals of the two organizations differ. Hospitals usually have multiple goals (for example, treatment, teaching, and research in varying degrees) which often conflict with each other. Primary ambulatory care, in contrast, usually has a somewhat simpler and more congruent goal structure, most typically to provide comprehensive and coordinated primary care to a defined population.

The orientation toward time tends to be different. Hospital staffs tend to think in terms of days and sometimes even weeks in making patient care decisions, whereas in ambulatory care the focus is in terms of minutes or, at most, hours.

In addition to the differences in time, there are also basic differences in the nature of staff-patient interactions and orientations. In hospitals, patients are captives of the staff, who come and go, and patients have little influence over staff or hospital policy. In contrast, in primary ambulatory care settings the staff are "captive" and it is the patients who come and go. Patients have the potential to exert somewhat more control over provider behavior through broken appointments, lack of adherence with medical regimens, and choosing to seek other providers, factors not generally present with in-patient care.

The nature of manager-physician relationships is fundamentally different in primary ambulatory care settings. In hospitals, managers have a somewhat more remote, impersonal, and more structured relationship with physicians through the extensive committee structure of the hospital and the nature of the relationship among the governing board, hospital administration, and medical staff organization. In primary ambulatory care, because of many of the above-noted differences, the relationships between managers and physicians are much more direct, immediate, and personal.

Although the specifics may differ, this kind of "cultural analysis" is equally applicable to managers of for-profit organizations operating in other industries. In the present case, these differences tended to reinforce each other, resulting in two distinctly different "cultures." These issues permeated and dominated the technical and political issues throughout the group practice's development. Further, because of the dominance of the cultural issue, the technical and political issues tended to blur. Among the primary technical issues considered were: (1) the recruitment and retention of physicians, including whether or not to develop a single-specialty or multispecialty practice; (2) the use of other professional staff, such as nurse practitioners, physician assistants, and residents; (3) the overall organizational design of the practice; and (4) the development of information systems. The two primary political issues involved (1) the degree of medical staff opposition to the idea and (2) the relative degree of autonomy required by the group practices. Environmental scarcity and environmental competition, along with the degree of hospital preparation or readiness to implement the program, influenced the way in which managers dealt with these issues. In the following section several examples of how managers dealt with these issues are discussed. This is followed by an examination of how one hospital overcame a number of technical, political, and cultural problems in making the transition to delivering primary care.

**Recruiting and retaining physicians.** A major challenge facing any manager about to develop a new organizational unit is the issue of staffing. In the current case, this meant the recruitment and retention of physicians. Also, central to this issue was the decision to start a single-specialty (in almost all cases, composed of family practitioners) or multispecialty group practice. A single-specialty practice composed of exclusively family practitioners offered the potential advantage of being easier to manage from the perspective of having physicians with similar training and practice styles, particularly with physicians of similar age. Multispecialty practices (for example, a family practitioner, an internist, and a pediatrician), while being perhaps more difficult to coordinate and manage, might have the advantage of appealing to a wider variety of patients. The decision of developing a single-specialty or multispecialty practice was the first important strategic decision facing management. It also had important "political" ramifications. For example, the decision to go with a single-specialty family practice was generally supported by specialists on the hospital staff because they stood to gain from the increased referrals which would be generated by the family practitioners. In contrast, in a number of sites, this decision was opposed by the existing family practitioners in the community who perceived the proposed new group of family practitioners as a competitive threat. On the other hand, the decision to start a multispecialty practice was more likely to be supported by the family practitioners in the community but met with some opposition from some specialists who felt that the internists and pediatricians, even though primary care-oriented, still had subspecialty interests (for example, in cardiology, gastroenterology, and so on) which might result in fewer patients being referred.

In approximately two thirds of the groups the decision was consciously made to develop one or the other form of practice. In the remaining one third, relatively little consideration was given to the issue; the groups were interested primarily in hiring the first qualified physician, regardless of specialty. In these cases, management had not given much thought to the overall role of the group in terms of the hospital's mission and strategic plan. It was also the case that several groups who initially planned to develop single-specialty family practice sites could not find suitable applicants and, instead, ended up hiring an internist or pediatrician and later on adding a family practitioner or two to become a multispecialty site rather than the originally intended single-specialty site.

In dealing with this issue, the first lesson that emerged was that the *actual methods or tactics used in recruitment* (for example, advertisements, contacts with residency programs, participation at recruitment fairs, word-of-mouth, and so on) were *less important* than whether or not the hospital had its own residency program to draw upon, had active and on-going involvement of the medical director in recruitment, and offered an incentive compensation arrangement based on productivity. Those groups which were associated with hospitals that had an active residency program enjoyed a distinct advantage over those which did not in that they could recruit physicians from the residency program. Where residency programs existed, the hospital-sponsored group practice was seen as more central to the hospital's overall teaching mission.

Almost without exception, those sites that were successful in physician recruitment and retention, whether single specialty or multispecialty, had the continuous and personal involvement of the medical director in recruitment activities. These physicians viewed recruitment as a key aspect of their role and did not leave it to hospital management alone or to chance. These physicians had a good idea of the kind of practice they wished to develop and the kind of physicians who would work well together in a group-practice setting. Groups which developed incentive compensation arrangements to supplement base salaries were also more successful at recruiting and retaining physicians than those which did not. Sixteen of the 53 grantees had such arrangements.[4] Thus, in general, it would appear that man-

---

[4]One incentive arrangement worked as follows. If a physician's billings exceeded base salary plus $10,000 practice expenses, the physician received 35 percent of the surplus up to $10,000 above salary and expenses; 50 percent of surplus generated between $10,000 and $20,000 above salary and expenses; 75 percent between $20,000 and $30,000 above salary and practice expenses; and 90 percent above $30,000 in salary and expenses. In order to protect themselves, management reserved the right to reduce the physician's base salary if after four years the physician wasn't producing that base.

agers of new vertically integrated organizations should consider whether special resources already exist for staffing the new unit, take an on-going personal involvement in staff recruitment, and consider special incentives for attracting staff and rewarding productivity.

From a life-cycle perspective, those groups which were initially successful in recruiting and retaining physicians remained so. To a considerable extent, once a nucleus of physicians was formed, groups were able to sell themselves to other physicians because there was tangible evidence of a viable working group. A common factor in groups that experienced difficulty was the presence of medical directors who did not culturally fit the goals of the group or the hospital. For example, one medical director emphasized specialty-oriented care rather than primary care, while others had severe personality conflicts with physicians within the group and on the medical staff. Another common factor among those groups that experienced difficulty in recruitment was the lack of incentive compensation arrangements.

**Using nurse practitioners, physician assistants, and residents.** Using nurse practitioners, physician assistants, or residents had the advantage of enabling a group to offer a broader range of services or, in the case of the residents, meeting institutional objectives regarding the teaching mission. At the same time nurse practitioners, physician assistants, and residents introduced additional uncertainty and complexity into the group. Twenty-six sites used nurse practitioners or physician assistants and 13 used residents; 5 sites used both. A number of communities were not prepared to accept either nurse practitioners or physician assistants, despite growing evidence regarding their productivity, quality of care provided, and patient satisfaction (Le Roy, 1982)

Generally, nurse practitioners and physician assistants faced two socialization problems, one with regard to patients and the second in regard to the group itself. The second proved to be the far more serious as the nurse practitioners for the most part were well accepted by patients. However, expected problems arose in regard to the nurse practitioners being incorporated into the group itself. In the sites with younger physicians, particularly family practitioners, there was conflict between the desire of both to have more direct patient contact. This problem was further exacerbated in the site with residents because of the residents' desire to obtain as much direct clinical experience as possible. Thus, they often performed functions and tasks which would also be performed by the nurse practitioner or physician assistant. In addition, in many sites there was lack of clear role definitions, particularly in the case of nurse practitioners. Role definition and clarification usually had to be continually negotiated. In one site the medical director's style in dealing with this issue was to let the nurse practitioners and physicians work out their own role relationships individually rather than developing a formal organization-wide policy on the issue. In another case, the medical director's style was to work out the role relationships through regularly scheduled management and subunit committee meetings. In both cases, the nurse practitioners became a viable part of the group practice over time. Typically, they had some of their own patients; performed screening, health education, and health promotion activities; made home visits; and conducted industrial exams.

Overall, three factors were associated with the successful use of nurse practitioners, physician assistants, and residents. The first was the degree to which their use was consistent with the overall goal and mission of the group and its sponsoring hospital. The second was compatibility with other providers in the group, and the third was clarification of their roles. General lessons which can be drawn are that managers of new vertically integrated units must carefully consider introducing new kinds of professional workers, paying particular attention to issues of compatibility and clarification of roles.

**Designing the practice.** A series of key decisions involved the overall design of the practice itself. While hospital-sponsored primary care group practice is an example of a divisionalized structure (Kaluzny and Konrad, 1982) in which the hospital is superimposed upon the primary care program, there is also the issue of choosing a design for the practice itself. This can be considered a "nesting" design decision within the larger divisionalized structure. Among the grantees the primary nesting design options included: (1) a *simple structure* characterized by few services and few providers and a managerial subsystem that is only beginning to emerge; (2) a *machine structure* characterized by a close relationship between the clinical and administrative systems, a relatively high degree of vertical and horizontal differentiation, and a high degree of formalized plans and procedures; and (3) a *professional structure* characterized by highly developed professional services that are very loosely tied to the management subsystem and characterized by limited vertical integration and a high degree of professional differentation (Mintzberg, 1979, Kaluzny and Konrad, 1982). Few of the grantees fit neatly into only one category but, in general, one of the above three designs tended to dominate.

In general, the "professional" design practices performed better than the "machine" design practices which, in turn, did better than the "simple" structures. The main problem with the simple structure was its dependence on one key individual. This limited the amount of input and experience available to the group and hospital. It also left the group and hospital vulnerable to that individual's leaving. The simple-structure sites had particular problems in recruiting and retaining physicians. They also tended to be located in areas where it was difficult to build patient volume. In general, they did not have sufficient depth or complexity of resources to cope.

Machinelike bureaucratically organized practices tended to be successful if they had strong medical-director leadership which could effectively represent the group's interests in dealing with hospital administration. In some of the more successful practices, the medical directors were influential persons within the medical staff and in larger hospital circles often carried the title of vice president for ambulatory care. In some other cases the medical director's interests were closely aligned to those of the hospital administration, such as in the case of helping the hospital to expand its teaching capacity. In cases where such strong leadership or coalignment of goals did not exist, the hospital tended to dominate the group, resulting in considerable conflict and physician turnover.

The professional design resembled closely the private practice of medicine model and, therefore, had the widest appeal to most physicians associated with the program. These practices were characterized by considerable physician involvement in decision making, more collaborative relationships among physicians and between physicians and hospital administration and, as will be subsequently discussed, a greater degree of autonomy in operating the practice. They were also associated with less medical-staff opposition and strong medical-director leadership. They did particularly well in physician recruitment and retention and generally developed viable practices. The general lesson for managers is that new units designed to provide new products or services to new markets may require a different organizational design and structure than that used by the parent organization. This "shift in design" is of particular importance when a high percentage of professional staff is involved in the new unit.

**Information systems.** Almost without exception, hospital information systems related to billing, accounting, budgeting, utilization, and related issues were inadequate for providing primary ambulatory care. Simply put, the information needs of primary care are different from those of inpatient care.

Many hospitals, for example, initially did the billing for their groups. However, such systems were established to do in-patient billing where most of the care is covered by third-party insurance. The systems could not be easily adapted to do primary care group-practice billing where there is less third-party coverage for care and more out-of-pocket payment to consider. As a result, collections and revenues suffered.

In the financial and utilization report areas, primary care groups require different information than in the in-patient area. For example, the amount of revenue generated per physician is important to a group practice in order to assess productivity and practice patterns, whereas such information is not usually required for in-patient care purposes.

Those managers who recognized early the need for different systems and who developed a collaborative approach with the group's medical director or administrator were more successful in developing useful information systems. To an important degree, the issue of information systems involved the larger issue of the relative degree of autonomy granted to the groups. The general lesson for all managers is that new units operating in new and different lines of business are likely to require new and different kinds of information systems which ought to be planned for in advance by working collaboratively with those involved in the new activities.

**Dealing with medical staff opposition.** Handling the technical issues noted above was made more difficult in those sites which experienced considerable medical-staff opposition. This was largely a political issue, with the sources of opposition stemming from multiple factors including: (1) philosophical opposition to the "corporate practice of medicine"; (2) fear of competition for patients; (3) fear of competition for hospital beds; (4) fear on the part of older physicians that the new, usually younger, group physicians would change and upgrade the standards of medical practice in the community; and (5) resentment that younger physicians should be given a subsidy to start their practices.

The degree of medical-staff opposition was centrally related to an early strategic decision facing hospital administrators, namely the extent to which the medical staff was involved in the original decision to apply for the grant. For most hospital administrators, the issue involved a major trade-off and risk. The importance of including people in decisions that affect them has become conventional wisdom, particularly when working with professionals such as physicians. However, by attempting to do so, hospital administration ran the risk of having the proposal turned down by the medical staff. Indeed, a few county medical societies voted against the proposal or passed it by a narrow margin. Most sites chose not to widely involve the medical staff in the development of the proposal or the plans for the group. They gambled that if the grant was successful, they could then provide details and ask for further input and support as necessary. Besides, the hospital might not get the grant and administrators felt there was little need to unnecessarily antagonize the medical staff.

This strategy had a price. For some, the price was high, involving active vocal opposition throughout the grant period, transfer of admissions from the funded hospital to a competing hospital in the community, and, in a few cases, lawsuits against the hospital. Such resistance significantly hindered recruitment of group physicians and marketing efforts. In many groups, little or no marketing was done for fear of reprisal by the medical community.

Those sites which made a concerted and conscientious effort to involve the medical staff in the planning process experienced significantly less medical-staff opposition. What opposition did exist could be dealt with in a more congenial fashion by leaders of both hospital administration and the medical staff. For example, one site ran into some resistance from specialists who felt the group physicians were not distributing referrals evenly. The medical director effectively dealt with this problem by agreeing to keep records on the volume of referrals going to the various specialists. These data showed that referrals were being evenly distributed and the issue quickly passed.

Several strategies were used by hospitals to deal with medical-staff opposition, whether the opposition was strong or mild. Perhaps the most effective strategy was the appointment of a respected older physician from the hospital's own medical staff to become medical director of the group. The appointment of such a person generally quieted whatever opposition existed. Many members of the staff still did not agree with the concept but were, at least, willing to go along and trusted the judgment of the respected medical director. Such medical directors were also generally adept at hospital politics and were able to work effectively with hospital administration on behalf of their groups.

A second strategy used to overcome resistance was to indicate how the group practice would benefit other members of the staff, particularly the specialists who would benefit from increased referrals. In similar fashion, in other sites it was "sold" to the staff because it would benefit the hospital's developing teaching interests by serving as a practice site for residents.

A third strategy used was to stress that the group practice was serving a population whose needs were not currently being met by physicians in the community. In some cases, this involved the poor and medically indigent. Thus, the group could be "sold" on the basis that it wasn't going to compete with private practitioners for patients. In fact, some private practitioners saw the group as desirable in that they could "transfer" some of their Medicaid patients to the hospital-sponsored group.

Some of the above strategies were used in combination and others singly. In general they worked particularly well where the hospital had a clearly defined idea regarding how the group fit into the hospital's overall mission and strategic plan, whether that was to serve the underserved, expand the hospital's market base in the face of growing competition, or develop an additional site for teaching residents. The above strategies were also particularly effective where demand for services was high. High patient volume could be used as evidence that the group was meeting a need in the community and that it was a viable undertaking. Where such volume did not exist, managers had a much more difficult time dealing with on-going medical-staff opposition.

Thus, managers can expect opposition to the development of new units and vertically related ventures. The above findings suggest that such opposition can be effectively dealt with through early and relevant involvement of the parties affected; through recruitment or co-optation of key respected organizational leaders to support or actively participate in the new organization; through indicating how the new unit and its activities will benefit other organizational members; through indicating how the new unit and its activities will deal with aspects of the firm's business that are generally unattractive to others; and by emphasizing how the new unit and its associated activities are consistent with the organization's overall mission and strategic plan.

**Structuring the degree of autonomy between the group and the hospital.** In the design of a new program or subunit, a major question emerges as to how closely it should be linked with the organization's existing programs, units and services. Weick (1976) has referred to this as the problem of "loose" versus "tight" coupling. This issue has also been raised by Miller and

Friesen (1980) as an organizational transition archetype involving "maturation" in which an organization recognizes that a group or subunit may require a greater degree of autonomy than more established departments, particularly where the new unit is quite different from existing units. As previously noted, this issue was particularly salient to the CHP grantees because of the fundamental differences between in-patient and ambulatory primary care. In general, these differences suggest that loose coupling, as reflected by granting considerable autonomy to the group, would be appropriate. On the other hand, the groups were intended to be hospital-sponsored and, indeed, a major purpose of the program was to provide a stimulus for on-going hospital sponsorship even after termination of the grant. Thus, hospitals had compelling reasons to exert considerable control and direction over the sites.

How the grantees dealt with this inherent conflict turned out to be a key factor in meeting the various performance criteria. Each hospital's structuring of its autonomy relationship involved a number of "political" issues concerning the allocation of power, authority, responsibility, and accountability. As shown in Figure 7–2, autonomy is a multidimensional concept composed of functional and structural dimensions on the one hand and administrative and clinical dimensions on the other. Functional autonomy refers to the group's ability to exercise relatively independent control over its budgeting, personnel, purchasing, and related decisions. Structural autonomy refers to the formal organizational and reporting relationships between the group and the hospital. The less formalized and hierarchical these relationships, the greater the degree of structural autonomy. Administrative autonomy refers to the group's ability to manage its own internal affairs without interference from hospital administration. Clinical autonomy refers to the ability of the physicians to develop their own principles of practice, refer to whomever they want, and admit patients based on their best judgment; in brief, to enjoy the same rights and privileges as other physicians on the medical staff. In addition, autonomy may be further characterized as "perceived" or "objective," depending on whether the in-

**FIGURE 7–2**    Dimensions of autonomy

|  | Administrative | Clinical |
|---|---|---|
| Functional | Budgeting, finance, and billing<br>Purchasing<br>Personnel | Patient care practices<br>Referrals<br>Admissions<br>Use of ancillary services<br>Physician recruitment |
| Structural | Reporting relationships with hospital administration | Reporting relationships with hospital and medical staff administration |

formation is based on a person's perception of the degree of autonomy involved or on an independent measure; for example, the degree to which persons perceive they have autonomy in purchasing decisions versus the actual level of dollar limit beyond which the hospital requires approval for a purchasing decision. The discussion which follows draws on both perceptual and objective measures of autonomy. Primary emphasis is given to administrative *functional* autonomy issues because it was in this area that most of the conflict existed. Further, the structural dimension of autonomy was primarily reflected in the functional issues.

Duncan (1979) suggests that a relatively more-open, decentralized, and less-formalized organizational structure is most appropriate during the adoption stage of a new program, whereas a more-centralized, formalized structure is more effective for actual implementation. This suggests that at the implementation stage most hospitals might have been better off exerting relatively tight control over the group practices. However, one also needs to take into account the nature of the program being implemented and, in this case, the fundamental differences between in-patient and ambulatory care. Further, it is important to recognize the highly professionalized members of ambulatory care centers, physicians in particular, with their associated needs and expectations regarding autonomy. These considerations would suggest the need for hospitals to exert relatively loose direct control over the group while, of course, maintaining final accountability.

Groups that enjoyed greater autonomy were generally characterized by the following features: (1) while many still followed the hospital's personnel policies, exceptions could be made and most importantly, the group had complete control over its own hiring and firing; (2) the hospital set a relatively high dollar limit for purchasing items before hospital administration's signature was required; (3) the group was allowed to use its own vendors where that made sense from a cost, quality, or volume viewpoint rather than being required to go through the hospital's purchasing department; and (4) groups did their own billing and enjoyed considerable discretion in the development and monitoring of budgets. In contrast, groups with less functional autonomy had to adhere more strictly to the hospital's personnel policies, had a low dollar limit (typically $100 to $300) beyond which the hospital required prior approval for purchases, and generally had little say over their own budgets and related financial matters.

In general, groups which encouraged greater functional autonomy experienced less medical-staff opposition and fewer physician recruitment and retention problems. The direction of causality, however, is not clear. It could be that low medical-staff opposition and successful physician recruitment and retention enabled the hospital to grant more autonomy to the group, while a high degree of opposition and poor recruitment suggested that the hospital needed to exert more active control. Or, it could be that where medical staffs saw the hospital granting more autonomy to the group, such that it functioned like a private practice, medical-staff opposition was less and the group was also better able to recruit and retain physicians. Certainly in the case of recruitment, the more plausible explanation, based on the grantees' experience, is that granting autonomy led to more-successful recruitment and retention than the other way around.

In general, those groups which enjoyed greater functional autonomy from their sponsoring hospitals experienced more favorable outcomes in terms of improving the organization of access to care, fulfilling the hospital's on-going commitment to primary care, becoming financially viable, and having a positive financial impact on the sponsoring hospital. However, it was also the case that, while autonomy may have been a necessary condition for more-successful outcomes, it was not a sufficient condition. What was also required was strong medical-director leadership and, often, administrative leadership as well. Several sites which did enjoy considerable autonomy experienced less-favorable outcomes because they lacked effective medical-director leadership. Thus, in order for autonomy to be effective, there needs to be at least a minimal level of expertise, experience, and leadership within the group itself. As previously noted in discussing the overall results, it was also important that the medical director be integrated into the hospital through active committee participation.

Some specific examples in the purchasing and personnel areas provide further illumination of the autonomy issue. In one case, the group proposed a major departure in the staffing of ambulatory care activities which involved replacing a number of nursing, clerical, and receptionist positions with a more broadly trained medical assistant. This required the development of a new, more appropriate job description, unique to the group; filling the position was expected to reduce staffing costs. The hospital at first resisted this change. Eventually the position was approved, but it created a lasting impression of hospital interference in the group's policy making.

Another example involved the group practice's needs for flexibility in using part-time employees. The hospital administrator refused to permit the hiring of a part time licensed practical nurse. The hiring had been approved by the assistant administrator who thought she had previously advised the hospital administrator of the decision. The hospital administrator then undercut his assistant's decision by reducing the group office manager to half time, again over the objection of the assistant and the group's medical staff. While the requirement of administrative or committee approval for staffing changes was relatively common among the groups, in this case the lack of a formalized system or method for reviewing approval heightened the strong feeling of arbitrary interference by the hospital in group management and further eroded the ability of the group's administrator.

The third example is afforded by a group which was required to fill vacant positions with hospital employees who wanted to transfer, even though the group could have recruited others at less expense. As a result, personnel expenses for support staff were unusually high, adding to the total operating expense of the practice.

In the purchasing area, most hospitals purchase supplies in large quantities and, because of the large inventory, are able to reorder well ahead of time. However, the primary care groups did not have large facilities for storing a vast number of items and, furthermore, their needs for additional supplies were more immediate and less standardized. As a result some sites had to purchase items on their own and then submit the bills for reimbursement. This caused strain between the group and the hospital because it was contrary to hospital policy and did not offer a practical long-term solution.

In other sites, the requirement for hospital approval for purchases above $300 caused a number of problems, resulting in endless delays in receiving needed materials. In one case, delays in processing a requisition resulted in the hospital missing a deadline for receiving Foundation funding for equipment.

The autonomy issues and examples raised above are also important from a life-cycle perspective on organization learning (Kimberly and Miles, 1980). Specifically, some of the hospitals learned from their early mistakes and granted their groups greater functional autonomy over the course of the grant. This is analogous to Miller and Friesen's (1980) notion of the "maturation" state of organizational transition. In almost every case, such autonomy was associated with improvements in physician recruitment and retention, better productivity, and a more smoothly functioning group.

In contrast, a number of hospitals chose not to grant such autonomy particularly where the group was doing poorly. This is a natural reaction since it is conventional wisdom (institutionalized in a number of management texts) to exert more control over a department or a unit experiencing difficulties. However, in almost every case the situation became worse, resulting in continued physician turnover, low productivity, and a generally unstable practice. Thus, for all managers, it appears that *more* rather than less autonomy is the preferred strategy when dealing with a small organization of professionals operating in a somewhat different environment and culture than the organization as a whole. This, of course, assumes that the subunit has at least a minimum level of expertise to carry out its functions.

The experience of the grantees also supports Peters and Waterman's (1982) findings that high performing organizations appear to have simultaneous "loose-tight" properties. In the present case a great deal of autonomy or "looseness" was conducive to higher performance but, at the same time, needed integration or "tightness" was also important, as exercised not by close supervisory control over the practice but through medical-director involvement in hospital committees and decision-making forums. The latter mechanism enabled the medical director to learn about new hospital plans and policies and, in turn, to indicate the primary care perspective on these plans and policies as well as advance new primary care plans.

The preceding discussion indicates how technical and political issues merge within the context of the larger cultural issues. Medical-staff opposition and problems associated with autonomy made it difficult for the hospitals and groups to deal with their technical issues of recruiting and retaining physicians, and designing the overall organization of the practice and its associated systems. These issues were, of course, embedded within the larger context of ambulatory primary care being fundamentally different than in-patient care. The issues were further compounded in sites serving a higher percentage of low-income and Medicaid patients and/or facing stiff competition from other hospitals and physicians. A further understanding of the complexity involved can be derived from examining a case in which a number of the above issues converged.

**Bucking the odds.** Consider the following scenario. A hospital applies for a grant to develop a primary care group practice. The hospital tells its medical staff the grant is simply a way to attract new primary care physicians to the area and that the physicians are free to practice without restriction. Further, they indicate that the hospital will get out of the practice as soon as it can. As it is, the local county medical society barely approves the proposal. The hospital tells its governing board very little about the intent or purpose of the grant. The board and management are preoccupied with implementing a merger with another hospital. The person who wrote the grant and is its leading proponent leaves the hospital shortly after the grant is received. The administrative person placed in charge of the project has no previous knowledge of it and little understanding of what it is supposed to achieve. He also has little time for it. The director of the local family practice residency program, sensing medical-community opposition and sensitive to the feelings of the competing hospital in town (which jointly sponsors the residency program), is neutral toward the idea. He neither encourages nor discourages graduates of the program to practice at the site. The first two physicians recruited leave after one year. The next physician recruited has a history of personal problems and has a practice style completely foreign to that of younger, more recently trained family practitioners, does not know what it takes to be a medical director, and has an active distaste for physician recruitment and for building a group practice. Meanwhile, the hospital's occupancy is declining, its long-term debt is increasing, and the local economy is in a downturn.

What are the chances that such a practice in such a setting will even survive—never mind having an impact on the other performance criteria? Yet the above was exactly the situation faced by one grantee. Not only did it survive, it went on to do quite well on a number of performance criteria. Why? How did management bring order out of seeming chaos, success out of impending failure?

Overall, 7 grantees did not survive and an additional 11 continued as independent practices without ongoing sponsorship. Thus, it is important to examine the key circumstances and events which enabled this site to overcome its problems and develop a relatively successful practice. The first ingredient was *perseverance*. Despite the board's lack of information and understanding of the project and therefore their lukewarm commitment, the hospital's chief executive officer was able to articulate the importance placed on providing services to those in need and to extending the hospital "beyond its four walls." In an important sense the group practice was a symbol of what the hospital in part wanted to become, even though the board knew little of the background of the idea or its implementation. This philosophical commitment enabled the hospital to turn down a $1 million offer for the group practice's building and property. Such commitment carried the hospital through the difficult period of developing a viable practice. Other grantees, some facing far less adverse circumstances than this grantee, lacked such commitment and effectively threw in the towel.

A second ingredient, related to the first, was the physical presence of the clinic building—an attractive facility well located in the community. This served as a *tangible reminder* of the hospital's commitment. It would have also served as a highly visible embarrassment if the hospital couldn't fill it with at least three or four primary care doctors and make good on their commitment to the community in which it was located.

The third ingredient was extremely important. Simply put, there was *demand* for the group's services. A high volume of satisfied patients makes everyone happy—physicians, hospital, and community. High volume can mask a number of underlying problems and issues which become major difficulties in the absence of such demand. Many of those sites which did not survive or did relatively poorly suffered from insufficient patient demand, either due to overestimation of the demand in the beginning, shifts in the socio-economic composition of the community served, or inability to develop services to meet pockets of community need. In the present case, there was never serious doubt that adequate patient volume existed. The question was whether the hospital could ever get a group of physicians to stay long enough to deliver care.

A fourth ingredient was a *relatively benign external environment* in regard to third-party reimbursement, regulation, and competition. Unlike some other grantees, this site had a relatively low percentage of Medicaid patients (approximately 13 percent in 1982), good payment relations with Blue Cross/Blue Shield, no rate review programs, no problem in obtaining regulatory approval for the practice site, and no direct competition in the target area from either other physicians in the community or from the other hospital in town.

Finally, as in other sites, *presence of a family practice residency training program* was conducive to development of a successful practice. While this grantee was slower and less able to take advantage of this resource because of the political issues involved with joint sponsorship by the competing hospital, its continuing presence was a source of encouragement for the hospital. They recognized it as a key factor in recruitment efforts and were finally able to break the logjam by recruiting two family practitioners from the residency program. This was a key event in turning the situation around.

The philosophical commitment of top hospital administrative leadership, combined with high potential patient demand and favorable environmental factors, bought the hospital time. Time to learn from early mistakes regarding the autonomy needs of the group. Time to deal with larger issues of implementing a merger and developing new building plans before realizing that the group practice also required attention. Time to eventually involve the board and medical staff to some degree through development of an advisory committee. And time to gradually convince the director of the family practice residency program as to the importance of the practice site in terms of the larger community. Given such time, the hospital was able to develop a stable group of three well-trained family practitioners after total turnover of physicians during the first three years of practice.

Figure 7-3 summarizes the relationships among the key variables influencing the outcomes of this grantee. As shown, the hospital created most of its own implementation problems, which served as inhibitors of the group's development. The number of favorable circumstances, described above, bought the hospital time and provided some motivation to deal with the problems. These served as facilitators. Thus, the hospital was able to learn from its past and make a number of changes in reporting relationships, functional autonomy relationships, giving more attention to the group, and to some extent educating the board and medical staff—all of which made it more attractive for recruiting family practice residents. Once this occurred, given the high potential patient demand and other favorable circumstances, the probability of a successful practice developing improved dramatically. As noted by the hospital's original vice president for planning and research: "To get a program of this type underway you're going to have to be a damn good artist of the behavioral sciences. You have to be able to interact effectively with physicians, above and beyond all else in ways that obtain and maintain consensus and commitments."

The above experience holds a number of lessons for all managers. They include the importance of maintaining commitment, learning to buy time, and a willingness to experiment and learn. At the same time, one must be confident that sufficient demand for the new product or service exists to make the above strategies viable.

## GUIDELINES FOR MANAGING ORGANIZATIONAL TRANSITIONS IN HEALTH CARE

We have examined the process and outcomes of one form of organizational transition—vertical integration jointly undertaken by hospitals and physicians through sponsorship of primary care group practices. We do not claim that the lessons learned from this experience are directly transferable in their specifics to other forms of transitions in health care delivery (for example, mergers, consolidations, shared services arrangement, and so on) nor to organizational transitions in other industries. However, some of the principles underlying the lessons do have managerial generalizability (as opposed to statistical generalizability) and it is these we wish to highlight.

For the most part the guidelines have to do with *environmental assessment* and *organizational assessment* in relationship to each other. In brief, in undertaking new ventures one needs to assess the degree to which the environment is favorably predisposed to the new venture and the degree to

FIGURE 7-3    Interrelationships among factors influencing performance

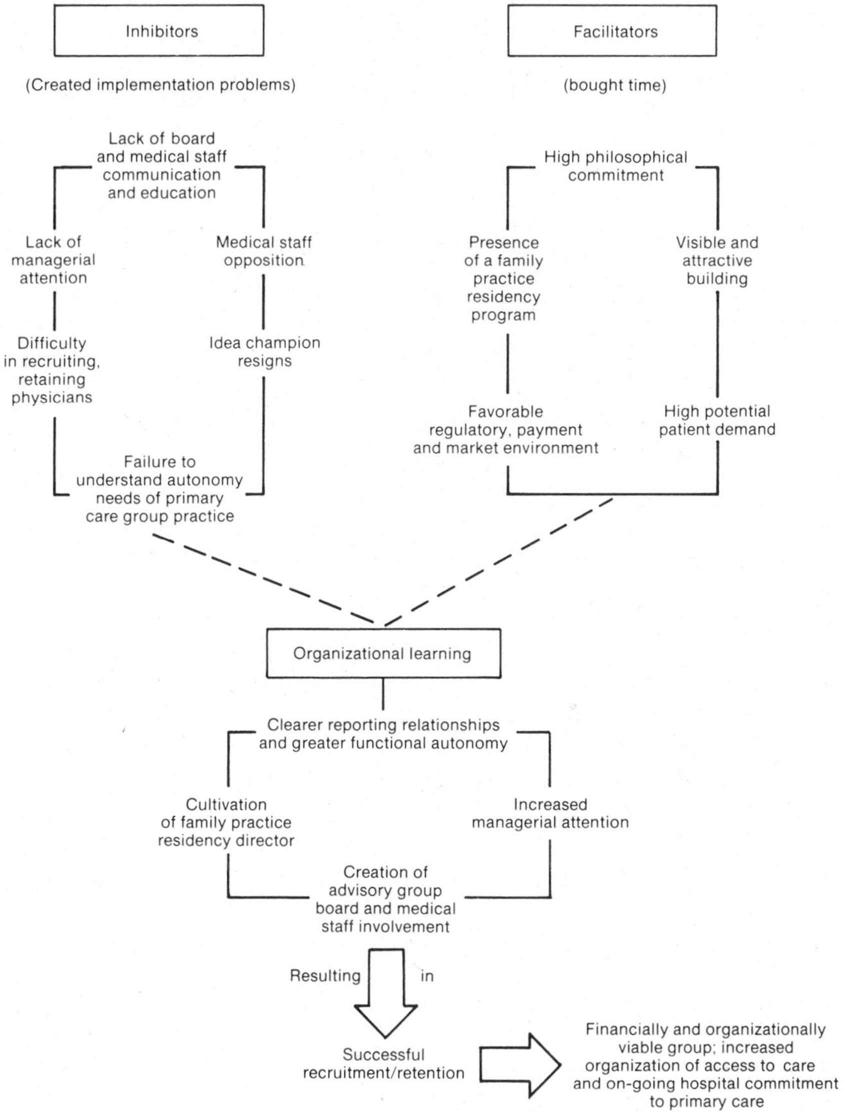

which the organization is capable of implementing it. Figure 7–4 provides a simplified framework which can be used by managers as a diagnostic aid. Briefly, where the environment is favorable and the organization has strong capability to launch the new venture, one is in a situation of having an almost "sure winner." Where the environment is unfavorable but the organization is strong in its capability one is faced with a calculated risk–type A. The type-A risk is that the organization will be strong enough to overcome

**FIGURE 7-4**   Simplified decision aid for diagnosing likely success of new ventures

|  |  | Environment | |
|---|---|---|---|
|  |  | *Favorable* | *Unfavorable* |
| Organizational capability | High | Likely winner | Calculated risk type A |
|  | Low | Calculated risk type B | Likely loser |

the unfavorable environmental circumstances. Where the environment is favorable but the organization is weak, one is faced with a calculated risk–type B. The type-B risk is that the environment will be favorable enough to pull the organization through. When the environment is unfavorable and the organization is weak one is faced with a likely loser situation. Among the relevant environmental factors to assess are the degree of competition in the market place, the strengths and weaknesses of one's competitors (Porter, 1980), the likely demand for the new product or service, and the availability of needed resources. Among the organization factors to be examined are the degree to which the new venture is seen as central to the organization's mission and strategic plan, the strength of available leadership, recognition of the new unit's needs for autonomy, and, at the same time, the degree to which the new unit can be appropriately integrated into the parent organization. The framework shown in Figure 7–4 was applied to the CHP grantees and found to be generally predictive of differences in performance (Shortell et al., 1984). For example, hospital-sponsored groups with high organizational capability and favorable environments experienced the highest performance scores on a variety of measures (ongoing commitment, improving the organization of access, financial viability, and having a positive impact on the hospital). The next-highest performers were those with high organizational capability, functioning in relatively unfavorable environments (calculated risk–type A).

The poorer performers were those with low organizational capability, regardless of whether the environment was particularly favorable (calculated risk–type B) or unfavorable (losers). Thus, based on present experience, organizational capability appears to be a somewhat better predictor of the likely success of new vertical-integration initiatives than the favorableness of the environment. Keeping Figure 7–4, in mind we turn directly to the guiding propositions.

## Centrality to organizational mission and strategic plan

*Proposition 1: The greater the degree to which the organizational innovation is seen as central to the larger organization's mission and strategic plan, the greater the probability of success.*

It is important that the organizational innovation be seen as central to the organization's mission and strategic plan. It must be a part of what the organization is all about and what it sees itself as becoming. This is different from merely being commited to a promising new idea. In the present case, those groups which were seen as central to the hospital's evolving mission to expand ambulatory care activities as a means of furthering hospital goals of community sevice and institutional survival and/or growth were generally more successful. This degree of centrality to the organization's mission also enabled hospitals to better withstand the technical, political, and cultural issues which arose. The principle is likely to apply to other organizational transitions as well.

## Recognizing and managing differences in culture

*Proposition 2a: The greater the differences in culture between the larger organization and the new unit, the greater the number and complexity of technical and political problems which will arise.*

*Proposition 2b: Given 2a, the greater the degree of managerial attention to cultural differences, the greater the probability of success.*

Managers seldom explicitly recognize the number of ways in which new organizational innovations may differ from the parent organization. Some of the ways in which new units may differ from parent structures include: (1) differences in technology, (2) differences in market served, (3) differences in scale of operation, (4) differences in specialization of functions, (5) differences in the percentage and types of professionals involved, (6) differences in orientation toward time (7) differences in orientation toward goals, and (8) differences in types of rewards. In brief, new units may represent distinct subcultures as the result of interactions among the above kinds of factors. As has been described, these cultural differences were particularly pervasive in the hospital-sponsored primary care group-practice setting. They strongly influenced the kinds of technical and political problems which emerged and required considerable managerial attention. While cultural differences may exert less influence in other situations, it is important for managers to give greater attention to conducting a "cultural diagnosis" or assessment of newly proposed organizational innovations or transitions. Failure to do so may result in unexpected implementation problems leading to failure.

## Recognizing and managing environmental variables

*Proposition 3a: The greater the degree of environmental scarcity and environmental competition, the greater the difficulty in implementing new organizational forms.*

*Proposition 3b: Given 3a, the greater the degree of managerial attention to environmental factors, the greater the probability of success.*

Scarcity influences the amount of resources available to launch new organizational ventures. Competition influences the probability that the new organizational form will acquire all the resources it needs for growth. Where both scarcity and competition exist, organizations face a particularly difficult challenge in initiating new organizational forms. In the present study, scarcity in the form of serving a high percentage of low-income patients and a high percentage of Medicaid patients and competition from other hospitals and providers did exert some influence on the probability of group success. Due to the subsidy in the form of the Foundation grant, these factors exerted less effect than they otherwise might have. Nonetheless, they had to be managed effectively through judicious physician recruitment, design of the practice, and through attempting to appeal to a relatively wide base of patients. Environmental scarcity and competition are generic factors which need to be considered by all managers faced with developing new organizational forms. The greater the extent to which scarcity and competition exist, the greater the amount of venture capital which may be required for the new undertaking and the stronger the organization needs to be (see Figure 7–4).

## Assessing the degree of coupling required

*Proposition 4: The greater the differences in culture and the greater the percentage of professionals involved, the greater the degree of loose coupling or autonomy which must be granted to the new organizational unit.*

The issue of coupling was originally raised by Lawrence and Lorsch (1967) in terms of the degree of differentiation and integration required by an organization. Organizations with a high percentage of professionals require a considerable degree of differentiation but, at the same time, require some degree of integration in order to achieve overall organizational goals. Results of the present study suggest that considerable functional autonomy is required where the new organizational unit consists of a high percentage of professionals charged with accomplishing a mission which is culturally quite different from the parent organization. In such situations, integration is maintained through committee involvement of relevant leaders (for example medical director) and other similar lateral linkage mechanisms (Galbraith, 1973). Similar findings have emerged from a recent study of hospital mergers (Starkweather, 1981). These findings are likely to prove useful to all managers of new activities involving a high percentage of professionals such as scientists, engineers, lawyers, architects, and accountants. Failure to follow them may lead to excessive turnover of professional staff, a significant threat to the success of the undertaking.

### Recognizing that organization design and management practices are themselves sources of uncertainty, complexity, and problem formation

*Proposition 5: The greater the degree to which continuous attention is given to organization design and management practices, the greater the probability of success.*

Typically, organization design, staffing, information system design, and related management practices are viewed as responses to uncertainty and complexity in the external environment and/or as ways of managing planned change. It is generally assumed that if they can be "matched" to the demands of the environment or the change situation, successful outcomes are more likely to occur. However, what is not recognized is that such "matching" is not a one-time-only process but, rather, is a subtle process requiring continual monitoring and adjustment. Based on the present study, these adjustments are *not* due only to on-going changes in the environment or in the nature of the planned change but are *also* due to additional complexity, uncertainty, and related problems created by the organizational design and management practices themselves. Thus, groups which started multispecialty practices to deal with environmental competition found that such practices raised other problems of internal coordination which, in turn, had to be managed through changes in the structuring of autonomy relationships and related means. The lesson is that organizational design and management practices associated with the development of new organizational forms must be managed *simultaneously* and *continuously* to increase the probability of successful implementation. Failure to do so leads to "organizational drift" which, if left uncorrected, leads to demise.

### Using multiple strategies to manage cultural, technical, and political issues

*Proposition 6: The greater the degree to which multiple strategies are used to manage cultural, technical, and political issues, the greater the probability of success.*

Too often managers adopt a single plan or strategy for developing and implementing new organizational forms. When the original plan fails, they become frustrated and frequently don't know where to turn. A major lesson from the present study and suggested by others (Kotter and Schlesinger, 1979) is that multiple strategies and plans are needed to successfully launch new organizational forms. Thus, managers who developed multiple ways of selling the idea to the medical staff and defusing opposition, who recognized the need for switching from multispecialty to single-specialty practices or vice versa, who recognized the need for redesigning autonomy relationships, and so on, were generally more successful.

The use of multiple strategies closely parallels Landau's (1973) ideas regarding the importance of redundancy. Contrary to the conventional wisdom that redundancy is inefficient, Landau suggests that in highly uncertain environments and situations, redundancy contributes to reliability of performance and adaptability. The present study of hospital-sponsored primary care group practices supports this notion. Those practices which had such built-in redundancy features as (1) multiple sources of patient referral, (2) multiple methods and sources of physician recruitment, (3) physicians who could cover for one another and provide overlapping patient care functions, (4) widely available hospital backup and support services, (5) dual information systems, and (6) alternative sources of funding generally performed better. In brief, managers of organizational transitions involving new organizational forms would appear to be well served by developing multiple strategies for implementation involving the incorporation of redundant features. This is likely to be particularly true where the environmental conditions are unfavorable. Failure to build in such redundancy restricts the organization's ability to learn and to switch to other strategies in order to increase the probability of successful implementation.

Based on present findings, these six guidelines relating to mission/strategy, culture, environment, coupling, design, and redundancy seem most important to managers of vertical integration initiatives. They are important because they tend to maximize organization learning. In the end it was the ability of the hospitals and their groups to learn quickly from their mistakes and make appropriate adjustments which proved critical to achieving their objectives.

## REFERENCES

Aday, L.; R. Andersen; S. Loevy; and B. Kremer. *Hospital-Sponsored Primary Care: A Study of Impact on Community Access.* Ann Arbor, Mich.: Health Administration Press, forthcoming, 1984.

Aldrich, Howard E. *Organizations and Environment.* Englewood Cliffs, N. J.: Prentice-Hall, 1979.

Becker, Selwyn W., and Gerald Gordon. "An Entrepreneurial Theory of Formal Organizations," pp. 315–44. *Administrative Science Quarterly* 11, December 1966.

Cameron, K., and D. A. Whetten. "Perceptions of Organizational Effectiveness across Organizational Life Cycles," pp. 525–44. *Administrative Science Quarterly* 26, 1981.

Carroll, Glenn R., and Jacques Delacroix. "Organizational Mortality in the Newspaper Industries of Argentina and Ireland: An Ecological Approach," pp. 169–98. *Administrative Science Quarterly* 27, 1982.

Daft, Richard L., and Selwyn W. Becker. *The Innovative Organization.* New York: Elsevier Science Publishing, 1978.

Denzin, Norman. *Sociological Methods—Source Book.* Chicago: Aldine Publishing, 1970.

Duncan, Robert B. "What is the Right Organization Structure? Decision Tree Analysis Provides the Answer," pp. 59–70. *Organization Dynamics* 3, Winter 1979.

Galbraith, J. *Designing Complex Organizations.* Reading, Mass.: Addison-Wesley Publishing, 1973.

Hannan, Michael T., and John H. Freeman. "The Population Ecology of Organizations," pp. 929–64. *American Journal of Sociology* 82, 1977.

Kaluzny, Arnold D., and Thomas R. Konrad. "Organization Design and the Management of Primary Care Services." pp. 33–67 *Management of Rural Primary Care—Concepts and Cases,* ed. G. E. Bisbee, Jr. Chicago: Hospital Research and Educational Trust, 1982.

Kimberly, John R., Robert H. Miles, and Associates. *The Organizational Life Cycle.* San Francisco; Jossey-Bass, 1980.

Kotter, John P., and Leonard Schlesinger. "Choosing Strategies for Change," pp. 106–13. *Harvard Business Review,* March/April 1979.

Landau, Martin. "On the Concept of a Self-Correcting Organization," pp. 533–42. *Public Administration Review* 33, 1973.

Lawrence, Paul., and J. Lorsch. *Organization and Environment; Managing Differentation and Integration.* Boston: Harvard Business School, 1967.

LeRoy, Lauren. "The Cost-Effectiveness of Nurse Practitioners." pp. 295–314 in *Nursing in the 1980's,* ed. L. H. Aiken. Philadelphia: J. B. Lippincott, 1982.

Marrett, Cora B. "Influences On the Rise of New Organizations; The Formation of Women's Medical Societies," pp. 185–99. *Administrative Science Quarterly* 25, 1980.

Miller, Daniel, and P. Friesen. "Archetypes of Organizational Transition," pp. 268–99. *Administrative Science Quarterly* 25, June 1980.

Mintzberg, Henry. *The Structure of Organizations.* Englewood Cliffs, N. J.: Prentice-Hall, 1979.

Murrin, Kathleen L. "Laying the Ground Work; Issues Facing Rural Primary Care." p. 19 in *Management of Rural Primary Care—Concepts and Cases,* ed. G. E. Bisbee, Jr. Chicago, Hospital Research and Educational Trust, 1982.

National Planning Association, Robert Wood Johnson Foundation Community Hospital—Medical Staff Sponsored Primary Care Group Practice Program, Washington, D.C., 1974, p. 5.

Nicoll, D. R. "Paradigm Reframing," pp. 1–7. *OD—Practitioner* 11, 1979.

Pennings, Johannes M. "Organizational Birth Frequencies; An Empirical Investigation," pp. 120–44. *Administrative Science Quarterly* 27, 1982.

Peters, T. J., and R. H. Waterman, Jr. *In Search of Excellence: Lessons from America's Best-Run Companies.* New York: McGraw-Hill, 1982.

Pfeffer, Jeffrey, and Gerald R. Salancik. *The External Control of Organizations; A Resource-Dependent Framework.* New York: Harper & Row, 1978.

Porter, M. E. *Competitive Strategy: Techniques for Analyzing Industries and Competitors.* New York: Free Press, 1980.

Shortell, Stephen M.; Thomas M. Wickizer; and John R. C. Wheeler. *Hospital-Physician Joint Ventures: Results and Lessons from a National Demonstration.* Ann Arbor, Mich.: Health Administration Press, 1984.

Starkweather, D. *Hospital Mergers in the Making.* Ann Arbor, Mich.: Health Administration Press, 1981.

Tichy, Noel M. "Problem Cycles in Organizations and the Management of Change," pp. 164–83. In *The Organizational Life Cycle,* ed. J. Kimberly and R. H. Miles. San Francisco, Jossey-Bass, 1980.

Weick, Karl E. "Educational Organizations as Loosely Coupled Systems," pp. 1–19. *Administrative Science Quarterly* 21, 1976.

Whyte, W. F. "Social Inventions for Solving Human Problems," pp. 1–13. *American Sociological Review* 47, February 1982.

Williamson, Oliver E. *Markets and Hierarchy; Analysis and Antitrust Implications.* New York: Free Press, 1975, p. 82.

Zaltman, Gerald; Robert Duncan; and John Holbek. *Innovations and Organizations.* New York: John Wiley & Sons, 1973.

# 8

A delete design model for
successful transitions

Stuart Albert
*School of Management*
*University of Minnesota*

## A DELETE DESIGN MODEL FOR SUCCESSFUL TRANSITIONS

Peters and Waterman in *In Search of Excellence* (1982) define the future organization as a hybrid that addresses three prime needs: a need for efficiency around the basics, a need for innovation, and a need to avoid calcification by being able to break the habits of the past. The latter, which includes: (1) a "willingness to regularly 'hive off' new divisions as old divisions get big and bureaucratic; (2) a willingness to shift products or product lines among divisions . . . ; (3) a willingness to take the top talent and bring it together on project teams . . . always with the notion that such accommodation is temporary; and (4) a generic willingness to reorganize and reshuffle the boxes . . . as needs arise" (p. 317), defines the problem of delete design, specifically, how to create flexibility and needed change[1] by regularly terminating the old (and sometimes replacing it with something new). The most biologically apt metaphor is how an organization can shed it's outworn habits and structure and so revitalize itself.

The past is not easily shed, however, and often organizations and the individuals within them fail in their attempt to do so. Indeed, the problems of creating change and transition are legion. Consider several examples:

---

[1] I use the term *design* to signify an interest in planned or intentional change.

1.   Philip Selznick in *Leadership and Administration* (1957), recounts a classic case of an organization unable to change its culture. Gar Wood, a manufacturer of high-quality boats, decided to mass-produce a low-cost speedboat, but production and sales alike couldn't alter their preoccupation with top-quality craftmanship. As Selznick indicates, "Members of the selling staff . . . could not shift emphasis from 'snob appeal' to price appeal. The quality commitment was so strong that an entirely new division—operating in a separate plant hundreds of miles away and therefore recruited from a different labor market—had to be created to do the job successfully" (pp. 54–55). In short, the old culture could not be changed.

2.   The case of the schizophrenic company. A manufacturing plant responded to the efforts of a new manager who tried to introduce Japanese-style participative management by neatly dividing itself into two halves: the older workers on the night shift who resisted and retained a more hierarchical structure, and the younger workers on the day shift who adopted a participatory style. The resulting schizophrenic existence ultimately proved so stressful that the manager lost his job and the company reverted back to its original style and structure.

In these examples, old ways could not be relinquished. It is common to think of these situations as ones in which people are threatened by something new, that they resist change. The delete design model will give us a new way of thinking about such occasions. It will, in some instances, suggest new tools for dealing with them.

Before we present the delete design model it is useful to locate it within a broader context that will define its growing significance.

At a very general level all efforts to produce change can be classified into one of three models (Albert, 1980a): add design in which change is introduced by the addition of new elements; delete design in which change is produced by the elimination or deletion of old elements; and replacement design or redesign,[2] in which change is accomplished by the conjunction of deletion and addition. The distinction between add design and delete is, of course, an analytic one. Most change is a composite of both processes occurring simultaneously, one sometimes leading and at other times lagging the other.

The model of add design, that of change by the addition of new elements, presupposes the existence of new and/or unused resources and a place to deploy them. The add design model is one of growth and expansion. Its roots are buried deep in the concept of a frontier, in the seemingly endless possibility of establishing new social, economic, organizational, and political forms on previously uninhabited or sparsely inhabited territory. Add design is the model of the New World.

As the environment becomes filled, however, when opportunity for growth and expansion becomes increasingly limited, change and renewal

---

[2]I am indebted to David Whetten for this phrase and for the insight that most design problems are more properly considered problems of redesign.

become possible only with a shift to a model of change by replacement, a model which requires delete design. It is not surprising that we have avoided seeing this shift for as long as possible, for the process of deletion is a painful and difficult one. Persons, groups, organizations must be disenfranchized. Processes of detachment, decommitment, deinstitutionalization must be effected. Questions of loss and justice surface. Problems previously solvable by a better information technology become replaced by dilemmas (Aram, 1976) that are not in principle solvable at all. For this reason, as well as others, organizations, nations, and individuals seek growth, the discovery of new resources, and the exploration of new frontiers. The possibility of change becomes bounded, not by the limits of man's rationality or imagination or by his inability to envision a future, but by his simple inability to extricate himself from his own past.

Over the last 200 years we have clearly witnessed a shift from add design to replacement design. Indeed, what is commonly unrecognized in the current widespread interest in innovation is that, in a world of finite resources, innovation is made possible only by dismantling old forms, by a redeployment of time and attention; in short, by delete design.

The link between innovation and the prior requirement of delete design is often lost, however, because although resources used for innovation come from somewhere, it is often difficult to tell where. An individual may withdraw resources (such as commitment and attention) in small amounts from many projects over a long period of time until something like a critical mass is assembled, sufficient to launch a new effort. Because the acts of deletion are dispersed among many objects and displaced in time, the link between cause and effect tends to be lost and innovation as a means of change tends to be treated as if it were a problem of add design when in many cases it is a problem of replacement design. As Biggart (1977, p. 410) stated:

> It is not generally recognized that change is an act of destruction as much as creation. Because most organizations do change slowly, experimenting with and selectively incorporating new forms, the destruction of old forms and methods is relatively obscured. But the destructive process must either precede or exist simultaneously with the creator. This act of undoing and dismantling is important theoretically; reorganization presumes the rejection or supercession of old methods in favor of the new and the organization must systematically destroy the former, competing structures.

Indeed, the more radical the change to be instituted, the more the past must be not only diminished but obliterated. As Winston Smith, in George Orwell's *1984*, comments:

> Do you realize that the past, starting from yesterday, has been actually abolished? If it survives anywhere it's in a few solid objects with no words attached to them, like that lump of glass there. Already we know almost literally nothing about the Revolution and the years before the Revolution. Every record has been destroyed or falsified, every book has been rewritten, every picture has been repainted, every statue and street and building has been re-

named, every date has been altered. And that process is continuing day by day and minute by minute. History has stopped. Nothing exists except an endless present in which the Party is always right. (p. 128)

The intent of this chapter is to develop four processes of delete design within organizations. The model of delete design that will be presented is useful both for the strategic choice (Child, 1972) and environmental adaptation points of view (Hannan and Freeman, 1978; Aldrich, 1979). The model will help both individuals and organizations plan for transition by identifying the processes that are involved in the production of smooth transitions. The delete design model will also help an organization that has experienced change, perhaps even discontinuous and revolutionary change, retrospectively construct whatever degree of transition is possible. Thus, the model has both prospective and retrospective uses.

## ORIGINS

The delete design model is not the inductive generalization of a well-defined and established body of data, nor is it designed with a particular transition in mind, nor does it present a case study, nor does it integrate, summarize, extend, quantify, or amend a previous tradition of research within organizational theory. Moreover, the set of processes comprising the model cuts across different categories of phenonema. For example, the model talks about retirement and culture change in the same breath. In doing so, it does not claim that these two phenomena are identical, merely that it is useful to entertain the notion that, in respect to problems of deletion, each may function in similar ways. Our aim, in fact, is to motivate the exploration of the model in as many diverse settings as possible. This motivation is congruent with its origin as an abstraction from diverse sites within organizational life. Thus, the model to be presented has no proper lineage. It is more a mongrel than a pure breed. The test, however, is not its ancestry, but the kind of work it can perform.

## THE DELETE DESIGN MODEL

The delete design model consists of a set of four processes:

I. A summary process (Albert, 1976, 1978, 1983) in which all important aspects of the past are evoked and summarized.
II. A process of justification (Albert, 1976, 1978, 1983) in which the grounds for termination are stated and defined.
III. A continuity process (Albert, 1976, 1978, 1983) in which a link is discovered or invented between past and future.
IV. A process we label $\Delta C$, a momentary increase in attachment for a project, idea, objective, etc., akin to a eulogy before the fact, in which the value of that which will be lost is celebrated in order to create the possibility of closure.

We now consider each process, stating its contribution to the termination of a past event and to the construction of a sense of closure.

## I. The process of summarization

A summary is defined as an abbreviated statement of the history of an event, occasion, project, etc. More specifically, it is the selective repetition of aspects derived from the history of the event presented in a condensed and symbolic form.

A summary may be explicit, formal, public, or it may be implicit, informal, private. It may be the product of individual or collective effort. It may be specifically motivated by a task that seems to require it, such as the compilation of data for a financial report, or it may be the by-product of other activities. Within an organizational context, one can think of a large number of sites where summaries are constructed and presented. For example, summaries occur as a result of the task of formulating an annual report, which is itself a summary. Summaries of past performance are almost always explicit parts of all planning documents. Names of organizations and companies are symbolic summary statements of a claimed identity. Organizational name changes almost always initiate and are initiated by summary statements of what and who the organization is and would like to be. Summary statements of corporate culture and identity are always implicit, if not explicit, in most training programs designed to socialize newcomers into the organization. At the individual level, summaries naturally occur as part of the performance appraisal process, as part of retirement dinners, as well as in the comments made to friends and family at the end of each day.

An examination of the times and sites of summarization suggests the thesis that summaries reflect points of change and transition. The core proposition of the delete design model is that summarization may create as well as reflect a sense of closure. One reason[3] is that a summary assembles considerable information in one place. The familiar adage that one can't know where one is going unless one knows where one has been is apt. Summaries locate and contextualize experience at the same time that they abstract its essential themes. In doing so they provide a launching pad for future action.

**Criteria of a successful delete design summary.**   One criterion of a successful summary as a closure-constructing device is that it somehow states the essence of that which it will terminate. How such a summary is to be arrived at is, at the present time, more art than science. A summary, at least an adequate one, is constructed according to an explicit or implicit theory about what is important. Moreover, a summary of something important is almost never constructed in one sustained burst of cognitive reflection but

---

[3]See Albert (1976, 1978, and 1983) for a more complete discussion of why a process of summarization may lead to a sense of closure.

rather is an on-going and incremental process of trial and error, judgment and reflection. If the object to be terminated is an entire organization, a theory of the organization as a whole is necessary to guide the summary process to what is essential. For this purpose there are innumerable conceptions of organizational life that provide guidelines about what is important. In fact, all measurement instruments are implicit theories about what is important (see Van de Ven and Ferry, 1980, etc.).

Another criterion of a successful delete design summary is that the summary be complete, that it not lead to the conclusion that something important has been left out. There are a number of ways to ensure completeness. For example, the adversary proceeding of the law court is an instance of a mechanism that is employed to ensure that all the facts of the case are present before a judgment is made, in short, that the summations of both sides form a whole without a gap. A similar device can be utilized to ensure the completeness of a summary intended to serve a delete design function, namely, to use those who fear the loss of the status quo to summarize its full meaning and significance. The danger, of course, is that in an adversary proceeding between those who favor change and those who do not, truth is more likely to be victim than victor. Historically, when extremely important matters are to be summarized, outside observers pledged to uphold and state the complete truth are almost always needed. Indeed, the construction of a complete and truthful summary is an important function of many professions, for example, auditor, journalist, historian.

A third determinant of whether a summary will create a sense of closure has to do with whether it is positive or negative. An extremely positive summary may create the illusion or correct perception that a goal has been reached, thereby creating the possibility of closure. On the other hand, an extremely negative summary may create grounds for the rejection of a course of action as impossible. A mixed or neutral summary provides the least impetus towards closure. These three propositions are, of course, open to test.

A fourth criterion of a successful delete design summary is that it highlight the distinction between means and ends, between enduring and desirable values and the instruments to achieve them. A summary that makes this distinction provides the groundwork for the claim that, while a specific object may be terminated, the values it stood for will not be, a claim which, if accepted, makes termination easier. We will take up this issue again when the continuity process is discussed.

A fifth characteristic of a successful delete design summary is the extent to which the summary makes the case, in so far as the facts allow, that the causes of past success are restricted to unique and transitory conditions. To the extent that this proposition can be supported, the possibility of terminating present activity is not only raised but also perhaps seen as inevitable.

Summaries differ both in the extent to which they make statements of causal attribution, and in the extent to which they assemble evidence that could be used for such purposes. Consider a concrete illustration. If a summary establishes that the past success of a company was due to a particular chief executive officer, then his departure calls into question the continued viability of the enterprise, i.e., it raises the issue of closure. What weight should be given to different antecedents of success and failure is an extremely difficult judgment to make and requires scientific procedures of inference and evidence that are rarely present. Because they are not, a historical summary of success or failure is more a political document in favor of or opposed to the continuation of the status quo than a scientific document. Writing history that includes on-going events is therefore a dangerous occupation at the organizational level for a certain kind of history may create the past as well as record it.

Sixth, to achieve a sense of psychological closure, regardless of the facts of any situation, whether it is really over or not, the summary of such an occasion must be a human document. It must tell a story of success and failure, of hopes and dreams, and of disappointments. It must do justice to the nature and intensity of the emotions involved. Just as no incomplete financial statement can be accepted, so no summary of the human involvements in an enterprise can create a sense of closure without expressing all that was emotionally as well as cognitively significant.

Finally, to be effective as a closure-creating device, a summary of any organizational event must be constructed on multiple levels, and/or there must be multiple summaries constructed, at least one for each level of analysis. For example, consider the termination of a project. Summaries of the project might be constructed at the individual, group, and organizational levels, each level providing a history of its involvement in the project. Some of these summaries would be individual efforts, others would be the result of a group effort. Of the summaries that result, no one is likely to encompass the truth, nor is agreement necessary or even desirable among competent summaries of the same set of affairs. Some sort of integrative mechanism might be set up to synthesize multiple summaries of an event, or the summaries might simply be left as separate documents. What is most important, however, is that, for a summary to maximally contribute to creating the possibility of closure, it must surface *all* of the factors that bind the organization to its present course, some of which may be subtle, and hence difficult to grasp, some of which may be unpleasant or private. It is in the service of this need for completeness that multiple summaries become useful.

In a sense, the prescriptive implication of the summary as a delete design process is that a flexible organization should adopt a procedure analogous to that of a newspaper and compile and constantly update obituaries of important projects, complete with eulogies, in order to maintain the possibility that closure, once needed, will not be delayed.

**Practical matters.**    How can the foregoing discussion be put to use? The following steps provide a rough guide.

1. Conduct an organizational inventory of summaries, noting the nature of each summary and the occasion on which it occurs. The previous discussion suggests some things to look for, such as completeness, etc.

2. Determine how each occasion of summarization could be expanded, made more complete, and how additional summaries might be evoked, commissioned, constructed. There are a large number of ways the number and kinds of summaries within an organization can be expanded. For example:

   a. Ask three historians of different persuasions to write a corporate or organizational history. Make no attempt to reconcile the different portraits that emerge; leaving them discrepant will provoke exactly the kinds of discussions that are valuable.

   b. Invite a research group to study the organization as a means of holding up a mirror to the organization.

   c. Ask persons about to retire to write a history of those things within the organization that are unseen but valuable, and put the work on display.

   d. Run a metaphor contest in the organization's newsletter: In what ways is this organization like: a religion, an army, a family, etc?

   e. In the Gar Wood case mentioned in the Introduction, a summary might consist of a Quality Museum to which each craftsman would contribute. The museum would attempt to record everything that was of quality, the final product, the tools employed, the care and precision of their use, etc.

3. Knowing where summaries take place within the organization and knowing how they might be expanded, now allows the analyst to consider whether in a specific case intensifying and expanding the process of summarization might plausibly lead to a greater sense of closure.

## II. The process of justification

Change and transition must be justified by reference to either internal or external factors (the task is over, the goal accomplished, so the task force can disband; or, there is an urgent need for personnel to help with project X which is more important than the one we are working on, and so we will disband, even though we aren't quite done yet). One must justify the nature and magnitude of the change to be initiated as well as the reason for initiating it now. The latter is often especially difficult if the general situation for the business or organization is deteriorating slowly rather than precipitiously. I call the classic formulation of this problem the Frog's Dilemma. Imagine a bucket of boiling water. A frog dropped into this bucket will surely try to jump right out. Consider a second bucket of cool water. Place a frog in this bucket and turn on the stove. As the water gets hotter, the frog begins to think, "Maybe I should jump out." But why now, he thinks. It is after all only a degree hotter than a second ago and the moment to jump didn't seem right then. Besides, maybe the future will bring cooler water.

With the slow incremental rise in temperature, right up to the boiling point, the frog remains in the bucket, and becomes frog's legs.

Just as it is absolutely obvious that change and transition require justification, similarly it is not so obvious how to deal with the Frog's Dilemma. The chief executive officer of a large manufacturing company is dealing with a common variant of this problem. Brought on board (actually promoted within the company) to affect a turnaround, the issue he faces as the economy and the company improve is how to retain the special commitment of the employees that was motivated by the crises. A task force within the company has been given the job of coming up with "a new banner that people can march to." Having had the advantage of a precipitious crisis, the chief executive officer faces the problem of how to maintain and create change as its justification slips away.

Because the process of justifying change is not always simple, I include it as part of the model. In incremental situations, action often awaits some external discontinuity that can serve as a justification for it.

### III. The continuity process

The third process of the delete design model is the search for continuity between events, ventures, or strategies, etc., that are being terminated and new ones that are beginning. The discovery of continuity creates the possibility of transition since it provides a link between past and future, a link that may blunt the force of revolutionary change.

An appreciation of the crucial role that the discovery of continuity can play in a delete design process can be obtained if we consider Selznick's process of institutionalization (Selznick, 1957). Selznick states that to "institutionalize is to infuse with value beyond the technical requirements of the task at hand" (p. 17), the test of which is expendability. That is "if an organization is merely an instrument, it will be readily altered or cast aside when a more efficient tool becomes available. . . . When value infusion takes place, however, there is a resistance to change. People feel a sense of personal loss; the "identity" of the group or community seems somehow to be violated; they bow to economic or technological considerations only reluctantly, with regret" (pp. 18–19). The problem of delete design confronts this problem directly. How is something that has been infused with value to be terminated? The most successful procedure is if the value is not terminated, but merely expressed in another location. The continuity process— or more accurately, the process of locating a dimension of continuity—is one part of the solution to the problem of deinstitutionalization, which is to locate another domain, product, or set of activities that allows the organization to preserve the values represented by the demise of the old product or project.

Continuity can take many forms. In his chapter on the crises at Antioch, Warren reports that Birenbaum was effective in part because he restated the Antioch themes—the connection between work and a liberal education, the need to provide an education to those who have been bypassed, disenfranchised, or left behind in America, etc., thus providing important evidence that the "new" and surviving Antioch would continue what was of value to the "old" Antioch.

Shortell, in his chapter on vertical integration, indicates how a single person can create a bridge between the old and the new when he points out how a respected older physician from the hospital's own medical staff defused opposition to the new unit when he was appointed as medical director of the ambulatory primary care unit which was being created. In terms of our own analysis, what is critical is that the new group practice be perceived as an instance of add design as a way to "serve the underserved, expand the hospital's market base . . . or develop an additional site for teaching residents," rather than be perceived as an instance of replacement or delete design. High demand for the services of the new unit is of course necessary to sustain the claim of add design, but it is by no means sufficient.

In general, there is no simple procedure for locating a dimension of continuity or for establishing its importance. A very complete and extensive summary may prove a useful way of locating potential sources of continuity. Closure, however, is determined more on the basis of the promise of continuity than on the fact of continuity which, after all, can be established with certainty only after a transition has taken place. What matters is the degree to which the promise of continuity can be believed in those cases in which it seems to be necessary.

**Practical matters.**   As a practical matter there are at least two roles, that of explorer and that of learner, which can be of use in most situations. What is constant in these roles is that the person who accepts and occupies them takes pleasure in approaching the unknown. The unknown becomes related, annexed, and assimilated to what is known. Regardless of what changes, the person's orientation to change remains constant. As Oppenheimer is reported to have said, "Change is the only constant." The organizational task, then, is to create, legitimize, sanction, and provide occasions for the performance of the informal or formal roles of explorer and learner.

Consider a related device, a formally defined transition role. When individuals change jobs within a company we often expect them to make the transition abruptly. To create continuity we might slow down this process and create a time when a person holds two job titles simultaneously, at the same time that we ask him to perform only his new job, thereby recognizing that a transition is necessary. Special performance appraisal devices could be created for such times in which the person is evaluated according to how well he masters the challenge and tasks of transition, one of which might be to state the dimensions of continuity and discontinuity between the new and old jobs. A variation would be to let the person determine when after a given length of time, such as six months, he wished to relinquish his old title. Some, embracing the Spanish tradition, may wish to retain a string of past job titles as a reminder of their genealogy.

Consider how continuity might be established in the Gar Wood case.

The craftsman's view of himself was linked to the production of a quality product. One way to create continuity is to enlarge the craftsman's self-conception, to have him become a craftsman-manager, where the new product being produced is a quality business. In short, quality would continue, but its origin would shift. For each craftsman to become linked to a new definition of quality might require a profit-sharing plan and other trappings and symbols of management, being paid every two weeks, etc. The conceptual tools of the manager would be added to the physical tools of the craftsman at least in some small way that would allow him to appreciate what quality market research and financial analysis involves.

To the extent that such a redefinition of role could be achieved for all the craftsmen en masse, one would have a potential source of continuity. Of course, it is possible that craftsmen want to remain craftsmen and not craftsman-managers, in which case the technique may simply fail.

IV.  The $\Delta C$ process: An increase in the strength of the bond to objects of future loss

It is well known that in almost all societies transitions are marked by ritual (Van Gennep, 1928/60). It is probably no accident that this is the case, for ritual from a sociological and psychological perspective is a societally evolved formula for dealing with the uncertainty and stress that are part of all occasions of real change: birth, death, marriage, etc. Our thesis is that we can find within rituals of transition some of the most powerful organizational processes for managing change in nonritual contexts. In the present example we abstract a process that we label $\Delta C$ from the ritual format of a retirement dinner. Our attempt is not to analyze all the features of such an occasion, but merely to abstract one core feature, remove it from its ritual context, and demonstrate how it may function in other settings as a device for creating closure.

If we think of a retirement dinner for a chief executive officer, one feature we note is the exchange of real and simulated praise. The company says how much it valued the work of the person leaving, and the person, how much he valued working for the company. The purpose of a retirement dinner is to honor the person for his service to the company by means of a public ceremony that creates and celebrates a positive bond between the individual and the organization he or she is leaving. The inducements-contributions balance (March and Simon, 1958), the basis of prior association, is panegyrically transformed into a contributions-contributions balance, which is now presented as the defining and enduring relationship between individual and organization.

One way to conceptualize the exchange of praise within the ritual format of a retirement dinner and indeed the place of the dinner itself within the history of association between individual and organization is in terms of what I call a temporal cohesiveness function (Albert, 1980a, 1980b, 1983), shown in Figure 8–1 on the following page.

**FIGURE 8-1**     Temporal Cohesiveness Functions

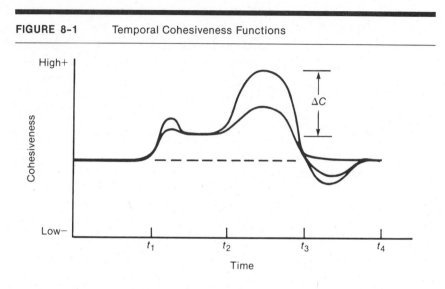

A temporal cohesiveness function is a plot over time of the degree to which the organization and the individual publicly express mutual liking, attraction, commitment, and cohesiveness. (For the purpose of developing this notion here we will treat these terms interchangeably. In other contexts and for other purposes they are, of course, distinct. When the model presented here is applied to a specific domain and measurement is both desirable and necessary, discussion of the different implications of each term is necessary.)

Assuming that there is some baseline level of attraction between individual and organization, then what we commonly observe during the ritual leave-taking of a retirement ceremony (as well as during the nonceremonial occasions associated with leave-taking) is an increase in the expressed degree of mutual cohesiveness, liking, and attraction between the individual who is leaving and those who will be left. This is illustrated by the rise in the curve at $t_1$. (The temporal cohesiveness function is also drawn so as to represent the exchange of mutual praise that typically accompanies the beginning of a relationship in which the individual and the organization both express how pleased they are to be entering into an association.)

The delete design model proposes that the magnitude of $\Delta C$ is given by the following functional equations:

$$\Delta C = f(W, N, O)$$
$$W = f(R, I)$$
$$N = f(D, V)$$
$$O = 1 \text{ or } 0$$

We will illustrate these equations within the context of a retirement dinner and then show how the terms in the equations apply more generally.

The magnitude of $\Delta C$ depends on whether it is warranted ($W$), held to be necessary ($N$), and whether opportunity ($O$) permits its expression. Whether it is warranted depends principally on the affective nature of the relationship between the individual and the organization, as well as on their degree of involvement ($I$).

If an individual is only peripherally a member of an organization, or a member for only a very brief time, an elaborate retirement dinner is unlikely. The individual must have a positive relationship[4] of some involvement with the organization to warrant a public expression of mutual affection during leave-taking. Thus, friends may embrace before a lengthy journey that will separate them, while strangers, whose relationship does not warrant that degree of heightened affection, will not. The term ($I$) can be best developed by analogy from the interpersonal case. Peter Marris (1974) comments that the "intensity of grief (as felt by the individual in mourning) is related to the intensity of involvement, rather than of love" (p. 33). I believe that the same is true for the separation of a person from a task, a group, an objective, an ideal, etc. and that this is true at the collective or organizational level as well. The difficulty of separation depends not only on whether the object of attachment was rewarding or pleasant, but on whether it was one of intense and prolonged involvement. High involvement is often, indeed hopefully, correlated with high reward, yet the force of Marris' observation is that we may expect separation to be difficult even when the object of separation is not a source of great reward. For this reason we include the term ($I$) as distinct from ($R$).

Whether an increase in cohesiveness is necessary ($N$) depends both on the expected duration of the separation ($D$) and how vulnerable ($V$) each party will be once separated. In the case of a retiring chief executive officer, the expected duration is infinite since the separation is usually intended to be permanent. To the extent that the chief executive officer was a key member of the organization, the organization might feel itself somewhat vulnerable without his leadership, as indeed the individual might feel somewhat diminished without his institutional affiliation, staff, identity, etc.

Thus, we expect retirement dinners to occur only if it is both warranted and necessary, and of course, if there is opportunity. (An organization may be so overwhelmed by crises that it cannot muster the time and energy to create a ceremony, or the individual may die before leaving the organization.) If an expression of $\Delta C$ is warranted (the person had a positive and significant association with the organization), but held to be unnecessary (the person is merely going on vacation), it will not occur. If it is perceived to be necessary (the person is leaving forever), but unwarranted (the person was only part-time or had been fired for poor performance, for example), then $\Delta C$ would also not occur.

---

[4]We will treat only the case in which $R$ is positive. If $R$ is negative, as might be the case at the individual level were the person to be fired after a fight with his boss, this would be indicated by a dip in the curve which would be the inverse of $C$. To state the general case, the probability of closure is a direct function of [$\Delta C$].

Thus, as shown in Table 8-1, the magnitude of $\Delta C$ is hypothesized to be a multiplicative function of whether it is warranted and whether it is held necessary, and is therefore expected to occur in only one cell of the table.

Thus, resistance to change will occur when an object of great and positive attachment is being relinquished forever, the absence of which raises a threat to the surviving organization. The delete design model proposes that when the expression of $\Delta C$ is substantially greater or less than that called for by $W \times N$, a smooth and successful transition will not occur.

The terms of these equations can be illustrated in other settings. Consider a firm that is re-evaluating its current business strategy. A plan for change that provides only economic justification for terminating an old activity will, if Selznick is correct, fail because it does not recognize that the past strategy may well be prized in excess of its value as an instrument of rational economic policy. The model of delete design proposes that successful transition will be facilitated to the extent that the organization can state and honor the deep and diverse sources of value that sustain its commitment to the old strategy, particularly if it can find sources of continuity so that cherished values can find expression in new projects.

The process of $\Delta C$ has a visibility function. It is a way of surfacing value commitments that have become attached to old projects, commitments that act to defend the status quo from change, but commitments that cannot always be seen or stated. For example, a project may have resulted in a bonus that was spent on a vacation that was particularly memorable. To terminate the project without the individuals involved giving at least private expression to those things for which it was the instrument is to fail to give an adequate summary of the history of the project.

$\Delta C$ as a celebration of past achievement provides evidence that whatever sacrifices were necessary to engage in instrumental activity (and to forego instrinsic or more immediate rewards) were warranted, not merely by the prospect but by the fact of future rewards. An organization that does not ade-

---

**TABLE 8-1**  The predicted magnitude of $\Delta C$ as a function of whether it is warranted and necessary

|  |  | Necessary | |
|---|---|:---:|:---:|
|  |  | No | Yes |
| Warranted | No | $\Delta C = 0$ | $\Delta C = 0$ |
|  | Yes | $\Delta C = 0$ | $\Delta C >> 0$ |

quately celebrate its victories will soon lose the will to pursue them, for organizations need to continually validate the purposefulness of sacrifice if they expect to command it.

One of the reasons $\Delta C$ as a process is interesting is that it appears to contradict a very common formulation of change—Lewin's three processes: unfreezing, a process of weakening an individual's attachment to his current position; movement to a new position; and the refreezing (Lewin, 1951; Schein and Bennis, 1965). $\Delta C$ proposes, in Orwellian fashion, that one way to weaken attachment is to momentarily and intensely strengthen it, much as a hug prepares the way for separation. There will no doubt be occasions when change is best instigated by attempting to directly weaken ties to the past, and other occasions when a momentary strengthening is best, and still others when some combination is desirable. This problem has not been investigated, largely, I suspect, because an alternative to Lewin has not been clearly stated. As a first approximation, one could state that unfreezing may be the technique of choice when the change agent has sufficient power to actually remove the individual physically and psychologically from the conditions that sustain his current belief and practice. When this is not possible, $\Delta C$ might be appropriate. In any case, unfreezing and $\Delta C$ appear to have opposite assets and liabilities. $\Delta C$ is unlikely to be resisted, as might be the case for direct unfreezing, but its enactment risks strengthening rather than weakening an individual's attachment to the past. This is quite unlikely in the case of unfreezing which, at worst, leaves things as they are.

**Practical matters.**     How might the notion of $\Delta C$ be applied in a concrete case? Consider the example of the engineer who is finding it difficult to make the transition to manager, an example we mentioned at the beginning of this chapter. The person leaving engineering might be given the task of defining a new prize for engineering, recognizing some special kind of excellence that is unique to engineering and distinct from management and which is not now given recognition, a prize that might bear his name, and which he would award. In this way the person is given the opportunity to identify and praise what was of personal value but which is no longer part of his job. His past has been given a proper eulogy.

**The paradox of delete design and the problem of reattachment.**     A flexible organization is not only one that is prepared to terminate involvement when necessary, but one that is capable of reactivating involvement once it has been suspended. There are few studies of how this process can be managed well in organizational life, for return is usually taken as a commentary on the original decision, namely, that it was an error, and/or that the individual or enterprise lacks consistent purpose, and hence strength. For a firm to reacquire a firm similar to the one it divested itself of a year ago is relatively unheard of. But in a turbulent environment in which the planning horizon must of necessity fall within the near rather than the distant future, such reversals may make eminent sense. In this section we discuss some of the obstacles to necessary reversal and how they may be managed.

In terms of our illustration of a retirement dinner, the larger the party, the greater the outpouring of affection, the more complete the praise for the chief executive officer's accomplishments, the more generous his retirement bonus, the more that intimacy is made possible by the knowledge that it will not have to be sustained, the more it should prove difficult for the chief executive officer to immediately return to the company and carry on as before. He is functionally in the position of the person for whom a great farewell party was staged only for the person to announce at the end of it— "Thank you very much, but I decided not to go . . . It's so pleasant here, you see." The degree of felt attraction for such a person might well be below baseline as indicated in Figure 8–1 in the period from $t_3$ to $t_4$. Typically, what makes the return of the chief executive officer possible at all is the claim of crises, the detailing of extraordinary circumstances. Formally, I propose that there is a monotonic relationship between the increase in cohesiveness that preceded separation and the depth and duration of what I call the refractory period—that time when the relationship between the individual and the group he has left cannot be restarted without discomfort.

The essential tension or paradox with which we have been dealing can be stated as follows: The more an organization prepares for the possibility of terminating certain commitments, decisions, ventures, tasks, etc., the more it will make difficult a return to those commitments, if necessary. Flexibility in creating the possibility of closure translates into inflexibility in reinstituting the same course of action. An apparent and indeed real solution would be to make termination decisions only after exceedingly careful thought and investigation. But of course it is precisely the public history of care that went into a decision that acts retrospectively to prevent its reversal. As in all dilemmas, the task is not to find a solution, which in principle a dilemma does not have, but the invention of an institutional form that can manage and make the most of its enduring tension.

Note that the argument of the preceding section applies equally to the reversibility of a sense of closure, not merely the reinstitution of something that was eliminated, divested, or terminated. The sense of closure is independent of the fact of termination, although there is normative pressure to have the two be coincident. When something is over, but not felt to be, or when something continues, but feels as if it is over, the individual or group typically experiences a disquieting and disruptive tension. The processes of the delete design model are intended to create both the fact and the sense of closure. However, success in doing so tends to create the conditions that make reversal of either difficult.

## THE DELETE DESIGN MODEL AND THE DOCTRINE OF EMERGENT PROPERTIES

The terms of the model, processes of summarization, justification, the discovery of continuity, $\Delta C$, and the functional equations that prescribe its magnitude and necessity are, in general, orthogonal to the usual distinctions between micro and macro levels of analysis. Summaries, for example, can be of individuals, groups, organizations, networks of organizations, etc. By developing the model in terms of a diverse set of illustrations we do not wish to imply an insensitivity to the doctrine of emergent properties or to the dangers of reductionism, but merely to advance the hypothesis that with respect to the conceptualization of a historical process such as a transition, it may be possible that different levels of analysis bear an essential similarity to each other.

## TWO MANIFESTATIONS OF THE DELETE DESIGN MODEL

Processes of delete design are present throughout a variety of settings and occasions. They occur as part of the planning process, as considerations in decision making, as part of a number of rituals. These processes, however, can be assembled in forms created especially for their enactment as a closure-creating device. We present two: the organizational funeral and the fire drill.

### Organizational funerals

One way to accomplish delete design is simply to perform the deletion without ceremony or fanfare. Work groups may be terminated, objectives may be abandoned with nothing more than a statement that termination is required. There are times, however, when this position simply won't work. Commitment and attachment may have become too great. A process of institutionalization may have taken place. In these cases, the minimalistic position is that separation requires nothing by way of either informal process or formal ceremony. An alternative is the design of a formal ceremony or funeral.

The three processes of the delete design model are, in fact, present in various forms within many funeral rituals in this culture. The individuals assembled at the funeral both constitute, create, and receive summaries of the life of the departed. The summary of the life of the departed, which is created both in public and in private, has the potential for evoking a powerful image of the departed person, and in doing so, presents to public view and private conscience a set of values and unfinished tasks that may be taken up and continued by the survivors. A eulogy ($\Delta C$) celebrates the value of the departed person, an increase in the display of affection that is both warranted and necessary. There are expressions of loss and mourning which also imply great attachment.

The process of eulogy and $\Delta C$ is illustrated in the Sales and Mirvis chapter on the collision of cultures. Soon after the takeover, the top-management group of the acquired company met, as Sales and Mirvis relate, to "grieve" the past and prepare for the future. Moreover, rather than accept loss, top management chose to preserve their own companies' values and to avoid being "steered" by the other company. As pointed out earlier, unless the $\Delta C$

process is handled appropriately, it may reinforce rather than diminish past commitments.

What might a termination ritual look like at the organizational level that would provide both an occasion to praise the achievements of the past and to mourn the loss of those things of value that do not continue? Since formal rewards such as pay are insufficient praise (while they stand for past success, they do not state its basis), one element of the ritual might be to create an oral history that would summarize the meaning and significance of what was being lost, a record that would both record and re-evoke the individual and collective success that was achieved.

Of course, an oral history is merely one vehicle for the operation of delete design processes as an explicit functional equivalent of a funeral eulogy. But whatever ritual form is selected or invented, part of the ritual should conjoin the new with the old. Just as future generations attend the funerals of the old, so the possibility of new products, organizations, ventures, etc. should be present, at least symbolically, at the demise of the old. One practical method for organizations to create something new out of something old is to delete more than is necessary and create something new out of the slack resources that have been generated.

There are, no doubt, other ceremonial occasions to which elements of a ritual funeral can be grafted. A retirement dinner could be held for a project and not a person. Just as divorce rituals have come to be invented within the last several years, so might some form of organizational funeral.

### Serious play: The delete design simulation

Fire drills are different from plans in that they require that people simulate and role-play the activities that would be required were a real fire to break out. Organizations that must plan for catastrophe know the value of behavioral planning, i.e., actual rehearsal, in addition to cognitive planning. The simulation of delete design processes within the organization call for a different set of meetings, agendas, emotions (for example, camaraderie—the suspension of formal authority, etc.). Their behavioral enactment asks individuals to suspend their usual activities and to simulate precisely what might occur were a large piece of their everyday world to be threatened with demise. What would happen if the company were acquired by a firm intent on changing its operating culture and philosophy, for example? The design of a yearly ritual fire drill would establish the organization as one whose virtue was flexibility. One would suspect that the ritual would be surrounded by humor, in part to relieve the seriousness of the issues that were being presented. For example, a fire drill for a university might create the apparatus for declaring financial exigency, complete with outraged editorials, eloquent speeches of questionable relevance, all of which could be performed as theater, perhaps by an internal repertory company. (There is, in fact, an absence of plays that deal with the problems of change and flexibility within large organizations. There is at the same time a vast literature that deals with these issues within the nuclear family.)

## RESISTANCE TO CHANGE: WHICH IS MORE UNKNOWN, THE PAST OR THE FUTURE?

There is a very large literature on the factors that produce resistance to change (see, for example, Zaltman and Duncan, 1977). The delete design model is compatible with many formulations. In some cases it provides an additional perspective, in others an alternative point of view. For example, Staw's lucidly argued theory of the escalation process contains a number of assumptions about the barriers to decommitment (Staw, 1980). If, for example, commitment is not relinquished out of a need to justify the past, then administrative procedures that reduce a sense of personal responsibility for past commitments should be effective decommitment devices. Staw's analysis is a good illustration of the relationship of the delete design model to much of the commitment literature; namely, the model complements existing work by pointing out that separation from past attachments may be difficult because individuals lack a set of exiting processes. In fact, the motivation to justify past behavior may arise out of default, out of the lack of procedures, rules, plans, or techniques for exiting when the motivation to do so is in fact present.

There is, however, a point of view for which the delete design model represents, if not an alternative, then clearly a difference in emphasis.

*Many formulations suggest that change is resisted because the future is unknown, and hence feared.* Consistent with this assumption, change is facilitated to the extent that it can be viewed as a transition, which means that what is new about the future is only gradually revealed. In fact, one of the reasons that planning as an organizational activity continues despite the failure of plans to anticipate the future is that at the moment it occurs, planning renders any hypothetical future less strange. This reduces fear of that future which, from a strictly behavioral conditioning point of view, reinforces the activity of planning. The fact that the plans don't work matters less than that the act of planning itself reduces fear better than any other rationally defensible alternative.

*The delete design model proposes a different source of resistance to change, namely, that the past is unknown.* This may be considered an odd statement until we consider the fact that we often don't know what something meant to us until we lose it. Its relational significance to other parts of our lives was not apparent, but rather implicit, taken for granted, unarticulated. This is the sense in which we mean that the past is unknown; namely, that we do not know the significance of the loss for the rest of the self. For an organization as well as an individual, the test is to know all the significant implications of all possible losses were each loss to occur without replacement.

The present, being yesterday's future, is the site of goals and dreams, the loss of which undercuts the validity of those past activities whose basis derived from their future promise. Given a loss in the present, the question is always how far back and to what matters do the consequences extend. The difference in emphasis supplied by the delete design model is that change may be resisted not merely because the new elements the future will supply are unknown, but because the significance and implications of any present loss are similarly unknown.

## SUMMARY AND CONCLUSIONS

The delete design model consists of a set of four processes. We state each in the form of a prescriptive principle.

Principle I:    *Summarize the past.* A summary is an abbreviated history of the past. If it is to create a sense of closure, it must summarize the meaning as well as the objective facts of the past, the hopes and dreams of the participants as well as their accomplishments. It must be a statement of all that was significant even though ephemeral, intangible, assumed, treating for the moment and for this purpose all significant background and context to past events as if they were foreground. To create a sense of closure a summary of the past need not be true, but if not, it must be a believable fiction.

Principle II:    *Justify a change.* Provide sufficient reason for doing something new. Find a sufficient reason why change is necessary and/or desirable such as the successful attainment of a goal, a clear instance of failure that cannot be reversed by additional resources, or a situation in which there is good reason to believe that success or failure will be perpetually unclear and in which there is a better alternative. Justification must state why *this* change is necessary or desirable, and why it is necessary or desirable *now*.

Principle III:    *Create continuity between the past and the future.* Since revolutionary change will always be resisted, motivate change by the promise that at least some valued elements of the past will be preserved and will continue in the new arrangement. Almost no situation is so dire that the individual would be willing to give up *everything* about it. (See, for example, Glenn Gray's classic, *The Warriors* (1970), for an account of the appeal of battle.)

   *Corollary: Mourn the loss of what does not continue.* It is never sufficient to deal with death by acknowledging its necessity, nor to argue that what has been deleted was not worth having. Some provision must be made to mourn the loss of a valued past. To manage change, one must accept this task or ensure that there are no survivors.

Principle IV:    *Eulogize the past (ΔC).* One cannot leave a valued course of action without acknowledging, giving expression, and celebrating the worth of what is being left. The appropriate image of this principle is that of a parting embrace. Sensitive management of this process is necessary however to ensure that the expression of $\Delta C$ does not reactivate reasons for continuing rather than terminating attachment.

The delete design model contributes to successful change in two senses. The first requirement of successful change is that it happen. The four processes of the delete design model, both individually and collectively, help to create a sense of closure for the past, which in turn makes change possible. Second, to the extent that abrupt change is resisted because of its revolutionary quality, the delete design model suggests how change can be made a transition, a transition which forms a bridge between past and future, and which makes passage between the two both easier and more likely.

As presented, the processes of the delete design model lend themselves to the construction of specific roles, techniques, rituals, etc., but they also define four categories of analysis and commentary that can be used as the logical format for speeches, memos, press releases that both announce and attempt to create change. Albert and Kessler (1978) suggest that there might be a preferred order to the four processes; namely, that they occur in the order I - II - IV - III. A speaker would summarize the past, justify a new direction, praise what was accomplished, and then assert that despite the impending change, important and valued elements of the past would continue. This order preserves a flow from past (summary statements) to future (continuity statements). One practical use of the model, therefore, is that it defines the tasks that need to be engaged as part of the symbolic management of change (Pfeffer, 1981).

*Postscript*:   As a test of the model I wrote the first draft of this chapter without a summary. The editors wrote, "At the end do a summary paragraph about delete design and the management of transitions." Q.E.D.

## REFERENCES

Albert, S. "Dynamics and Paradoxes of the Ending Process." In *On the Endings of Wars*, ed. S. Albert and E. Luck. Port Washington, N.Y.: Kennikat Press, 1980a, chap. 1.

_____. "The Sense of Closure." In *Historical Social Psychology*, ed. K. Gergen and M. Gergen. Hillsdale, N.J.: Lawrence Erlbaum Associates, 1983.

_____. "Towards a Theory of Successful Separation across the Life Cycle." Paper presented at the American Psychological Association Meetings, Montreal, 1980b.

Albert, S.; T. Amgott; M. Krakow; and H. Marcus. "Children's Bedtime Rituals as a Prototype Rite of Safe Passage," pp. 85–105. *Journal of Psychological Anthropology* 2, 1979.

Albert, S., and S. Kessler. "Ending Social Encounters," pp. 541–53. *Journal of Experimental Social Psychology* 14, 1978.

_____. "Processes for Ending Social Encounters: The Conceptual Archaeology of a Temporal Place," pp. 147–70. *Journal of Theory of Social Behavior* 6, 1976.

Aldrich, E. *Organizations and Environments*. Englewood Cliffs, N.J.: Prentice-Hall, 1979.

Aram, John D. *Dilemma of Administrative Behavior*. Englewood Cliffs, N.J.: Prentice-Hall, 1976.

Biggart, N. W. "The Creative-Destructive Process of Organizational Change: The Case of the Post Office," pp. 410–26. *Administrative Science Quarterly* 22, no. 3, 1977.

Child, J. "Organization Structure, Environment and Performance: The Role of Strategic Choice," pp. 1–22. *Sociology* 6, 1972.

Galbraith, J. R. "Designing the Innovating Organization." *Organizational Dynamics*, Winter 1982.

Goodman, P. S. et al. *Change in Organizations*. San Francisco: Jossey-Bass, 1982.

Gray, J. Glenn. *The Warriors: Reflections on Men in Battle*. New York: Harper & Row, 1970.

Hannan, M. T., and J. N. Freeman. "The Population Ecology of Organizations. In *Environments and Organizations: Theoretical and Empirical Perspectives*, ed. M. W. Meyers and Associates. San Francisco: Jossey-Bass, 1978.

Kimberly, J. R. "Initiation, Innovation, and Institutionalization in the Creation Process." In *The Organizational Life Cycle*, ed. J. R. Kimberly and R. H. Miles. San Francisco: Jossey-Bass, 1981.

———. "Managerial Innovation." In *Handbook of Organizational Design*, ed. P. C. Nystrom and W. N. Starbuck. New York: Oxford University Press, 1980.

Lewin, K. *Field Theory in Social Science: Selected Theoretical Papers*. New York: Harper & Row, 1951.

March, J. G., and H. A. Simon. *Organizations*. New York: John Wiley & Sons, 1958.

Marris, P. *Loss and Change*. New York: Pantheon Books, 1974.

Orwell, George. *1984*. New York: New American Library, 1981.

Peters, Thomas J., and Robert H. Waterman, Jr. *In Search of Excellence: Lessons from America's Best-Run Companies*. New York: Harper & Row, 1982.

Pfeffer, J. "Management as Symbolic Action: The Creation and Maintenance of Organizational Paradigms." In *Research in Organizational Behavior*, ed. C. C. Cummings and B. M. Staw. Greenwich, Conn.: JAI Press, 1981.

Schein, E. H., and Bennis, W. *Personal and Organizational Change through Group Methods*. New York: Wiley-Interscience, 1965.

Selznick, P. *Leadership in Administration*. New York: Harper & Row, 1957.

Staw, B. M. "Rationality and Justification in Organizational Life." In *Research in Organizational Behavior*, ed. B. Staw and L. Cummings, Vol. 2. Greenwich, Conn.: JAI Press, 1980.

Van de Ven, A. H. "Early Planning, Implementation and Performance of New Organizations." In *The Organizational Life Cycle*, ed. J. R. Kimberly and R. H. Miles. San Francisco: Jossey-Bass, 1981.

Van de Ven, A. H., and D. L. Ferry. *Measuring and Assessing Organizations*. New York: John Wiley & Sons, 1980.

Van Gennep, A. *The Rites of Passage*. Chicago: The University of Chicago Press, 1960.

Zaltman, G. and R. Duncan. *Strategies for Planned Change*. New York: John Wiley & Sons, 1977.

# PART III

Revitalizing

# 9

## Managing transitions in organizational culture: The case of participative management at Honeywell*

Rosabeth Moss Kanter
*School of Organization and Management,*
*    Department of Sociology*
*Yale University*
*and Goodmeasure, Inc.*

Many large American corporations today are particularly concerned about changing their cultures, based on mounting evidence that more participative, employee-centered cultures benefit both short-term productivity and longer-term potential for innovation and adaptation. But the very idea of culture change in a large organization suggests a difficult, long-term process that can easily become sidetracked, bogged down in contradictions, undercut by residual structures and practices, or confined to rhetoric without corresponding changes in organizational patterns.

Unlike those types of organizational transitions that have both tangibility and clear temporal boundaries (for example, mergers, leadership changes, formal reorganizations, new plant openings), transitions in organizational culture are more difficult to identify with precision because "culture" itself is so elusive. Because this kind of transition lacks identifiable pivotal events corresponding to an "on/off switch" for a new organizational state, but rather consists of subtle shifts in a large number of organizational patterns, it is equally difficult to manage a "culture change" with either certainty of short-term results or clear signs that the transition has indeed occurred. Furthermore, "culture" is an aggregate concept, summarizing numerous events and patterns, combining the behavior and values of numerous actors—and not just reflecting the decisions or official pronouncements of leaders. Leaders, for example, can make the decision to acquire another company and force this transition to occur, at least at the level of formal record, whether or not all actors are prepared, voluntarily, to shift their actions to reflect it; adjustment at the level of norms and behavior patterns comes *after* an organizational "switch" is thrown. But transitions in culture cannot be said to have occurred until the point at which a high proportion of organizational events have occurred independently and which *together* reflect a new pattern of values, norms, and expectations. In short, a few examples of new practices scattered here and there throughout an organization do not represent "culture changes"; they need to be woven into the entire fabric of the system. (Kanter, 1983)

But at the same time, to point to these characteristics of organizational culture does not mean that culture is purely ideational and voluntaristic— dependent on individual attitudes and changes in individual "consciousness." Culture manifests itself through numerous organizational structures; it is made concrete by organizational events. And, thus, it can be managed; it can be shifted by changing concrete aspects of an organization's functioning. For example: *values* do not exist independently of *rewards*; *preferences* do not exist independently of *political signals* from power holders; expectations about *activities* do not exist independently of *action vehicles* or programs permitting the activities.

This chapter uses the establishment of participative management as its example of transition in organizational culture. Through a case study at Honeywell's largest division, it points to some typical problems in attempts by organizations to move to more-participative cultures and then describes an effective set of solutions developed at Honeywell to guide that kind of transition.

The Honeywell case provides an instructive example of the model of organizational culture and strategy change that I set forth in *The Change Masters* (Kanter, 1983). Grass-roots innovations, or local departures from tradition, in the form of new behavior or new programs at middle or lower levels of the organization, begin to accumulate until there are competing models for "how we do things around here." Then, crises or galvanizing events focus management's attention on the need for strategic decisions; often the grass-roots innovations form the basis for an explicit new direction which is now announced and publicized to the organization and managed at the top. To solidify the new direction, prime movers continually push for it, and the change gets reflected in a wide variety of systems and practices which institutionalize it. Along the way, contradictions and problems of implementation must get resolved, and the whole organization must be mobilized for new behavior. These five forces (grass-roots innovations, gal-

vanizing events, strategic decisions, prime movers, and multiple action ve-
hicles/systems changes) were present in the Honeywell case.

## BACKGROUND

Honeywell is one of a number of companies currently recognizing the
value of employee involvement for organizational effectiveness in business
success, as well as responsiveness to what has been described as the "new labor force." For the Aerospace and Defense Units of Honeywell, an interest
in teamwork and participation grew organically out of the technology and
resulting organizational structure as well as deriving from a push by leaders
to be progressive forces in the new work environment. The value of collaboration and teamwork has long been well understood in the aerospace
business, as necessary for pulling together functional specialists to work on
complex projects, and a number of "matrixed" roles, such as program managers, were designed to accommodate this need. These parts of Honeywell
were also early users of Quality Circles, thus developing a history of participative activities somewhat earlier than other major corporations who are
mounting activities in the current business climate.

While the interest in what has come to be called "participative management" or "employee involvement" among top managers in many U.S. corporations has been growing, terms like "participation" and "participative
management" have become buzz words signifying new management fads
sometimes seen to be recklessly pursued by zealous advocates without regard for the costs or consequences. The term participation sometimes con-
jures up unfortunate images, even for supporters, of "voting booths" or "all
decisions by committee" or employee veto power, or disgruntled employees
who use the concept as a club to further batter beleaguered first line supervisors.

Some of the problems are merely definitional, resolved once managers
and employees become clear about the limitations of the concept and the
parameters surrounding its use. For one thing, there is a strong and striking
difference between the meaning of participation in the political arena—the
origin of images of unbridled democracy or voting booths—and increased
employee participation in work organizations. For governments and other
representative bodies, the goal of participation is to secure consent—legiti-
mization for policies that cannot be pursued unless a specified number of
constituents agrees. But in business organizations, the goal of participation
is quite different; it involves mobilizing more people for problem solving in
the interests of task performance. Occasionally employees may gain a larger
voice in policies affecting their own jobs, but tasks and jobs—organizational
outputs—are much more clearly the focus of participative management.
Thus, participation should take its place as one of a number of tools used by
management to ensure organizational effectiveness in the interest of meeting the needs of the business as well as employees.

But a confusion as to the proper meaning and role of participation in an organization's functioning seems to be more common than not at this stage in the development of American corporations.(Kanter, 1983; Stein, 1983; Goodmeasure, 1982) And it is related to a lack of awareness on the part of many managers about how to build participative vehicles into their ongoing operations in an effective and result-producing way. This article builds on my experiences as a consultant to Honeywell's Defense Systems Division in developing a strategy and structure for managing participation. It outlines the typical problems created by a failure to manage participation and illustrates them with examples from the division's early experiences. It then describes how the formation of a top-management steering committee, with a set of strategies and procedures supporting it, has helped make participation not only manageable but also beneficial to both employees and the division. (While I write about this in the third person, my colleagues and I were actively involved in working with the division to shape each step of the process.)

## THE PROBLEM

Even in the best-managed companies, with leadership truly dedicated to making participative management an integral part of the culture, we have noted a tendency to forget the principles of good management when an activity comes under the label of "participation" or "employee involvement." (Kanter, 1983) Participation is too often treated, not as delegation or increased involvement, but as "abdication": managers in effect stepping aside and disclaiming responsibility for the activity or the results. Then the organization is faced with situations like these—all real examples:

1. Participative vehicles such as Quality Circles for hourly employees get elaborate and costly training, but the equivalent task forces for salaried personnel and managers get none, and the people on them begin to express frustration with ineffective meetings and unfocused goals. The managers involved begin to wonder whether participation is just a costly waste of high-priced time.

2. Quality Circles are left to set their own goals, with no information coming from top management about relevant problems of value to the facility. So many of the Circles take on problems that management considers trivial, like the layout of the parking lot. When production pressures increase, facility managers cut down the time the company allows for Circle meetings from an hour a week to an hour a month.

3. Because of turnover of managers, employee task forces established under a former manager to make recommendations on personnel programs have only a vague sense of when to finish or to whom to show their products. One solves this by badgering the general manager for an appointment. Another decides to go to each key executive individually for a meeting and approval—eight in all. Meanwhile, personnel

department specialists have strong, not-yet-voiced, concerns about some of the recommendations and do not plan to take over implementation without a fight.

4. Top management makes clear that it requires more "participative management," which other managers equate with task forces and committees. So at the drop of an issue, no matter how trivial, a task force is formed. Soon the number escalates so much that there is the equivalent of one task force for every five nonexempt employees. But participation is not evenly spread, and some people are so overloaded with task forces that managers begin to resent the whole idea, flipping back to a belief that directive management and individual assignments are better.

5. Every time a new employee problem arises or a zealous manager decides to get some credit for doing something creative for his/her people, a new award or motivation program is put in place. Soon there is a long list of programs in use *somewhere*, but no one really knows who they affect, how much they cost, whether they are worth it, or how to use them elsewhere. There is a piecemeal jumble of activities: a few Quality Circles here, a team-building effort there, a new incentive system somewhere else, a special push to reward excellence in still another area. In addition, there is a tendency to start many more of these activities but to follow through on very few. And some are directly competitive: for example, task forces assigned by different people to overlapping problems.

6. The company makes an elaborate fuss over its employee activities for lower-level workers, and the more publicity these activities get, the more cynical supervisors and middle-level managers become. The managerial work force sees no difference in the demands and constraints on *them*; indeed, they feel vaguely punished and resentful every time there is another exhortation from the top about participation, because many of them feel unrewarded for their efforts anyway, and some of them have been practicing employee-centered management. Then, to cap it all, the same management that has been pushing "participation" plans and executes a reorganization in secret.

7. Meanwhile, most of the Circles and teams and task forces and motivational programs go on without respect to business needs or strategy; nor do the strategy formulators take them into account.

It is important to note that most of these traps do not become clear until employee-involvement activities have been underway for some time; they are issues of "maturity" rather than initiation. Indeed, in the first flush of enthusiasm connected with starting something—for example, forming teams or Quality Circles, running surveys, or listening sessions—companies often forget to consider or plan for the wider-system issues that inevitably come up later, sometimes reflected as "symptoms" such as cynicism, frustration, or disaffection. For Quality Circles, for example, the lull seems to come after about 18 months.

Because it had developed employee-involvement activities earlier than other comparable companies, Honeywell's Defense Systems Division (DSD) encountered a number of management crises around participation before there were very many organizational models at Honeywell—or for that matter, elsewhere in American industry—for planning to avoid them or quickly repair them. Both the problems and the solutions thus provide instructive examples for other companies.

## HISTORY OF "IT" AT DSD

At the time of this writing, DSD was the largest and most profitable division of Honeywell, part of its Aerospace and Defense Group within Honeywell Control Systems. It was composed of three major operations, two based in Minneapolis and one in Seattle, along with a subsidiary acquired in 1982 and a few remote facilities. DSD had begun an active program of Quality Circles in 1978 and thus had already experienced the successes that could come from employee involvement at lower levels. Then division management decided to extend participative opportunities to the salaried work force in 1980.

In 1980 a number of external pressures and challenges facing Honeywell in the Minneapolis area brought managerial attention to questions of quality of work life, especially for technical and administrative employees. The then-general manager, Matt Sutton, developed, in consultation with his staff, seven management principles, to make clear DSD's commitment to a people-centered culture. A chief engineer was given the assignment to serve as project manager for the effort to translate the principles into practice, under the project name, "Managing Today's Work Force." A cross-hierarchical task team was formed for each principle, involving 57 employees in 7 teams making recommendations for steps needed to realize each principle. (Both chairs and members were selected by the project manager.) A member of the employee relations department staff began to work with the project to support the process.

Assessments from each team were compiled by the project manager and staff person in the late fall of 1980, realigned into four major areas of primary employee concern: appraisal, career development, communications, and quality of work life (work environment); these results were reported to the general manager. Many members of the original seven teams were enthusiastic about their participation and wanted to continue to be involved in next steps as four teams were formed in the four major issue areas. At the same time, and somewhat independently, two other task teams had been formed: one on pay (stemming from wider Honeywell directives and the initiative of a DSD employee relations manager), which had largely completed its work of designing a new pay program; and one on equal employment opportunity/affirmative action. Most of the members of the pay team could immediately move on to the closely related performance appraisal team.

Then in January 1981, as the four new teams (involving 47 employees) were getting started, a new general manager (Richard J. Boyle) came on board (see Boyle, 1984), and the project manager returned to his engineering assignment. The logical "home" for "Managing Today's Work Force" seemed to be employee relations, with a loosely attached "advisory committee" of a few key executives. The director of employee relations became project manager, and the teams began their work of making recommendations for short- and long-range action in each issue area.

But six months into the process, several problems were identified, and it was clear that DSD had to develop a better way to manage this form of participation—as well as related questions of organizational strategy and change.

These comments from task team chairs were typical:

> We once went into a meeting with the advisory committee, made a report which I thought was quite good, and at the end everybody just turned to each other and looked blank. Maybe the report was not as good as I thought, but I think something else was wrong. The fact is that it was never clear to members of the advisory committee what, exactly, their authority was. While they were all managers in the division, this whole program had never been worked out carefully enough so that people knew what they were supposed to do in that setting. We simply had no direction at any level. It was not fair to have people go into a room, make a report, and then have the people to whom they were reporting look totally bewildered and blank.

> We had a hell of a time figuring out exactly what it was that we were supposed to be doing. We really got very little help or assistance from the advisory or steering committee. For a long time there was simply no communication. There were no regular meetings scheduled, or specific check points. I think it would have been useful if people knew that at x time they were going to have to have a report. A related problem was that we might make a recommendation or suggestion, but it was never clear that anybody on the advisory committee knew what to do with that. In other words, we might feel that we got something done or accomplished, and nothing would happen.

Among the first-order problems and concerns were those reflecting design and management of the project itself:

1. There was "lip service" from management about supporting the "Managing Today's Work Force" process. The project actually had little in the way of thoughtful strategic or tactical support from top management at DSD. When the advisory committee met it was unclear how it was to operate, what decisions it was supposed to make, or what direction it wanted the effort to take.

2. There was a lack of clear understanding of the ground rules for task teams and their chairs: their roles, the areas in which they could act

autonomously or should seek approval, the extent to which they could communicate directly with the organization or route communications through project "management," and so forth.

3.  The roles of the advisory committee and the project manager were ambiguous. There were questions about who was ultimately in charge, and who authorized what kinds of actions.

4.  The question of accountabilities, standards, timetables, and deadlines for the task teams was largely unresolved. It was not clear who, if anyone, was holding the task teams accountable and how results would be measured. Among other things, accountability would have provided task teams with boundary conditions that would have facilitated their internal deliberations, and it would have provided the division and the participants with methods of evaluation.

5.  Design and development of the project, while extremely well-intentioned, did not include the task teams themselves, and therefore was not modeled on participative management. In consequence, some of the teams mirrored a top-down process. The project was typical of the way many managers view participation: the top telling the middle what to do for the bottom.

6.  There was no clear mechanism for convening new task teams and dissolving them when their work was completed. Was the advisory committee the appropriate body to do this? Procedures were unclear or nonexistent, as was the role of the project. For example, would the effort disappear when these task teams were finished? Was this a one-shot effort?

7.  The project was not connected enough to the whole organization. Relatively few people really saw it or understood it outside of the hundred or so active participants. There was little visibility and considerable skepticism. Line managers wondered if they would ever see results.

A second set of concerns revolved around how the task teams themselves operated:

1.  Some of the task team members and chairs benefited greatly from the "team"-oriented, participative nature of the project, learned to work in groups, and transferred learning from the project to routine operations. This was not true of everyone. Some participants were relatively authoritarian. So others on the team wondered what "participation" really meant.

2.  Some task-team chairs appeared to have strong ownership of their teams' project and occasionally conveyed, to varying degrees, a sense that they would get "their" programs implemented independently of the MTWF project, or that the team members were there to assist them in "their" project. While the chairs' enthusiasm was positive, some of the impact on team members and on the project was not.

3.  Hierarchical or organizationally dependent relationships between task-team members and the chairs probably inhibited task-team mem-

bers from expressing disagreement or contributing fully. It was difficult or impossible in many cases to address and resolve this issue.
4.  In the beginning, task teams appeared to flounder without much di-
    rection or guidance, and this was a source of frustration. It took longer
    than many people found useful to develop a satisfactory mode of oper-
    ating and, hence, several teams took a long time to make progress on
    their tasks. Much of the progress was unfacilitated hit or miss. As one
    chair commented:

> One of the things that I have learned very clearly during this whole thing is
> that the learning process for teams is time-consuming. It is time-consuming in
> ways that are hard to anticipate and understand before you start. It took us a
> long time to collect data about existing pay and increases, how they hap-
> pened, when they happened, and what information people were given about
> them. It also took us some time to collect data about how people felt about all
> that. That was one part of the learning process; a second part was just learn-
> ing to work together and that takes time.

5.  The teams had a tendency to look inward and to "suboptimize"—that
    is, to get so caught up in the intrinsic interest of their task that they for-
    got about the fact that they are supposedly representing the rest of the
    organization and that other parties had a stake in what they were do-
    ing. Further, they didn't take sufficient advantage of the resources/
    wisdom/experience/concerns available in the rest of the organization
    without prodding.
6.  The teams varied greatly in their awareness and knowledge of imple-
    mentation strategies. In some cases, they were consciously aware of
    what it took to "sell" a proposal (although perhaps not as informed
    about implementation itself). In other cases, it was not clear whether
    they had given any thought to these issues.

A third set of concerns revolved around coordination among task teams:

1.  There was no clear mechanism to link task teams directly (other than
    the advisory committee and project manager, which were weak and
    indirect connections) so as to coordinate areas of overlap in their tasks
    and proposals or to communicate items of useful information. Teams
    did not see themselves as part of a larger, coherent effort with a clear,
    shared direction.
2.  Task-team chairs (and, we infer, members) did not evidence much in-
    terest in the activities/progress/experiences/results of other task teams.
    When teams worked on issues that overlapped with matters of concern
    to another team, they became competitive and resented the "intrusion"
    of the other teams on "their" turf.
3.  Task teams did not seem to view each other as resources for the ex-
    change of useful insights about task or process.

Finally, there were questions about the role of the employee relations
function in this process, since the teams were concerned with traditional

personnel matters. While the employee relations director was interim project manager, little else was clear:

1. The role and leadership of employee relations was not particularly visible in this project, and consequently there was a tendency on the part of some task teams to ignore employee relations, to forget that employee relations staff were "pros" in the task-team areas, or to "blame" employee relations for some of the lack of direction in the beginning.

2. It was not clear whether the employee relations members of the teams were identified as special resources. It was not clear whether they should be so identified and play a public role as experts in their groups.

3. The employee relations staff had not clarified (or, at least, communicated with each other) its own hopes and concerns for the project nor defined the appropriate role for employee relations staff in this project as it continued. This was relevant both because of the expertise the employee relations staff represented and because the task-teams' tasks fell within employee relations areas.

## THE FORMATION OF THE "IT" STEERING COMMITTEE

DSD management resisted concluding either that each problem should be addressed piecemeal or that "clearly participation does not work." Both are typical conclusions many American executives would draw when faced with these kinds of issues. For the general manager and other key managers, the clear solution lay in a single major step: putting the process of participation in organizational change under better management control. This step served two purposes: (1) to extract the maximum value from the participative activities already underway and (2) to develop a coherent and guided framework for involving employees in organizational innovations to solve problems and recommend changes as the need arose (Boyle, 1984; Kanter, 1983).

The vehicle for doing this was a top-management steering committee, composed of representatives of all major functions and facilities, chaired personally by the general manager. This steering committee was the executive body for a "parallel organization," in effect, a second, supplementary organization that could bring people together across the hierarchy to solve problems on a temporary ad hoc basis. It would be as though DSD had two organizations: the conventional one represented by the formal organization chart for routine, ongoing operations; and a second, much flatter, more flexible, and continually grouping and regrouping, for the purpose of managing change via increased participation. (Kanter, 1983) The link between the two organizations was the steering committee, whose composition would ensure that concerns of the ongoing operations would be reflected in parallel organization activities, and, in turn, that results of the participative problem-solving teams could be incorporated into ongoing operations.

The steering committee was formed in late summer of 1981 and got underway with a day-long strategic planning meeting in October, which I designed and ran for the top management staff. At this strategy session the group:

1. Received short briefings on the theory behind a parallel organization.
2. Reviewed the seven management principles for continued relevance and wrote a mission statement integrating employee involvement into DSD's business direction.
3. Defined the value that employee involvement would have for the business, for employees, and for managers.
4. Developed objectives for the culture/climate of DSD over the next several years—which made innovation a central consideration.
5. Reviewed for coherence and completeness all of the strategies currently in use at DSD that were related to those objectives—including the "Managing Today's Work Force" task teams, the Quality Circles, and a large number of communication and reward mechanisms.
6. Identified gaps in the current strategies that represented areas for future action.
7. Reached agreements about the composition and operation of the steering committee itself.
8. Defined next steps to keep the process moving toward results.

The steering committee struggled with how to identify the effort they were engaged in, with whether to give it a name. "Managing Today's Work Force" was a limited project, and that name disappeared into the larger, more-encompassing attempt to guide the division toward increased effectiveness, with participation as one tool. The more the committee thought about all the things contributing to their desired new way of working and managing, the less adequate any single phrase seemed. "It" was not simply a productivity improvement program, because attention to employee needs was also important. But neither was it simply quality-of-work-life effort because the company expected bottom-line payoff. Participative management was important, but more as the method for achieving results, than as an end in itself. And none of the phrases in current use captured the ideas of "quality" and "innovation" to the satisfaction of the division's executives. So they decided, somewhat tongue-in-check, to call it IT. And the top-management team guiding this effort is known as the IT Steering Committee.

Division executives were clear that IT was to be a total way of managing the business to generate payoffs for the company, its managers, and its employees. IT would begin with the existing division-wide task teams and gradually extend the number and kind of vehicles managed by the steering committee.

The functioning of the IT steering committee was straightforward. The committee consisted of all of the direct reports of the division general manager, including the vice president of major operations, the controller, the strategic planner, and the personnel director, as well as other key managers responsible for large numbers of people, including the director of engineering, and the location managers of the two major facilities in the Minneapolis area. (Periodically, the steering committee would review its composition for appropriateness, given the issues with which it was dealing.) The committee met monthly, and the vice president of the most distant operation, in Seattle, was connected to the meeting via a speaker phone, so that he and his employee relations director could participate. An agenda for the meeting and advance materials were prepared by the staff to the steering committee, from the Human Resource Development Department, who also made sure that steering committee members were sufficiently informed of all major activities and that task teams were making progress according to their schedules.

Effective staff work meant that monthly meetings could be maximally efficient and that busy executives could indeed put in the time it took to manage this additional set of activities. Longer meetings were scheduled for task-team reports or other special events, like the report of a special study on innovation. In addition, a day-long strategic planning meeting was held about every nine months, to review objectives and progress for the previous period and to set priorities as well as establish teams for the next generations of issues.

Both the composition of the steering committee and its division-wide view of events (bringing in the perspective of every major function as well as the general management concern for the health of the overall business) ensured that there was appropriate integration between employee involvement and business effectiveness. This ideal did not always work perfectly or smoothly, of course, but the steering committee's structure enabled rather rapid adjustments to be made when the two sets of considerations were out of phase.

## RESULTS ONE YEAR LATER

There were a number of concrete results of the IT steering committee's first year of operation, including the products of the first set of task teams which reported to it. When the committee was formed, there was a great deal of concern that participative activities were out of control and not tightly enough focused. In a relatively short time, management was able to reassess these activities, bring them under control, and develop a comprehensive plan for proceeding into the future. The IT steering committee focused on developing a theoretical base for effectively managing participation. At the point at which they had a firm understanding of what it was that they were trying to do and an idea of how to go about accomplishing it, they put in place a series of procedures which guaranteed that these efforts would be brought under control and be tightly focused. They determined how a task team would be proposed, how the proposal would be evaluated, how the actual team would be formed, who would be eligible to lead a team, what kind of resources would be available to task teams, how the team would report to the steering committee, and, perhaps most important, how a task team would be brought to a close. They also directed a number of other policy reviews and activities oriented toward improving innovation.

Other accomplishments are less tangible. The first is the increased capacity, spirit, and enthusiasm that appear to have been generated by these activities. Team members put this in terms of overall enrichment and increased effectiveness. As one team chair put it:

> There's no question in my mind that employees who have been a part of this experiment are, frankly, better employees. I feel at the moment myself as though I could be a paid consultant on appraisal systems. I've really learned a lot during the process of developing a new performance communication program. I'm not sure that I'd feel exactly the same way about compensation systems, but the fact is that I stretched myself in a way that I never had before. I've learned things about other aspects of our business and the organization, and that makes me a more valuable employee. I'm not just speaking for myself. I believe that this is a characteristic of how other people feel who are a part of this experiment.

These sentiments were echoed by other employees at DSD. A key executive, indeed, felt it had made *his* job more rewarding.

The IT steering committee has now begun to hook this process into the organization as a whole. Although the job is far from complete, there have been major strides made in the last nine months in educating the organization and middle managers. And, in addition, more employees lower down in the organization are convinced that top management within DSD is committed to significantly changing the way in which DSD is managed and operates.

There were also a number of specific results from the task teams:

1. Members of the Equal Employment Opportunity/Affirmative Action task team were proud of the fact that their own personal attitudes had changed as a result of being on the task team. It was clear to them that over the course of working on these issues and problems they had learned a great deal and enriched their own lives. They were the architects of a five-year comprehensive Equal Employment Opportunity/ Affirmative Action plan; in addition they developed and fostered better communications between nonwhites and whites within the organization and helped to increase management's awareness of the problems of minority groups within the organization. They put into place a minority scholarship program, a minority career development program within DSD, and a management appeals process, or due process procedure, which they worked out specifically for Equal Employment Opportunity and affirmative action problems.

2. The performance-appraisal task-team members designed a new performance communication process, as part of creating a new climate and concept within DSD regarding personnel reviews. The program centers around the idea that review of a person's performance is not a one-way street. In the future, DSD reviews will be give-and-take discussions, as opposed to one-sided sessions in which a supervisor or manager appraises past performance with little input from the employee. The team supported the concept with a comprehensive brochure and training program; the training program has been successfully implemented, with an enthusiastic response not only from supervisors and managers but also from employees. For many DSD employees, this program is a concrete sign of a new culture in the division.

3. The communications task team defined the issue in terms of several projects. They designed an introductory brochure to give existing employees and new employees a thumbnail sketch of the way in which DSD is organized, including customer contacts, operations, officers, and how DSD relates to Honeywell as a corporation. The task team is still working on mail distribution control systems and an assessment of what kind of information is known about specific employees and employee groups. This information will be useful in breaking out communications in such a way that DSD will be able to target specific groups and individuals so that management will be able to more effectively communicate with all employees.

4. The first accomplishment of the career development task team was to gather information in order to define the issue appropriately. With the philosophical bases clear, the team is now ready to follow through. A specific plan and program will be developed over the next two to three years.

5. The quality-of-work-life task team developed a wellness proposal for DSD, carried out a comprehensive study on flextime which resulted in its adoption, and produced an information guide called the DSD Yellow Pages. Having completed its work effectively, the team disbanded.

6. In addition, a special study of innovation at DSD by Goodmeasure, Inc., was commissioned by the steering committee, to compare middle management of the Defense Systems Division with a national data base (Kanter 1982, 1983). Forty-four middle managers were interviewed in depth about their major accomplishments, and from this study were extracted a number of recommendations for policy changes and development programs at DSD to spur more innovation and maintain consistency with the division's direction. The results were fed back to the steering committee first, then to the directors and other steering committee members, each of whom developed his own plans for how to disseminate the data further and to act on recommendations relevant to his piece of the organization.

Within two major staff departments, participative activities blessed by the steering committee have flourished. The finance department has a particularly wide array of activities, under the tongue-in-cheek name of FinD IT, for the finance department version of IT. A new employee-run newsletter appropriately called "The Bean Counter" is used to convey news of a number of task-team activities, including one on productivity improvement via better use of computers, one named "People" concerning career development, work load, and physical conditions, and a task team on training. The most noteworthy accomplishment of the training task team to date was the establishment of "FUD," or the Finance University of DSD. It is also investigating job transition and establishing a department library. A shorter-term task team on productivity measurement issued its report after six months of work, establishing appropriate guidelines for a field in which productivity is notoriously hard to measure. The humorous labels attached to various finance department activities should not be taken lightly; they are serious indications of the new spirit with which people are approaching their work, in which they feel that their creative spirit is unleashed and their opportunities for self-expression and contribution are heightened.

Similarly, the employee relations department, in conjunction with Goodmeasure, Inc., carried out an in-depth study of its own functioning, to reorient its own activities to the existence of participative problem solving at DSD; in the course of doing so, it launched its own teams, including secretarial Quality Circles, a strategic planning committee, and a computer systems user group (Pesso, 1984). In both the finance and the employee relations departments, active steering committees linked to the IT steering committee via the director who sits on both managed the array of problem-solving teams within the departments, acting as the division-wide steering committee does to ensure that priorities are set and accountability is met.

At the end of the first nine months of the steering committee's active functioning, a second strategic planning meeting was held to review progress and set priorities for the next round of teams and for the attention of the committee itself. At this meeting, the steering committee extended IT in a number of significant directions.

A study group was formed to examine cooperation with the union and to recommend possible union involvement in IT activities. A task team was also chartered to communicate IT process, status, and results throughout the division as well as to prepare educational programs for all employees on participative management. The composition of the steering committee was enlarged to include four rotating representatives of middle management. And eight employee-generated proposals for the formation of new teams were considered, several of them on significant business-related issues. This was one dramatic sign that IT was catching on with the whole salaried work force and was seen as a vehicle for solving problems in all domains, not just those bearing on employees' quality of work life. Among the new teams chartered were ones concerned with obsolescence of technical personnel, business information systems planning, and the productivity implications of work and family issues. Several proposals were considered inappropriate as division-wide IT issues but were sent to the relevant bodies for action; for example, a proposal for a team to look at engineering assignments in order to reduce production costs was referred to a group-wide production council and to a location manager who was the communication link with the group's council, and another proposed team on typewriter/computer interface selection was referred to an existing task team on office automation.

Both the chartering of new teams and the channeling of employee initiative toward existing activities were signs that the IT steering committee was indeed working as the management body for keeping participation under control and beneficial to all concerned.

The overall goal to which the steering committee was directing itself was "total employee involvement." But members were also clear that this was not possible without continued top-management commitment and support. As one of the steering committee's members said, "IT must be *believed* to be *seen*." In short, the results from IT activities were possible only as long as top management believed they were worth investing in.

## CONCLUSIONS: THE NEED TO MANAGE PARTICIPATION

Many companies using some sort of "participation" or programs concerning quality of work life do so in a way that ultimately creates problems that prevent the full realization of initial objectives (Stein, 1983; Kanter, 1983). DSD's own efforts, in the early stages, ran the risk of falling into some of these traps, before the formation of the steering committee and explication of the roles that it might carry out. Indeed, a major part of the steering committee's activities, and of the issues it tackled, were related to understanding these issues, considering alternatives, and establishing the mechanisms that would avoid the problems in the future. These traps fall into five broad categories.

### Abdication of managerial responsibility in connection with the participation

There is often a tendency, not always clearly recognized, to assume that participative mechanisms essentially require management to back off and that exercise of conventional managerial responsibilities is inappropriate. However, this confuses the particular kinds of responsibility that might appropriately be exercised with the notion of maintaining some responsibility. If there is none at all, then the participation is not connected to on-going tasks, is not appropriately coordinated, and lacks the support that alone will enable it to be fully effective.

Specifically, this often leads to two categories of problems. First, it leads to a failure to plan, monitor, and control activities, which are just as necessary in this case as they would be for any project. Yet, these activities are probably even more important in participative management than in other cases, the more so as it needs to be demonstrated that the participative approach can appropriately coordinate its efforts with the on-going tasks of the organization, the special responsibility of management. The second trap is that this abdication of managerial responsibility tends to leave employees foundering without support and therefore both wastes resources and leads to frustration on the part of those involved in the mechanism. Managerial responsibility, after all, does not necessarily mean control. On the contrary, it can be the most effective way of demonstrating that management, representing the organization broadly, is demonstrating its support and the importance of the activities underway. Whether or not a group of people can solve the resource problem themselves, the lack of managerial attention may lead to the feeling of simply "playing in a sandbox" without being connected to the significant work of the organization.

### Development of disjointed, uncoordinated, and possibly contradictory programs

Since the participative mechanisms are often, as at Honeywell/DSD, fairly broadly distributed, and since they therefore may involve many people in a variety of different task groups or activities, it is critical to make sure that these add up to a coherent program with coordinated effort. There are at least four ways that these problems show up in practice, and that need to be addressed by a mechanism such as the steering committee provides.

First, the programs may lack appropriate relationship to the business strategy and plans for the organization at large. To the extent that people are simply allowed to select or invent a task that seems relevant to them, or that is drawn from a larger list made available by the organization, the efforts may be insufficiently focused on immediate issues, may not be closely connected to the strategic issues at the time, and may be carried out in ways that are less than ideal, even though the general thrust is important.

Second, if anyone, anywhere, can start or stop anything, as might be the case if task forces or local units can simply launch efforts on their own initiatives, unnecessary competition may result. Since, almost by definition, many people in an organization tend to see common issues, this can lead to several different groups springing up to attack the same problem. This *may* be useful in the sense that different approaches can be constructive and a certain amount of healthy competition can be fostered. This cannot be ensured unless there is some overall coordinative mechanism. In its absence, what may result is dysfunctional competition or simply waste of resources.

Third, whether or not there is waste overlap and duplication of effort, there is likely to be very little transfer of experience. Activities do not learn from each other; people who develop skills and new insights into both their programs and the ways of dealing with them are not readily enabled to teach those abilities to others, and so the organization fails to take systematic advantage of the benefits of the new approach. Worse yet, people and groups may tackle things in a way that is not effective and could readily have been avoided if they had had a chance to learn from others' experiences. In a certain sense, since much of the management of participation is inevitably wrapped up in helping an organization learn how to behave in systematically different ways and to support that with appropriate mechanisms, the ability to learn from that experience and to use it in shaping ongoing efforts is perhaps fundamental. Yet, the lack of coordination and systematic exploration makes that impossible.

Finally, without coordination and overall systematic effort, there may well be gaps and holes that are never recognized, so that important things fall through the cracks. The result is often very good work which is, however, incomplete.

### Emergence of a "quick fix" mentality

For a number of reasons, including the pressure of other, ongoing work, and the general tendency for most organizations to reward short-term results more powerfully than long-term ones, there may be a number of traps that result. Three deserve specific mention.

First, there may be a tendency to mount brief campaigns and grab anything off the shelf that seems to respond to the immediate pressures. This leads to the tendency to solve symptoms rather than problems, and to provide the appearance of action without its substance.

Second, there may be a temptation to assign specialists to make the "fix." Neither management nor those who might be able to either contribute to the problem or learn from the solution have a chance to be involved, even if the solution is effective. More frequently yet, the conventional specialists may be precisely those least likely to do anything innovative because they are more invested in maintaining the status quo than almost anyone else.

Third, people often have narrow motives for quality of work life or participation. Without special attention and learning and without a chance to understand in much greater depth the rationale underlying these programs, the inclination may be to do anything that seems to make the employees feel better, or to work on relationship issues, rather than to look for the potential to use new insights, ideas, and experience to solve problems by finding better ways to deal with them in the first place. Participation is *not* simply a psychological device by which people become more committed to action. On the contrary, it is a powerful way to tap expertise and capacity that are not used and to actually modify the operation of the organization so that tasks are done more effectively and problems are likelier to be reduced in the future. A strong steering committee and ongoing coordinative mechanisms can help avoid these problems.

### Insufficient development of vehicles to institutionalize the programs

The management of participation, and the systematic launching of mechanisms to engage people's fuller capacities, as is the case at Honeywell/DSD, means that the focus is on changing the way the organization operates in the long run so that those new capacities can both be developed continually and be more fully engaged in problems as they emerge. That means the programs need to be institutionalized, in the sense that they become a part of common working practice, supported and rewarded throughout the organization. Yet without specific attention to the ways of doing this and the launching of specific mechanisms that make it happen, this may never come about. Many programs that start out very effectively ultimately fail because the organization never really changes or learns from the initial successes. There are several specific issues that need to be addressed and that the steering committee at DSD has been attacking.

First, there needs to be a mechanism to ensure continuity of effort when managers rotate or turn over in their roles. If the effort is largely coordinated and controlled by what is in the manager's head, then transfer to another person means another process that is reinitiated and whose outcome may not be the same. There need to be vehicles and mechanisms that allow the manager to make concrete what he or she is learning, and that, in turn, help anyone else in the same position to build on the past and move further down the same road. A particular task for the steering committee is to help ensure that this happens.

Second, there need to be mechanisms for follow-up, to make sure that things are not simply started but that accessible benefits are utilized. This means not only that it is possible to learn from what happened, in the sense of doing better the next time, but more specifically that ideas capable of implementation and potentially useful for the organization are put into practice. Many groups, in the absence of a coherent and integrated system, develop very good ideas or carry out changes in their own areas that never become available for implementation in the organization at large. Ideas are dropped, things that need extra resources to implement fail to be used, and even powerful and implemented ideas remain isolated rather than being diffused broadly. In particular, steering committees can and should often seek to create new roles or establish new functions that can routinize what has been learned by particular groups. This incorporates in the on-going life of the organization the benefits that have been developed through the participative or innovative mechanisms.

Third, there needs to be a way to add new issues, shift the focus of effort toward new priorities, and make sure that the activities underway, whatever their specific nature, are appropriately oriented to issues addressing the organization and attacking its contingencies as they change. A particular advantage of greater participation is, indeed, that it enables more local flexibility and quicker response, but that needs to be appropriately coordinated and information needs to be available. It does not simply happen by itself. Here, too, a steering committee or equivalent coordinative mechanism is essential.

### Assumption that "participation" is an end in itself, rather than a path to other goals

Strikingly often, organizations engaged in participative management or its equivalent under some other label, do not recognize its connection to business effectiveness, organizational structure, productivity, innovation, or the organization's capacity to respond effectively and accurately to employees and the community environment (Stein, 1983; Kanter, 1983). The link is seen, rather, as a psychological one. People who participate feel a sense of psychological ownership, therefore develop a greater commitment to the effort, and therefore work harder and are likelier to do the right things. To the extent that such a model is underlying organizations' efforts in this direction, then it makes little difference what people participate in so long as they have a *feeling* of being more involved. This grossly misunderstands the essential significance of participation in the organizational environment. These psychological mechanisms do, of course, exist; they underlie much of what has long been referred to, often inappropriately, as the "Hawthorne effect." And it is certainly true that, to the extent that people are able to be influential or feel that they are influential in an area, they are likelier to be committed to the decisions that result.

However, the main reason for supporting participative management and mechanisms to enhance quality of work life in organizations is not purely psychological, because those activities are both short-term and, ultimately, likely to boomerang. On the contrary, the real merit of these mechanisms is that they generate and help take advantage of concrete ideas for action, make it possible for definite and useful experience of those in the organization to be brought to bear on the solution of specific and important problems, provide a greater likelihood that people's capacities can be used in connection with the specific problems, and help to create an organization, including its most specific and concrete manifestations, which are appropriately brought to bear on accurately recognized problems and priorities. The root of participation and its impact does not lie in its psychological dimensions, but in its organizational dimensions. It engages people's full energies, draws on their genuine strengths and advantages, and helps to create mechanisms that produce the organization's results with greater effectiveness.

The other problem that arises from considering participation an end in itself rather than a path to objectives, is that it often leads to the use of "participation" inappropriately or where it really does not fit. For example, it is sometimes assumed that people ought to be asked their opinions, because that is consistent with the idea of participation, whether or not they know anything about the subject, whether or not they have any stake in the outcome, whether or not the person asking has any intention of using the comments, and whether or not there will really be any impact, simply in the assumption that this is a more "participative" approach. We know from a great deal of research, as well as experience, that participation in this sense can be extremely dysfunctional. In fact, it can make matters much worse. More often, perhaps, it is simply a waste of everyone's energy, but at the very least it makes it less likely that important initiatives in the future will be seen as significant. All of these reasons, and others, make it essential that the steering committee help educate the organization broadly, so that both in principle and in practice, and in terms of people's expanded knowledge and understanding, these participative mechanisms are increasingly linked to the organization's real purposes, operate in ways that are genuinely useful for the organization and the people, and provide for significant growth in business effectiveness as well as individual contribution and reward.

## EXTENSIONS

The steering committee structure, and the set of operating procedures and objectives surrounding it, solved the immediate problems faced by DSD—bringing disparate efforts under control. After all, the division-wide task teams and other related activities predated the existence of a conscious participative management or quality of work life strategy for the division. The idea of a steering committee was thus embraced wholeheartedly by managers as a way to create *more* control. This is ironic, of course, because the launching of such vehicles in many companies is seen as beginning a process of loosening of controls rather than strengthening them. One obvious implication is that it may not be necessary to begin participative management in all cases with a conscious strategy, but rather to begin by experimenting with a number of action vehicles, developing a steering committee or guiding mechanism or strategic plan after the organization has accumulated some experience and does indeed have activities to manage. This is the model of culture and strategy change I develop in *The Change Masters*: grass-roots innovations and "crises" or galvanizing events *preceding* strategic decisions and making them possible (Kanter, 1983).

Yet the model of a well-organized steering committee is applicable elsewhere, especially for organizations wishing to begin with a plan. It is typical in many companies to begin these kinds of organizational change efforts by assigning specialists to design or plug-in a program—install so many Quality Circles or create the employee involvement plan. But the DSD steering committee model suggests that such organizations can start by designing an integrated, manageable set of problem-solving activities with the commitment of top executives by developing the steering committee first.

For example, at another Honeywell operation, the Training and Control Systems Operation, we built in part on the successful experiences at DSD to develop a top-management team, vision, and commitment to serving as a steering committee before launching any other employee involvement activities.

First, the executive staff held a series of meetings planning for the future of the business, improving communication across functions, and solving problems that required the involvement of the top. They combined these problem-solving meetings with discussion of a pending reorganization and the launching of increased employee involvement, building in part on the rationale behind the reorganization. Two off-site meetings, a month apart, lasting a day and a half, tackled business problems, resolved questions about the reorganization, and defined a draft set of management principles for the treatment of people, along with a plan for disseminating them and implementing them in the organization. Then meetings were held with all supervisors to announce the reorganization, refine the principles via supervisors' input, and identify volunteers willing to take the results to the levels below.

At a third off-site the executive staff agreed to serve as an explicit steering committee, on an interim basis, managing these activities. The group reviewed and refined the plan for involving employees in problem solving while continuing discussions of necessary actions with respect to the business. They also established a variety of teams and special projects aimed at addressing technical work problems. Then, all employees were brought together in groups of 15 with a volunteer facilitator to examine the principles and define the issues that employees felt were priorities for management attention to improve the work environment in the interests of increased performance.

At the next off-site meeting, the executives reviewed these data, made decisions about actions on employee concerns that could be addressed immediately, and established four task teams to work on the highest-priority issues. Thus, the steering committee in this facility has become the guiding body for problem-solving activities involving employees as well as a large number of business problems. It sets direction and manages a series of temporary problem-solving teams.

The steering committee model makes sense even when no new teams or committees are being established. At still another Honeywell facility, the steering committee is serving as the policy-formulating group, providing and maintaining a coherent direction for a number of ongoing quality-of-work-life activities as well as new initiatives related to the growth of the business, such as the design of a new physical plant.

In general, the idea of a management structure for participation helps guard against the problems we outlined at the beginning of this article (or if they are not obviated, at least a mechanism exists for making sure that managerial concerns are taken into account). It is the existence of a body or a mechanism like a steering committee that is the important thing, not any particular concrete events, efforts, programs, or initiatives that might be undertaken under steering committee auspices. The particular nature of employee involvement—whether it involves task teams, Quality Circles, communication programs, or simply a more responsive organizational structure and management style—should be guided by local conditions and preferences, and these activities can come and go as circumstances change. But what should be seen as a permanent part of the organization's existence is a parallel structure headed by a steering committee for managing strategy, planning, and implementation of any new initiatives to ensure the best results all around.

The steering committee is the bridge between routine operations and the need every organization has to manage change. The existence of a steering committee can ensure appropriate involvement of employees in policy review and reformulation, problem solving, and innovation. This model helps make "participation" both responsible and relevant to the needs of the business. And it guides a major culture change so that this kind of more abstract transition can take hold.

## REFERENCES

Boyle, R. J. "Wrestling with Jellyfish," pp. 74–83. *Harvard Business Review*, January–February 1984.

Goodmeasure. *Productivity and the Management of Participation.* Cambridge, Mass.: Goodmeasure, Inc., 1982.

Kanter, R. M. *The Change Masters: Innovation for Productivity in the American Corporation.* New York: Simon & Schuster, 1983.

Kanter, R. M. "The Middle Manager as Innovator," pp. 95–105. *Harvard Business Review*, July–August 1982.

Pesso, T. "Changing Personnel Departments: The Honeywell Case," pp. 75–80. *Personnel*, January–February 1984.

Stein, B. A. *QWL in Action: Managing for Effectiveness.* New York: American Management Association, 1983.

# 10

Transitioning to change: Lessons
from NSC

A. Lee Barrett, Jr.
*Vice President*
*Responsive Organizations, Inc.*

Cortlandt Cammann
*Institute for Social Research*
*The University of Michigan*

## INTRODUCTION

By May of 1981, H. M. (Pete) Love, the chairman and president of National Steel Corporation, faced a challenge. NSC's markets were deteriorating, the cost of capital was increasing, and profits were under extreme pressure. While people within NSC were aware of the financial conditions facing the company, cyclical downturns were nothing new in the steel industry, and NSC had some of the most efficient production facilities in the industry. Production levels had been cut back sharply because of a significant drop in orders over the past eighteen months, but many felt that the company was not doing particularly badly, since it was doing as well as or better than others in the steel industry. Yet Love saw otherwise. Only stringent cost reductions and drastic adjustments of operating rates had enabled the corporation to stay in the black (1980 Annual Report p. 2). Existing products were being produced efficiently, but few major new products or markets were being developed and the existing markets were declining as a result of both foreign competition and the increasing use of nonsteel products. Further, while the company was vertically integrated, managers in different groups were intent upon maximizing individual unit profitability and did not always act in the best interests of the corporation as a whole.

The problems facing NSC are familiar to many managers in mature industries. The organization had grown and successfully matured over a period of decades. However, the environment in which it operated changed significantly. The very methods and approaches that had produced success in the past were now inhibiting the changes that were required. National Steel faced the challenge of changing from a corporation that could function effectively in the 1960s and 70s to one that would succeed in the 1980s and 90s.

The purpose of this chapter is to examine the early stages of this transition process at National Steel. The chapter will focus on issues faced by a large, mature, and stable organization that wants to create an environment in which meaningful organizational change is possible.

### The problem: Creating a climate for change

The initial problem facing Pete Love was to create a climate that would facilitate change. NSC, like many mature organizations, had developed a relatively stable culture that did not promote adaptation and change. People in the organization understood its methods of working, its structure of authority, and its position in the marketplace. They understood their own jobs and objectives as well as those of others. Generally, each individual did his job, guarded his territory, expected to be rewarded when he did well, and otherwise minded his own business. Open conflict was generally avoided, and each individual showed most of the characteristics of what Alderfer[1] has labeled "overboundedness." As the economic environment became more turbulent, this became increasingly problematic.

In situations such as this, the first step in effecting change is creating a willingness to change. No individual, not even the chief executive officer, can change the culture of an organization by himself. Changing the people who hold positions of responsibility can bring new talents and knowledge to bear. But new appointees are likely to experience the same pressures, expectations, and lack of responsiveness as did their predecessors, and in all likelihood will end up behaving in the same ways. Changing responsibilities and organizational structures will affect who is responsible for resolving specific problems, but when changes are required in the way most people approach problems, changing structures will not be enough. More drastic changes (for example, changing the whole top-management team and replacing them from the outside) might create change in the culture of the organization. Such changes may also produce such a loss of personnel and trauma that the organization risks death from the "cure."

Moving an organization's culture to one that is more open to information, more willing to change and innovate, and more diffuse in its alloca-

---

[1]C. P. Alderfer. "Boundary Relations and Organizational Diagnosis," in *Humanizing Organizational Behavior*, ed. H. Meltzer and F. R. Wickert (Springfield, Ill.: Charles C Thomas, 1976).

tion of responsibility requires that large numbers of people in the organization begin to change the way they think about the organization's purpose, the way they view their roles and jobs, the risks they are willing to take, and the way they deal with other organization members. Such changes cannot come about until sufficiently large numbers of people understand the need for them and until they become willing to help make change happen. In Love's case, this meant creating conditions where large numbers of people were willing to change their views of the purposes of National Steel as a corporation, the way it should work to accomplish these purposes, and the role they should play in making the corporation successful. If this could be done, then the human resources of the corporation could be turned to the problem of coping with a depressed and changing economic situation.

**The context: The steel industry and NSC**

The difficulties which Love faced in creating change at National Steel were largely rooted in the history of the corporation and the nature of the steel industry. The National Steel Corporation was formed in 1929 by the merger of the Weirton Steel Company, the Great Lakes Steel Corporation, and certain interests of the M.A. Hanna Company. The men who ran these businesses felt that they could work more effectively as an integrated entity than as separate businesses. The separate organizations continued to operate relatively autonomously, and the arrangement proved generally beneficial to all. As years passed, additional units were added for strategic business reasons, and the general pattern of coordinated but relatively independent organizations continued to develop.

By 1980, National had evolved into an integrated steel producer with additional businesses in aluminum, fabricated metal products, energy resources, and financial services. Steel and steel products represented the core of the company's business (over 85 percent of gross revenues), and the company had four relatively modern and efficient steel mills that produced its products. The company was self-sufficient in terms of its key raw materials—iron ore, coal, and limestone—and had operations in 25 states, employing over 33,000 people. In 1979, the company had revenues of $4.3 billion and profits of $126 million. The corporation was still managed as a series of essentially independent companies whose activities were coordinated by the chief executive officer and corporate staff, but this did not generally cause major problems since each company had relatively well-defined spheres of activity.

As might be expected, the recent economic downturn in the steel industry caused major problems for NSC. High inflation, slow economic growth in the United States, and competition from foreign producers in a variety of markets began to affect severely the steel business in 1980. The decline in domestic car sales and the general market shift away from tin cans were particularly troublesome for National. The company managed to stay competitive in these and other key market areas, but its revenues declined 9 percent, and its profits 33 percent in 1980. Shipments were off 20 percent that year and overall employment had declined by nearly 5,000 people.

When Love took over as chairman of the board in the spring of 1981, he faced a bleak situation. The economic situation was deteriorating, and many people were saying it would not improve dramatically. The corporation had a number of effective businesses but there was a minimum of cooperation among them, and in many cases it was not clear that they were individually adaptive enough to change with the times. The company was not generating sufficient profits to allow it to continue to meet its capital needs, and it faced many of the problems of product cost and foreign competition that were endemic to the steel industry. In many ways the company was better off than its competitors, but the situation was clearly serious.

### The first steps

One of Love's first moves was to reorganize the top management of the corporation so that a coordinated approach could be taken to dealing with the company's problems. He chose Jim Haas, formerly vice president of National's steel distribution business, as the executive vice president of a newly created Steel Group, with all four steel division presidents reporting to him.

In addition, he began to talk about changing the culture of the corporation, beginning with the senior management. He felt that people needed to accept and accomplish more aggressive financial goals, that the corporation had to become more innovative in its approach to business planning and technological improvement, and that the style of the corporation had to become more participative with higher commitment and improved quality of work life throughout.[2] The senior management felt that these changes would be difficult to accomplish, and not all of them were convinced that they were necessary. Everyone recognized that the company was in trouble, but not everyone agreed on the way to respond.

In the summer of 1981, a consulting firm, Responsive Organizations, Inc., was contacted by one of NSC's steel divisions to assist in implementing labor-management cooperative efforts. As part of the preparation for that project, the consultants talked with NSC's corporate management to determine whether there was top-management support for the cultural changes desired at the division. Love decided to use this contact as an opportunity to stimulate change at the senior management level and asked the consultants to do a diagnosis of the top group and to help them work on their own internal relationships.

---

[2]In a confidential management bulletin published shortly after he became chairman, Love established his personal objectives for the corporation. These included financial, technological, and human resource elements, and were regarded as very ambitious by the senior management. Financial objectives: 7 percent return on sales in 1983, 8–10 percent in 1985, 11–12 percent in 1987. Technology objectives: to become a technology leader. Human objectives: stress participative management and quality of work life.

A series of nondirective interviews was conducted among the 12 managers reporting directly to Love, and the results were fed back to that group. From the interviews, which generally were open and candid, the following perceptions emerged:

1. Operating units were functioning quite autonomously, even to the extent of competing with each other for customers, products, and employees.
2. The role of the corporate staff had been minimal and often not welcomed in the operating units when exercised.
3. There had been little coordinated group interaction among senior management officials. Coordination that had existed was usually instigated by the chairman through individual conversations with subordinate managers.
4. Conflicts between and among executives had been addressed indirectly, if at all.
5. Communications between operating units, organization levels, and senior management had been sketchy and sporadic.
6. The recent creation of the Steel Group required managers to coordinate with and assist each other much more than in the past, and many managers were uncomfortable with this change.
7. There was major concern on the timeliness of introducing participative management in the company at the same time that drastic measures were needed to reduce costs and improve financial performance.

### Determining a common organizational direction

Once the interviews had been completed, Love held a meeting of the people interviewed to discuss the findings and consider a proposed course of action. The group decided to begin by having the 13 senior managers work together to develop an agreed-upon strategic direction for the corporation and a statement of what it would like National's human resource philosophies and practices to be in the future. This course of action was chosen both to accomplish a very specific and necessary task (agreeing upon NSC's strategic direction), and to provide this group of managers with an opportunity to examine and improve the way they worked together.

The senior managers agreed to begin meeting in a series of half-day sessions to define their common strategic direction. At the first meeting, held in October 1981, the group examined its understanding of current management practices and strategies in eight areas: marketing, innovation and creativity, human organization, financial resources, physical resources, productivity, social responsibility, and profit requirements.

The group found that they had considerably different views of the current situation. Some felt that the current marketing emphasis was on selling more profitably to existing markets, while others thought the emphasis was on identifying new markets. Some managers held the view that the company was doing a good job of selecting the most-qualified people, while others thought that it was not doing a good job of matching jobs and individual abilities. Some people believed the company was managing financial resources adequately to meet its objectives, while others said that financial resource management was minimal. Disparities also existed in beliefs that physical resources were being optimally used and in perceptions that productivity was a high-priority problem area.

In its second meeting, the group discussed what the corporation's goals should be for the next decade in each of the eight areas. Again, opinions and points of view varied widely. In marketing, for instance, some felt the goal should be to aim at high-margin products and markets, others that it should be to become a customer-oriented company dedicated to solving problems, and still others that it should be to continue present trends of marketing. In other areas, such as financial and physical resources, goals were often stated in vague terms related to supporting marketing plans or supporting corporate strategies.

As the discussions progressed, it became increasingly evident that members of senior management had substantially differing opinions and perceptions of what the company's present strengths and weaknesses were and what its long-term strategy should be. The group soon recognized the need to develop a common basis of understanding for these differences to be resolved. They decided that the creation of an overall statement of the company's general direction or mission might serve as such a basis. The need for an overall corporate mission statement was felt particularly strongly by those members of the group who managed operating divisions—steel, aluminum, fabricated products, etc. They felt it was the corporation's responsibility to provide them with some direction in this regard. In addition, the recent reorganization had raised a number of issues about responsibility for decisions that needed to be resolved.

Not all the senior managers agreed that a corporate mission statement was needed. Some felt it represented an unnecessary change in the status quo. Moreover, it was a potential threat to their long-held and highly valued independence. Nonetheless, because the issue of lack of corporate mission arose regularly in discussions, the group agreed to develop such a statement.

After several more half-day meetings failed to produce agreement on a mission and organizational objectives, the group decided that it needed a longer period of concentrated effort and agreed to hold a 2 1/2 day off-site meeting of all 13 senior managers. The first day and a half of this meeting were spent on obtaining agreement on what the elements of the mission statement should include and on drafting the statements for each of the elements. After a final review of each element of the statement on the third morning, the group spent considerable time discussing what this mission statement really meant to the organization and to each member of senior management. Several people underscored the importance of commitment, both by each individual and by the group as a whole, if the mission was to be meaningful.

A later version of the mission is shown in the appendix. It is substantially the same as the mission which was developed by the senior managers in this meeting, although it does reflect some changes that were made later based on questions and critiques by other managers in the corporation. There are a number of aspects of this mission that represented substantial departures from the past practice of NSC.

1. The return on invested capital (ROI) objectives were substantially higher than anyone expected could be accomplished if National kept the business configuration it currently held. In order to accomplish these objectives, NSC could not remain primarily a basic steel producer. The top managers agreed that ROI objectives similar to those in the mission statement were required for the corporation to survive, but this meant a fundamental change in the nature of the company and its business approach.

2. The focus on innovation, customer-driven marketing, and low-cost, high-quality production represented significant departures from past definitions of purpose at NSC. It represented a new approach to defining what businesses the corporation should be in and what objectives managers of these businesses would try to accomplish.

3. The focus on participative management represented new principles for how people in the organization would deal with each other. In the past, managers had used whatever style was comfortable, and many had not been particularly participative. Making participative practice a part of the mission represented a new expectation that would require many managers to change their operating styles.

Taken together, these objectives represented a definition of significant business and cultural change for the organization. To make the mission a reality would require changes in the things people within the corporation did, the criteria for evaluating how well they did them, and the methods which they used for doing them. The members of the senior management group recognized that it would be difficult to get these changes accepted and implemented throughout the organization. A number of the senior managers were themselves not sure they agreed with the new directions, and so, although they were committed to support it, they were unsure how well the mission would be accepted.

### Beginning to implement the mission

To generate acceptance for the new mission, the senior managers developed a three-step plan for communicating its content. The first step was to hold a meeting with the people who reported directly to the senior managers. This meeting was to cover the economic conditions facing the company, the mission, and plans for further communications. It was to allow sufficient time for discussion and critique, and senior management was to use the input from the meeting as a basis for revising the mission statement which they had developed. Much of the discussion was to be conducted in small groups facilitated by outside consultants.

This meeting was to be followed a month later by a meeting of the top 250 managers in National Steel, where the process would be repeated and plans developed for communicating the mission to all employees of the organization. Small-group discussions at this meeting would be led by NSC managers trained to act as facilitators.

The final step was for each organizational unit to communicate the mission within its own organization and to start developing plans for implementation.

The first of the two planned meetings to communicate the new mission was held in late February 1982. It involved the 13 senior managers who had been instrumental in preparing the mission and the 49 managers who reported to them directly. The meeting accomplished a variety of objectives. The senior managers had to explain, clarify, and defend the mission. They had to speak as a team with a unified voice, and they tried to model participative, nondirective behavior with subordinates. These behaviors provided some concrete evidence that senior management was serious about the new mission.

Discussion of the mission produced both a reasonable understanding of the mission by the managers who had not seen it before, and some legitimate critiques that required changes be made by the senior managers who had originally created it.

One specific outcome of this meeting with the top 62 managers of NSC was the creation of a plan and structure for implementing the mission. The effort was given a name, National's Action Plan (NAP), and an NAP Mission Statement implementation document was prepared. It described the purpose of the mission statement, and contained a set of guidelines for implementing the mission and the initial steps to be taken. Among those steps was the formal designation of those 13 senior managers who had initiated the development of the mission as the senior management group charged with overall responsibility for overseeing the mission implementation. A coordinating committee, made up of seven members of this group, was established to coordinate the implementation of the mission statement within all parts of the organization. Three task forces were established (human resources, strategic plans, and policies and procedures), made up of participants from the February meeting. These task forces were responsible for reviewing systems and procedures within specified areas for consistency with the mission statement. They were asked to make recommendations for changing those systems or procedures as necessary. In addition, a group of middle-level employees was selected and trained to help facilitate the forthcoming meeting with the top 250 NSC managers.

Throughout this period, the financial situation in the steel business continued to deteriorate. After numerous alternatives were explored, it was decided that the company could no longer continue to operate its steel plant in West Virginia. The plant, long regarded as the company flagship, had been forced to shut down all but two of its blast furnaces for several months during 1980, while layoffs had exceeded 3,000 employees. Its major product, tinplate, was competing in a declining tin can market. Upgrading facilities and shifting production to other steel markets would create a cash drain that the company could not afford. In searching for a solution to this problem that would be consistent with the human-organization and social-responsibility aspects of the mission, as well as with its financial-performance goals, management decided that the fairest option was to offer the plant to the employees under an Employee Stock Ownership Plan (E.S.O.P.). The sensitive nature of this decision, and the deliberations surrounding it, forced Love to postpone the meeting with his 250 top managers until April. The decision to offer the West Virginia plant as an E.S.O.P. to its employees was announced in mid-March.

The subsequent letter of invitation to the April meeting created some concern and confusion. People were aware of the financial difficulties facing the company, but to many the West Virginia plant decision was a shock. To hold a meeting of 250 people to discuss the company's new mission was an event unique in the company's history. Thus, many of the participants arrived puzzled and somewhat apprehensive.

The meeting structure was similar to that of the February conference. It began with a general session in which Love described the current financial situation and discussed the necessity for a new direction for the corporation. The mission statement and National Action Plan document were distributed to all participants. Most discussion occurred in small-group meetings which were facilitated by the 20 middle-level employees who had been trained for that purpose. Those who attended the February meeting were spread among the small groups to explain, discuss, answer questions, and serve as resources to the groups in a participative and nondirective manner. After the documents were discussed thoroughly, groups from the same division or location met to begin preparing plans for implementing the mission at their locations. The conference concluded on the second day with a review by Love of the meeting's objectives, an urging that participants recognize this as the first step in a lengthy process to make National a different kind of place to work, and a reminder that they now had the job of continuing to move the company in the direction which had been spelled out, including helping the 99 percent of the company's employees not at the meeting to begin moving in that same direction.

The meeting produced a variety of responses. For some managers the effect was depressing. The information about the economic situation confirmed the bleak picture they had received from other sources. For others, the meeting was a hopeful sign because it signaled that necessary changes were going to be made and that they would be involved in making these changes. Many of the managers in the steel businesses of the corporation developed questions about their futures because they could not see how their businesses could meet the ROI objectives in the mission. The announced sale of the West Virginia plant served to demonstrate top-management's commitment to the change. Managers in nonsteel businesses understood that the emphasis on basic steel products might decline, but they still felt that the main focus of top-management attention was steel-directed. Probably the most typical reaction, however, was one of skepticism. Many managers felt that the espoused direction was sensible, but did not believe that the senior managers were serious enough about change to make it happen. In spite of this skepticism, the meeting did generate a lot of interest and anticipation of change.

Immediately following this meeting, the middle-level employees who had served as facilitators for the meeting met with the consultants who had assisted in the meeting to review their performance and to discuss what their future role in the NAP implementation process might be. By and large they were satisfied with how they had done and were increasingly committed to doing something further to assist in carrying out the mission. The group developed a recommendation to the coordinating committee to designate this group as a continuing resource of facilitators who would assist managers in creating desired changes.

### The transition structures in operation

The coordinating committee convened its first meeting shortly after the April conference. It approved some suggested changes to the mission statement that resulted from the April meeting. It also agreed to the suggested role for the internal facilitators and approved additional training for members of this group to help them improve their skills. The members of the coordinating committee decided to answer all the questions raised in the April meeting and send them out to all attendees. The committee also began to work on the preparation of a plan for monitoring and controlling the change activities throughout the corporation.

The three task forces began their work shortly after the April meeting. Each took a slightly different approach to its work. The policies and procedures task force began by looking over the list of issues and concerns that had come out of the April meeting. It then developed a list of 16 possible areas where policies or procedures might be impairing attainment of the corporate mission. These included such items as transfer pricing, financial reporting, purchasing, and creativity. Next they developed a questionnaire to send to all 250 participants in the April meeting, asking where they felt changes in policies, procedures, or practices were needed. By far the most frequently mentioned item was transfer pricing between business units. The group recommended that a set of teams representing each transfer price issue (for example, purchase of coal by the steel group, etc.) be set up to work out an agreement that would be acceptable to each business unit involved. This process was designed to push the decision making to the lowest level practical. The group found no other issues of significance to report to the coordinating committee.

The strategic planning task force decided that the critical issue it should examine was the adequacy of existing business-unit strategic planning processes. The group arranged to hear reports from all business units on their methods of planning. Most were found to be adequate, although some needed improvement. The group also examined the overall corporate strategic planning process. There was considerable discussion about the role of the corporate planning function, with two conflicting points of view. One view, held most strongly by the steel group, was that the corporate staff should be "facilitators" of the planning process, which should take place directly between the business-unit head and the corporate officer responsible for that business. Others felt that the corporate planning group should take on a more active role of evaluating and consolidating the plans of business units and presenting them to the chief executive officer with their recommendations. These differences of opinion were never completely resolved by the task force, and as a result they made no significant recommendations for changes in strategic planning to the coordinating committee.

The human resources task force had the most difficult time. After struggling for several meetings with their charter and the issues they should examine, the group concluded that the corporation needed to resolve a number of structural issues before the task force proceeded. The primary issue which the group felt should be resolved was the relationships and division of responsibilities between corporate staff, business-units' staffs, and divisional staff in areas related to human-relations policy.

During the months following the April meeting, the senior management group continued to meet on a regular basis. It discussed its role in the mission-implementation process, continued its team-building activities, and tried to identify further the changes necessary to make the mission a reality.

Concurrently, the newly formed internal facilitator group was establishing itself as a resource for assisting in the change process throughout the corporation. The external consultants conducted a series of training sessions to strengthen their facilitation and change skills, and the facilitators began to help conduct mission communications meetings throughout the corporation. One member of the group was designated as the full-time administrator to coordinate NAP activities.

At the same time, business units and functional (staff) offices began communicating the corporate mission within their organizations and developing their own plans for accomplishing the corporate mission. At corporate headquarters, a cost-conservation task force was set up in response to concerns by field managers that severe cost-reduction measures had been instituted at the plant level, but that no similar "belt-tightening" efforts had been undertaken within the corporate offices. As a response to these concerns, Love asked for volunteers to serve on a task force to look into ways that the corporate offices could cut back on costs. A surprisingly large number of people volunteered, and a group of 20 was selected, representing a cross section of headquarters employees from vice presidents to secretaries. The group examined opportunities to save money in over a dozen categories which had been identified through a questionnaire sent to all headquarters employees. Both an oral and a written report were made to members of the senior management group, including Mr. Love. The activities of this group were similar to actions that were taking place throughout the organization, and provided evidence that the upward flow of information in the organization was improving and that responsiveness at the top was beginning to increase.

### Emerging organizational issues

As the coordinating committee, the task forces, and the business groups tried to figure out how to implement the mission statement, increasingly they ran into problems with the organization's structure. Managers had difficulty determining what they could do, and they were reluctant to initiate action without a clear definition of responsibility. The people in charge of different businesses often disagreed about the best solutions to problems, particularly when their self-interest was involved. Since they didn't have clear performance criteria to use to resolve differences, they could not make decisions about what to do.

The senior management group soon recognized that it needed to assume responsibility for dealing with these organizational issues. A first step was to elaborate on the broad concepts of the corporation contained in the mission statement by stating that the company would become a diversified operating company with comparatively autonomous business units. This statement was a clarification of the notion that the company would no longer function as it had in the past, with nearly all decisions being made by the chairman. On the other hand, the corporate officers would not operate as passively as they might under a holding-company concept. The term "diversified operating company" was meant to convey an operating style somewhere in between these two extremes.

This decision helped clarify uncertainties that existed around roles, although many people felt that the existing organizational structure was not compatible with the concept of a diversified operating company. The existing structure did not give managers the freedom to make business decisions independently, and the reward structure put them in conflict with other managers. To deal with this, Pete Love realized that a further reorganization was needed. His desire was to create a structure where teamwork was easier to achieve, where individual operating units were clearly defined, and where participative management was modeled and encouraged.

As a result, Love, with the advice and consultation of several of his key managers, created an entirely new structure for the company. A four-person group called the "Office of the Chairman" was created. This group, consisting of Love as chairman and chief executive officer, two vice chairmen, and Jim Haas as the president and chief operating officer, was given responsibility for overall strategic planning and corporate-wide policy formulation. Five operating units, called business groups, were designated, each as a self-contained profit center. They were: the Steel Group, which included the four steel plants plus all iron ore, limestone, and steamship operations; the Aluminum Group; the Fabricated Products Group; the Distribution Group; and the Energy Group, which included the company's coal, oil, and gas resources. These business groups reported to the chief operating officer and were to operate with their own staff offices, augmented and supported, where required, from the corporate staff. Each of the two vice chairmen had several operating units and staff functions under his purview. A newly constituted senior management group, made up of those people reporting to members of the Office of the Chairman, was maintained in the new organization. Its purpose was to ensure that information was shared across business groups and staff functions. While each member of the Office of the Chairman had specifically designated responsibilities, the group was designed to function as a team and individual members were given wide latitude to make decisions, provide guidance, and speak for the company. Wherever possible, however, decisions were to be made in a collaborative manner involving not only the entire Office of the Chairman but the senior management group as well. The Office of the Chairman was seen as spending the majority of its effort on issues of strategic direction. This new organizational structure was designed to accomplish the following:

1.  To implement and institutionalize a more participative management culture.
2.  To reflect the concept of a diversified operating company.
3.  To emphasize the planning process and the participation of senior management in it.
4.  To designate clearly the separate business units of the company and provide more autonomy to them.

Initial reactions to the reorganization were quite positive throughout the corporation. It was a clear signal that the implementation of the mission was occurring in a visible and significant manner. It legitimized certain people and groups working together that had not cooperated well in the past. It provided a structure in which energy could be channeled more efficiently to carry out the new mission at all levels of the organization. It allowed business-unit heads to get together on issues that they had been unable to resolve in the past.

In the Steel Group, in particular, the reorganization was received with a great deal of relief. It created a feeling that steel could get on with the task of turning its financial condition around with a much greater degree of control over its own destiny. This feeling, coupled with the aggressive development and communication of a mission statement by the Steel Group itself in support of the corporate mission, also countered fears that steel might not be seen as capable of meeting the corporation's financial goals.

By putting new faces into new positions, the reorganization also underscored the notion that implementing the mission would require new skills and new ways of doing things. Furthermore, by creating a team concept of management at the top levels of the corporation, both in the Office of the Chairman and the senior management group, the reorganization furthered the concept that the job of managers involves a responsibility for cooperating and working with others in the company, and is not just a matter of managing one's own work well.

The new organizational structure is now in the early stages of implementation. While initial indications of its success are good, it remains to be seen whether it will achieve its intended results and whether the issues remaining to be addressed in the change process will be dealt with effectively. For instance, while it should help certain groups to work together more easily, it does not resolve all issues of interdependency. Line-staff issues, while being recast, will not disappear. A strategic planning process still needs to be put in place. Reward systems, both formal and informal, still need to be realigned for consistency with the mission. New communication flow patterns and information and reporting mechanisms will be needed. The members of the Office of the Chairman will have to develop an effective way of working with each other and with the senior management group. Mechanisms, such as the coordinating committee, will need to be continued to ensure that a focus is provided for other aspects of the mission implementation process that were underway before the reorganization.

## Results of the change process

What was accomplished at NSC between the beginning of 1981 and the reorganization which took place in September 1982? Clearly, the changes were limited. Financially, the period was a poor one for the corporation, ending in a large loss for the first six months of 1982. Strategically, there was little change in the organization's business mix. The decision to sell the West Virginia plant represented a major strategic shift, but the sale had not yet been completed; and while a number of businesses had been pruned and others acquired, no major shifts had yet been made.

Organizationally, the results were more significant. The creation of the Steel Group had led to a series of significant internal changes. The marketing organization, for example, had previously been changed so that separate NSC marketing organizations were no longer in competition for the same sales. The reorganization carried this a step further, separating the energy suppliers and steel-fabricating units from the steel business so that they could more profitably manage their assets and so that profits (and losses) could be attributed more accurately to the businesses where they occurred. Similar clarifications were made in the missions of the other business groups.

Structurally, only a few changes had been made in the systems that affected organizational behavior. The pay system was being examined at the top- and middle-management levels, but had not been changed. The manpower planning system for tracking and developing high-potential managers was not extensive and had not altered. The accounting and control systems were not particularly sophisticated and, while they were being overhauled, the changes had not yet been implemented. The strategic planning and capital allocation mechanisms were also being altered but, again, the changes had not gone into effect.

At the lower levels of the organization, people knew that changes were occurring, but they hadn't yet seen them reach their levels. They had seen the new mission statement, but tended to be skeptical, waiting to see if changes would really happen. In some of the plants, programs to involve employees in decision making were beginning to reach the hourly worker levels, but concern for the uncertain future was probably a more-prevalent attitude than confidence in the new direction.

What had changed was the attitude toward change and the capacity to change. All members of the organization had at least some understanding of the problems facing the corporation. Managers had heard that the style and direction of the corporation were changing, and they had begun to see concrete evidence that it was happening. At many locations, the managers were being involved in planning the changes that were to happen. The reorganization reduced the constraints on organizational units and made it easier to focus on necessary changes. It also mobilized energy to examine and revise the systems and procedures, and established new values to guide the behavior of NSC employees.

## Characteristics of a transition from stability to change

It is possible to use this case to identify a number of processes that characterize the shift from stability to change in a large, mature organization. It also illustrates a variety of dilemmas that must be dealt with and resolved by people who are interested in facilitating such a transition and creating the conditions that allow cultural change to occur.

**Creating a need for change.** The first step in any change process is the creation of a felt need for change.[3] If no one in an organization feels a need to change anything, significant change will not occur. More importantly, however, the need for change must be felt by the people whose energy is required for change to happen. This is a particular problem in mature, stable organizations where each person has well-defined limits on his/her roles and responsibilities. If the people who feel a need for change are not directly responsible for the changes to be made, conflict may occur, but change probably will not.

The NSC case is particularly interesting in this regard because one of the individuals who felt a need for change in the culture was the chief executive

---

[3]Michael Beer has referred to this as dissatisfaction and views it as one of the three key elements in any planned change process. The other two elements referred to by Beer are a model of what the end result of the change should look like and a process for carrying out the change.

officer. He wanted to create a more innovative organization that allowed employees more opportunity to initiate and take responsibility for change. He wanted to develop an organization committed to excellence and improvement. The problem he faced was that he, alone, could not make all of the changes required for the new culture to develop. As a consequence, he needed to initiate a plan of action that would build a broad-based understanding of the need for change and a general commitment to making the change occur.

To create this need for change, Love used a variety of tools. The first was a series of presentations about the nature of the problems facing the corporation. In personal meetings and in a videotape presentation he tried to communicate to all the employees in the corporation that the situation facing the company was not simply another cyclical downturn. All employees knew that the economic situation was bad, but Love's message was that it reflected fundamental changes in the environment, not just another downturn that would eventually improve. He emphasized that the organization needed to change fundamentally the way it did business to survive. This message provided a signal that the current situation could not be dealt with in the way other downturns had been dealt with in the past. The severe, prolonged nature of the market downturn seemed to give this message credibility.

The second tool was the series of management meetings that occurred. Each began with a description of the problems facing the organization and provided managers with an opportunity to discuss their economic problems with people from other parts of the business. This process helped managers understand that the problems they faced on their jobs were also facing people in other parts of the company. It helped highlight that the problems could not be solved unless people throughout the corporation started to work together to find creative solutions.

The third tool was making critical symbolic decisions. The decision to sell the West Virginia plant, in particular, provided a clear signal that the people at the top of the organization recognized the seriousness of the situation and the need for drastic action. Similarly, the personnel shifts that resulted from the reorganization indicated that changes were necessary.

The final tool was the business planning process. Love and the key managers reporting to him began to use the planning process to require shifts in business direction and managerial behavior. This tool was only partially developed at the time of the reorganization, so its use was limited until after the period described in this case.

**Creation of a standard.**    A second element in creating an openness to change is the development of standards that indicate the areas where change is necessary. Simply understanding that change is necessary is not sufficient. Individuals also need to know where to direct their efforts in making changes. To provide this direction, they need a set of standards that they can use to determine the areas in which they need to do things differently.

In the NSC case, these standards were provided by the new mission that was developed by the senior managers. This mission provided some general guidelines that individuals could use to determine areas where change was necessary. If a business unit was not helping the organization accomplish its ROI objectives, changes were clearly required in the business. If the decisions which were being made would not produce the type of market leadership described in the mission, new decision-making criteria needed to be employed. If the way decisions were made was not sufficiently participative, new decision-making processes needed to be developed. If organizational units were not sufficiently responsible community members, new methods of dealing with communities needed to be developed. The effect of the mission statement was to help employees throughout the organization recognize where change was necessary. It provided standards for helping them decide which aspects of their current activities needed attention.

One important aspect of the NSC mission is worth noting here. While it provided standards for determining what had to be changed, it provided little guidance for deciding the changes to make. It is fine to specify that a business had to eventually meet certain profitability requirements, but that doesn't help managers decide how this can be done. It is easy to say that decision making needs to be more participative, but this does not provide managers with models they can use to alter their behavior in a more participative direction.

As a consequence, one effect of the mission statement was to create frustration. Organization members could begin to identify what they were doing wrong, but had a hard time figuring out how to change so that they could do things right. The effect of this frustration was that managers started searching for new approaches, and identifying barriers to creating change. As they identified barriers, their frustration increased, and their frustration stimulated the top officers of the corporation to reorganize into more-independent business groups. The reorganization gave managers a structure within which to use the energy the mission statement had created.

It is difficult to conclude whether or not this mission statement was an effective tool for creating change. It clearly sent the message to the organization that change was required, but its lack of specificity made it difficult for managers to figure out how to change. Yet, it was the frustration that this produced which led lower-level managers to take more responsibility for initiating change and which resulted in the reorganization that formally located responsibility for change at lower levels. On balance, it seems that the mission was useful in creating conditions for change, but that it did not represent a sufficiently clear model of the desired end state to facilitate the process of changing.[4]

---

[4]Beckhard and Harris (1977) and Beer (1980) are among the theorists who have identified the importance of a clear set of objectives for the change effort in making the change effort successful.

**The development of transition structures.** Many theorists interested in organizational change have stressed the importance of transition structures in the change process.[5] The critical activities at NSC demonstrate that these structures can be important even in the very early stages of a change effort. The creation of the senior management group was a useful tool in building a powerful coalition that could communicate the need for change throughout the organization. The creation of the coordinating committee provided a mechanism to focus the energy of key top managers on the change process. It helped them monitor the results of the mission communication within the organization, ensure that there was adequate information sharing about problems and successes, and provide resources for change activities to groups that needed them. The NAP task forces provided structures for examining areas where changes might be needed and for ensuring that barriers to change were identified and dealt with by the appropriate people. These task forces were most useful in identifying the need for a change in the structure of organizational responsibilities as a method for clarifying responsibilities for change within the organization. The creation of the internal facilitator group provided a structure for training a group of middle-level people in the skills of facilitating change, and also provided a communication channel between people within the organization and those at the top, which was outside the normal chain of command.

The transition structures used at NSC also demonstrated that such mechanisms can face severe problems. The managers who were a part of them generally experienced tension between the demands of dealing with change and the demands of their regular jobs. In some cases, this led them to try to minimize the effort they put into activities associated with transition activities. In others it produced attempts to define the tasks of transition groups in ways that minimized the effort they would require. These reactions are not surprising since these managers were being asked to operate outside of the basic authority structure which had provided the context for their activities throughout their careers in the organization. It meant, however, that the managers needed to have a clear understanding of what they were doing, of its importance to the organization, and of the value which the senior executives of the organization placed on their activities. When these understandings were clear, the groups seemed to function well. When they were not, problems resulted. Temporary structures are a useful part of any change effort, but if the experiences of managers at NSC are generally applicable, managers who are not experienced in working in them require help in understanding their roles and support in carrying them out.

**The emergent nature of transition planning.** The change activities in this case illustrate the emergent nature of transition planning during the early stages of the change process. When Pete Love began his attempts to change the culture of National Steel, he may have had a clear image of

---

[5]Beckhard and Harris (1977) clearly articulate the importance of these transition structures.

where he wanted to go, but he did not know how he was going to get there. At each step, the results of the last activities and random events influenced what would happen next. The central point here is that in any organization, planning for cultural change will always have this characteristic. External events such as the severe downturn in the steel business can never be fully anticipated, and the consequences of activities such as the communication of the organizational mission can never be completely predicted. As a result, transition planning is always an iterative process in which each new activity is based on the results of the last one.

More importantly, however, cultural change is an organizational activity. It can occur only if a large number of people alter their beliefs about how the organization works and what their role is within it. Therefore, executives and change agents can only set the process in motion and create structures to guide it. The changes will occur as a consequence of the interaction of people and events with the programs and activities designed to create change. This process is too complex to plan centrally. It can happen effectively only if there are people in positions throughout the organization who can monitor events and invent change plans that are appropriate as conditions warrant. Thus, the process of creating cultural change involves developing people who understand the changes that are desired, who have the skills to create them, and who can continually invent new programs and structures to reinforce and accelerate the process of changing. There can be no fixed plan for accomplishing this goal, only a continual process of planning what to do next to accomplish it.

**Relation of individual and organizational change.** Finally, this case demonstrates that creating conditions for cultural change involves both individual and organizational change activities. The behavior of people within an organization is influenced by both the organizational structures and systems which exist and the beliefs and competencies the individuals have developed over time. In order for the systems and structures to change, key individuals need to understand how new structures and systems can be designed and used to produce different results.

By the same token, if systems and structures change, but individuals do not develop a new understanding of their purpose and new skills for making them work, then behavior may be affected but it will not be qualitatively different. In the case of National Steel, for example, if the responsibilities of senior managers had been altered, but there had been no change in their image of what the business of the corporation was going to be or the types of activities required to succeed, the effect would probably have been negligible. Changing the mission and the characteristics of the people who made up the senior management group gave the reorganization more meaning. Similarly, developing, at various levels in the organization, specific programs intended to encourage collaborative problem solving represents an activity that is consistent with the mission and change. Such programs can be successful, however, only if the individuals who are part of them can learn to work together in groups and to use participative methods for making decisions.

The need for both individual and organizational change has important implications for cultural change efforts. It means that the strategies for creating change need to include methods for creating changes in organizational structures and systems and methods for creating changes in individuals. It also means including strategies that create a felt need for change at both levels. Change approaches that focus on only one level or the other are unlikely to succeed.

## CONCLUSION

Many mature organizations reach a point where a shift in their basic purpose and culture is desirable. This chapter has examined the first phase of such a change in the National Steel Corporation. The primary purpose of this phase is to create conditions where changes in activities, structures, and beliefs are supported and can be made with relative ease. Conceptually, this represents the first stage in a larger transition process, but it also represents a transition from stability to flexibility. This initial phase of change has all of the characteristics of a transition. It requires the development of a felt need for change, an articulation of the type of change that is desired, and a structure for facilitating the change process. The outcomes of the initial phase are a commitment to changing the culture of the organization, a model of the desired state to be accomplished, and an understanding of how the broader change will occur.

In the case of National Steel, these results have generally been accomplished. What remains is for the people in the organization to devote their energy to implementing the change and making the new culture a functioning reality. It requires coping with a fluid and difficult external environment, and resolving problems that are created when old structures and beliefs begin to change. It is impossible to predict what the result will be or how National Steel will function in the future once the changes have been made. It is clear that creating a new National Steel will not be an easy task, but it is also clear that the process of change has begun. Whatever emerges, the corporation is clearly in a state of change and the way the organization functions in the future will not be the same as the way it has operated in the past.

## REFERENCES

Beckhard, Richard, and R. T. Harris. *Organizational Transitions: Managing Complex Change.* Reading, Mass.: Addison-Wesley Publishing Company, Inc, 1977.

Beer, Michael. *Organization Change and Development: A Systems' View.* Santa Monica, Calif.: Goodyear Publishing Company, Inc., 1980.

## APPENDIX: MISSION STATEMENT NATIONAL STEEL CORPORATION

National Steel Corporation is a diversified firm whose Mission is as follows:

To provide a superior and consistent financial return to its stockholders.

This mission will be carried out within the framework of the Corporation meeting its social responsibility to its employees and the communities in which it operates, conducting its business with the highest ethical behavior, and providing its customers with high-performance products and services.

The Mission will be supported by the following key elements:

A. Financial Goals
   1. National will develop a portfolio of businesses which, in the aggregate, can produce consistent growth in earnings per share and a 20 percent minimum return on invested capital.
   2. This portfolio will include businesses which generate cash and businesses whose growth prospects merit investment. Both types of businesses are needed to ensure continued progress for the Corporation.
   3. These goals specifically comprehend an on-going evaluation and upgrading of the Corporation's portfolio of businesses by investment, acquisition, and/or divestiture in order to achieve a 15 percent return on equity and a corresponding increase in shareholder value and a balance sheet that will support these goals.
B. Marketing
   The marketing goal for the Corporation is to provide products and services to its customers which are of the highest performance and value for their specific requirements, through leadership in the following areas:
   1. Quality Leadership will be the responsibility of all employees and will be emphasized from the research and development effort through the entire manufacturing and distribution process.
   2. Price Leadership will be established by attaining the low-cost position through productivity and capital investment.
   3. Market Leadership will be achieved in those several markets in which the Corporation focuses its financial and human resources in order to establish product and service differentiation.
C. Human Organization
   National's human organization objectives are as follows:
   1. Develop a participating management style with a lean, high-quality group of employees who receive continuous training and development regardless of economic conditions.
   2. Define criteria for all jobs which are clearly understood by all employees.

3. Provide and maintain clean and safe work areas.
4. Provide open communication channels to all employees concerning corporate goals, objectives, strategies, etc., so that employees are better informed.
5. Provide an atmosphere which will enhance employee pride in their jobs and the Corporation.
6. Maintain the concept of superior compensation for superior performance, which is essential for the accomplishment of the Corporate Mission.
7. Provide opportunity for all employees regardless of age, sex, color, religion, or national origin.

D. Creativity and Innovation
It is essential that management create an environment which encourages and rewards creativity and innovation through entrepreneurial management within the strategies and objectives of the Corporation.

E. Productivity
Productivity is the responsibility for all employees of the Corporation and is a key element in successfully carrying out the Mission of the Corporation. In order to improve organizational effectiveness, productivity goals will be established. The minimum goal will be productivity increases which exceed increases in employment costs.

F. Social Responsibility
The Corporation recognizes its social responsibility to its employees and the communities in which it operates. In order to meet its social responsibilities, the Corporation must be a profitable business. National is committed to maintaining an improved environment and it encourages employee participation, according to the highest ethical standards, in serving the needs of the communities in which its plants are located.

# 11

## Revitalizing organizations: The leadership role

Noel Tichy
David Ulrich
*Graduate School of Business Administration*
*The University of Michigan*

### INTRODUCTION

General Motors, American Telephone & Telegraph, Citibank, Honeywell, TRW, General Electric, International Business Machines, and U.S. Steel are among a long list of major U.S. corporations investing in major organizational transformations to ensure long-term vitality. In some cases, transformations occur while companies experience financial success; for others change happens after pressures from foreign competition, economic shifts, and technological change have exacted a financial toll. In either case, the challenge is fundamentally the same. Mature corporations need to revitalize via new products, services, or markets, or by increased productivity, quality, or innovation, to compete in increasingly tough environments. Firms such as GM and U.S. Steel represent whole industries where revitalization is necessary, while firms such as GE or IBM fear gradual loss of world competitiveness. Transforming and revitalizing such massive institutions requires a special brand of leadership different from leadership requirements during decades of growth in relatively stable markets.

To revitalize organizations, leadership needs to help organizations develop a new vision of what they can be, then mobilize the organization to change toward the new vision. This new leader is similar to what Burns (1978) characterized as the "transformational" leader, one who commits people to

240

action, who converts followers into leaders, and who may convert leaders into moral agents (p. 4). This leader contrasts to the "transactional" leader who merely exchanges such things as jobs, money, and security for compliance. Organizational revitalization calls for visionary, charismatic leadership. One of the most dramatic examples of transformational leadership and organizational revitalization in the early 1980s has been the leadership of Lee Iacocca at Chrysler Corporation. He provided the leadership to transform a company from bankruptcy to success. He created a vision of success and mobilized large factions of key employees toward enacting that vision. Due in part to Iacocca's leadership, by 1983 Chrysler made profits, attained high employee morale, and helped employees generate a sense of meaning in their work and a desire to challenge themselves to experience success. Whether Chrysler will be able to sustain this organizational phenomenon over time remains to be seen. If it does, it will provide a solid corporate example of Burns' (1978) transformational leader.

Lee Iacocca's high visibility may symbolize a missing element in management, namely the existence of transformational leaders. This chapter argues that a new brand of transformational leadership is central to revitalizing institutions. In the chapter, concepts are presented to help understand dynamics of individual and organizational transitions. Guidelines for transformational leadership are also presented.

## RATIONALE FOR REVITALIZATION

Technical, political, and cultural pressures will likely shape organizations throughout the 1980s. Figure 11-1 lists environmental forces which will impact organizations. While these forces may not unfold as predicted in Figure 11-1, we assume that environmental technical, political, and cultural forces will be destabilizing to organizational technical, political, and cultural systems. These environmental forces represent both threats and opportunities, depending on the organization. Dealing with these forces may result in new missions and strategies, massive reorganizations, and major restructuring and revamping of the financial, marketing, production, and human resource systems. In addition, internal political systems, as reflected in who gets ahead, how they get rewarded, and who has the power to make decisions, will face major overhauls. Finally, because of environmental forces, new cultures will be required. Old organizational norms and values must shift to new ones which are better aligned with the new organizational strategies and structure, with values of a changing workforce, and with emerging societal values.

Specific pressures for change may vary across industries and companies, but pressures listed in Figure 11-1 illustrate some external forces. Technological changes, symbolized by the computer revolution with easy access to and manipulation of information, will probably move organizations to become more service-oriented and automated. Continued economic uncertainty around inflation, productivity, national deficits, interest rates, and

**FIGURE 11-1** The mandate for organizational transformation

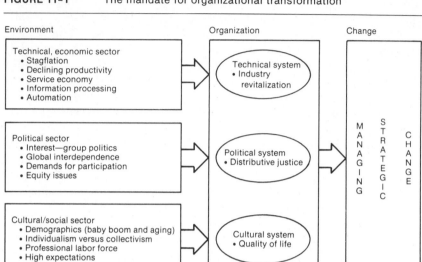

Source: Noel M. Tichy, *Managing Strategic Change: Technical, Political, and Cultural Dynamics* (New York: Wiley-Interscience, 1983).

innovation may force organizations to retain flexibility and manage change. In the cultural arena, demographic changes, individualistic values, and highly educated employees with high job expectations may lead to new organizational cultures. A tumultuous change may also affect organizational political systems where realignments and rewards reflect power. Power decisions are reflected in compensation programs, career decisions, budget decisions, and informal power in organizations. Unlike the technical area where formal tools such as strategic planning and organization design inform decision making, in the political area concepts and language are less formal and often less overt. Nonetheless, with environmental pressures, much management time and attention will be allocated to strategic political changes required to revitalize organizations. The political arena is illustrated by the time and attention given to key leadership decisions, such as American Bell reshuffling leadership, resulting in the resignation of Archie McGill, the "brash," aggressive marketing leader hired from IBM to transform AT&T. McGill's resignation purportedly reflects a political realignment within the new American Bell organizations to shift power back into the hands of more traditional AT&T managers who were reacting against the brash outsider. Overall, environmental forces will require that revitalized organizations adapt to environmental pressures and work to overcome internal resistances to change.

### Internal resistance to change

Given environmental pressure, organizational change is a pressing need. However, accomplishing organizational transitions is more challenging and difficult than merely recognizing the need for change. Environmental pressures and uncertainties in Figure 11–1 not only provide an impetus for change but also trigger individual and organizational resistances to change. These forces of resistance are generated in each of the three interrelated systems which must be managed in the process of organizational transitions: technical, political, and cultural (Tichy, 1983). Managing technical systems refers to managing the coordination of technology, capital, information, and people to produce products or services desired and used in the external marketplace. Managing political systems refers to managing the allocation of organizational rewards such as money, status, power, and career opportunities and exercising power so employees and departments perceive equity and justice. Managing cultural systems refers to managing the set of shared values which guides the behavior of members of the organization. Organizational revitalization must overcome individual and organizational resistance to change in these three systems (Tichy, 1983).

Technical system resistances include:

1. Resistance due to habit and inertia. Habit and inertia cause task-related resistance to change. Individuals who have always done things one way may not be politically or culturally resistant to change, but have trouble for technical reasons in changing behavior patterns. A very simple example is the difficulty some office workers have shifting from electric typewriters to word processors, due to habit and inertia.
2. Resistance due to fear of the unknown or loss of organizational predictability. Not knowing and having difficulty predicting the future create anxiety and hence resistance in many individuals. Again, the introduction of automated office equipment has often been accompanied by such resistances.
3. Resistance due to sunk costs. Organizations, even when realizing that there are potential payoffs from a change, are often unable to enact the change due to sunk costs of the organization's resources in the old way of doing things.

Political system resistances include:

1. Resistance due to threats to powerful coalitions. A common threat is found in the conflict between the old guard and the new guard. One interpretation of the exit of Archie McGill, previously president of the newly formed AT&T American Bell, in mid-1983, is that the backlash of the old-guard coalition exacted its price on the leader of the new-guard coalition, Mr. McGill.
2. Resistance due to resource limitations. In the days when the economic pie was steadily expanding and resources were much less limited, change was easier to bring about as every party could gain. Such was the nature of labor management agreements in the auto industry for decades. Now that the pie is shrinking, decisions need to be made as to who shares with a smaller set of resources. These zero-sum decisions are much more politically difficult. As more and more U.S. companies

deal with productivity, downsizing, and divestiture, political resistance will be triggered.

3. Resistance due to indictment quality of change. Perhaps the most significant resistance to change comes from leaders having to indict their own past decisions and behaviors to bring about a change. For example, Roger Smith as chairman and chief executive officer of General Motors, must implicitly indict his own past behavior as a member of senior management when he suggests changes in General Motors' operations. Psychologically, it is very difficult for people to change when they were party to creating the problems they are trying to change. It is much easier for a leader from outside, such as Lee Iacocca, of Chrysler Corporation, who does not have to indict himself every time he says something is wrong with the organization and its management.

Cultural system resistances include:

1. Resistance due to selective perception (cultural filters). An organization's culture may highlight certain elements of the organization, making it difficult for members to conceive of other ways of doing things. An organization's culture channels that which people perceive as possible; thus, innovation may come from outsiders or deviants who are not as channeled in their perceptions.

2. Resistance due to security based on the past. Transition requires people to give up old ways of doing things. There is security in the past. One of the problems in change is getting people to overcome the tendency to want to return to the "good old days." One of the problems in General Motors is that there are still, in 1983, significant members of the white collar work force who are waiting for the "good old days" to return.

3. Resistance due to lack of climate for change. Organizations often vary in their conduciveness to change. Cultures which require a great deal of conformity often lack much receptivity to change. A company such as General Motors with its years of internally developed managers must overcome a limited climate for change.

With all of these resistances to change, senior managers need to continually pose basic questions: What business(es) should we be in? Who should reap what benefits from the organization? What should be the values and norms of organizational members? Answers to these questions do not come easily, and require intensive soul-searching, then transformational leadership. Transformational leaders must be willing to lead dialogue around these issues and work to implement new answers by proactively managing individual and organizational transitions. The next section identifies the dimensions of the transition process which leaders need to understand and master.

## THE NATURE OF TRANSFORMATIONS

Organizational transformations take time, often three to five years, to unravel conflicting, paradoxical forces which put extreme demands on organizational leadership. It is important to understand that:

> Change requires exchanging something old for something new. It is important to recognize that all change requires exchange. People have to unlearn and relearn, exchange power and status, and exchange old norms and values for new norms and values. These changes are often frightening and threatening while at the same time potentially stimulating and providers of new hope. One must recognize the nature of exchanges: there are costs and benefits which must ultimately be balanced in favor of the benefits side. This can mean that transition managers have to help the balancing by reducing expected costs and enhancing expected benefits. At the simplest level, organizations sometimes provide monetary benefits for people to make change. They also increase the costs for some by firing them.
>
> (Tichy, 1983, p. 332)

To revitalize organizations, both individual and organizational dynamics must be considered. Transformational leaders must deal with both dynamics. At each level we identify phases through which the successfully revitalized organization must pass. These phases will be described, followed by a closer examination of specific tasks of transformational leaders.

### Organizational dynamics

**Trigger event.** Change is often triggered by environmental pressures. Many of the technical, political, and cultural environmental forces listed in Figure 11–1 will trigger organizational change for the next decade. For AT&T, technological and political forces led it to undertake its massive transformation. For General Motors, economic factors of world competition, shifting consumer preferences, and technological change are driving it to change. Not all potential trigger events lead to organizational responses. The external trigger event must be perceived and responded to by internal leaders in the first phase of the transformation process.

**Felt need for change.** As a result of the trigger event being perceived by the organizational leaders, the dominant group in the organization must experience a dissatisfaction with the status quo. Thus, in the late 1970s, John DeButts, chairman and chief executive officer of AT&T, was not satisfied with the long-term viability of AT&T as a regulated telephone monopoly in the age of computers and satellite communication systems. When Roger Smith became chief executive officer at General Motors at the start of the 1980s he could hardly be satisfied with presiding over the first financial loss for General Motors since the Depression. The felt need provides the impetus for transition, yet such impetus is not uniformly positive.

Just as the felt need for change releases energy for revitalizing organizations, it also releases defensive forces. The technical, political, and cultural resistances reviewed above are most evident during early stages of an organizational transformation. At General Motors, the early 1980s were marked by tremendous uncertainty about many technical issues, including marketing strategy, production strategy, organization design, factory automation, and development of international management. Politically, many powerful coalitions were threatened. The UAW was forced to make wage concessions and accept staffing reductions. White collar workers saw their benefits cut and witnessed major layoffs within the managerial ranks. Culturally, the once dominant managerial-style no longer fit environmental pressures for change. "GM way" was no longer the right way. Losing market share and money, layoffs, and cuts in compensation were not part of a culture General Motors employees had learned to expect. Even with environmental triggers for change, technical, political, and cultural resistances made the transition very difficult.

These resistances to change can lead to organizational stagnation rather than revitalization. In fact some managers at GM in late 1983 were waiting for "the good old days" to return. Such denial exemplifies an awareness of or dysfunctional reaction to the felt need. As indicated in Figure 11–2 a key to whether resistant forces lead to little or adequate change and hence organizational decline or revitalization is leadership. Defensive, transactional leadership will not rechannel resistant forces. International Harvester appears to have had defensive transactional leadership. The result at International Harvester in the early 1980s was lack of a new vision and mobilization of employees to engage in new behaviors. In contrast, Lee Iacocca has been a transformational leader at Chrysler by creating a vision, mobilizing employees, and working toward the institutionalization of Chrysler's transition. Creation of a vision, mobilization of commitment, and institutionalization are three key activities for transformational leaders.

**Creation of a vision.** The transformational leader must provide the organization with a vision of a desired future state. While this task may be shared with other key members of the organization, nonetheless, having a vision remains the core responsibility of the transformational leader. The leader needs to integrate analytic and creative, intuitive, and deductive thinking. Each leader must create a vision which gives direction to the organization while being congruent with the leader's philosophy and style. At General Motors, after several years of committee work and staff analysis, a vision of the future was drafted which included a mission statement and eight objectives for General Motors. This statement was the first articulation of a strategic vision for General Motors since Alfred Sloan's leadership. This vision was consistent with the leadership philosophy and style of Roger Smith. Many people were involved in carefully assessing opportunities and constraints for General Motors. Meticulous staff work culminated in committee discussions to evoke agreement and commitment to the mission statement. Through this process a vision was created, paving the way for the next phases of the transformation at GM. At Chrysler, Lee Iacocca developed a vision without committee work or heavy staff involvement. In-

**FIGURE 11-2** Change leadership

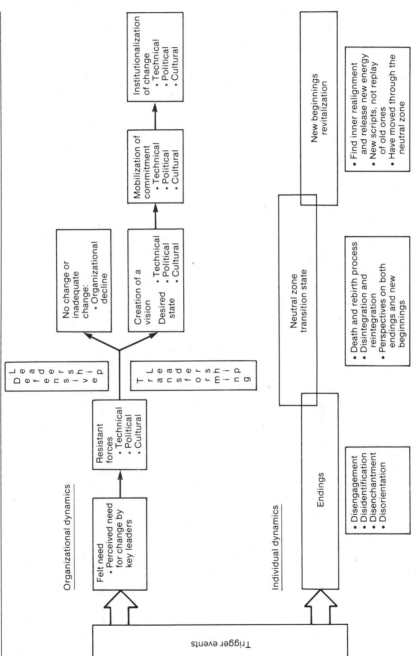

Source: W. Bridges, *Making Sense of Life's Transitions* (New York: Addison-Wesley Publishing, 1980).

stead, he relied more on his intuitive and directive leadership, philosophy, and style. Both GM and Chrysler ended up with a new vision because of transformational leaders proactively shaping a new organization mission and vision. The long-term challenges to organizational revitalization are less "how" the visions are created and more the extent to which the visions correctly respond to environmental pressures and create transitions within the organization.

**Mobilization of commitment.** In mobilization of commitment, the organization, or at least a critical mass of it, accepts the new mission and vision and makes it happen. At General Motors, Roger Smith took his top 900 executives to a 5-day retreat to share and discuss the vision. The event lasted five days, not because it takes that long to share a one-paragraph mission statement and eight objectives, but because the process of evolving commitment and mobilizing support requires a great deal of dialogue and exchange. Mobilization of commitment must go well beyond five-day retreats. It is in this phase that transformational leaders tap into a deeper sense of meaning for their followers. Maccoby (1976) acknowledges that leaders who will guide organizations through revitalization are distinct from previous leaders and gamesmen who spearheaded managers to be winners in the growth days of the 1960s and early 1970s. In more recent years Maccoby argues:

> The positive traits of the gamesman, enthusiasm, risk taking, meritocratic fairness, fit America in a period of unlimited economic growth, hunger for novelty, and an unquestioned career ethic. The negative traits for manipulation, seduction and the perpetual adolescent need for adventure were always problems, causing distrust and unnecessary crises. The gamesman's daring, the willingness to innovate and take risks are still needed. Companies that rely on conservative company men in finance to run technically based organizations (for example auto and steel) lose the competitive edge. But unless their negative traits are transformed or controlled, even gifted gamesmen become liabilities as leaders in a new economic reality. A period of limited resources and cutbacks, when the team can no longer be controlled by the promise of more, and one person's gains may be another's loss, leadership with values of caring and integrity and a vision of self-development must create the trust that no one will be penalized for cooperation and that sacrifice as well as rewards are equitable.
>
> (Maccoby, 1976)[1]

After transformational leaders create a vision and mobilize commitment, they must determine how to institutionalize the new mission and vision.

**Institutionalization of change.** Organizations will not be revitalized unless transactions result in new patterns of behavior within the organiza-

---

[1]Michael Maccoby, *The Gamesman* (New York: Simon & Schuster, 1976). Copyright © 1976 by Michael Maccoby. Reprinted by permission of Simon & Schuster, Inc.

tion. Transformational leaders need to transmit their visions into reality, their missions into action, their philosophies into practice. New realities, actions, and practices must be shared throughout the organization. Alterations in communication, decision making, and problem-solving systems are tools through which transitions are shared so that visions become practice. At a deeper level, institutionalization of change requires shaping and reinforcement of a new culture which fits with the revitalized organization. The human resource systems of selection, development, appraisal, and reward are major levers for institutionalizing change. Tools for institutionalizing transitions will be discussed later in the chapter.

### Individual dynamics

The previous section outlined requisite processes for organizational revitalization. Although organizational steps are necessary, they are not sufficient to create and implement change. In managing transitions, a more problematic set of forces, focused on individual psychodynamics of change, must be understood and managed. Major transitions unleash powerful conflicting forces in people. The change invokes simultaneous personal feelings of fear and hope, anxiety and relief, pressure and stimulation, leaving the old and accepting a new direction, loss of meaning and new meaning, threat to self-esteem and new sense of value. The challenge for transformational leaders is to recognize these mixed emotions, act to help people move from negative to positive emotions, and mobilize and focus energy necessary for individual renewal and organizational revitalization.

Figure 11–2 also provides a set of concepts for understanding individual dynamics of transitions. The concepts, drawn from work by Bridges, propose a three-phase process of individual change (Bridges, 1980). First come endings, followed by neutral zones, and then new beginnings. During each of these phases there is an identifiable set of psychological tasks which individuals need to successfully complete to accept change.

**Endings.** All individual transitions start with endings. Endings must be accepted and understood to proceed with the transition. Employees who refuse to accept that traditional behaviors have ended will be unable to begin new behaviors. The first task of an ending is disengagement, which often accompanies a physical transaction. When transferred from one job to another, individuals must learn to disengage from the old position. They must learn to accept the new physical setting and disengage from the previous setting. When transferred employees continually return to visit with former colleagues, they have inadequately disengaged. The second task is disidentification. Individual self-identity is often tied to job position; thus, when a plant manager is transferred to corporate staff to work in the marketing department, he or she must disidentify with the plant and its people, and the self-esteem felt as a plant manager. At a deeper personal level, individual transactions require disenchantment. Disenchantment entails recognizing that the enchantment or positive feelings toward past situations cannot be replicated in the future. Chrysler, GM, AT&T, or U.S. Steel employees who remember the good old days need to accept disenchantment from those feelings as the present reality is different and self-worth cannot be recaptured by longing for or thinking about the good old days. A new enchantment centered on new circumstances needs to be built. Finally, individuals need to experience and work through disorientation, which reflects the loss of familiar trappings. Endings are necessary for individuals to accept transitions. As mature organizations become revitalized, individuals must disengage, disidentify, disenchant, and disorient with past practices and discover in new organizations a sense of worth or value.

To help individuals, transformational leaders need to replace past glories with future opportunities. However, in helping individuals pass through endings, leaders must acknowledge individual resistances and senses of loss in a transition. Leaders must also encourage employees to face and accept failures as learning opportunities before moving onto new opportunities. Holding on to past glories and memories without coming to grips with failure and need to change may be why companies such as W. T. Grant, International Harvester, and Braniff were unsuccessful at revitalization. There is a sense of dying in all endings. It does not help to treat transactions as if the past can be buried without effort. The past should provide new directions, not old memories.

**Neutral zone.** The key to individuals being able to fully change may be in the second phase which Bridges (1980) terms the neutral zone. This phase can be interpreted as a seemingly unproductive "time out" when individuals feel disconnected from people and things of the past and emotionally unconnected with the present. In reality, this phase is a time of reorientation where individuals complete endings and begin new patterns of behavior. Often Western, and especially U.S. culture, avoids this experience and treats the neutral zone like a busy street, to be crossed as fast as possible and certainly not a place to contemplate and experience. To run across the neutral zone too hurriedly does not allow the ending to occur nor the new beginning to properly start. A death and rebirth process is necessary so that organizational members can work through the disintegration and reintegration. To pass through the neutral zone requires taking the time and thought to gain perspective on both the ending—what went wrong, why it needs changing, and what must be overcome in both attitude and behavioral change—and the new beginning—what the new priorities are, why they are needed, and what new attitudes and behaviors will be required. It is in this phase that the most skillful transformation leadership is called upon. A timid bureaucratic leader who often reels in the good old days will not provide the needed support to help individuals cross through the neutral zone. On the other hand, the militaristic dictatorial leader can try to force a new beginning that does not allow people to work through their own feelings and emotions. The purported backlash toward the "brash" Archie McGill at American Bell in June 1983 may have been an example of trying to force people through the neutral zone to a new beginning. Archie McGill was known to rant and rave about the stodgy, old-fashioned, and noninnovative "Bell Shaped Men" at AT&T. While he was trying to help and lead individuals to become innovative and marketing-oriented, he may have not allowed them to accept the endings inherent in the transition. His enthusiasm may have been well placed, but his sensitivity to individual endings and neutral phases of transactions may have been lacking.

Failure to lead individuals through the neutral zone may result in aborted new beginnings. At International Harvester, the organization in 1983 appeared stuck in the neutral zone. The new beginning at International Harvester must enable people to find a new identification with the future organization while accepting the end of the old organization so that new energies can be tapped. This transformation has occurred at Chrysler Corporation, where morale and esprit de corps grew with the new vision implanted by Lee Iacocca. Organizational revitalization can occur only if individuals accept past failures and engage in new behaviors and attitudes.

Transactions which lead to revitalized organizations and renewed individuals must pass through the stages reviewed in Figure 11–2. Successful transformational leaders need the ability to understand, emotionally cope with, and inspire vision and commitment on the part of self and followers. Leaders can mobilize organizations; they can inspire and lead individuals through transactions; and they must play a central role in revitalizing organizations. The remainder of this chapter sets forth a set of concepts and tools available to transformational leaders engaged in revitalizing organizations.

## LEADERSHIP WHICH CAN REVITALIZE

Above, we have argued for leaders who can revitalize; below we set out some guidelines and characteristics of those whom we feel can fill the role. This section first presents an outline of general characteristics of transformational leaders, followed by a set of tools for each major phase of the organizational transformations: trigger and felt-need phase, vision-creation phase, commitment phase, and institutionalization phase.

### General characteristics of transformational leaders

Transformational leaders are called upon to create something new out of something old. They must develop and communicate the new vision and get others not only to see the vision but to be committed to it. Transactional managers, in contrast, make only minor adjustments in the organization's mission, structure, and human resource management. Transformational leaders not only make major changes in the organization mission, structure, and human resources systems, but evoke more fundamental changes in the basic political and cultural systems of the organization. It is the revamping of the political and cultural systems which most distinguish transformational leaders from the transactional. At Chrysler, until Lee Iacocca took over as leader, the basic internal political structure had been unchanged for decades. It was clear who reaped what benefits from the organization, how the pie was to be divided, and who could exercise what power. Mr. Iacocca needed to alter these political traditions, starting with a new definition of Chrysler's link to external stakeholders. The government was given a great deal of control over Chrysler in return for the guaranteed loan that staved off bankruptcy. Modification of the political system required other adjustments, including the trimming of fat in the management ranks, limiting financial rewards for all employees, and receiving major concessions from the UAW. An indicator of a significant political shift was the inclusion of Douglas Frazer on the Chrysler board of directors as part of UAW concessions. This brief list gives examples of the extent to which the political system was revamped as part of Mr. Iacocca's role.

Equally dramatic was the change in the cultural system. First, the company had to recognize its unique status as a recipient of a federal bailout. This needed bailout came with a stigma. Mr. Iacocca had to change the cultural values from a loser's to a winner's feeling. Employees were not going to be winners unless they could in cultural norms be efficient and more innovative than competitors. This change had to be accomplished with fewer resources than those of their competitors. The molding and shaping of the new culture was clearly and visibly led by Mr. Iacocca, who not only used internal communication as a vehicle to signal change, but used his own personal appearance in Chrysler ads to reinforce his internal messages. Quickly, the internal culture was transformed to that of a lean and hungry team looking for victory.

So what does it take to transform an organization's technical, political, and cultural systems? The transformational leader must possess a much deeper understanding of organizations and their place both in the wider society and in the lives of individuals. It is this deeper understanding of social systems that the transformational leader must either intuitively know or have been formally prepared to comprehend. The ability to build a new institution requires the kind of political dialogue our founding fathers had when Jefferson, Hamilton, Adams, and others debated issues of justice, equity, separation of powers, checks and balances, and freedom. This language may sound foreign to corporate settings but when major organization revitalization is being undertaken, all of these concepts merit some level of examination. At Chrysler, issues of equity, justice, power, and freedom underlay many of Mr. Iacocca's decisions. Thus, as a beginning, transformational leaders need to understand concepts of equity, power, freedom, and the dynamics of decision making. In addition to modifying political systems, transformational leaders must understand and realign cultural systems.

Culture plays two central roles in organizations. First, culture provides organizational members with a way of understanding and making sense of events and symbols. Thus, when confronted with certain complex problems in an organization, employees "know" how to approach it the "right" way. For example, at IBM it is very clear to all insiders how to form a task force to solve problems since task forces and problem solving are a way of life in IBM's culture. Like the Eskimos who differentiate five types of snow and have a vocabulary to describe it, organizations create vocabularies to describe how things are done in the organization.

A second role that culture plays in organizations is to provide meaning. It embodies a set of values which help justify why certain behaviors are encouraged at the exclusion of other behaviors. Companies with strong cultures (Deal and Kennedy, 1982) have been able to commit people to the organization and to identify very personally and closely with the organization's success. Superficially, this is seen in the "hoopla" activities associated with an IBM sales meeting, a Tupperware party, or an Amway distributor meeting. Outsiders often ridicule such activities, yet they are part of the process by which some successful companies manage cultural meaning. On one level it is analogous to rituals carried out in religious groups. The key point in assessing culture is to realize that to transform an organization the culture that provides meaning must be revamped. The transformational leader needs to articulate new values and norms and then to use multiple change levers ranging from role modeling, symbolic acts, creation of rituals, revamping of the human resource systems, and management processes to support new cultural messages.

In addition to managing political and cultural systems, transformational leaders must make difficult decisions quickly. Leaders need to know when to push and when to back off. Finally, transformational leaders are often seen as creators of their own luck. These leaders seize opportunities and know when to act so that casual observers may perceive luck as a plausible explanation for success, whereas, in reality, it is transformational leaders knowing when to jump and when not to jump. Again, Mr. Iacocca can be viewed as a very lucky person or else the possessor of a great ability to judge when to jump and when not to jump. These general characteristics of transformational leaders will now be incorporated into a more detailed look at the transformational leadership role as it is played out across the phases of an organizational change. In the next section we identify a set of leadership behavior and tools which can help an organization move toward revitalization.

### Transformation leadership role and skills

At each phase of organizational transitions, transformational leaders can engage in practices which revitalize the organization. Below we highlight leadership skills at each phase which transformational leaders may practice for revitalizing organizations.

**Trigger/felt-need phase.**   Identifying triggers for change and sensing felt needs require environmental scanning capability which is linked to the transformational leader's need to process information and make decisions. Environmental scanning may also be done by projecting future environmental conditions which a company may face. For example, a company's future environment may require increased technical skills for continued organizational success. In this case, the transformational leader must create a vision for technological growth and development. Environment scanning occurs by assessing economic, political, and cultural trends and by projecting how those trends may affect organizational practices. When the automobile industry started in the early 1900s, cars were designed for the "average" family of four to five people. However, as families became smaller in the 1960s and 1970s, smaller cars could more easily meet family transportation needs. While the economic oil crisis may have speeded up small-car production, cultural trends may have eventually produced the same result. Transformational leaders must continually scan environmental changes and prepare organizational visions to match these changes.

Another major factor in organizations experiencing an appropriate felt need for change is transformational leaders performing stakeholder analysis. Stakeholders are actors external to an organization who play major roles in organizational success. Organizations are supported by a complex web of stakeholders. Relevant stakeholders include competitors, customers, suppliers, regulatory agencies, distributors, unions, stockholders, employees, and financial institutions (Ulrich, 1984). Each of these stakeholders interacts with the organization to receive necessary services. Transformational leaders must understand what stakeholders give to and receive from their organizations, so that stakeholder relationships can be maintained during organizational revitalization. During revitalization, changes are likely to occur in stakeholder relationships. When Lee Iacocca solicited government funds, he had to simultaneously maintain relationships with financial supporters, unions, and customers. These stakeholders had to modify their relationship with Chrysler as Mr. Iacocca made changes with government stakeholders. In setting strategies to revitalize organizations, the goals and influence of each stakeholder must be considered to determine efficient allocation resource.

The skill of identifying and responding to stakeholders is central to its revitalization strategy. An organization's multiple goals need to remain balanced with multiple goals of stakeholders. If, in developing a revitalization strategy, key stakeholders are not considered, these stakeholders will be less likely to help the company reach its revitalization goal. In an organizational transition, the ability to adapt to different stakeholder groups is critical. Since different stakeholders may have different expectations of organizations, transformational leaders need to work with each stakeholder and communicate how the organizational transition will affect each group. Lee Iacocca communicated to Chrysler workers that the short-term transition, although painful, would be essential to Chrysler's future. He also communicated to federal agencies, financial supporters, suppliers, and customers the new direction of Chrysler and how each stakeholder would be benefited by the transition from larger to smaller automobiles. He was adept at showing the importance of Chrysler to the overall economy of the United States to federal agencies, to convincing the financial community that their short-term patience would lead to financial gain over time, to suppliers that they needed to endure some shortages in orders, and to customers through advertising that Chrysler was changing to meet consumer needs. Identifying and responding to interest groups is critical to both strategy formulation and organizational transition.

Stakeholders often trigger need for change. Low customer demand moved GM to design small cars. Financial institutions and loss of investor confidence triggered Chrysler's need for government support. Government legislation triggered AT&T's transition to a deregulated company. Foreign competitors triggered change in U.S. Steel. In these and other cases, triggers for revitalization came from stakeholders. Transformational leaders who maintain contact with stakeholders respond more quickly to triggers for change. Once there is an appropriate felt need for change, the transformational leader must overcome resistant forces by moving throughout the next phases of organizational transition.

**Creation of a vision phase.** In order to overcome the resistant forces triggered by a felt need for change, organizations need a vision which people can become committed to achieving. Transformational leaders need to spearhead the creation of this vision. The future vision must be shared throughout much of the organization so that members have a clear idea of where they are heading. Martin Luther King's "I have a dream" speech symbolizes such a vision. Charles Brown, chairman of AT&T, articulated a vision of AT&T after the breakup of the system. Other leaders such as Tom Watson at IBM and Walter Reuther at UAW are remembered for their ability to shape organizational visions.

An important skill in developing a vision is to be able to define a firm's distinctive competence. Without this vision, the strategy which is formulated may be unrealistic and inconsistent with the firm's capabilities. Therefore, a key transformational leader skill is to identify a firm's strengths and weaknesses, its distinctive competence. This is accomplished by leaders knowing the overall business and the areas of the business which are the firm's distinctive competencies vis-a-vis competitors. By defining a firm's distinctive competencies, transformational leaders can make decisions about where to allocate resources to maximize the probability of reaching strategic goals. Resources of the firm can be allocated to those areas which will provide the firm success over time. In the electronics industry, a number of firms have attempted different strategies. IBM's distinctive competence is its size, its ability to offer a total range of services, and its marketing ability to convince customers of its service and reputation. Some electronics firms such as Burroughs and Honeywell have tried to compete with IBM in all parts of the electronics industry. Their experience has been unsatisfactory as the distinctive competence of these firms is not the same as IBM's. In contrast, some electronics firms have worked to become market leaders in a particular niche. Intel specializes in components and chips. They have not tried to imitate some of the other multiproduct electronics firms, but identified their distinctive competence in one area and worked to leverage that distinctive competence to their advantage. Cray Electronics has worked to become a leader in very large hardware computer technology. Strategic decisions based on the distinctive competence of the firm provide clear direction. In particular, as organizations undergo revitalization, distinctive competencies must be identified, developed, or enriched. AT&T's distinctive competencies of telecommunications, market share, name recognition, and technology must be conserved as a basis for new markets with the reorganization. However, new competencies must be developed at AT&T to compete in unregulated markets.

For managing organizational transitions, defining a firm's distinctive competence also allows transformational leaders to focus on how the transition will position the firm in the marketplace. Having a clear definition of a firm's distinctive competence helps the organizational transition define where organizational changes are necessary. For example, Intel's commitment to being a supplier of components allows Andrew Grove, founder and president of Intel, to focus on ensuring a stable customer demand to use their components. When IBM purchased 12 percent of Intel's stock, Intel's major customer ensured a long-term relationship with the firm, thus guaranteeing that the firm's distinctive competence in components would be supported by the marketplace. A similar agreement between IBM and Rolm Corporation, a telecommunications company, signifies the breadth of efforts to link firms with complementary distinctive competencies. Also, to define a firm's distinctive competence requires an awareness of the overall business so that strengths and weaknesses in the business can be managed. Recognizing these strengths and weaknesses allows organizational revitalizations to occur in a realistic and systematic pattern. By creating a vision through emphasis on distinctive competencies, transformational leaders take a valuable step toward organizational revitalization. Following creating of a vision, commitment to the vision occurs.

**Commitment phase.** It is during the commitment phase that the psychodynamics of changing people can make or break the transformation. This is the phase when an individual organization member must be helped through his or her neutral zone to find a new beginning. The process skills required of leaders in this phase are considerable, involving key individuals or the dominant coalition in the formulation of the change plans. Those individuals need to be more connected and involved in central transactions of the organization change.

In addition to involving key individuals, managing the process involves setting goals which can be visible and reinforced by success. Managing the process implies achieving early success in part of the transition and using those early successes to reinforce other required changes. These early successes are often communicated through stories about how an employee was particularly successful by attempting new behaviors. As such stories proliferate, patterns emerge that reinforce the transition changes (Peters, 1978). Another skill in managing the process of transition is to have gatekeepers make public statements about their response to the transition. Such public statements reinforce behavior in others as well as the gatekeepers.

It is during this phase that leaders must always be aware of the critical importance of arousing subordinates to accept the vision and to see how the vision and future will meet their needs. This means that leaders must be sensitive and responsive to employee needs and able to help individuals manage their mixed emotions about endings, neutral zones, and beginnings.

Transformational leaders will need to act as role models for subordinates. These leaders will embody the attitudes and behaviors which subordinates should work to attain. Ghandi, although a political example, set the example for passive resistance to British rule. His goal was to communicate, by example to others, alternative actions against British rule. Transformational leaders need to look for opportunities to exhibit the behaviors embodied in the desired state vision. Leaders work to create in followers a sense of moral commitment to the company and its cause. In new firms the founder often instills this sense of moral commitment. A religious cult may be built around working for the company. Employees are seen as "Intel" persons, which encompasses much personal life. In organizations which are being revitalized, transformational leaders must instill this same moral commitment that the founders did. This is precisely what happened at Chrysler.

To accomplish this commitment and moral identification, the leader must systematically use symbols to create meaning. Slogans are created, rituals and ceremonies are scheduled, and visual signs are prepared, all to reinforce the new cultural values. The use of symbols, rituals, and visual signs is part of consistent communication from leaders who keep repeating and repeating the same messages about the vision and desired state. It is the consistent and constant repetition through multiple channels which helps generate the commitment.

**Institutionalization phase.**   The final phase of transitions, once the commitment phase has been successfully completed and individual new beginnings are underway, is to ensure that the transformation is institutionalized and does not slip away. Four major sets of tools will be discussed in this section to help transformational leaders institutionalize transformation: organization structure, management processes, culture management, and human resource management systems.

*Manage the organization structure to meet strategic goals.*   The study of organization design has been the focus of much theory and research. While the study of organization design serves many purposes, we highlight the role which organization design plays in institutionalizing organizational transformations. Transformational leaders need to ensure that an organization's structure matches its strategic goals. Chandler's (1962) classic work identifies how at Sears, Roebuck, Du Pont, and GM the strategy was closely aligned with organization structure. At GM the strategy set by Alfred Sloan was to offer a car for every potential buyer. The five divisions allowed a structure where Chevrolet, Oldsmobile, Pontiac, Buick, and Cadillac automobiles could be produced for different income levels. If the structure matches the firm's strategy, the firm is more likely to be successful in meeting its strategic goals. For example, as AT&T made strategic shifts by entering new markets, a number of organization structure changes followed. Divisions became profit centers, marketing departments became more involved in decision making, and managers assumed more profit/loss responsibility as AT&T moved to being a competitor in the telecommunications marketplace. The structure at AT&T changed to fit with the new strategic direction of the firm. In modifying structure, leaders have a primary tool to institutionalize transitions. Structure can be one means to implement a firm's strategic goals.

As leaders define a firm's strategic goals, decisions also must be made on how to structure organization to meet those strategic goals. Decisions need to be made about centralization versus decentralization of the firm. Centralization has advantages of economies of scale, control, and stability. Decentralization has advantages of profit centers, autonomy, and clear indicators of responsibility. Decisions also must be made in regard to the organization's structure: functional versus product versus geographical versus matrix. Each organization structure is appropriate in different environmental circumstances and managers must decide which structure best matches organization and environment needs. Organization decisions also need to be made about roles, rules, and responsibilities.

Efforts need to be made to define what reporting relationships will be used during the transition period. Roles need to be defined so that individuals know their responsibilities in the organization and how the organization is structured. Job responsibilities and who has responsibility for ensuring performance during the transition need to be defined and specified. Clear descriptions of what the organization structure will look like after the transition also need to be made to reduce uncertainty during the transition. These clear descriptions need to include clarification of roles (who will report to whom), rules (policies which might be modified by the transition), and responsibilities (who will be held responsible for different actions). Just as the organization structure needs to fit with the strategic direction of the firm, so also the organization structure needs to be managed during the firm's transition.

*Manage management processes.* In managing transitions, tools of planning, programming, and budgeting can be used by transformational leaders. Skills in these areas are central to institutionalizing revitalization.

For effective planning, skills are needed in setting objectives and in specifying resources required to reach objectives. These same skills are needed for managing transitions. Objectives for the transition period need to be set. Methods, or alternative plans and procedures used in the transition period, need to be specified. Resources such as people, financial support, facilities, time, and equipment which are needed during a transition period also need to be identified. Where resources are lacking, efforts need to be made to increase those resources.

Programming refers to making specific program decisions about how to institutionalize strategic goals of a firm. Strategic programs may include new products, product modifications, new facilities, or market shifts (Stonich, 1982). When a strategic program is defined, funds must be allocated to a program so that the changes will occur. Program management requires skills in setting clear objectives about specific projects and following through with the project until its completion. Transition management requires the same skills. Defining an entire transition project is important for leaders. Allocating funds so that transitions occur smoothly is also an important ingredient to transition management. Budget decisions also need to be made which institutionalize transitions. Managing the budget strategically requires allocation of resources to ensure that neither current nor future goals are compromised. It requires that leaders make decisions to support future programs while maintaining current standards. In managing transitions, the same skills are necessary. Organizational transitions also require balancing current and future financial demands. To balance current and future budget demands while in transition, leaders need to design an effective budget allocation process which identifies key decision nodes.

*Culture management.* Corporate culture is a leadership tool in institutionalizing transformations. Culture refers to the shared values and norms inherent within a firm (Deal and Kennedy, 1982). An organization's culture must be managed to help organizations stabilize changes. To manage culture requires that transformational leaders identify their personal philosophies and how those philosophies are translated into organizational values and practices. Books by Alfred Sloan of General Motors, Ray Kroc of McDonalds, and Willard Marriott of Marriott Hotels are written as statements of philosophy and culture. In revitalizing organizations, a leader needs to make explicit his or her philosophy and the desired corporate culture consistent with that philosophy.

In addition to defining personal and corporate values, transformational leaders need to identify existing and desired cultures within their organizations. Corporate cultures can be identified by the patterns of behavior and existing practices within the company. Wilkins (1978) was able to identify existing cultures in companies by examining stories which employees continually told and which became legends and myths within the company. Transformational leaders should recognize existing cultures so that, as companies engage in transitions, the changes will be enacted around specific practices and beliefs. As AT&T changes from a regulated to unregulated industry, the culture Charles Brown must work to instill is one that goes from little worry about incentives, profits, and aggressiveness in the market to one with much emphasis on these things. This change in culture will be central to AT&T's success in a competitive environment.

As new cultural statements are defined from the leader's philosophy, those cultural premises must be shared with management and employees throughout the organization. By transformational leaders knowing their personal philosophy and their desired corporate culture, they can communicate through speeches, memos, informal discussions, and formal presentations the culture of the revitalized organization. Lee Iacocca was explicit about Chrysler's need to change from a culture of defeatism to one of aggressiveness and success. He communicated this culture to employees though a variety of leverage points. As employees caught the vision which Mr. Iacocca shared, they became more committed to the future success of Chrysler.

Finally, culture can be institutionalized through rewarding practices and activities consistent with desired values, staffing key positions with individuals who have a clear cultural bias, and developing the new cultural norms in formal training events. At General Electric, the corporate culture is a key component of the formal development programs. Managers who attend GE's training programs learn the "GE way." In addition to classroom training about GE's culture, for each group of managers who attend GE's programs, Jack Welsh, the chief executive officer, speaks about his philosophy and vision for GE and the requisite culture to accomplish his vision. For institutionalizing change, culture is a key management tool. In the transition state, leaders need to identify the elements of the culture that need to be maintained, eliminated, and introduced. As this is done, transformational leaders can communicate the new culture throughout the company.

*Manage human resource management.*   Perhaps the most powerful means for institutionalizing change are the people systems in organizations, that is, the human resource processes of staffing, appraising, developing, and rewarding direct energies and activities. When it comes to institutionalizing change, these systems need to be redirected.

Managing the staffing function requires projecting present and future staffing needs, fitting people to roles, and setting up day-to-day monitoring systems. It also requires managing succession politics, such as who gets ahead and how they get ahead, and requires selection and placement of key gatekeepers of the desired culture. In particular, leaders might address the following staffing decisions:

1.   What types of individuals need to be hired to support a future desired state after the transition is complete?

2. What individuals do we need to hire during the transition to signal to employees and other stakeholder groups the direction of the transition?
3. What staffing needs can we meet within the company to signal the direction of the transition?

For transformational leaders, the above issues are salient. Jack Welsh, chief executive officer at GE, has stated that "strategy follows people." He believes that if correct people are placed in appropriate organizational positions, revitalizations are more likely to occur. In addition, selection and succession of employees during a transition serve as important clues to employees of the company's future vision and the leader's commitment to allocating resources to ensure that the transition will occur.

Managing development systems requires that attention be paid to both formal training programs and on-the-job training programs. These development programs need to be consistent with transition needs of the firm so that as the transition evolves to a new desired state, key individuals in the transition will have acquired necessary skills to fulfill their modified responsibilities. Transformational leaders manage development systems by deciding which individuals and departments will receive developmental efforts and by responding to the following questions:

1. What training do we need to provide current employees so that they fit with future goals of the company?
2. What will be the impact on careers from the transition?
3. What socialization procedures are in place to help new employees understand the direction of the firm? What individuals are running this program? Could we involve other key gatekeepers of the organization's transition to orient new employees?

Development requires identifying the key individuals who will be required to support the transition and working with those individuals to voice their public commitment to the transition process. Development efforts can also be made to mold and shape the organization's shared values. The formal development programs should be consistent with the culture implicit in the organization's transition. This may involve socialization of new employees to the organization's pivotal values (Schein, 1968) and increasing awareness of current employees to new values inherent in the transition.

Appraisal systems need to be developed which determine the behaviors which will be rewarded, how to measure performance, and how to administer benefits and compensation during and after the transition. The appraisal system must also be designed to deal with issues of equity (are different groups in the organization appraised equitably?) and involvement (who is involved in the appraisal process?). In addition, transformational leaders might address the following appraisal issues:

1. What skill mix is critical to meeting the objectives set forth in the transition plan?

2.  How will future appraisal systems match with goals of the firm?
3.  How do we manage short-term appraisals (while in transition) and how will those appraisals be consistent with future appraisal systems?

During the transition, these issues become sensitive as new roles are assumed and changes are enacted. The appraisal system must also be designed to measure behaviors which are consistent with the culture implied by the transition. As AT&T moves from a regulated environment to the competitive telecommunications environment, new appraisal systems must be developed which focus on behaviors consistent with the desired state implied by AT&T's transition. The culture changes which will be needed for AT&T to accomplish its transition will need to be built into the appraisal system.

Reward systems also must be consistent with the transition. Linking the reward system to the desired state of the transition is important to focusing individual attention and embarking on new beginnings. Designing rewards and specifying performance criteria for rewards during and after a transition enable the transition to occur quickly. Issues of who gets what and how are central to reward systems during organizational transitions. Having key gatekeepers rewarded for working toward the desired state implied by the transition overcomes some of the resistances to change. Reward systems during transitions must also fit with the desired culture implied by the transition. Some specific reward issues include:

1.  How will the reward system need to be modified for the transition to occur? In particular, how will gatekeepers in the firm need to be rewarded to get their commitment to the transition plan?
2.  How do we motivate other employees to see the value of adopting the transition plan for their personal needs and desires?
3.  What alternative rewards might we employ to gain commitment to a transition plan?

Rewards need to be designed to shape and reinforce the culture of the organization both during and after the transition. Incentive systems need to be designed to motivate individuals to work toward accomplishing the transition (Lorange & Murphy, 1982).

As the human resource management systems of staffing, development, appraisal, and rewards are used to institutionalize change, transformational leaders should be more able to revitalize organizations. By working human resource management issues during transitions, leaders and organizations should accrue the following benefits:

1.  A sensitivity to people. Organizations do not make transitions, people do. Working explicitly on managing the issues most critical to individuals (staffing, development, appraisal, and rewards), leaders can direct the transition so that it occurs smoothly and effectively.
2.  An ability to prepare managerial and technical talent during and after the organizational transition. Ensuring that the right people are in the

right place at the right time (staffing) and with the right skills (development) will help the organization institutionalize a new vision.
3. An ability to overcome resistance to the transition. Using appraisal and reward systems consistent with the firm's future desired state should help overcome technical, political, and cultural resistances to change.

Issues addressed by human resource management concepts can help an organization institutionalize change. In linking human resource management concepts and organizational transitions, a number of key skills can be practiced by transformation leaders to institutionalize the transition process.

Implicit in the above discussion about institutionalizing change is the fact that, for transitions to last, transformational leaders need to spend more time thinking about, discussing, and working on human resource management issues. Some of this time may be shared by forming a transition team, which includes experts in human resource management, to raise questions such as those reviewed above. Spending time with human resource management issues should help stabilize organizational transitions.

In addition to spending time thinking about human resource management issues, efforts need to be made to collect and process information about human resource management. Collecting information on human resource management and strategy might help transformation leaders allocate resources to stabilize organizational revitalization.

## CONCLUSION

While it is difficult to project all dilemmas which organizations will have to overcome in the future, two likely dilemmas can be posited. First, increasing economic, political, and cultural environmental pressures for change will likely force organizations to continually make changes to respond to such externally triggered demands. Second, the next decade is likely to be a less resource-rich environment. Organizations which succeed will have to do so by managing scarcer resources more efficiently. To successfully lead organizations in times of change, transformational leaders are necessary. Transformational leaders move organizations from current to future states, create visions of potential opportunities for organizations, instill within employees commitment to change, and instill new cultures and strategies in organizations which mobilize and focus energy and resources. Transformational leaders are necessary to lead individuals and organizations through transition.

Transformational leaders help individuals work through endings, neutral zones, and new beginnings during transition states. Transformational leaders move organizations through transitions by working through the transition phases of trigger/felt need, creation of a vision, commitment, and institutionalization. In this chapter, we have identified skills which transformational leaders can practice to allow individual and organizational transitions to come to fruition.

Transformational leaders are not born. They arise when mature organizations face environmental problems which cannot be solved by slow evolution. They assume responsibilities for reshaping organizational practices to adapt to environmental triggers for change. They proactively direct organizational changes which instill confidence in employees for new ways of doing things. They help overcome resistance to change by creating visions which evoke confidence in new organization practices. Over the next decade, transformational leaders will become more evident in organizations able to respond to changing, resource-scarce environments.

## REFERENCES

Bridges, W. *Making Sense of Life's Transitions*. New York: Addison-Wesley Publishing, 1980.

Burns, J. M. *Leadership*. New York: Harper & Row, 1978.

Chandler, A. *Strategy and Structure: Chapters in the History of American Industrial Enterprise*. Cambridge, Mass.: MIT Press, 1962.

Deal, T. E., and A. A. Kennedy. *Corporate Cultures*. Reading, Mass.: Addison-Wesley Publishing, 1982.

Lorange, P., and D. Murphy. "The Human Resource Dimension in the Strategic Planning Process: Systems Design Considerations." Paper presented at National Academy of Management, New York, 1982.

Maccoby, M. *The Gamesman*. New York: Simon & Schuster, 1976.

Peters, T. J. "Symbols, Patterns, and Settings: An Optimistic Case for Getting Things Done," pp. 63–79. *Organizational Dynamics*, Autumn 1978.

Schein, E. H. "Organizational Socialization and the Profession of Management," pp. 1–15. *Industrial Management Review* 9, 1968.

Stonich, Paul (ed.). *Implementing Strategy: Making Strategy Happen*. Cambridge, Mass.: Ballinger Publishing, 1982.

Tichy, N. *Managing Strategic Change: Technical, Political, and Cultural Dynamics*. New York: Wiley-Interscience, 1983.

Ulrich, D. "Specifying External Relations: Definition of an Actor in a Firm's Environment." To appear in *Human Relations*, 1984.

Wilkins, A. *"Organizational Stories as an Expression of Management Philosophy."* Ph.D. Dissertation, Stanford University, 1978.

# PART IV

# Reviewing

# 12

## Rabbits, lynxes, and organizational transitions

Kenwyn K. Smith
*The Wharton School*
*The University of Pennsylvania*

### INTRODUCTION

This is a chapter about *how we think*—how we think about the transitions organizations pass through. Recently writers have used life-cycle metaphors (Stotland and Kobler, 1965; Greiner, 1972; Sarason, 1972; Kimberly and Miles, 1980), evoking developmental images: creating and bringing organizations to life, nurturing them into maturity, or supporting them through the death process.

This is an encouraging sign, for we face a national dilemma in terms of the viability of our organizations. The current average life of profit-making organizations in the United States is less than 12 months. This means that one out of every two organizations created each year will not survive past "infancy"—an "infant mortality" rate of crisis proportions. In addition, many of the organizations that do survive should not. Many are kept alive by public funds that act like a respirator to a dying patient. If the plug of public funds were pulled and criteria of efficiency were applied, many of these organizations would become moribund instead of merely examples of living death. Some of these organizations once served a functional purpose but they have become old and should be allowed to go out gracefully. Others hardly got past infancy before they became stuck on some type of developmental plateau.

If it were human babies that were dying or merely existing in a living death, we would label this a national disaster, have endless presidential commissions and legislative investigations, and see literally billions of dollars poured into research, together with an enormous national commitment to "solve the problem." However, organizations are not human babies, at least not literally, and no special attention is being paid to this issue. Instead we're focused on concerns such as the national debt, unemployment, inflation, and productivity and there is no loud voice proclaiming that at the root of all these national economic ills is the problem of "infant mortality" and "living death" of organizations.

These concerns are not new. Ever since the emergence of consciousness man has reflected on how he organizes. Events such as wars, the building of governments, the institutionalization of marriage, exploring space, etc., all contain within them the constant cycling of birth, life, and death of organizations. These life-cycle processes are very easy to see. But we have virtually no way of thinking about them. And history is replete with examples of people disliking one system of organizing, becoming committed to creating alternatives, only to find years later that the alternatives evolved into conditions as undesirable as the ones they were designed to replace (Michels, 1915; Sarason, 1972).

It is easy to describe an organizational transition once it has occurred, using before and after to contrast what happened. However, these transitional times are difficult to understand while we are in the midst of them. They are hard to predict in advance or to accurately picture what life will be like after the transition.

In this chapter, I draw upon a system of thinking known as Cybernetics II to formulate some ways to reflect on what actually occurs during transitions. I do this with the hope that someday we'll be able to formulate action theories that will: (1) give us alternative ways to think about phenomena (such as transitions) than those we gravitate to while embroiled in the dynamics of those phenomena; (2) provide a framework for generalizing from our particular experiences to similar experiences in different situations or at different times; and (3) sketch clear guidelines for action when other guides such as intuition, precedent, or whatever are muddied, obscured, or nonexistent.

**Three tales**

Sometimes the most appropriate way to speak is allegorically, for often a fanciful story contains within it truths more richly stated than can be captured in logical propositions or mathematical equations. The special value of such a story is that the reader or listener, rather than seeking "the truth" can create out of the fabric of the allegory the truths that fit for that particular situation.

As a way of sketching the conceptual terrain of this chapter, I would like to tell three stories: The Tale of the Polyploid Horse; Stories of Parallel Processes; and the Visitation of the Martians. In these stories we can find many truths relevant to understanding the problems we become embroiled in with our organizing and the powerfully unexpected transitions that occur as a consequence of our best-laid plans.

The first story—the Tale of the Polyploid Horse—is told by Bateson (1979). In the late 1980s a great geneticist was awarded the Nobel Prize for creating a horse twice the size of an ordinary Clydesdale—twice as long, twice as high, twice as thick, with four times the usual number of chromosomes.

But alas, by the time it was fully grown it was unable to stand on its four legs, for it was too heavy, being, of course, eight times the weight of a normal Clydesdale. Each morning it had to be raised to its feet by a crane and suspended in a special frame so it could take the weight off its legs.

The polyploid had to be continuously hosed to keep it at a normal temperature for its skin and dermal fat were twice as thick as normal while its surface area was only four times that of a normal horse. It didn't cool properly and without the hoses the innermost parts would begin to cook.

And there was an enormous problem with eating. Every day it had to eat eight times the amount that would satisfy a normal horse and had to push all that food down an esophagus only four times the caliber of the normal. The blood vessels too, were reduced in relative size, making circulation difficult and straining the heart.

This fable illustrates a problem so often encountered in our organizing. We are all painfully familiar with the organization built and surviving at a particular size which is allowed or encouraged to grow to twice its size. And then suddenly it dies. There were no special signs of problems until suddenly a threshold of some kind was passed and all the original systems that functioned when the organization was smaller ceased to function effectively, even when they too were doubled in size. As the experience of the polyploid horse suggests, doubling size may require some functions to be multiplied by two, others to be halved, some to be raised to the third power, and so forth. And the problem is we don't know in advance, at least not at this point, which set of functions should be altered in which way. For we have no idea when changes in two or more interacting variables, whose curves are discrepant, will push the system across critical thresholds (Bateson, 1979).

Our second story deals with the parallel processes that may exist between the microcosm and the macrocosm. Our world of experience is filled with similarities and differences. For example, if we look into a powerful telescope and then into an electron microscope there can be great similarities in what we see. The relationships of the sun, the moons, and the planets all create images similar to those created by tiny molecules as they relate to each other. In social systems these parallel processes can be seen in the following examples.

In a conversation I once had with a White House staff member of the Kennedy Administration, she indicated it was always easy to gauge the emotional climate in the relationship of the president and his wife. When I asked how, she reflected that when President and Mrs. Kennedy were clashing, their two personal staffs seemed unable to coordinate their respective activities. The hairdressers and the transport people would become locked into irresolvable conflict. When JFK and Jackie were relating well with each other, the two staffs found ways to settle "differences of opinions" amicably, avoiding tendencies to polarize. This illustrates how organizational conflicts at one level of the system, such as the interpersonal clashes between division heads, get played out in parallel forms by conflicts between workers in the divisions they supervise. These parallel processes involve the aligning of intergroup relations at one level of the system with interpersonal dynamics at a higher level.

The alignment however may go in a number of different ways. Newfield (1969) in his memoir on Robert Kennedy reported that "the circle of staff and advisors Kennedy drew around himself mirrored the divided, discontinuous layers of his biography as well as the latent tensions between what he was and what he was trying to become." In this statement, Newfield suggests that the inner tensions of the intrapsychic can be seen played through in the interpersonal relations of those who surround a leader.

The converse of this mapping of the various dimensions of our inner being onto the external relations may be seen in how the Western press for years speculated on the health of Soviet Party Chairman Brezhnev. From time to time reporters suggested Brezhnev's illnesses could be used as an index of the intensity of the major clashes in the relationships among the main factions of Soviet politics. The thought went as follows: As leader, Brezhnev had to take into himself the interests of all the factions that his power and position depended on; if these factions were clashing, so also were the introjects of their interests he carried around inside himself. Hence he experienced inner stress that was a parallel manifestation of external tensions and these expressed themselves in the form of physical illness. Whether this was actually true is unknowable. However, in this speculation we can see a way of thinking that suggests conflict among groups can be transformed into intrapsychic tensions for those who identify internally with all or several of those clashing groups.

The parallel processes story focuses the idea that what is being experienced in a particular group or in a set of relationships may in fact be a playing through of dynamics at another level of the system with which they're aligned. What is experienced as an internal transition may simply be a playing through of a much larger dynamic. In fact an internal change may be a way for the larger system to remain fundamentally the same or vice versa (Simmel, 1955).

The issue of parallel processes may prove to be one of the most complex themes we have to learn to deal with in the management of organizational transitions. For if the place where transitional dynamics are evident is not the place where the real changes are occurring, we will obviously need some radically different ways of thinking than those we currently use.

The third story comes from a historical event. It was Sunday, 8 P.M., October 30, 1938. CBS was about to present H. G. Wells' famous novel *The War of the Worlds* in which the Martians arrived via a mysterious meteorite that crashed to Earth in New Jersey. Orson Welles was the announcer, but for various reasons few people heard the introduction telling that this was a performance of a piece of literature. However, over the next few minutes a large number of people tuned in to the dramatization and came to believe that what they heard was a live account of something happening right at that time. Within a short period of time the whole nation was thrown into pandemonium.

Within half an hour of the beginning of the show, people were reporting that Martians, as tall as skyscrapers, were about to wade across the Hudson River and that clouds of heavy smoke were rising from Newark and New York. Even the Secretary of the Interior came onto the air to exhort calm, giving in the process credence to the story being dramatized by Orson Welles and his collaborators.

After a commercial break the announcer, in preparation for the second half of the show, restated that this was a CBS dramatization of an H. G. Wells novel. It was only at this time that Orson Welles and his group, the Mercury Theatre of the Air, learned of the pandemonium that had been created (Houseman, 1948).

In this "Invasion of the Martians" story can be found many truths relevant to organizational transitions. (1) An event such as a simple radio broadcast when *framed* as a live news report can create radically different meanings and unleash remarkably powerful forces. The critical issue, however, resides in how the event was *framed*, not the actual event in and of itself. For example, when the second half of the show proceeded with everyone understanding it was a dramatization, the events conveyed were hardly even listened to, let alone given any power. (2) When we are dealing with human consciousness, the impact of powerful ideas, especially if they are grounded in primal fears, can be absolutely overwhelming and all-determining of collective action. (3) Content, such as history and current events, can provide a dampening or fueling effect on such an occasion. For example, this broadcast occurred just before the Munich crisis and the nation had grown anxious and news-hungry. There was an air of expectation of disaster. "The Invasion from Mars" fulfilled the anticipations of an anxiety-riddled time.

From these three stories—the polyploid horse, parallel processes, and the Martians—several underlying themes for understanding organizational transitions may be extracted: (1) All-important is the frame placed around experience: alter the frame and you can radically alter the meaning of the experience; (2) planned changes can produce catastrophic consequences despite the best of intentions; (3) what occurs in the microcosm may be a reflection of what's taking place in the macrocosm and vice versa. These are the central themes that undergird the spirit of this chapter.

## Cybernetics I

For the past three decades there have been many attempts to understand planned organizational changes and, since Ashby (1956), Katz and Kahn (1966), Miller and Rice (1967); Thompson (1967) and von Bertalanffy (1968), a rich set of metaphors have been borrowed from open systems theory. In many ways it would make sense for us to attempt to formulate our images of transitions in terms congruent with the systems theory we learned to apply from the biological sciences: inputs, throughputs, and exports; the cyclical nature of system activities; the concept of dynamic homeostasis; the tendency of systems to become increasingly differentiated; and the view that systems are equifinal (Katz and Kahn, 1966). These basic concepts, fruitfully augmented by the role of boundary systems as articulated by Rice (1969) and elaborated by Alderfer (1976), would seem the most logical place to start.

But there's a snag.

Since the late 1960s there has been a quiet revolution taking place in scientific thought, especially as it relates to evolution and the dynamics of change. Long-standing beliefs in principles such as the "survival of the fittest" have crumbled. Hence, if we wish to draw on metaphors from man's knowledge of the universe and from theories of evolution it is necessary first to appreciate the theories that are replacing those we've relied on for years. Although these new theories are still in their embryo they contain great potential for radically different types of thinking. I refer to the theory of dissipative structures developed first by Prigogine (1967) in the field of chemistry but now applied to a wide range of disciplines, from biology to sociology, from embryology to consciousness (Jantsch, 1976; Bateson, 1979; Jantsch, 1980).

### The shift

For a long time scientists had thought about evolution in the Darwinian framework that tended to separate the microcosm and the macrocosm from each other, viewing the environment as fixed and the survivability of a particular species as dependent on how it fared in competition with other species within this given environment. Of course, in a more general sense there was some recognition that the macrocosm too was evolving, but at a very different pace and in such a different way that from a pragmatic perspective it could be treated as fixed. Thought was rarely given to the idea that what was occurring at the level of the microcosm might influence and be influenced by the evolution of the macrocosm and vice versa. Then the change occurred. It came in a simple way, but it was provocative. "What about the possibility that the microcosm and the macrocosm are co-evolving?"

This shift in thinking was fueled by the recognition that the actions of individuals (hunting practices, automobile pollution), corporations (toxic wastes), nation states (nuclear fallout), etc. were influencing the ecology. Hence it became more and more essential to start viewing social processes as impacting powerfully on the future evolution of the ecology as a whole. In fact it became theoretically self-evident that the very actions of those dedicated to obtaining a competitive advantage in the survival game might well destroy the very conditions necessary for that survival (Schön, 1971).

There are numerous cybernetic concepts that can contribute to how we think about transitional phenomena. In this chapter, I would like to elaborate some of these concepts and point to some of the ways these various cybernetic concepts are interlinked in everyday experience, introducing the texture of a future cybernetic theory of transitions. The topics to be elaborated include: dissipative structures, stability versus resilience, autopoiesis, novelty and confirmation, microcosmic evolution, symmetry breaks, catastrophe theory, morphostasis, morphogenesis, symbiosis, self-transcendence, paradox, and framing.

## CYBERNETICS II

This new system of co-evolutionary thinking, Cybernetics II, stretches radically beyond the parameters of open systems theory and what is referred to now as Cybernetics I. At the center of this new thought are two concepts—dissipative structures and autopoiesis (auto = self; poiesis-production).

The theory of dissipative structures is based on the field of nonequilibrium thermodynamics and postulates the principle of "order through fluctuation." In this sense it formulates a very different role for fluctuation than was prevalent in Cybernetics I. Traditionally, fluctuation has been viewed as equilibrium-disturbing. Hence for a system to remain stable, it has been believed that fluctuation must be minimized. In Cybernetics II, however, fluctuation is viewed as a major vehicle for *creating* order, not destroying it. In fact, the theory of dissipative structures suggests that near-equilibrium order is destroyed, whereas far from equilibrium order is maintained (Prigogine, 1976).

The concept of "order through function" may be illustrated by considering a typical predator-prey relationship. Imagine a territory inhabited by rabbits who are the prey for the predatorial lynxes (Tustin, 1952). When rabbits are abundant the lynx population increases, but as the lynxes become abundant, the rabbit population falls because more rabbits are caught. As the number of rabbits diminishes, the lynxes go hungry and likewise decline, making possible the relative increase in rabbits again. The system, in other words, is in oscillation; its order depends upon the patterns of fluctuation.

The power of this example can be seen if we consider the plight of a particular rabbit who wants to be sure to behave in ways that will contribute to the long-term survivability of its species. Its dilemma is it cannot work out what to do—whether to try to escape or simply let itself get caught and eaten. It depends entirely on the point of the oscillation as to whether surrender or escape best serves the goal of long-term survival. To decide this the rabbit would have to get into a "lofty" enough perspective to pick up on the overall order of the cycle (a tall order!). Then it might recognize that sometimes escape would be the best contribution, other times to give itself up to be eaten would be wiser. However the rabbit doesn't (can't) do this. It operates according to an internal set of rules which it believes will best serve it goals; that is, it always tries to escape (Smith, 1982b).

The theoretical point we can learn from the rabbits-lynxes story is provocative when applied to how we manage our organizations. For example, when something goes into chaos, our automatic response is usually to try to restore order as quickly as possible. That's what our internal set of rules says we should do; so we do this believing that both long-term and short-term viability will be augmented by this action. However, it may well be that the most appropriate action for system viability is to encourage the chaos, doing the equivalent of the rabbits' offering themselves up to be eaten. The reality is, of course, from the inside we simply don't know what would be best. But we can say that *sometimes* doing what we always do, i.e., applying the standard internal rules and regulations is the worst thing we can do, even though while we're doing it we may well believe it's for the best.

How we think in these situations where there are large fluctuations is critical. I'd like to illustrate by describing an occasion on which I felt management might have benefited greatly had they chosen to think in cybernetic terms. We were working with the Buildings and Maintenance Division of Weymouth State Hospital (a pseudonym). For years workers had been depressed. This depression expressed itself in high absenteeism and turnover, poor morale, and a very lethargic attitude toward work. For months we had been encouraging workers to become more vocal about concerns they were refusing to express. Mostly they talked about poor pay. Certainly salaries were low. But their constant focus on pay conditions, something unchangeable given the state system, provided a smokescreen for their discontent over other issues which they could influence. These other things were small, but their cumulative impact was very potent.

Then one day their rebellious spirits became engaged. The State Hospital Commission for weeks had been promising workers an announcement of anticipated salary increases. But week after week, there was no news.

There was one very influential shop within Buildings and Maintenance—heating and air conditioning. It so happened that 11 of the 15 men who worked in this shop had received job offers elsewhere. But they liked Weymouth, felt a great degree of loyalty, and knew that if they all left suddenly, the hospital, since it was the middle of winter, could be in real trouble. So they delayed leaving as long as possible, hoping the anticipated raises might be sufficient to enable them to stay. But as the weeks went by and they heard nothing these workers became furious, threatening to all take sick leave on February 2nd if they did not hear by February 1st, not what their raises would be, but simply when they would be told about their raises.

It so happened that the deputy commissioner had the announcement ready by the last week of January. On hearing the threat of industrial action, he refused to make the announcement so the workers would learn "they could not push management around," as the top ranks of Weymouth expressed it. The heating and air conditioning group carried through on their threat, catalyzing a sympathetic progressive "sick out" by virtually all workers over the next 10 days. In many ways the "sick out" was disruptive. In many other ways it was cleansing—like the whole Buildings and Maintenance Division taking a bath. A great deal of pent-up emotion was expressed through this event. In addition, the workers had been very careful to avoid all being absent at the same time so that the safety of patients and medical staff would be preserved. For a few brief days there was within Buildings and Maintenance a spirit of intense cooperation. They covered for each other. The place became alive. Certainly no one was depressed.

From an outside perspective, this was the most vital we had seen the workers over a 12-month period—a chance for great change, if only it could be understood in those terms.

The Hospital Commission did not share this perspective. They interpreted the industrial action as chaos to be suppressed and moved quickly and punatively to do what they described as "preserving order." Raises were delayed an extra two months; virtually all of the air conditioning and heating workers left and a year later the place was again lethargic and depressed, with absenteeism and turnover as high as ever. The atmosphere was tinged with bitterness.

The order and stability, so vigorously controlled by the Hospital Commission, was effectively killing both the Buildings and Maintenance Division and the people who worked there. For a few brief moments of chaos, the place seemed alive. Cybernetic thinking would have encouraged this turbulence, viewing it as a time for renewal and rebuilding.

### Stability versus resilience

The idea that near equilibrium order is destroyed, whereas far from equilibrium order is maintained is counterintuitive to most of the ways we think. So this requires some elaboration. A distinction Holling (1976) made between stability and resilience is helpful in this regard. He defines *stability* as the capacity of a system "to return to an equilibrium state after a temporary disturbance; the more rapidly it returns and the less it fluctuates, the more stable it is." On the other hand *resilience*, according to Holling, may be viewed as a "measure of the persistence of a system and of its ability to absorb change and disturbance and still maintain the same relationship" with other entities in its ecosystem. With these two concepts in place it is possible to think of an entity becoming more unstable as a result of large fluctuations, but that knowing how to survive with these fluctuations makes for greater resilience in that a lot of changes can be absorbed.

Waddington's (1975, 1976) work in embryology provides a framework for thinking about the critical conditions of stability and resilience. In embryology, the role of fluctuations can be observed clearly for a fertilized egg is hovering in a nonequilibrium condition. It insists, as it were, on changing. The only way to stop it from changing is to kill it. To symbolize the development of an embryo, Waddington (1976) suggests we have to understand both the trajectories projected by the potential within the cells of the embryo and the system of constraints which together become like an epigenetic landscape.

The fluctuations of a system may be understood in terms of the cross-sectional shape of the valleys. For example, in a canyon it would be difficult to divert the flow from the very bottom of the system. Should a strong enough force be available to create such a diversion, the system would return to the bottom of the valley the moment the influence ceased. In Holling's (1976) terms such a system is very stable. A system with little stability would be one shaped like a broad river flood plain. For here it would be easy to divert the system from the lowest point and it would return to that point only after considerable meandering. To understand the resilience of the system, Waddington (1976) suggests we examine not the shape of the valleys but the height of the watersheds on each side of it, for they prevent the system from being provoked, through minimal disturbance, into unknown territory.

Waddington's main argument is very simple but has powerful ramifications. When a system is near the point where equilibrium cannot be sustained, small fluctuations may alter the system, because a small fluctuation may carry it across the watershed so it falls under the potent influence of another epigenetic landscape. And once this has happened there may never by a way back to the original landscape. Recent experiments in embryology have thrown some light on this issue. For example, one group of researchers asked the question, "What would happen if we took a cell from the stomach of a bird and placed it in its eye? Would the cell which normally produced nerves to help contain digestion continue to produce such nerves, or would it generate reflex nerves that facilitated the dilation of the pupil?" Earlier theory suggested that the stomach cell would always grow into a stomach neuron because that's what its genetic code would instruct it to do. If the replacement environment were too foreign, it might die. But it would become stomach nerve or nothing. However, it has been found that switching to a new epigenetic landscape can cause the exact opposite to happen, such that the transplanted cells take on the identity of the new site rather than of their source (Begley & Carey, 1982). In one experiment, outer belly cells of a toad were grafted onto the head of a newt embryo. The cells remained toad. In this sense they did not betray their genes. However, they did not become belly cells. Rather, they created toadlike suckers on the side of the newt's head, displaying an amalgam of the forces from the genetic trajectory and the epigenetic landscape.

The distinction between resilience and stability highlights two radically different ways for thinking about how to manage resources in human and ecological systems. Since the stability view emphasizes equilibrium, within this framework it becomes all-important to pour resources into maintaining a predictable world (a *fail-safe* world). On the other hand, a resilience view suggests the energy be focused on persistence, with the emphasis being upon keeping options open, examining events from a regional rather than local perspective (a *safe-fail* world). The assumption here is that the future will be unexpected rather than expected. Within such a resilience framework, whatever stability there is will be seen as a result, not of a static regime, but as an equilibrium created out of a dynamic network of the complex intersection of internal and external forces. A safe-fail approach treats with caution the idea of trying to shrink fluctuations, recognizing that such attempts may be just as likely to produce an effect opposite to that desired (Simmel, 1955) by triggering, through some catalytic event (Maruyama, 1963), unexpected changes. Out of resilience thinking, the conclusion is that for an entity to persist, it must be able to make a companion out of disturbance, variability, and uncertainties.

## Autopoiesis

Cybernetic theory has always emphasized the importance of the relationship of an entity with its environment. For an entity to thrive it must be linked to a network of relations which constantly recreates the conditions necessary to sustain it (Maturana, 1981). An entity capable of doing this may be described as autopoietic. The basic principle of autopoiesis is that an entity must be proactive and responsible for the creation and sustenance of that network. If it does not, it is essentially parasitic and likely to die off once the energy available to it from the networks with which it interacts expires. Those entities that link their actions and reactions to their networks in a recursive way are the ones capable of being self-creative.

Autopoiesis may be autocatalytic or cross-catalytic. By *autocatalysis* is meant that entities can participate actively in interactions which directly help the formation of entities such as themselves. *Cross catalysis* refers to participating in the formation of entities of an intermediate kind, which in turn support its own (Jantsch, 1980).

Autopoietic structures may interact with and even create webs of interaction that are unpredictable. However, throughout they are singular in purpose. They attempt to maintain themselves in the most consistent manner possible. To do this they must constantly monitor their environment, themselves, and their interactions with the environment, making adjustments according to some model or other of "appropriate" behavior. In this regard an autopoietic structure may be viewed as an information processing system.

Weizsäcker (1974) discussed two complementary aspects of communication—novelty and confirmation—that provide a good basis for understanding the central idea of what is meant by an autopoietic entity. Pure novelty, or uniqueness, stands for chaos. It is the condition where there is no order. Hence it does not contain any usable information. On the other hand, pure confirmation brings nothing new and as such stands for stagnation. Another way to say this is that 100 percent confirmation is the equivalent of a system in thermodynamic equilibrium. In contrast, 100 percent novelty is like a period of intense instability where the old structure is no longer being confirmed but where, as yet, no new structure has been established. Jantsch (1980) suggests that autopoiesis may be found in the region represented by the *balance* between these two extremes of novelty and confirmation.

An autopoietic structure exists in a condition of paradoxical tension generated by the powerful mix of novelty and confirmation. Jantsch (1980) summarizes this paradox: "Living near boundaries of a stable domain (i.e., in sufficient nonequilibrium) is a precondition for a system's capability of evolving; of changing to another, qualitatively different stable domain (Prigogine, 1976); but at the same time, apparently through more effective flexible coupling of the subsystems (Prigogine, 1976) it enhances the system's resilience, or capability for persistence in the original domain (Holling, 1976) which, in turn, tends to increase the fluctuations until they are big enough to drive the system to a new regime (Prigogine, 1976)." The question, as yet unanswerable, is whether a large number of fluctuations contributes to both an entity's capacity to persist and its transformability. And, more particularly, at what point and via what mechanisms does structural persistence relinquish its "grasp" in favor of long-term viability via some transformation?

Perhaps the most fruitful way to capture the essence of what is meant by autopoiesis is to tell the story of the beginning stages in the evolution of the microcosm. In this story we find entities creating changes in the macrocosm that in turn create the conditions necessary for the microcosm to evolve into new forms. Not that the microcosm organism "knew" in advance that this is what it was up to. Nevertheless, in hindsight this is what happened. For this description I draw heavily on the work of Jantsch (1980).

**Evolution of the microcosm.** In microcosmic evolution, the first "structures" to form were the dissipative ones that involved chemical and biochemical reactions. Then came a symmetry break. The primitive cell developed. At this point, what emerged was a thing called a membrane. The membrane became a vehicle for both the separation and the reinforcement of biochemical pathways and cycles. The membranes became a way to keep nonequilibrium systems contained so that one nonequilibrium system didn't "spill over" into another. This enabled numerous dissipative structures of microcosmic size to be contained within a single cell, facilitating as it were the miniaturization of structures. These miniaturized structures were very much like the complex, multiple, interacting dissipative structures typical of higher-level systems, except that they were microcosmically small. They operated on the same principles as the microcosm and as such represent the earliest-known parallel processes.

These microorganisms, called *prokaryotes*, can be thought of as the second stage of development. They are the substances such as bacteria and algae which reproduce themselves via cell division. This is a multiplication process through which the complete genetic information in a cell is reproduced in several copies. No natural death separates generations, for each cell lives on and, through many steps, becomes a very extended structure that stretches across space and time.

A third stage of development in microevolution, following dissipative structures and prokaryotes, was the emergence of *eukaryotic* cells. They came soon after the appearance of free oxygen, an ecological necessity for them, for this type of cell breathes. The eukaryote has a real nucleus in which the genetic material, organized into chromosomes, is aggregated. Theory about how these cells developed is controversial. However, Margulis (1970) suggests that the process involved a type of fusion without loss of the participants' identities. The participants in this fusion were the various prokaryotes. Thus the eukaryote contains within it the earlier forms from which it evolved, namely the prokaryotes. The thing that is critically different about the eukaryotes is that they carry within themselves their own genetic material and mechanisms to reproduce themselves. The earlier prokaryotes could be viewed as a huge, common gene pool, like a generally accessible "central library" to which temporally defined "species" could go to "select" the particular genetic material they needed to survive in their environments. In contrast, the later eukaryotes were more like "private genetic libraries" where the genetic possibilities would be inherited via a process such as sexuality.

We should point out that in each of the transitions—from dissipative structures to prokaryotes to eukaryotes—each lower level contributed to the creation of the conditions that enabled the later organisms to surface. For example, it is easy to see that the emergence of free oxygen in the environment provided the "kick" necessary to trigger the development of the eukaryotic cell. But where did the oxygen come from? This was not known until recently. Scientific work over the last few decades on unicellular microfossils, which existed thousands of millions of years ago, has indicated that the earliest dissipative structures and prokaryotes were primarily responsible for a tremendous transformation of the earth's surface by in fact creating free oxygen in the atmosphere. In this sense they created the preconditions necessary for their next stage of evolution, for it so happens that cell tissues and multicellular organisms are made up of oxygen-breathing cells. The process was long and complicated because it involved the oxidation of the entire surface of the earth, which was done in stages. Initially, a small quantity of oxygen was produced, providing a beginning shield from the sun's ultraviolet radiation. This shield enabled a variety of changes in the earth's ecology to occur (Jantsch, 1980). And, in turn, these ecological changes then helped fuel the overall oxidation program.

What's of special importance in this story is that the actions of the pro-karyotes, across millions of years while their own microevolution was mod-est, produced changes that were responsible for a dramatic alteration in the evolution of the macrocosm in which they were embedded. In turn, the changes in the macrocosm created the conditions for a radical change in the microcosm. Of course the converse of this could also be stated. The macro-cosm created the conditions to enable the microcosmic prokaryotes to gen-erate oxygen that in turn changed the macrocosm. In short, this example il-lustrates both the pattern of co-evolution and what we mean by the term autopoiesis. While an organism may be busily adapting to an environment on the one hand, that very adaptation may be in the process of driving the evolution of that same environment on the other hand. At the micro level we may be observing evolution playing itself through on the basis of *confir-mation*, the preservation of "what is." In parallel, however, we will find at the macro level that the evolution will be operating on *novelty*, changing "what is." Or vice versa. When the balance increases from both sides, as confirmation moves in the direction of novelty, and novelty in the direction of confirmation, the middle-range conditions become created that enable autopoiesis to occur.

**An organizational example.** To illustrate some of these dynamics oper-ative in a contemporary organization, I'd like to describe briefly some events that occurred in the development of Dexter (pseudonym), a psy-choeducational facility for adolescents in a very wealthy county near a large Eastern city. In this example we can see: (1) the transportation of dyn-amics in the ecosystem into the internal operations of the new organization, (2) the tensions between novelty at one level of the system and confirmation at another, and (3) the creation of recursive networks that helped produce the ecological conditions necessary to sustain the development of the facil-ity. Before illustrating this first issue, I need to provide a little background. Lassiter County for years had argued that they needed a residential place-ment facility for emotionally disturbed adolescents. To date, these individ-uals were being inappropriately incarcerated in state psychiatric hospitals, being left uncared-for until they encountered trouble with the law, or being a constant disruption to otherwise normal, middle- to upper-middle-class families. Numerous organizations became involved in advocating the building of a place eventually to be called Dexter; they included the county healty department, the county school system, the state department of men-tal health, the state department of education, the local judiciary, a group of private psychiatrists, numerous parent groups, and a variety of social ser-vice agencies. All agreed that the county needed and deserved a first-rate psychoeducational residential center where the best mental health and educational specialists that money could buy would "save" these disturbed adolescents. They didn't say it this way. But that was what they meant. For 14 years planning took place and although everyone could agree on an overall goal, there was no agreement as to how to proceed or which organizations were to be responsible for what. Conflicts raged, sometimes delaying planning by literally years as task forces were created and disbanded in considerable disarray. At one point it was agreed the county health department would run the clinical and residential sides of Dexter, while the county school system would provide the educational component. Funding was to come from the state. However, in the year before Dexter was to open and well after construction of a complex of buildings had begun, the county health department withdrew. This left the state department of mental health with either a multimillion dollar albatross as a memorial to planning folly or the task of running the facility itself. Reluctantly, the state resolved to take on the operational responsibilities and negotiated with the county school board a precarious, though implementable, contract to provide a school for 200 children and adolescents.

During the first year of operation four broad conflicts were constantly operative in the life of Dexter (Smith, Simmons, Thames and Marx, 1983). They were the following.

1. *Whose needs does the facility serve?* The county school board saw Dexter as a place to send emotionally disturbed students who, by law, had to be provided for educationally. The judges wanted placements for adolescents coming through the court system. The clinical staff had dreams of controlling the population admitted because they had an investment in the treatments they wished to offer. For months, staff at Dexter struggled over how admissions would occur, via the school system, or the judgment of the clinicians, or at the discretion of the judges.

2. *What model of treatment was to be appropriate for Dexter?* This question ended up revolving around who would have control. Would the medical model be dominant, with psychiatrists the main determiners of treatment, or would it be a truly collaborative psychoeducational program with clinical and educational needs being equal co-partners? The struggle took the form of whether Dexter would be primarily a treatment center with residential and school components grafted on or whether it would be primarily a school with clinical and residential annexes.

3. *What constitutes "success" for Dexter?* Dexter was to be judged on some broad criteria such as how many adolescents were returned to normal and how quickly. Whenever clinicians found their "patients" too hard to handle or unresponsive to treatment there was a tendency to recommend transfer to a hospital, claiming that the "failure" was due to the inappropriateness of the original placement decision. There also surfaced a strong norm of each element of Dexter trying to hold others responsible for the things that did go wrong. Clinicians blamed the school. The school blamed the clinicians. The residential wing blamed . . . etc.

4.  *Who pays for what?* For months there was controversy over who would pay for what services. The state had agreed to forward a lump sum figure calculated on a per child basis to the county board of education to run the school. However, this was cut by the state legislation budget system after the agreement had been made. Then there was the question of third-party insurance money. Could this be collected and, if so, to whom would it be paid and what portion of it would be poured back into Dexter? There was also another catch. Originally, when the county health department had planned to run Dexter, they intended to pay county salaries, which were considerably higher than the state rates. There was no way good staff could be attracted to Dexter at the lower pay scales. Yet Dexter, now a state facility, was obliged to keep pay consistent with the other hospitals under its jurisdiction. Lassiter was outraged by this, feeling that since it carried on its back so much of the state by its large tax contributions, due to its wealth, the least the state could do would be to give them higher pay. Otherwise the original goal of a first-class establishment would be undermined from the beginning.

For most of the first year of Dexter's life these four conflicts raged. Nothing anyone did seemed able to drive them away. At times they went underground, only to resurface potently and disruptively at the most inopportune moments. In reality, staff did good work during that first year, but at every crossroad these problems reraised their heads, demanding an inordinate amount of time and, in some cases, some battle casualties such as the first medical director, who was fired, in large part as a fall guy.

What was particularly intriguing, however, was that these conflicts were the same ones that had undergirded the complex and convoluted 14 years of Dexter's prehistory (Simmons, 1983). The larger society, namely the county, the state, the various groups of professionals, and interested parents, had been unable to grasp these conflicts and bring them to any kind of resolution. But once Dexter was built, these conflicts could be transported, as it were, from the amorphous struggle of social and political life and deposited within the walls provided by the bricks and mortar of Dexter.

Once those walls were built, the fluctuation of the dissipative structure of the macrocosm could be miniaturized and repeated, in localized form, within the microcosm. And the inner dynamics of Dexter proceeded to be played through, in parallel with how they'd been handled in the macrocosm.

To illustrate the second point, namely the tension between novelty at one level of the system and confirmation at another, we can pick up on another aspect of the Dexter story. At one stage it became almost ludicrous to observe the struggles between novelty and confirmation. The larger society wanted something new, some novel ways to deal with old problems. Dexter was to be this place. However, no sooner was it created than the larger systems in which the facility was embedded acted to undermine the very things it had established Dexter to do. For example, it was decided that the adolescents should live in small units, like families, eating their evening meals in their residences. However, every bureaucratic obstacle conceivable was placed in the way of doing this. The law stated that, in institutions such as this, dishes had to be cleaned at water temperatures much higher than those in the residence halls. However, procurement policies, established in another part of government, made it impossible to order the necessary equipment to heat the water to the required temperature. There's no need to tell the details of this story. We all know how situations like this unfold for they are so common. Each solution created a further problem that demanded yet another solution ad infinitum until the whole system caved in and everyone decided it would be less psychologically damaging for all concerned to feed the residents in a central dining hall, cafeteria style. This undermined the family meal concept, but it saved the system from another type of insanity.

Here we see novelty at the macrocosm being, as it were, put into the microcosm. Then the macrocosm returned to its pattern of confirmation. Change—represented by the microcosm—and status quo—represented by the macrocosm—then proceeded to clash swords until some stability regime was implemented. In this case of the meals, status quo predominated over novelty; as a result nothing new was created, and at least on this dimension Dexter became no better than the other institutions it was designed to replace.

There was one major event in the first year of Dexter's operation that illustrates perfectly the creation of recursive networks that help produce the ecological conditions necessary to sustain the development of the system. A few weeks before Dexter was slated to open, the state department of mental health went into a budget crisis. Funds were being cut everywhere and hiring freezes were applied. Dexter was exempt from many of these restrictions, but it became evident during this time that there was no way for the facility to operate at the level everyone expected unless they received more money. Requests were sent up through state channels but repetitively they were rejected. Pleas were sent to the governor. All to no avail. The message was clear. Dexter must make do with what they had. This meant some staff would have to be fired and the vision of what Dexter could offer had to be reduced to about the level of a baby-sitting function of disturbed adolescents.

The staff became outraged and under the skillful leadership of the chief executive officer, who constantly pulled the strings while keeping a very low profile, a network of influential parents of potential Dexter residents was created. Many of them were well-connected professionals who in no time created a tremendous uproar about how the state was cheating Lassiter County; having promised them the sky originally it was now about to provide services at the level of the banal. "Given all we do for the state, we *deserve* better," was the battle cry. The news media and the local press were pulled in and for a brief period the political pressure placed on the governor was enormous; so much so that he could not continue to ignore the situation. He gave in, promising that Dexter would be provided with the necessary funds.

In this event we can see the entity, Dexter, using many of its resources to influence one part of its ecosystem (the parents and powerful professionals of the county) to pressure another part of the ecosystem (the governor and the department of mental health) to behave in a way that would support and sustain rather than subvert and undermine the interests of Dexter. Of course, in the long run, the extra funds Dexter was given were taken from other projects equally deserving, though less politically volatile. So it's hard to believe that anything like distributive justice occurred. However, in this event we can see the behavior of an entity being directed toward creating in the macrocosm conditions that will enable the microcosm to persist in its particular forms.

**Another look at the evolutionary patterns.** One of the remarkable things that modern science has taught us about evolution is that it does not proceed in gradual steps, but with dramatic jumps. These jumps are most visible in the breaking of patterns of symmetry, either spatial or temporal symmetry, or both. If we look at these symmetry breaks, we can learn a great deal about what is really involved in the transitional process. For example, as the eukaryotes developed they folded into themselves contributions of the prokaryotes such that the new organisms contained, as it were, their predecessors within them. This folding in, however, did not occur in an additive way. Rather, a new system of combination of prokaryotes was especially created in the formation of the eukaryote, generating thereby a system of *complexity* that had not previously existed.

There are numerous examples of the new levels of complexity created at this stage of evolution. Three will suffice.

The first is that at this point the cell nucleus became able to break down in an orderly way such that the genetic structures could be passed from one generation to the next. This stood in stark contrast to the never-ending multiple cell division process in which the prokaryotes engaged. This new reproduction system was made possible by the development of sexuality, which introduced both systematically enhanced variety and, for the first time, the concept of natural death of individual organisms. In fact, while reproduction had been by asexual cell division there had been no such notion as death. It came with sexuality—all part of the same package.

Apart from sexuality and death emerging with the evolution of the eukaryotic cell, we also find the development of the capacity to live off other organisms. This is our second example of increased complexity. Up to this time the prokaryotes got their energy via photosynthesis, a process which converts solar energy into chemical energy. But from this point on we have a new organism that can gain sustenance by eating plants or eating other organisms that have eaten plants that did the original solar-chemical energy conversion.

A third example is that, with the eukaryote, for the first time we have an organism that is able to recognize self and other in new ways and to communicate with other cells of a like kind. We have an organism capable both of bonding with others of its kind and of acting as an independent agent. Consider, for example, slime mold which is a temporary aggregation of prokaryote-eating eukaryotes. In periods when it's easy to get food they act independently. But when food is scarce they attract each other and, in the process, develop a system for moving along the ground in search of more favorable feeding places. After arriving at new pastures they unhook from each other and act individually again until the next period of scarcity (Jantsch, 1980).

The evolution of the eukaryote brought with it sexuality, death, the capacity to live off other organisms, communication, and the capacity to act individually and collectively. Quite a contribution!

There are many different themes we could pursue out of this microevolutionary story and Jantsch (1980) elaborates many of them for us. However, in this chapter, apart from using the dissipative structure, the prokaryotes, and the eukaryotes as examples of autopoiesis which we've now done, I would like to focus on the question, "What are the essential symmetry breaks represented in the transitions from one organism to another?" The nature of these symmetry transitions is likely to give us significant clues about the type of evolution dynamics at play in current organizational changes.

Jantsch (1980) indicates that the essential symmetry breaks occur in the spatiotemporal domain. For example, the emergence of dissipative structures marks a break in *spatial* symmetry. With the self-reproduction of the prokaryotes we see emerging for the first time a break in the *temporal* symmetry of experience, accompanied then, in turn, by special *time-binding processes*. When the eukaryote emerges, we find, for the first time, the breaking of *both* spatial and temporal symmetry. For here, with the development of sexuality and death there is the systematic inclusion of experience from the past which has been accruing in the ancestral tree. In these symmetry breaks several dynamics are evident: (1) The past becomes distinguishable from the future; (2) hence, new forms of bonding need to become established to enable the now distinguished past and present to remain linked (that is, the symmetry break provides the precondition for a new autopoietic system to emerge); (3) the transitions occurred basically in *steps*; (4) the process of self-reproduction is based primarily on changes in the underlying governing rules; and (5) the survivability of the new organism depends on establishing the right balance between novelty and confirmation (i.e., change and stability).

## Morphogenesis

In cybernetic theory, change may be thought of in two broad ways. There are those changes that are of a developmental nature. They operate according to the instructions encoded within the system. For example, a kitten and a duckling, as they mature, become transformed into a cat and a duck, respectively. The duckling under no circumstances will ever become a cat. This type of transition/change may be thought of as *morphostatic* (morpho = form; stasis = stable). Form is preserved. There is another type of change, called *morphogenesis*, where the basic governing rules or instructions, like the genetic codes upon which form depends, actually become altered. Such changes, once they have occurred, eliminate the possibility of an entity returning to the condition it was in before the change.

One of the central problems with trying to understand transitions of a morphogenic kind is that they are marked by chaos. The models that are appropriate for understanding the system both before and after the change break down completely when the instability threshold that marks the transition from one structure to another is reached. During this transitional time, it is not the general or the average that is of decisive importance, as is often the case in normal times; it is the particular (Jantsch, 1980). For example, the precise moment of the occurrence of an essential genetic mutation, or of a new species in an ecosystem, cannot be predicted. Nor can we know in advance how it will relate to its environment while the transition is actually occurring.

Until recently it has been very difficult to capture the dynamics of morphogenic change. However, the development of a new type of mathematics called catastrophe theory (Thom, 1975; Zeeman, 1977) and of a field called macrodynamics (Abraham, 1976) has provided a way for these transitional aspects of natural systems to be represented. The central element of catastrophe theory is recognizing the *discontinuous effects* of *continuous processes*, the problem posed in the tale of the polyploid horse. Any stable system can, on hitting an instability threshold, go through radical changes so that a new structure based on a new ordering principle emerges. The instability threshold, which becomes visible only when it is reached, is a consequence of multiple variables interacting unpredictably. Of course there are many paradoxes embedded in the very idea of an instability threshold. For example the very possibility of fluctuation *depends* upon the restraining character of the structure within which it is occurring. Were it not for the constraints of the structure, the extreme fluctuations would not have been experienced as extreme fluctuations and the jump to a new level of system would not have occurred. In other words, the tighter the structure, the less permissible are fluctuations within the systems, therefore the greater the probability that fluctuation will provide a threat to that structure.

A good example of morphogenesis can be seen in Figure 12-1. Here we can consider the graph paper upon which the "object" is drawn as metaphor for governing variables. While the entity remains unchanged in its superficial form, it can become dramatically transformed at another level by altering, as it were, the epigenetic landscape upon which it is mapped.

### Symbiosis, communication, and fusion

For a long time it was claimed that the ecological system operates on the basis of survival of the fittest. Cybernetics II suggests we restate that principle as "survival of the *symbiotic*." What do we mean by symbiosis?

**FIGURE 12-1**

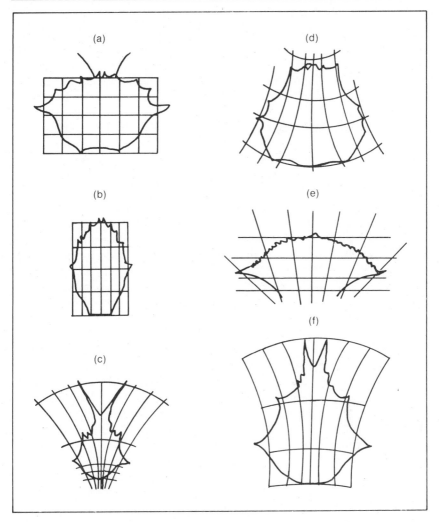

Source: D'Arcy Thompson. *On Growth and Form* (Cambridge, England: Cambridge University Press, 1961).

When two autopoietic entities interact, what happens is that usually one of the following three patterns emerges.

1.  The two entities may make some inner adjustments to each other so that there is a greater alignment between elements in one and elements in the other. However, these realignments are carried out in such a way that they in no way diminish the total autonomy of each entity. When this occurs we call it *communication*.

2.  The exchange may occur in such a way that both entities sacrifice a part of their respective individual autonomies so that the superordinate sys-

tem of which they are part may have greater autonomy in its relationship with other systems in its ecosystem. This is called *symbiosis*.

3. The individual entities may respond by treating their superordinate systems as all-important and surrender totally their individual autonomies so that the superordinate system will be maximally autonomous in its relationship with other entities of its kind in its larger ecosystem. This is *fusion*. By the entities giving up their autonomy in the interests of the superordinate system, they undermine their own capacity to continue as autopoietic structures. Instead they become reduced to the status of elements in a larger autopoietic system.

Symbiosis thus falls in the middle of the continuum from communication to fusion. At the communication end, total autonomy of the entities is maintained. At the fusion end, autonomy of the entities is surrendered entirely. In symbiosis we find the letting go of some autonomy, but it is only partial. The result is that with symbiosis we end up having autopoietic structures at both the level of the entities and of the superordinate system. Hence, it is, needless to say, a very complex system. Because a symbiotic system has particularly autonomous, self-producing activities going on at two levels it has to develop ways of determining if and when the autonomies at the lower level should be given priority over those at the suprasystem level and vice versa. To deal with this problem, we find the emergence of some type of hierarchy, which adds significantly to the complexity of the system.

In human systems based on symbiosis, we can observe two very different kinds of hierarchy. One may be characterized by the existence of a central planning center where overall policy for the collectivity is formulated and then passed down to the parts in terms of specific actions for them to take in the service of both themselves and the collectivity. The alternative is a pooling process where the ideas of component groups are raised and then debated as mutual adjustments are made. The U.S. Congress is illustrative of the former while the SALT or START talks between the Soviet Union and the United States are like the latter.

Symbiosis is usually understood in terms of the relationships among two or more entities. However, if we think of it more in terms of symbiosis of processes a clearer picture surfaces. For example, in the predator-prey relationship the actual entities of the prey species may be destroyed, but these deaths may end up sustaining a dynamic evolutionary process, such that both species benefit even though the individual entities do not.

The concept of process symbiosis provides a way for us to think about co-evolution. When one entity enters into a communicative exchange with another, some internal realignments take place so that the two entities can "understand each other." However, each entity is invariably an element of a larger system and the adjustments made at the micro level to facilitate communication may provide a stimulus for changes at other levels. Likewise, when a symbiotic or fusion process has occurred the increased complexity in the entities that have undergone changes may be communicated to neighboring entities, thereby serving as a catalyst for change there as well. For these reasons we can think of the constant interplay of communication, symbiosis, and fusion as the building blocks of the co-evolutionary cycle.

This type of thinking suggests to us that the important issue in the vitality of living systems is not *control*, as earlier versions of systems thinking emphasized, but *dynamic connectedness*. It is not an issue of adaptation or nonadaptation as Parsons (1949) argued. Rather it is the dynamic interplay between adaptation and nonadaptation. As Maruyama (1976) expresses it, the future belongs to the symbiotic systems, those that can develop relations with others that are mutually beneficial. There is no longer room for parasitic relationships where what one gains is another's loss, nor *antibiotic* relations where one, in its self-interest, actively harms the other.

I must provide a cautionary note to this discussion. To date what we "know" about symbiosis we have learned from ecology and biology. But this knowledge is based on symbiotic relationships that have already been developed. Nature arrived at its system of symbiotic relations at the cost of the extinction of species that were less symbiotic. At the societal level, however, we are in the position of constantly confronting new patterns and new social arrangements which allow for the possibility of creating symbiotic relations out of parasitic or antibiotic relations. Every time trade and cultural interdependence is developed in place of potential war between nation states, we have the transformation of antibiosis into symbiosis. As colonial and imperialist powers are exited from third- and fourth-world countries we have the possibility of symbiosis developing out of something previously parasitic. In social evolution none of us would be interested in simply waiting around passively to see what individuals, groups, organizations, etc. die off to enable "nature" as it were to define the symbiotic patterns which we end up "discovering" retrospectively. We want a way of thinking about symbiosis that enables us to be proactive and which can control or prevent parasitic or antibiotic relations from occurring.

### Alternative ways of thinking

It is very evident that we need different ways of thinking for our social relations than for those that have been used for exploring ecological and biological systems. Here the assumption has been made that species and plants don't "think" about alternatives and that there is value in not disrupting the balance of ecological relationships. In our social thinking, however, we are forever seeking out alternative paths to goals and virtually no one would argue that the balance of social relationships should be maintained as it currently is.

Maruyama (1976) is quite pointed about how inappropriate our traditional ways of thinking are for social issues. He describes them as "unidirectional, uniformistic, competitive, hierarchical, quantitative, classificational and atomistic," and argues that we need systems of thinking that are "mutualistic, heterogenistic, symbiotic, interactionist, qualitative, relational and contextual." Like Bateson (1979), Maruyama describes our problem as being the same as that of looking at the world through one eye. With monocular vision we are unable to see the world in more than two-dimensional terms. But by adding a second eye, we gain the possibility of depth perception. We see the same world, but it looks different, for depth has been added. Obviously the more eyes we have the greater the possibility of multiple perspectives. The question however is what do we do with the information gathered from the various vantage points. Traditional epistemologies suggest that we focus on that which is in common between them all or that the information be added or averaged to create a "reliable" picture of the whole. An alternative is to treat the differences latent in the observations from multiple vantage points as the equivalent of adding an extra eye, giving the flavor of different color overlays of the same picture. Or perhaps a stereophonic record player is a better metaphor, where the difference in the sounds between speakers enables one to listen to music multidimensionally. What is especially important here is to note that, if we eliminate the parts of the images on which the two eyes "disagree," what is left is *much less* than the single image obtained in monocular vision.

Playfully Maruyama (1976) asks, "What if we were to live in four-dimensional space?" To which comes the Eastern reply, "You need a third eye (I)." Might it be that to dwell in the N-dimensional space of our social universes we need $N-1$ eyes?

The literature of Cybernetics II suggests that there is a difference between naturally occurring autopoietic structures and those of social entities that engaged in self-reflection. For the latter, the task of autopoiesis has the flavor of self-trancendence, the functional equivalent of learning how to jump over one's own shadow. Self-transcendence, symbolized by Baron Münchhausen's pulling himself up by his own hair, may be viewed as the capacity to change one's point of view and therefore explore one's situation through a different light. Clearly self-transcendence is very difficult but it is essential if social entities are to develop ways to "step out" of the grooves that standard evolutionary processes are carving out for them.

Self-transcendence is a very difficult thing to even talk about because it becomes embroiled in the problems of self-referential thinking. For a social entity such as an organization to reflect on itself, it must have a system of representing both itself and the context in which it's embedded. To be able to talk and think, however, in self-transcendent ways, we need languages that are themselves self-transcending. This is a real problem. Consider, for example, the task of trying to determine how the rules of grammar shape the way we think. To do this we have to use a language that is governed by those rules of grammar to explore the impact those grammatical rules have on our thinking. To really understand, we would have to use a metagrammar. But that metagrammar in turn will be shaped by a meta-meta-grammar and so forth. In other words, the concern becomes one of whether we can examine our systems of thinking without using those systems of thinking as our vehicle for thinking.

While this is a real problem, it is one we can deal with so long as we can develop ways to transcend our usual ways of thinking about language. Pankow (1976) points out that what we need is a language that is able to make a statement and a statement about that statement (metastatement) at the same time. This means that we must be able to move out of a logical approach to language and to treat language as a multidimensional system. Consider Pankow's example of the instruction given to the mailman "to fetch mail from the post office only for those people who do not fetch the mail themselves." A logician would argue that this order is unresolvable, because indeed the mailman is allowed to fetch his own mail only if he does not fetch it and vice versa. This problem, however, is created because in this instruction there was a statement and a metastatement that belonged in different frames. So long as the frames are kept separate there is no logical dilemma. However, when the multiple frames are collapsed into a single, undimensional structure, problems of self-referential logic emerge.

Self-referential language that is treated in a logical way ends up either in the binds of self-confirmation which becomes tautological, reduced to banalties such as "if P is true, P is true," or self-renunciation which becomes paradoxical as in the statement "I am lying." Perhaps the clearest problem of paradox can be seen in Hofstadter's (1980) example of:

> The following sentence is false.
> The preceding sentence is true.

Taken separately these two sentences are harmless enough. Yet when put together they generate paradox because each comes to frame the other in the binds of self-renunciating self-reference. The paradox, however, does not lie within the statements themselves. Rather, it is created by the process of framing. The paradox ends up lying, as it were, in the space between the sentences, manufactured by a frame that makes the system of thought self-referentially double-bound.

To alter one's system of thinking one needs to be able to *reframe*, for all meaning ends up residing in the relationship between a statement and its context (Wilden, 1972; Smith, 1982b) as was evident in our *Invasion of the Martians* story. What do we mean by this process of reframing? A simple example will help.

Consider the situation of a child watching a play with a parent. The child asks, "What's that man doing now?" The parent's reply could be any of the following:

*a.* He's hitting the other man.
*b.* He's acting in a play.
*c.* He's making people laugh.
*d.* He's earning his living.
*e.* He's creating an image of himself as a dramatic artist.
*f.* He's spreading culture to the masses. (Smith, 1982a).

Each of these responses may be a valid comment in response to the one piece of data; however, each is framed by a different context. And as a result each answer is of a very different kind. Imagine, however, if the exchange had gone as follows:

> The child asks: "What's that man *doing* now?"
> Parent: "He's hitting the other man."
> Child: "No. What's he *doing*?"
> "I said he's hitting the other man."
> "That's not what I mean! What's he doing?"
> Parent, angrily: "I told you. Now be quiet!"

It might well be that the child knows the play and knows that, according to the script, the man should not be hitting anyone. Rather he should be playing with the dog or whatever. So the child's question "What's he doing now?" is not a request for a description but a question about why he's stepped out of role. It's a question in a totally different frame than the one the parent is thinking within. The exchange becomes exasperating because neither child nor parent understands the need to move to a metaframe, as it were, to first talk *about* what frame they're using. They do not know to say "You're listening to me through frame x. But I'm asking my question in frame y" (Smith, 1983).

The concept of reframing (Watzlawick, 1978) is very helpful for the task of thinking about organizational self-transcendence. For a system to generate alternatives it can simply take its experience and plug it into as many alternative frames as possible. In so doing it will begin to create a hybrid of multiple realities that will quickly replace the singular reality system it operated within when it saw itself and its world through monocular vision. The concepts elaborated in co-evolutionary theory provide some fruitful pointers as to where to look for new frames. Since the critical breaks came via disruption of symmetry patterns of the spatiotemporal structure, it is evident that by switching time frames (see McGrath and Rotchford (1983) for a review) or spatial frames, radically different realities may be created. We saw earlier in the figure from D'Arcy Thompson how dramatically different an object can look simply by altering the underlying dimensions of the coordinates upon which it is mapped.

For a human system to be autopoietic it must be able to be self-transcendent. That means moving out of its own construction of reality and entering into dialogue with the multiple realities it can create by framing its own and others' experiences in as many different frameworks as possible. Such activity may produce a lot of internal and relational fluctuations and may in fact keep the system in a somewhat unstable condition. However, it also will create a resilience that will give this system a chance to create, sustain, and change, where necessary, its symbiotic relations with other entities in its ecosystem.

## REFERENCES

Abraham, R. "Vibrations and the Realization of Form," pp. 134–49. In *Evolution and Consciousness: Human Systems in Transition*, eds. E. Jantsch, and C. H. Waddington. Reading, Mass.: Addison-Wesley Publishing, 1976.

Alderfer, C. P. "Change Processes in Organizations." In *Handbook of Industrial and Organizational Psychology*, ed. M. D. Dunnette. Chicago, Ill.: Rand McNally, 1976.

Ashby, W. R. *An Introduction to Cybernetics*. New York: John Wiley & Sons, 1956.

Bateson, G. *Mind and Nature*. New York: Bantam, 1979.

Begley, S., and J. Carey. "How Human Life Begins." *Newsweek*, January 11, 1982.

Coser, L. A. *The Functions of Social Conflict*. New York: Free Press, 1956.

Greiner, L. E. "Evolution and Revolution as Organizations Grow," pp. 37–46. *Harvard Business Review* 50, 1972.

Hofstadter. D. R., *Gödel, Escher, Bach: An Eternal Golden Braid*. New York: Random House, 1980.

Holling, C. S. "Resilience and Stability of Ecosystems," pp. 73–92. In *Evolution and Consciousness: Human Systems in Transition*, eds. E. Jantsch, and C. H. Waddington. Reading, Mass.: Addison-Wesley Publishing, 1976.

Houseman, J. "The Men from Mars." *Harper's*, 1948, reprinted in *Systems and Processes*, eds. M. Reda, E. Fappiano, and L. Czikowsky. New Haven, Conn.: College and University Press, 1968.

Jantsch, E. "Evolving Images of Man. Dynamic Guidance for the Mankind Process," pp. 230–42. In *Evolution and Consciousness: Human Systems in Transition*, eds. E. Jantsch, and C. H. Waddington. Reading, Mass.: Addison-Wesley Publishing, 1976.

_____. *The Self-Organizing Universe*. New York: Paragon Press, 1980.

Katz, D., and R. L. Kahn. *The Social Psychology of Organizations*. New York: John Wiley & Sons, 1966.

Kimberly, J. R., and R. H. Miles. *The Organizational Life Cycle*. San Francisco: Jossey-Bass, 1980.

Margulis, L. *Origin of Eukaryotic Cells*. New Haven, Conn.: Yale University Press, 1970.

Maruyama, M. "The Second Cybernetics: Deviation-Amplifying Mutual Causal Processes," pp. 164–79 and 250–56. *American Scientist* 51, 1963.

_____. "Toward Cultural Symbiosis," pp. 198–213. In *Evolution and Consciousness: Human Systems in Transition*, eds. E. Jantsch, and C. H. Waddington. Reading, Mass.: Addison-Wesley, 1976.

Maturana, H. R. "Autopoiesis." In *Autopoiesis: A Theory of Living Organization*, Series Vol. 3, ed. M. Zeleny. New York: North-Holland, 1981.

McGrath, J. E., and N. L. Rotchford. "Time and Behavior in Organizations," pp. 57–101. In *Research in Organizational Behavior*, Vol. 5, eds. L. L. Cummings, and B. M. Staw. Greenwich, Conn.: JAI Press, 1983.

Michels, R. *Political Parties*. New York: Dover, 1915.

Miller, E. J., and A. K. Rice. *Systems of Organization*. London: Tavistock, 1967.

Newfield, J. *Robert Kennedy: A Memoir*. New York: Dutton, 1969.

Pankow, W. "Openness as Self Transcendence," pp. 16–36. In *Evolution and Consciousness: Human Systems in Transition*, eds. E. Jantsch, and C. H. Waddington. Reading, Mass.: Addison-Wesley, 1976.

Parsons, T. *The Structure of Social Action*. New York: Free Press, 1949.

Prigogine, I. *Thermodynamics of Irreversible Processes*, 3d ed. New York: Wiley-Interscience, 1967.

_____. "Order through Fluctuation: Self-organization and Social System," pp. 93–133. In *Evolution and Consciousness: Human Systems in Transition*, eds. E. Jantsch, and C. H. Waddington. Reading, Mass.: Addison-Wesley Publishing, 1976.

Rice, A. K. "Individual, Group and Intergroup Processes," pp. 565–85. *Human Relations* 22, 1969.

Sarason, S. B. *The Creation of Settings and the Future Societies*. San Francisco: Jossey-Bass, 1972.

Schön, D. A. *Beyond the Stable State*. New York: Norton, 1971.

Simmel, C. *Conflict and the Web of Groups —Affiliations*. Translated by K. H. Wolff and R. Bendix. New York: Free Press, 1955.

Simmons, V. M. "Conflict in Open Systems: Planning for a New Organization." Unpublished Ph.D. Dissertation, University of Maryland, 1983.

Smith, K. K., *Groups in Conflict: Prisons in Disguise*. Dubuque, Iowa: Kendall/ Hunt, 1982a.

_____. "Philosophical Problems in Thinking about Change," pp. 316–74. In *Change in Organizations*, ed. P. S. Goodman and Associates. San Francisco: Jossey-Bass, 1982b.

_____. "A Role for Community Psychologists: As Participant-Conceptualizers." *Australian Psychologist* 18, no. 2, 1983.

Smith, K. K., V. M. Simmons, T. B. Thames, and J. A. Marx. "Organizational Growth: The Impact of History, Context and Conflict." Unpublished manuscript, University of Maryland, 1983.

Stotland, E., and D. L. Kobler. *Life and Death of a Mental Hospital*. Seattle, Wash.: University of Washington Press, 1965.

Thom, R. *Structural Stability and Morphogenesis*. Reading, Mass.: Benjamin, 1975.

Thompson, D'Arcy. *On Growth and Form*. Cambridge, England: Cambridge University Press, 1961.

Thompson, J. D. *Organizations in Action*. New York: McGraw-Hill, 1967.

Tustin, A. "Feedback," pp. 48–55. *Scientific American* 187, 1952.

von Bertalanffy, L. *General Systems Theory: Foundations, Development, Applications*, rev. ed. New York: Braziller, 1968.

Waddington, C. H. *The Evolution of an Evolutionist*. Edinburgh: Edinburgh University Press, 1975.

_____. "Concluding Remarks," pp. 243–49. In *Evolution and Consciousness: Human Systems in Transition*, eds. E. Jantsch, and C. H. Waddington. Reading, Mass.: Addison-Wesley Publishing, 1976.

Watzlawick, P. *The Language of Change*. New York: Basic Books, 1978.

Weizsäcker, C. F. von (ed.) *Offene System I: Beiträge zur Zeitstruktur von Information, Entropie und Evolution*. Stuttgart: Klett, 1974.

Wilden, A. *System and Structure*. London: Tavistock, 1972.

Zeeman, E. C. *Catastrophe Theory: Selected Papers*, 1972–1977. Reading, Mass.: Addison-Wesley Publishing, 1977.

# 13

---

# Paradox, planning, and perseverance: Guidelines for managerial practice

Robert E. Quinn
*The Nelson A. Rockefeller College of*
*Public Affairs and Policy*
*State University of New York at Albany*

John R. Kimberly
*The Wharton School*
*The University of Pennsylvania*

---

## INTRODUCTION

Several decades ago a missionary station was established among a tribe of nomadic aborigines known as the Yir Yoront. Traveling in small bands over a vast territory, the Yir Yoront particularly depended on stone axes which were the primary tools in the production of food, shelter, and warmth. The stone axe played both a technical and a symbolic role in the tribe. It represented masculinity and respect for elders. The axe was owned by men and used by women and children. Axes were borrowed from husbands, fathers, and uncles according to an elaborate system which was prescribed by custom. The axes were secured through trade with other tribes at seasonal fiestas. In elaborate rituals, the Yir Yoront would exchange spears for the stone axes.

As the missionaries worked among the Yir Yoront they determined to improve living conditions by distributing new, more efficient steel axes. They did this through the giving of gifts and using the steel axes as pay for services rendered. The axes were distributed to men, women, and children. There was little resistance to the steel axe, except for the fact that the older men, distrustful of the missionaries, were reluctant to accept the new tool. But because of the efficiency of the steel axe, it rapidly replaced the stone version.

The introduction of the steel axe brought some changes in the life of the Yir Yoront. First, their relations with other tribes were disrupted as interest in bartering for stone axes rapidly declined. Second, the status system became disrupted as old men became dependent upon women and children, often being forced to borrow the new axes. Third, the value system and social structure became greatly altered as many older men began to prostitute their daughters in exchange for the use of a steel axe. These unexpected outcomes were naturally of great concern to the missionaries. (Case reported by Sharp in Rogers and Shoemaker, 1971.)

The story may be apocryphal for the management of organizational transitions. The missionaries had an objective in mind and set out to make a relatively simple intervention into a system for which they felt some responsibility. The simple intervention, however, initiated a transition whose undesirable side effects nearly overwhelmed the gains in efficiency realized in changing from stone to steel. In introducing the steel axe, the missionaries were particularly naive about the complexities, tensions, and paradoxical connections that were part of the context in which they were working. As we pointed out in the introduction, managers (like the missionaries) tend to focus on the technical side of change. Here there are often what appear to be clear choices (steel axes are "better" than stone axes). They tend to focus less on the behavioral side. They do not see the organization as a tribe with a culture that is highly complex, full of tensions and paradox. Hence they are often surprised, frustrated, or demoralized by the change process. As we review the chapters in this book, and note the pervasiveness of this problem, it seems fair to conclude that modern managers might do well to remember the story of the missionaries and the steel axe. We will refer to it often.

In this chapter we present eight guidelines for the management of transitions in the world of practice. To introduce these guidelines, in the early part of the chapter we build a conceptual foundation. The resulting interpenetration of theory and advice creates a new and useful basis for managerial action. (The reader who is less interested in the conceptual foundation may prefer to skip ahead to the discussion of Figure 13–2 and the eight guidelines for transition management.)

### Culture and management

The concept of culture, until recently, has not been heavily emphasized in the literature on management. This is rapidly changing. In this book there is hardly a chapter that does not in some way point to the concept of culture in the management of transitions. Indeed, culture is the aggregate concept which consumes and connects the strategic, political, interpersonal, and institutional aspects of organizational life. Our purpose here is to review what we have learned and extend our thinking about culture so we can better understand its role in the management of transitions.

Like nomadic tribes, or any other social system, organizations have cultures. From the chapter by Sales and Mirvis (Chapter 6) we learn that these organizational cultures have a surface level and a deeper level. The surface realm has to do with more tangible things such as language, knowledge transmission, and behaviors. Here traditions, customs, and rituals are organized according to norms, roles, and role-relationships. The deeper level has to do with meaning, the values, and assumptions people use to make sense of the world. In different organizations we find very different world views. Consider the Sales and Mirvis examples of DC and GrandCo. When these two companies merged they had entirely different assumptions about the most basic aspects of organizational life. This phenomenon also occurs in different parts of a single organization. Contrasts between sales and accounting or production and research and development are often illustrations of such differences.

It is the deeper realm that Lundberg has in mind when he states, "culture is anchored in the epistemological structures which dominate among a culture's members." He argues that concepts of reality vary in two dimensions: Wholeness—fragmentation and stability—change. From this argument he develops four types of cultures and transition strategies (see Figures 4–3 and 4–4).

Lundberg's approach is one example of efforts to identify the understructure of perception and information processing. From these efforts, we distill four different ways of processing information and generating meaning among organizational members (Mitroff and Mason, 1982; Quinn and Hall, 1983).

**The hierarchical perspective.**   This objective perspective is oriented toward empiricism or the systematic examination of externally generated facts. It tends to be a present-oriented approach which describes *what is*. In processing information the problem tends to be analyzed from a static, cross-sectional view and the subject is seen as if in a photograph, frozen in time. In making decisions, people with this orientation tend to have a single focus. They take a long time to gather and systematically analyze the facts. The objective is to obtain the single best answer or optimal solution. This hierarchical perspective is oriented toward security, order, and routinization and tends to emphasize standardization and perpetuation of the status quo.

**The developmental perspective.**   This perspective is oriented toward idealism or the reliance on internally generated ideas, intuitions, and hunches. It tends to be a future-oriented approach which considers *what might be*. In processing information the problems tends to be analyzed from a dynamic, longitudinal view and the subject is seen as if in a moving picture. In making decisions, people with this orientation tend to have a multiple focus. They make decisions very quickly but continue to gather information and adjust the decision as they go along. This subjective perspective is oriented toward creativity, risk, and growth. It tends to emphasize adaptability and external legitimacy.

**The rational perspective.** This is a very purposive orientation. With rationalism, there tends to be an a priori logic which structures information processing. This is a very functional or instrumental outlook which tends toward the use of general principles, rules, or laws. In making decisions, people with this outlook tend to have a single purpose or focus. They make rapid decisions and, once the decision is made, it is final. This perspective is very achievement-oriented and tends to emphasize logical direction and the initiation of action.

**The group perspective.** This perspective provides a considerable contrast to the above. This one is more oriented to feelings than to facts. This is a more existential view, which suggests that the world can be known only through human interaction. Meaning is discovered through process. The individual case is more important than the general rule, hence there is a much greater tolerance for individual exceptions and spontaneous events and behaviors. In making decisions, people with this outlook tend to have a multiple focus. They take the time to seek out diverse opinions and search for solutions that integrate the various positions. This perspective is oriented to affiliation and tends to emphasize harmony and consideration of the individual.

These four orientations can be used to explore the deep structures of organizational culture, the basic assumptions that are made about such things as the means to compliance, motives, leadership, decision making, effectiveness values, and organizational forms (see Table 13–1). They suggest four types of culture.

*The hierarchical culture* is permeated with assumptions of stability. Here it is believed that people will behave appropriately or comply with organizational needs when roles are formally stated and reinforced by rules and regulations. Surveillance and enforcement are important. In this legalistic view, it is assumed that the individual's primary need is for security and order. Leaders should be conservative and cautious, primarily providing technical expertise and seeing that the basic structure is maintained. As decision makers they should proceed slowly, objectively documenting the process, thus ensuring the accountability of the outcome. It is assumed that the effective organization emphasizes stability and control and that the ideal form is the hierarchy, pyramid, or bureaucracy.

*The developmental culture* is permeated with assumptions of change. It is believed that people will comply with organizational needs because of the importance or ideological appeal of the task that is being undertaken. In this dynamic view, it is believed that the individual's primary need is for growth, stimulation, and variety. Leaders should be inventive and risk-

**TABLE 13-1**     The world views in four types of organizational cultures

|  | Hierarchial culture | Developmental culture | Rational culture | Group culture |
|---|---|---|---|---|
| Compliance | Rules | Ideology | Contract | Affiliation |
| Motivation | Security | Growth | Competence | Attachment |
| Leadership | Conservative, cautious | Inventive, risk-taking | Directive, goal-oriented | Concerned, supportive |
| Decision making | Documentation, accountability | Adaptability, external legitimacy | Efficiency, conclusiveness | Participation support |
| Effectiveness values | Stability, control | Growth, resource acquisition | Productivity, efficiency | Development of human resources |
| Organizational form | Hierarchy | Adhocracy | Market | Clan |

taking, paying particular attention to envisioning new possibilities and acquiring additional resources, visibility, legitimacy, and external support. As decision makers they should proceed rapidly, making the most legitimate decision, later adapting the conclusion as more information is collected or as external conditions change and demands are altered. Compromise is important. It is assumed that the effective organization emphasizes growth and resource acquisition and that the ideal form is the adhocracy, organic system, or matrix.

The *rational culture* is permeated with assumptions about achievement. It is believed that people will comply with organizational needs if individual objectives are clarified and rewards are predicated on accomplishment. Compliance thus flows from formal contracting such as the MBO process. In this linear view, it is believed that the individual's primary need is to demonstrate competence and experience the successful achievement of predetermined ends. Leaders should be directive and goal-oriented, constantly providing structure and encouraging productivity. As decision makers they should proceed with reasonable haste, making logical, efficient decisions which are conclusive, decisive, and final. There is no place for wavering. It is assumed that the effective organization places emphasis on planning, productivity, and efficiency, and that the ideal structure is the market form or "Theory A" organization (see Ouchi, 1981).

The *group culture* is permeated with assumptions about human affiliation. It is believed that compliance flows from trust, tradition, and long-term commitment to membership in the system. In this process view, it is believed that the individual's primary need is for attachment, affiliation, or membership. Leaders should be participative and supportive, showing consideration and facilitating interaction. As decision makers they should proceed slowly, ensuring that all affected people participate and that the solution is supported by all members of the system. It is assumed that the effective organization places an emphasis on the development of human resources and that the ideal form is the clan, family, or "Theory Z" organization (Ouchi, 1981).

The four cultures are pure types. No organization is likely to reflect only one culture. Instead, as can be seen in Figure 13–1, we would expect to find combinations of values, with some being more dominant than others. Here we have profiled an approximation of the two organizations described by Sales and Mirvis. The profile toward the top of Figure 13–1 is a representation of the culture at DC, whereas the profile toward the bottom is a representation of the culture at GrandCo. Notice that each organization has some aspects of all four cultures but that the areas of emphasis are very different. These differences are at the heart of the conflict described by Sales and Mirvis. Understanding such conflict is one key to the effective management of organizational transitions.

**FIGURE 13–1**      The cultural profiles of two organizations

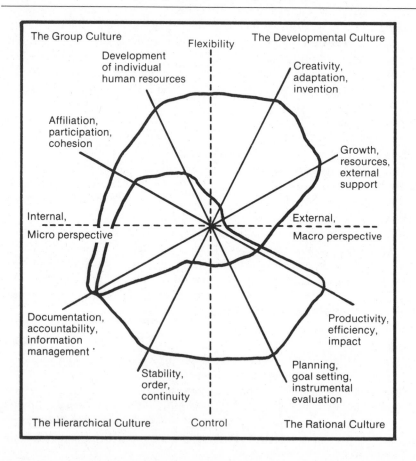

## The concept of transition

An organizational transition is a major change. The precipitants of transition are many and varied: the emergence of new political or economic conditions, an advance in research, or a change in performance demands. Whatever the stimulus, a complex process is initiated and the organization eventually moves to a new, less-turbulent condition. This period between more stable periods is what we mean by a transition. It is a time of fluctuation which results, among other things, in a new alignment of values in the overall culture.

**Tension and paradox.** Transitions are a dynamic, high-pressure context in which tensions and puzzles constantly frustrate linear thinking. During transitions, the emergence of paradox is a common source of managerial frustration. Consider the following illustration.

> The persistent paradox of Birenbaum's strategy is that he had to put the vast majority of his time and resources into short-term solutions to guarantee the ship would not sink; and yet he was aware that the solution to Antioch's crisis was to chart a course toward markets, imaginative programs, and cultivation of liberal-progressive sources of money in the country.

In making the above statement about the president of Antioch College, Warren illustrates a theme that runs through every paper in this volume. That theme is the emergence of managerial choices which embody both tension and paradox. The following are just a few of the many that are mentioned in the various chapters:

| | |
|---|---|
| Decentralization | Centralization |
| Trust | Authority |
| Individuals | Structure |
| Process | Purpose |
| Commitment | Accomplishment |
| Internal | External |
| Micro | Macro |
| Fragmentation | Whole |
| Short-term | Long-term |
| Present | Future |
| Developmental Change | Morphogenic Change |
| Continuity | Disruption |
| Confirmation | Novelty |
| Stability | Resilience |
| Destruction | Creation |
| Control | Fluctuation |
| Fusion | Symbiosis |
| Order | Dynamic Connectedness |

In discussing the problems of managing transitions, the chapter by Quinn and Andersen (Chapter 2) points out the fact that, as tensions mount, resources become strained and slack diminishes. The ramifications of decisions become magnified. Strategies that have proved successful in the past often seem only to make the problem worse. As an illustration they cite the death of the old *Saturday Evening Post*. The more management followed established strategies of success, the worse things became. In the young, Midwestern, high-tech firm described by Quinn and Andersen, management could not comprehend how to move from strategies compatible with the values of group and developmental cultures (top of Figure 2–1) and which figured importantly in their success to strategies which required different values seemingly antithetical to the firm's identity.

Smith points out in Chapter 12 that a paradox is created through the process of framing. Two things may be harmless and uninteresting when taken alone. But when framed together they may become a source of paradox and tension. In organizations, such paradoxes emerge when the contrasting values of group, developmental, hierarchical, and rational cultures begin to compete. In the case of Antioch cited earlier, for example, the president was consumed by short-term brush fires. As he worked on these he realized the need for long-term strategies. This realization became a source of increasing tension as he sensed the need to work on both. In his case the values in the upper right corner and lower left corner of Figure 13–1 were in conflict.

Which value should he have emphasized? At certain times one emphasis will bring considerable payoffs with minimum costs. At another time the same emphasis will bring little payoff at great costs. To arrive at the best answer the manager, like Smith's rabbit in Chapter 12, must transcend and reframe. The right choices will, over time, bring a reduction in the oscillations. A new culture or combination of values will emerge. The answer depends on timing. During a transition the system is in oscillation. There is an underlying dynamic which is not easily understood.

Reframing has much to do with novelty, confirmation, and transcendence. After explaining that 100 percent novelty would be complete chaos, and 100 percent confirmation would be complete order, Smith suggests that the capacity for transcendence, the creation of a new, more acceptable condition (a new equilibrium) exists in the tension generated by a powerful mix of novelty and confirmation. From such conditions comes a new order, a system state with new governing rules (a different culture or deep structure). Barrett and Cammann's (Chapter 10) description of the steel company after the process of revitalization would be one of several illustrations. After going through the transition, the company operated much closer to the assumptions embedded in the developmental culture. A new set of governing rules stabilized the system in a new and more participative pattern of operation. They shifted toward the upper left corner of Figure 13–1.

Understanding the centrality of opposition, paradox, and transcendence is the key to the effective management of transitions. At the heart of every significant transition in art, literature, music, and science, Rothenberg (1979) found evidence of what he called Janusian thinking. Named for the Roman deity Janus, whose faces looked in opposite directions at the same time, Janusian thinking often is a complex process in which two apparently contradictory ideas or concepts are conceived to be equally operative. Arising from psychological or intellectual conflict, Janusian thinking has a dreamlike, mirror-image quality and results in a creative leap which generates new insights. Einstein's observation that an object falling from a roof could be simultaneously moving and at rest is one of many such examples.

When organizations are in transition, deep structures begin to crash into one another. Because of some important change like the introduction of a steel axe, the passing of a new law, or the death of an important person, things cease to work smoothly. People begin to question norms and press for new directions. These questions and pressures challenge the deep assumptions about the patterns of social action represented in Table 13–1 and Figure 13–1. People become conflicted as paradoxes emerge. To move through a transition successfully, creative information processing is required. The ability to reframe and transcend is enormously helpful. To quote Smith's paper:

> Maruyama (1976) is quite pointed about how inappropriate our traditional ways of thinking are for social issues. He describes them as "unidirectional, uniformistic, competitive, hierarchical, quantitative, classificational and atomistic," and argues we need systems of thinking that are "mutualistic, heterogenetic, symbiotic, interactionist, qualitative, relational and contextual." Like Bateson (1979), Maruyama (1976) describes our problem as being the same as that of looking at the world through one eye. With monocular vision we are unable to see the world in more than two-dimensional terms. But by adding a second eye, we gain the possibility of depth perception. We see the same world. But it looks different, for depth has been added.

This statement suggests two ways of thinking. The traditional mode reflects assumptions of the rational and hierarchical cultures. Maruyama's preferred mode reflects the assumptions in the group and developmental cultures. Yet the orientations reflected in each of the cultures are essential to effective management. At one point in time, one orientation is more appropriate, at another point, a different orientation is more appropriate. During periods of transition the assumptions of the developmental perspective are clearly more important than ever, but the key to effective management is to know which orientations to emphasize in what combinations at which points in time.

Transitions are themselves transitional. As they evolve, different emphases on a different combination of values and assumptions may be required. When a change is initiated, existing patterns are disrupted and this results in a period of uncertainty and conflict. If key people accept and support the change, novelty turns to confirmation and eventually the innovation is routinized. As this process unfolds, managers are required to take on different orientations and styles. We see four areas of concern: strategic readjustment, political adaptation, cultural redevelopment, and structural routinization (see Figure 13–2). Figure 13–2 tends to suggest that these concerns are sequential. In reality, managers will often have to shift from one concern to its opposite or even simultaneously demonstrate several concerns. For this reason we have placed the four arrows in the center of Figure 13–2. Each word in Figure 13–2 (such as analysis, clarification, support, etc.) refers to a management principle. These are discussed in the next section.

## EIGHT GUIDELINES FOR MANAGING TRANSITIONS

With the above concepts in place we can proceed with the presentation of eight guidelines for managing transitions. The guidelines are not mutually exclusive but tend to overlap with their neighbors, yet are very different, even paradoxical to those guidelines that are juxtaposed in Figure 13–2.

### Strategic readjustment

No. 1. Analysis. *There is failure in success. Systematically diagnose the tensions.* Transition management begins with the diagnosis of building tensions. While tensions are always present in the management of an orga-

---

**FIGURE 13–2**    Shifting concerns in the management of transitions

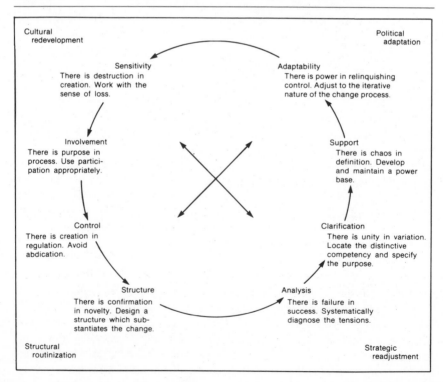

nization, the tensions are highlighted during transitions. Some key figure or figures determine that a major readjustment is necessary. The chief executive officer of the steel company in the chapter by Barrett and Cammann (Chapter 10) is an example. Although financial downturns were nothing new in the steel industry, he determined that the bleak conditions facing his company were part of a new and lasting pattern that required an entirely different kind of response. Hence he triggered a major change process. In each case a similar group or individual process occurs.

Obviously, analysis is the key to determining if a transition should be initiated but the question is how to go about such an analysis? This is a particularly difficult problem because the organization has strategies which worked in the past. Often it is these very strategies and values which are connected to the present difficulties and this failure of success poses a difficult paradox. In confronting this problem, Quinn and Andersen (Chapter 2) suggest a technique they intended for young organizations facing the transition toward formalization. The scheme, however, would seem to be useful for diagnosis in the early stages of any transition. It begins with a consideration of strategic alternatives, and then focuses on an analytic model which locates specific tensions in eight areas of performance: flexibility, growth, productivity, planning, stability, communication, cohesion, and human resource development. Based on the data generated in the first two steps, an informal dynamic model is developed. This particular step is a very attractive part of their scheme. Given the importance of paradox, as discussed in the previous portions of this chapter, the ability to identify counterintuitive alternatives is critical. In the case they describe, dynamic modeling helped top management to locate the problems that were driving the transition, helped them to realize that the strategies that had made them successful in the past were now contributing to their problems, and forced them to consider possibilities which were antithetical to their present value system.

Many managers will not have access to the kinds of expertise and resources described by Quinn and Andersen. Nevertheless, there is a basic lesson which can be of advantage. In making a systematic diagnosis, avoid unidimensional thinking by employing a wholistic model (such as the one in Figure 13-1) or set of questions which transcend all four cultural perspectives. In the process constantly search for the counterintuitive insights that help to locate the paradoxical tensions associated with transition.

**No. 2. Clarification.** *There is unity in variation. Locate the distinctive competency and specify the purpose.* Managing an organization is a very complex task. There are many coalitions of interests, both internally and externally, that hold different perspectives on what the organization is and what it should be. In times of transition, it is particularly important to find some unity in the variation. A purpose needs to be specified, one that people can support. This is no small order. Sometimes this clarification means a statement about the purpose of the change, as in the case of some restructurings, at other times it means an entirely new mission statement. In nearly all of the cases described in this volume energy was devoted to the development of a mission statement. Tichy and Ulrich (Chapter 11) discuss this process at some length and make a particular point about the need to determine the "distinctive competencies" of the organization. The *distinctive competencies* of an organization are its unique assets, those things which make it different from and give it an advantage over competitors. They cite, for example, IBM's size, its ability to offer a total range of services, its marketing ability to convince customers of its service and reputation. Two other examples from the electronics industry are Intel's capacity in components and chips, and Cray Electronics' leadership in large hardware computer technology.

Determining the distinctive competency allows for realistic strategy which is consistent with the organization's capacities, it clarifies where resources should be allocated in order to maximize the probability that goals be reached and it helps management to locate the places where changes should be made. When combined with the kind of analysis described under Rule No. 1, the determination of a distinctive competency can be most useful in the generation of a new mission statement. At times the transition may represent a conscious choice to move away from the distinctive competency and into an entirely new area of activity. Even in this case, however, a specification of distinctive competency is probably a crucial step in the transition process.

The generation of a mission statement is not necessarily an easy task. In the small corporation described by Quinn and Andersen (Chapter 2) it was necessary to go through a fairly structured process in a retreat setting. Once this was done, however, agreement was reached with relatively little conflict and reasonable commitment. At People's Express, a simple venting of frustration by the chairman led to a clarification of purpose and an informal statement of direction. In the larger and more diverse steel company, a series of half-day meetings only served to clarify the diversity of opinions that existed. Eventually 13 senior managers also went to a retreat setting and spent two and a half days in order to generate a new document. At Antioch, Birenbaum, operating in an environment of high conflict, elected to generate the mission statement himself.

Despite the diversity of techniques that were used, in each case the establishment of the mission statement signaled that a transition was underway. It provides for the integration and channeling of energy. It is a key reference point in the midst of the chaos that is characteristic of organizational transition.

### Political adaptation

**No. 3. Support.** *There is chaos in definition. Develop and maintain a power base.* Developing a new mission statement is a political process. Once the statement is generated, that process tends to become more heated.

While a clarified statement of purpose will bring the support of some, it will stimulate resistance in others. The issue of power becomes central. Tichy and Ulrich (Chapter 11) note:

> Unlike the technical area where formal tools such as strategic planning and organization design inform decision making, in the political area concepts and language are less formal and often less overt. Nonetheless, with environmental pressures much management time and attention will be allocated to strategic political changes required to revitalize organizations. The political arena is illustrated by the time and attention given to leadership. An example is American Bell's reshuffle which resulted in the resignation of Archie McGill, the "brash" aggressive marketing leader hired from IBM to transform AT&T. McGill's resignation purportedly reflects a political realignment within the new American Bell organization, designed to shift power back into the hands of more traditional AT&T managers who were reacting against the "brash" outsider.

In considering the maintenance of political relationships, the fate of Archie McGill might be fruitfully contrasted with Warren's description of Birenbaum at Antioch:

> Birenbaum understood that the power of his presidency rested with the trustees. He never confused popular sentiment with the specific governing authority reserved in the hands of the trustees. Therefore, he maintained a steady flow of paper from his office to all members of the board of trustees. He was in telephonic communication on a regular basis with members of the executive committee, particularly the chairman of the board and chairman of the executive committee. Birenbaum was mindful that his predecessor, James Dixon, had been unseated unceremoniously by the board of trustees for failing to maintain their confidence. This was a mistake he was determined not to make.

The dissemination of a new mission statement represents a very vulnerable point in the transition process and political sensitivity is particularly important. Birenbaum, for example, not only tended to the interests of the board but he fired a number of people and surrounded himself with people he could trust. He was building a base of power that could support and protect the new vision.

In the conceptualization of the new vision Tichy and Ulrich make the somewhat obvious but important point that managers engage in a stakeholder analysis. Such an analysis recognizes the network of significant others who interact with the organization. "This includes competitors, customers, suppliers, regulators, distributors, unions, stockholders, employees, and financial institutions." (Ulrich, 1983) What do these groups provide? What do they require? How will the new strategy affect them individually and collectively? The point we would like to emphasize is that once the mission statement is developed, the concern for stakeholders not only continues but intensifies. Transition management becomes as much a sales effort as an analytic process. Shortell and Wickizer (Chapter 7) report empirical support for the importance of new primary care units being perceived as central to the mission of their host systems and they suggest that considerable managerial attention be devoted to the maintenance of the perception. This suggests constant interaction with stakeholders. In selling the new image and maintaining the necessary political support, several guidelines can be derived and adapted from a review of the implementation literature (Howes and Quinn, 1978). The following are some of the most often violated principles.

1. Commit enough time for an adequate orientation.
2. Identify what will change and how the strategy will unfold.
3. Make clear the relative advantage to the stakeholder.
4. Demonstrate the likelihood of success.
5. Demonstrate your other sources of support.
6. Indicate what you need from the stakeholder.
7. Explore how you might support the efforts of the stakeholder.
8. Maintain frequent contact.
9. Continuously clarify expectations.

No. 4. Adaptability. *There is power in relinquishing control. Adjust to the iterative nature of the change process.* The continuous clarification of expectations suggests that at this point the change begins to take on a life of its own and authority, control, and design begin to give way to learning and adaptation. If the last rule suggests the establishment of a power base, this one suggests that the maintenance of power requires adaptation on the part of the designer. Change is not something which is envisioned, dictated in a memo, and then forgotten.

Making the assumptions embedded in the rational and hierarchical cultures, managers, when challenged, tend to grasp for the scepter of authority. At this point in the transitional process complexity, tension, and paradox tend to be at the maximum. The natural inclination, the intuitive response, is often to attempt to gain control. Smith's commentary on Weymouth State Hospital comes to mind. Needing to "preserve order," the administration moved quickly and punitively against workers engaged in an industrial action. This caused a key set of employees to leave the organization and locked the system into its original state of lethargy and depression. Had the opposite response been called forth, there is at least the possibility that the system would have moved toward a revitalized state. In this instance, management was like Smith's concerned rabbit in the story of the rabbit and the lynxes and it chose the most natural reaction (control) while the appropriate reaction was counterintuitive (adaptation). Management was locked into a one-dimensional view which reflected the assumptions in the rational and hierarchical cultures.

As Kanter points out in her chapter (Chapter 9) on the quality-of-work-life program at Honeywell, instrumental values often lead managers to search for the "quick fix." When reward systems are tied to short-term performance values, there is a considerable incentive to engage in "brief campaigns," to attack symptoms, or to generally give the appearance of making a change. In managing transitions, the "quick fix mentality" is a liability. The interative nature of change must be recognized. When the chief executive officer at National Steel (Barrett and Cammann) developed his mission statement, he knew where he was headed but had no idea how to get there. At each interval, random influences and the outcomes of the previous step set the constraints for the next decision. These could not be predicted ahead of time. A similar point is made by Shortell and Wickizer. Proposed designs and solutions to problems are themselves sources of uncertainty and complexity. A medical group may come up with a creative solution to the problem of coping with competition by introducing a multispecialty practice. However, when this is actually done, problems of internal coordination tend to emerge, requiring changes in structure and in levels of autonomy. Transitions call for solutions which generate new problems calling for additional solutions.

For this reason, managers must be prepared to embrace the assumptions embedded in the culture of development, even if only on a temporary basis. Standard operating procedures must be relaxed, redundancy encouraged over efficiency, and task forces and matrix designs become appropriate. The need is to engage in organizational learning, which includes the encouragement and consideration of criticism.

### Cultural redevelopment

**No. 5. Sensitivity.** *There is destruction in creation. Work with the sense of loss.* In his chapter on delete design, Albert quotes a particularly insightful statement from Biggart (1977, p. 410):

> It is not generally recognized that change is an act of destruction as much as creation. Because most organizations do change slowly, experimenting with and selectively incorporating new forms, the destruction of old forms and methods is relatively obscured. But the destructive process must either precede or exist simultaneously with the creator. This act of undoing and dismantling is important theoretically; reorganization presumes the rejection or supercession of old methods in favor of the new and the organization must systematically destroy the former, competing structures.

Recognizing the destruction in creation is one of the most important steps in the management of change. Most of us assume that resistance is linked to a fear of the unknown future. Albert raises the very intriguing idea that resistance may come from the fear of the unknown past. Over time, instrumental tools (like a steel axe or office layout) become infused with meanings. Often we do not know what these meanings are until after something has been removed or replaced. The Tichy and Ulrich and the Albert chapters both provide insightful discussions of the endings in beginnings and the need to help people through the period of loss. Albert's model of delete design suggests four basic principles.

The first principle involves summarizing the past. The summary states the essence of what it is that will terminate and hence provides a sense of closure, locates a context for knowing the meaning of the past; it honors the hopes, dreams, and accomplishments that were embedded there. Summaries will be made effective if they are comprehensive, reflecting all the viewpoints and interpretations. They must also be credible.

The second principle is justification. This is a statement of the new direction, an explanation of the nature and magnitude of the change and of why it is necessary now.

The third principle is continuity. There is a need to link the future to the past, to locate a domain, product, or activity that preserves past values. Birenbaum's statement arguing for the preservation of the original core values in the Antioch vision is a fine example.

The fourth principle is eulogize the past. This point recognizes that grief and loss are not as much a function of pleasurable experience with an object as they are a function of prolonged, intense association. One cannot leave a prolonged pattern of action without some ritual that aids in dealing with the associated uncertainty and stress. Here again, a significant paradox emerges. Albert suggests that the way to weaken a tie is to intensify the bond. The embrace of two loved ones, immediately before a separation, is such a ritual. This idea is again a counterintuitive solution to a paradox in the change process. The more-intuitive action is to simply get on with things. If the old business strategy is no longer effective, then the instrumental thing to do is to replace it as soon as possible. In fact, the old strategy may be infused, like the stone axe, with meaning, and replacing it requires summary, justification, continuity, and eulogy. This insight also allows us to better understand why organizations experience such crises when old success strategies become sources of failure. People like the management team in Quinn and Andersen's young high-tech firm had such intense and prolonged association with the group and developmental cultures that a shift toward the rational and hierarchical cultures meant an enormous sense of loss. Formulation management was a first step in the surfacing of the issues but additional rituals would probably facilitate such transitions.

Creation means destruction. A manager who is insensitive to individuals and their sense of loss will probably experience considerable resistance during the transition process. The four steps suggested by Albert represent one approach to managing the consequences of destruction.

**No. 6. Involvement.** *There is purpose in process. Use participation appropriately.* Meaning, emotion, and commitment are part and parcel of organizational life. Participation is a vehicle for dealing with these issues. To ignore them or hope they don't exist is to invite problems. As Kanter (Chapter 9) points out, participation is not an end in itself but is deeply connected to all aspects of an organization's capacities for effective performance. Most people assume that if people feel involved they are more likely to be committed. Kanter indicates that this assumption is misleading. The real merit of participative mechanisms is that they generate concrete ideas, make it possible for these ideas to be taken advantage of, connect people to the definition and solution of critical problems, increase the likelihood that people's relevant capacities will be utilized, and increase the probability of effective organizational performance. Participation is not an end in itself but a path to performance.

In the organizational change process, participation is critical. The problem is designing and using it appropriately. As Kanter indicates, it is often assumed that people should be asked their opinions, whether or not they know anything about the subject or have a stake in the outcome, whether or not the person doing the asking cares about the opinions of group members, or whether or not there will be any impact. In such cases participation is likely to cause more difficulties than it solves.

In the Honeywell case, a steering committee, among other things, ensured that participation was linked to real purposes, operated in genuinely useful ways, and provided increased organizational effectiveness rather than just individual satisfaction. While participation is clearly necessary in transition management, leaders, even in smaller companies, would do well to heed the guidelines provided by Kanter.

### Structural routinization

**No. 7. Control.** *There is creation in regulation. Avoid abdication.* Once a consultant and a manager were discussing change. The consultant had just presented a list of things that must be remembered in the management of transitions. The executive thought for a moment and said:

> I just realized something. I love to design change but I do not like to manage it. I am always starting new projects. When I think back, it seems that most of them die away. Before they are institutionalized, my interests have shifted to a new concern. I am attracted to designing, not institutionalizing.

The statement is important because it illustrates one of the most frequent traps in transition management. Kanter is particularly helpful in this area. Discussing participation she notes that managers have a real tendency to abdicate responsibility. They assume that participation requires them to back off. Hence there is a failure to plan, monitor, and control activities. This leaves employees to flounder, results in frustration, and wastes resources. Before the mechanisms of control were established, Honeywell was inundated with uncoordinated programs. The programs lacked relationship to the overall business strategy, spawned unnecessary competition, provided no transfer of experience, and allowed things to fall through the cracks. The establishment of the steering committee with its related objectives and operating procedures brought these various problems under control.

In discussing tools for the control of the change process Tichy and Ulrich (Chapter 11) discuss various program planning and budgeting tools that can aid in the management process. These tools are meant to smooth the shift toward institutionalization. Again from a review of the implementation literature by Howes and Quinn (1978) we can identify several principles which are often violated.

1. Set up adequate support and control networks.
2. Produce and make supportive services available.
3. Set up appropriate training programs.
4. Clarify and develop role expectations.
5. Encourage and reward the use of vertical and horizontal communication channels.
6. Integrate and provide frequent contact between change agents, managers, and members.

**No. 8. Structure.** *There is confirmation in novelty. Design a structure which substantiates the change.* Transitions may bring reorganizations. This statement holds because the strategic orientation, political relationships, and cultural meanings have all been reconstructed. In order to institutionalize the change, the structure almost always has to be modified. As Tichy and Ulrich point out:

> If the structure matches the firm's strategy, the firm is more likely to be successful in meeting its strategic goals. For example, as AT&T made strategic shifts by entering new markets, a number of organization structure changes followed. Divisions became profit centers, marketing departments became more involved in decision making, and managers assumed more profit/loss responsibility as AT&T moved to being a competitor in the telecommunications marketplace. The structure at AT&T changed to fit with the new strategic direction of the firm. In modifying structure, leaders have a tool to institutionalize transitions. Structure can be means to implement a firm's strategic goals.

The structure must be matched not only to the strategy but to the environment and the internal culture. While there is no general rule on how to design the structure, there are a number of issues that should be taken into consideration. Has the mission statement been altered? What is the organization to accomplish? How have the external forces been realigned? What are the forecasts for future external conditions? What are the internal cultures like and how do they interface? How do they vary in terms of technology, markets served, scale of operation, specialization of functions, percentages and types of professionals, time orientations, goals and rewards? To what degree should they be centralized or decentralized?

Answering such questions is not an easy task. Reorganization is a complex process. Sometimes it seems an endless process. It is essential, however, that the manager pay continued and close attention to the design of structures that routinize support and institutionalize the desired change.

## SUMMARY AND CONCLUSION

Like the missionaries introducing the steel axe, most managers underestimate and fail to understand the complexity of the change process. In this chapter we discussed the deep structures or competing assumptions in the cultures of organizations. Transitions may require shifts from one pattern of values to another. During these shifts cultural tensions emerge and paradoxical problems present themselves. These put a premium on creative, multidimensional thinking. Nevertheless transitions are themselves transitional. This means that at different points in the transition process, different managerial orientations may be required. Every transition, whether it represents an instance of restructuring, repositioning, and/or revitalizing, engages strategic readjustment, political adaptations, cultural redevelopment, and structural routinization. Our eight guidelines are intended to help the manager pick his or her way through the complexities of the transition process and emerge with a sense of accomplishment.

The model is, of course, itself an oversimplification, a neat abstraction to facilitate communication. Change is highly complex. The eight guidelines are themselves paradoxical. At one point, for example, they urge you to encourage openness, learning, and creativity, while at another point they call for control and the generation of structure. If change unfolded in a predictable sequence, it would make your job (and ours) easier. That it does not makes the shaping of new futures difficult and is the essence of the challenge in transition management.

## REFERENCES

Howes, N. J., and R. E. Quinn. "Implementing Change: From Research to a Prescriptive Framework," pp. 71–84. *Group and Organizational Studies* 3, no. 1, 1978.

Mitroff, I., and R. O. Mason. "Business Policy and Metaphysics: Some Philosophical Considerations," pp. 361–70. *Academy of Management Review*, no. 7, 1982.

Ouchi, W. G. *Theory Z: How American Business Can Meet the Japanese Challenge*. Reading, Mass.: Addison-Wesley, 1981.

Quinn, R. E. and R. H. Hall. "Environments, Organizations, and Policy Makers: Towards an Integrative Framework." in *Organization Theory and Public Policy*, eds. R. H. Hall and R. E. Quinn. Beverly Hills, Calif.: Sage Publications, 1983.

Rogers, E. M. and F. F. Shoemaker. *The Communication of Innovations*. New York: Free Press, 1971.

Rothenberg, Albert. *The Emerging Goddess: The Creative Process in Art, Science, and Other Fields*. Chicago: University of Chicago Press, 1979.

Ulrich D. "Specifying External Relations: Definition of an Actor in a Firm's Environment." Working paper, 1983. Available from author, Business School, University of Michigan.

# Index